The Language of Fictional Television

Also available from Continuum

Evaluation in Media Discourse, Monika Bednarek
New Discourse on Language, Monika Bednarek and J. R. Martin (eds)

The Language of Fictional Television

Drama and Identity

Monika Bednarek

continuum

Continuum International Publishing Group
The Tower Building
11 York Road
London SE1 7NX

80 Maiden Lane
Suite 704
New York NY 10038

www.continuumbooks.com

First published 2010
Paperback edition first published 2012

British Library Cataloguing-in-Publication Data
A catalogue record for this book is available from the British Library.

ISBN: 978-1-4411-5585-6 (hardcover)
978-1-4411-8366-8 (paperback)

Library of Congress Cataloging-in-Publication Data
A catalog record for this book is available from the Library of Congress

Typeset by Newgen Imaging Systems Pvt Ltd, Chennai, India
Printed and bound in Great Britain

D'oh (Homer Simpson)

Contents

Acknowledgements

The research described in this book was supported by a number of people and institutions, and I would like to express my thanks to them here. First, much of the research for this book was undertaken at the University of Technology, Sydney (UTS) on a Chancellor's Post-doctoral Research Fellowship, and I am very grateful to the university for their generosity. I also wish to thank the Faculty of Arts and Social Sciences at UTS, in particular Education and Journalism, for their support throughout my time there, and Alastair Pennycook for valuable academic advice, discussion and support on draft material. I also appreciate Tim Gooding letting me audit his class on scriptwriting for television at UTS, and for discussing aspects of professional practice with me.

Theo van Leeuwen, Michele Zappavigna, Naomi Knight and Sophie Reissner kindly agreed to read individual draft chapters, and their advice has been much appreciated. Needless to say, all remaining mistakes are mine. Helen Caple read and commented upon the whole manuscript and also provided the detailed illustrations used in Chapter 7 – it could not have been done without her.

Important inspiration also came from discussions at the University of Sydney initiated by Jim Martin on identity and interpersonal meaning, and it was also very helpful to have had the opportunity to present parts of my research at research seminars and conferences in Australia and Canada, which provided important feedback from the audiences. Thanks also go to the linguists who answered my query on LinguistList regarding existing linguistic research on popular culture.

I also wish to say thanks to Gurdeep Mattu for commissioning the book and the staff at Continuum for their editorial support. I am grateful too to Bettina Fischer-Starcke for bibliographical advice and for access to parts of her PhD thesis, and to Claudia Bubel for allowing me to reproduce a figure from her PhD thesis in this book. I would also like to thank Mark Assad for help with the corpus design as well as Abigail Brown for help with statistics and Michele Zappavigna for technical advice and other helpful suggestions.

Last, but certainly not least, I wish to thank my partner, my friends, and my family for the assistance, support and encouragement they have provided throughout.

Chapter 1

Introduction

1 Introducing *The Language of Fictional Television*

In this book I analyse the language of fictional television series, in particular, how it differs from 'naturally occurring' language, and how it is used to create drama and identity (of characters). By way of introducing some of the topics of this book, consider example (1), a scene from an episode from *The Simpsons* (FOX, 1989–):

[Homer has been subject to intense, negative media coverage after allegedly groping baby-sitter Ashley Grant and being accused of sexual harassment, although in fact he was just reaching for a piece of candy. For a detailed plot summary see http://www.imdb.com/title/tt0701109/plotsummary. After watching this media coverage Homer is feeling very dejected. (underlining indicates emphasis)]

(1)

Homer:	Aw, I need a hug.
	[Lisa and Bart only hug him after a pause]
	How come you guys hesitated?
Lisa:	Sorry, Dad, we <u>do</u> believe in you, we really do.
Bart:	It's just hard not to listen to TV: it's spent so much more time raising us than you have.
Homer:	Oh, maybe TV <u>is</u> right. TV's <u>always</u> right! [Homer walks upstairs]
[Bart and Lisa hug the TV]	
Homer:	[from upstairs] Are you hugging the TV?
Bart/Lisa:	No . . . [They kiss the TV]

(*The Simpsons*, 6.09, *Homer Badman*, 27/11/1994)

We can look at this scene with respect to several issues: First, we can consider the points that are being made about our relation to television through the use of metafictional comments, and through Lisa's and Bart's non-verbal behaviour: 'it's hard not to listen to TV', 'it's spent so much more time raising us than you have', 'TV's always right', 'are you hugging the TV?', Bart and Lisa hugging and kissing the TV. These are (humorous) points about the role of television in promoting certain truths, representations or ideologies, in being what Hartley calls a 'transmodern teacher' (Hermes 2005: 12). The points also relate to the affective responses we have with respect to television and its contents – theorized for instance with respect to 'parasocial interaction' (Giles 2002) and pleasure (Fiske 1994).

Another way in which we can look at this *Simpsons* scene is as an extract from a television series itself, and we can explore this with respect to scripted dialogue and its similarity/difference to 'real' language. We can also consider its communicative context such as its process of production, or its relation to the audience, its relation to other genres of fictional television (both animated and non-animated), how characters such as Lisa, Bart and Homer are construed through dialogue, or how audiences are attracted to buying *The Simpsons* DVDs. Issues concerning the communicative context of fictional television, its audience, its genres and especially its construal of characters (hence the subtitle of this book: *Drama and* ***Identity***) are in fact some of the questions that inform this book.

So how hard is it not to listen to TV? And should we listen to it (e.g. analyse it) at all? This book argues that it is time to take television dialogue seriously and to incorporate its many forms and genres in the linguistic enterprise as a whole, that is, to analyse not just news broadcasts, political interviews or reality TV shows, but also the diverse genres of *fictional* television. My interest in this book is particularly in the genre of 'dramedy' – a hybrid genre that combines elements of comedy and drama (hence the subtitle of this book: ***Drama*** *and Identity*) – though many points will be relevant to other fictional television genres.

More generally, this book studies television from a linguistic perspective. Drawing on the genre of dramedy and using case studies, it provides an introduction to the linguistic analysis of fictional television series, their dialogue and their characters.

The research framework is

- multi-methodological in that it tries to combine both quantitative and qualitative linguistic analysis and both 'manual' and computational (corpus) analysis;
- multi-theoretical in that it tries to incorporate insights from corpus linguistics, pragmatics, multimodal research, and stylistics;
- inter-disciplinary in that it tries to take into account to some extent insights from media/television/film/cultural studies while being firmly rooted within linguistics.

For students and researchers in media studies, it may be useful to note that my approach in this book is what media/communication studies calls 'textual analysis', combining elements of narrative analysis (with a focus on characters), discourse analysis (with a focus on language), conversation analysis (with a focus on spoken interactions, albeit scripted), and critical analysis (investigating ideology) (see Weerakkody 2008: chapter 14). From the perspective of linguistics, it is perhaps best called a 'corpus-based discourse analysis' (Baker 2006: 6) of television dialogue, as the book makes use both of computational corpus analysis (automatic analysis of large datasets/corpora) and close reading (manual analysis of individual texts). These methodologies will be introduced in more detail in individual chapters as relevant.

2 Structure of this Book

The Language of Fictional Television is divided into two parts. Part I, *Fictional Television: Dialogue and Drama* (Chapters 2–4) is about the analysis of fictional television in terms of its communicative context, genre, audience and dialogue. Part II *Fictional Television: Character Identity* (Chapters 5–8) concerns the construal of televisual characters through dialogue and other semiotic resources. The focus of Part II on characterization was chosen because of the paucity of research on characterization and television dialogue, with few serious attempts to model characterization in both linguistics and media studies.

Chapter 2 deals with characteristics of fictional television, in particular television series. Its different sections explore the rationale behind the analysis of television and the significance of television in our lives, important television forms and genres, and communicative aspects of television series: their communicative context, their inherent multimodality, their adherence to the code of realism, and the general nature of television characters. Chapter 3 applies the concepts set up in Chapter 2 to the analysis of an exemplar of one of the prevalent contemporary TV genres – the hybrid 'dramedy', which has elements of 'soap drama' and comedy, and which is seriously under-researched in television studies. It also includes an analysis of the language of DVD advertising discourse used to attract an audience to buying DVDs of fictional television series. Chapter 4 considers features and functions of television dialogue and explores differences between dialogue in dramedy and naturally occurring conversation. Chapter 5 uses corpus linguistic methodology to investigate differences in the language of 'dramedy characters'; Chapter 6 introduces the concept of 'expressive' character identity and features a corpus analysis of emotive interjections; Chapter 7 provides an in-depth analysis of the multimodal construal of expressive character identities in one scene; and Chapter 8 explores expressive character identity in terms of ideology and shared attitudes. Chapter 9 concludes the book with some final remarks.[1]

Throughout the book, the main points about fictional television series will be mostly illustrated through case studies of a particular contemporary popular US American television series, the dramedy *Gilmore Girls* (Warner Brothers, 2000–2007), that has had a global impact. It is worth noting that there is a tradition of focusing on one cultural product or author both in media studies, with individual monographs and edited volumes (Akass & McCabe 2004, McCabe & Akass 2006, Allen 2007) on television series such as *CSI* (CBS, 2000–), *Desperate Housewives* (Touchstone Television/ABC, 2004–), *Sex and the City* (HBO, 1998–2004) and in Stylistics, with research on individual authors such as Dickens (Mahlberg 2007) or Austen (Fischer-Starcke 2007). Most linguistic research (Rey 2001, Bubel 2006, Bubel & Spitz 2006, Quaglio 2008, 2009, Stokoe 2008) also addresses a particular television series only, whether this is *Star Trek* (NBC/Paramount, 1966–1969, 1987–1994, 1993–1999), *Sex and the City*, *Ally McBeal* (FOX, 1997–2002) or *Friends* (NBC, 1994–2004). In the context of this book, this focus on one series has the clear advantage that it allows us to elaborate extensively on the background and context of a series in which the linguistic analyses of its dialogue are embedded; it means that the analyses are coherent throughout, and we can see how the different analyses can illuminate various aspects of a television series. However, reference will also be made to my own and other linguists' analyses of *Golden Girls* (NBC, 1985–1992), *Dawson's Creek* (Warner Brothers, 1998–2003), *Friends* and *Lost* (ABC, 2004–), and I will frequently refer to other fictional television programmes and try to generalize to them. That is, the case studies of *Gilmore Girls* are employed for illustrative purposes only, demonstrating analytical frameworks and methodologies, and findings are related to other television series as much as possible. The television programmes that will be mentioned in this book are a mixture of contemporary (at the time of writing, for example, *Lost*), 'classic' (e.g. *Golden Girls*) and 'cult' (e.g. *Friends, Sex and the City*) series, mainly from the United States. The majority of these are available as DVD box sets and reruns of most of the classic and cult series are broadcast by cable television networks in the United States or can be viewed online.

Note

[1] A note on the use of notes in this book: The majority of the notes are used simply to direct the reader to further studies or research on discussed topics, or to point to alternative linguistic frameworks/methodologies that can be used in the analysis. This information has been delegated to the notes, so as to not 'break the flow' of reading. At other times, the notes will give information on methodological or terminological issues.

Part I

Fictional Television: Dialogue and Drama

Chapter 2

Analysing Television

Chapter 2 begins with describing some of the motivations behind analysing television before giving an introduction to some of the important aspects of fictional television: its forms and genres, its communicative context, the various modes/modalities it combines, the code of realism and the nature of televisual characters.

1 Why Television?

Pennycook (2007) comments on the widespread tendency to dismiss popular culture, which, as he says,

> has a long history: from a culturally conservative point of view, popular music and entertainment are the shallow interests of a populace devoid of an interest in higher culture; from a more leftist point of view, popular culture is mass culture, soporific entertainment to passify [sic] the people . . . . I argue by contrast that there are social, cultural, political, aesthetic, philosophical and educational grounds for seeing popular culture in more complex terms. (Pennycook 2007: 13)

As part of popular culture, television also has a long tradition of being attacked, and with other popular cultural products has been cast 'as the degraded, the illegal, or the immoral' (Fiske 1994: 243) despite the 'empowering pleasures' (Fiske 1994: 254) it has to offer. The analysis of 'popular' fictional television series of the kind studied in this book may thus need some justification. Without offering an exhaustive discussion, some key points will be made below as to why we should study television, especially fictional television.

First, the very 'popularity' of television entails a huge influence of it in our daily lives, as 'we spend more time viewing television programmes than on any other leisure pursuit, including going to the cinema, listening to CDs or even playing computer games' (Marshall & Werndly 2002: 8). Undoubtedly, television is a popular and important global medium that we engage with socially on an everyday basis: 'there is an argument in terms of scale – if popular culture is indeed so popular, and, moreover, closely bound up with English and globalization, we would be foolish to ignore it or to reduce it to dismissive comments about "pop culture" or "mass culture"' (Pennycook 2007: 81). In cultural and media studies products of popular culture, including television series, have been studied precisely because of this 'popularity', and the argument for taking popular culture seriously 'is an argument that would not be necessary for a cultural studies audience' (Pennycook 2007: 13). Lacey (1998) states: 'From a Media Studies perspective all media artifacts are worthy of investigation, particularly if they are popular. They are worthy of study because they have much to teach us about how societies are organized and how societies create meaning' (Lacey 1998: 84).

Indeed, the popularity of and our engagement with television is not just limited to viewing television programmes. Not only do we watch television, we also talk about it and even use it to negotiate our identities. Even those of us who (say they) do not watch television use that very claim to construe an aspect of their identity. Undoubtedly, we negotiate our identities partially through how much television or what television programmes we watch (e.g. in Australia *World News Australia* on SBS vs. *Today Tonight* on Seven; e.g. in the United States *The NewsHour with Jim Lehrer* on PBS vs. *Fox News Watch* on Fox). People frequently watch television together and/or talk to each other about it, both at home, among friends and at the workplace. As 'uses and gratification theory' argues, television fulfils needs for social interaction, relationship and identity building, by helping viewers both to bond with characters, to talk to others about television series and to compare our own identity with those of televisual characters (Selby & Cowdery 1995: 186). For instance, it has been suggested that television programmes, like other products of popular culture, have a crucial part to play in consumers' making sense of everyday reality, constructing identity and constructing desires (Pennycook 2007: 81, de Kloet & van Zoonen 2007: 337). To elaborate briefly on one of these aspects, Hermes (2005), drawing on Mepham (1990) and Hartley (1999), argues that television works as a transmodern teacher, telling stories 'to which people can turn in their efforts to answer questions which invariably spring up through their lives. What is possible for me, who can I be, what can my life consist of, how can I bring this about? What is it like to be someone else, to be particular kinds of other people, how does it come about that people can be like that?' (Mepham 1990: 60, quoted in Hermes 2005: 12). From his personal experience, the British novelist Nick Hornby writes:

> I spent as much time watching telly and films when I was a kid as I did lying around reading books. I think it's crazy that writers are only allowed to say that certain books have influenced them. I'm of a generation where that has not happened and, yes, there are writers that influenced me very much

> but the formative experiences of childhood were cinematic or television. (Totaro 2009)

Philosopher Mark Rowlands also alludes to this in the title of his book *Everything I Know I Learned from TV: Philosophy for the Unrepentant Couch Potato,* and Critical Discourse Analyst Ruth Wodak argues that fictional television series such as *The West Wing* (NBC, 1999–2006) offer

> a specific perspective (*event model*) on how 'politics is done' for the American lay audience (and because the series has been dubbed in many languages, for a much bigger global audience). In other words it offers a model of how all of us are supposed to believe politics is done! (Wodak 2009: 22)

A brief note in this context (of the importance of television) on new media: While some people may argue that television is 'old' media, and while it may face increasing challenges from the new media, 'free-to-air television can deliver one thing that nothing else can – millions of people, in the same place, at the same time' (Idato 2009: 3). Further, television content often 'migrates' from television to other platforms. As Australia's Channel Ten chief programmer David Mott puts it, 'So the ability to put the content out there [on other platforms] where they [people] want to see it is fantastic. But at the end of the day, the content has to start somewhere, and globally it is still driven by television' (quoted in Idato 2009: 3). Fictional television plays a big role in this context, with DVD box sets available to buy of many past and current series, and with the possibility to download individual episodes from platforms such as iTunes.

The significance of television in our lives is further shown by the level of academic attention it has attracted (outside linguistics) as evidenced by the existence of over 3000 articles on television studies in journals since 1995 (Allen 2004: 11). With respect to the interdisciplinary field of television studies (Allen 2004) and the more general field of media studies (Miller 2009), the main focus has been on television institutions, ownership/control, technologies of television, effects of television/audience research, global and local contexts of television, television and the new media, television genres, television production and reception, television narratives, and television and ideology/representation/content (e.g. gender, race, age), with methodologies ranging from textual (image/semiotic/structural) analysis to content analysis and ethnographic surveys (Selby & Cowdery 1995, Burton 2000, Allen & Hill 2004). In contrast, television dialogue is a neglected topic in linguistic research in line with a general tendency where 'the language of popular culture has been largely overlooked in applied linguistics and TESOL' (Pennycook 2007: 9). As shown by the variety of topics investigated in media/television studies there are many aspects that a linguistic analysis of television dialogue could focus on systematically, such as humour/comedy/pleasure, genre analysis or television narratives, with the emphasis in this book on some of the more neglected aspects of fictional television series – the genre of 'dramedy' (a comedy/drama hybrid), dialogue and the televisual character.

As a matter of fact, there are also good reasons for focusing on fictional television series in particular, which we can briefly consider now. First, the importance of fictional television becomes clear when we look at audience figures. For instance, considering broadcast (rather than cable) TV usage in the United States for the week of 20 April 2009 (Monday through Sunday) figures show that six fictional television series (*CSI* [CBS, 2000–], *Criminal Minds* [CBS, 2005–], *Grey's Anatomy* [ABC, 2005–], *Desperate Housewives* [Touchstone Television/ABC, 2004–], *The Mentalist* [CBS, 2008–], *NCIS 9P-Special* [CBS, 2003–]) feature in the top ten (the top four broadcasts are different versions of *American Idol* [FOX, 2002–] and *Dancing with the Stars* [ABC, 2005–]), with viewers ranging from 14.6 millions to 12.6 million (www.nielsenmedia.com). In Australia the currently most watched weekly television drama (*Packed to the Rafters* [Seven Network, Australia, 2008–]) has 2 million viewers (Idato 2009). In Britain, serial fictional television programmes such as *Coronation Street* [ITV, UK, 1960–] and *Eastenders* [BBC, UK, 1985–] repeatedly feature prominently among the weekly top ten programmes (www.barb.co.uk/report/weeklyTopProgrammes?, figures accessed for 4–10 May 2009; compare also the figures for 1992 reported in Selby & Cowdery 1995: 77).

Second, it is worth noting that the dialogue featured in fictional television series can have a significant influence on learners of English in non-English speaking countries, who may buy the DVDs and watch the original versions. For such learners, 'television programmes and films may be one of the best opportunities to hear a foreign language spoken. This also means that film [and TV, M.B.] language becomes an influential model for advanced learners of English' (Mittmann 2006: 575). From an ESL perspective, Quaglio (2008) also argues for an analysis and use of television dialogue in the English language classroom. Broadening this argument, the language shown on television may also have an impact on native speakers, for example the borrowing by speakers in the United Kingdom of particular expressions from television series (Coupland 2007). As part of the mass media, television helps to shape the 'sociolinguistic environment' (Coupland 2007: 185). Scripted television language may also have an influence on other languages when it is dubbed into these languages (Mittmann 2006, Díaz-Cintas 2009).

Third, fictional television series also engage audiences in particular ways. Creeber notes that 'in terms of hours alone the series and serial can produce a breadth of vision, a narrative scope and can capture an audience's involvement in a way equalled by few contemporary media' (Creeber 2004: 4). It is television series in particular that feature active fan involvement (Mittell 2004: 177). As Roman also points out, '[t]elevision programs and characters have a unique ability to become an intimate part of a household and family' (Roman 2005: 130, see also Esslin 2002: 42). In fact, audiences interact with television series and characters in diverse ways, ranging from being consumers to being fans, cultists, enthusiasts (de Kloet & van Zoonen 2007, citing Abercrombie & Longhurst 1998) and ranging from (wishful or not) identification with a character to affinity/liking and parasocial interaction (Cohen 1999, Giles 2002).

While there are hence a number of reasons for exploring fictional television, the decision to start this exploration with English-speaking culture (this book mentions mainly programmes from Australia, the United Kingdom and especially the United States), and to focus on American series is supported by the fact that television is becoming more and more globalized. The United States is a forerunner in its development: 'All of the main television formats – news, soaps, drama, game shows and advertising – were invented in America' (Machin & van Leeuwen 2007: 12). This is one reason why I have chosen a US American television series (*Gilmore Girls* [Warner Brothers, 2000–2007], cf. Chapter 3) as a particular focus in this book. American popular culture is a truly global phenomenon in the twenty-first century, with America supplying most of the world's entertainment (Olson 2004: 115). It 'has become the popular culture of the world at large. American television is thus more than a purely local phenomenon. It fascinates – and in some instances frightens – the whole world' (Esslin 2002: xv). At the same time, my perspective as a 'stranger' or 'outsider' to American language and culture (as someone who grew up in Germany and currently lives in Australia) will hopefully allow me to perceive interesting cultural points about a television series that someone all too-familiar with the culture may not notice. Regarding the point of nationality, global television in fact transcends national identity and is a major source for construing cultural identities (Barker & Galasiński 2001: 8), affiliation and bonding. As Hermes puts it, 'In everyday life, our allegiances and feelings of belonging often relate more easily and directly to (global) popular culture than to issues of national or local governance' (Hermes 2005: 1).

2 Television Forms and Genres

Sections 2 and 3 introduce some analytical concepts that can be used in the analysis of fictional television and that will be applied to a particular series in Chapter 3. This section explores television forms and genres, before Section 3 deals with the communicative context of fictional television.

Distinguishing between different forms and genres is a common way of differentiating television broadcasts, allowing us to group television broadcasts together in certain categories. While there are many different forms/genres of television in general, such as documentary, talk show, news broadcast, reality television, game show, television commercial, variety show, television movie or talent show, this section focuses on serial/serialized fictional television genres (contemporary examples from the United Kingdom and the United States are *Black Books* [Channel 4, UK, 2000–2004], *Spaced* [Channel 4, UK, 1999–2001], *House* [FOX, 2004–], *Desperate Housewives* [Touchstone Television/ABC, 2004–], *Grey's Anatomy* [ABC, 2005–], *Lost* [ABC, 2004–]), in particular television series that have a dramatic element.

A first important distinction to make in this context is that between a television *series* and a television *serial* (e.g. Huisman 2005b). Series usually feature the same characters, theme and settings, and stories are usually completed in one episode even though there may also be a few meta-narratives and mini meta-narratives across episodes and/or seasons, for example, in *Friends* (NBC, 1994–2004) or *Ally McBeal* (FOX, 1997–2002). Multiple plotlines can also exist, and minor characters (e.g. boyfriends/partners/friends) as well as settings can occasionally change (e.g. from school to university in *Dawson's Creek* [Warner Brothers, 1998–2003]). Each episode is relatively self-contained although there are occasional cliff-hangers across episodes and characters have a memory of (meaning the audience has to know) what has gone on in previous episodes. Although viewers do not have to watch each episode in order to follow the story, a series does demand some audience loyalty. *Serials* have more continuing storylines where the narrative is very open-ended, extends across individual episodes, and 'will go on for as long as audience interest and advertising support endure' (Huisman 2005b: 154). Soap operas such as *Neighbours* (Ten network, Australia, 1985–) are a typical example of a serial, but the more action-oriented *24* (FOX, 2001–) or *The Wire* (HBO, 2002–2008) would be two others. In fact, many programs today fall between a series and a serial (Dunn 2005: 132):

> While the series is still continuous and never-ending, storylines now often develop from one episode to another (even introducing cliff-hangers). This produces a cumulative narrative of sorts that does not exactly prevent viewers watching episodes in any order but which can be (and often are) watched in sequence. (Creeber 2004: 11)

The 'flexi-narrative' of series and serials can be regarded as reflecting the dynamic nature of the television medium (Creeber 2004: 2), and they have been argued to adequately 'reflect and respond to the increasing uncertainties and social ambiguities of the contemporary world' (Creeber 2004: 7).[1] This book will not say much about serials but deals mainly with television series, which, incidentally, are popular in the world of television because they offer

> a mixture of familiarity – the freedom from the need to make an intellectual effort, to think oneself into each new episode – and novelty: the recurring

> characters who will have become as familiar as members of one's own family, will, each week, appear in new and different situations and circumstances. Each week's episode will have this same mixture, but with a slightly different flavor. In short, the series provides the viewer with a sense of security, a structure that allows him to find his way through the chaos. (Esslin 2002: 37)

In other words, series are appealing because they simultaneously provide the viewer with intimacy/continuity/security and suspense/entertainment/novelty: 'once people engage, they want to remain engaged' (Idato 2009: 3), creating what Australia's channel Ten chief programmer David Mott calls 'stickiness' (in Idato 2009).

Several units of analysis can be distinguished in television series (see Huisman 2005b: 170):[2]

- the **series** as a whole;
- several **seasons** of a series (one season features several episodes and spans a certain period of time);
- several **episodes** (a specific number per season);
- several **segments** within episodes (units between advertisements);
- several **scenes** (a unit shot on the same location or studio set) within segments;
- several **shots** (with the same camera angle) within scenes.

With respect to the typical content and narratives of television series, different genres may be distinguished such as a sitcom (which can further be broken down into, for example, domestic sitcoms), action series, police series, science fiction series, detective series, fantasy series, prison series, mystery drama, soap drama etc. A more general generic distinction would be between 'drama' and 'comedy'. In fact, the term *genre* is a very fuzzy one; sometimes the series and the serial are themselves talked about as 'genres', and 'there is no agreed list of television genres' (Dunn 2005: 138).[3] Generally speaking, a genre is a 'category or class . . . marked by a particular set of conventions, features and norms' (Neale 2001: 1). The categorization of television broadcasts into genres can include differences in story-telling, plot, performance, style, content and other aspects: 'there are no uniform criteria for genre delimitation – some are defined by setting (westerns), some by actions (crime shows), some by audience effect (comedy), and some by narrative form (mysteries)' (Mittell 2004: 173). For example, the genre of 'soap drama' (e.g. *Friends* [NBC, 1994–2004], *Sex and the City* [HBO, 1998–2004], *Queer as Folk* [Channel 4, UK, 2000–2005]), which combines elements from the genres of soap opera and drama, is defined by its use of close-ups, its focus on dialogue, its quick editing, and its multiple storylines (Creeber 2004: 115). The soap drama is also a good example of the widespread contemporary phenomenon that 'television plays fast and loose with genre boundaries, embracing the hybrid genre . . . and self-reflexively referencing other genres' (Dunn 2005: 138). Thus, while the term *genre* is fuzzy and television broadcasts frequently conflate different generic elements, Turner (2001a) shows how it is used by audiences, academic researchers and critics and the television industry to select, understand, segment, and relate televisual texts to each other. Dunn (2005) as well as Mills (2005) also point to the widespread use of genre by the media industry and audiences:

> genre is still a much-used concept in relation to television, by audiences and by the television industry, even if they might not use the word itself. In marketing terms, genre is a way of distinguishing between programs for audiences; it is also a way of 'branding' broadcast channels . . . . It is a way of identifying whole TV channels, some of which are named by genre: the movie channel, the comedy channel, music television (MTV) and so on. (Dunn 2005: 138)

> media industries are commonly structured around departments making certain kinds of programmes; programmes thus contain material which can be read as conforming to generic structures; and audiences make sense of texts by comparison to genre expectations. And these three aspects respond to one another, with audiences selecting certain texts because of their preference for certain genres, and production responding to audiences' understandings of the products it supplies. (Mills 2005: 26)

Neale (2001: 3) argues that genre is multidimensional and can be put to different analytical uses.[4] In terms of genre in this book we will particularly look at the popular, contemporary and hybrid 'dramedy', a mixed 'drama-comedy' genre that will be introduced in Chapter 3.

3 Characteristics of Television

The following sections briefly discuss the most important characteristics of fictional television with respect to four aspects:

1. communicative context;
2. multimodality;
3. the code of realism;
4. character identity in television.

3.1 Communicative context

Scripted dialogue, whether in plays or in television is very different from ordinary, naturally occurring conversation with respect to its communicative context. It is not spontaneous talk but pre-planned, construed dialogue that is controlled by its author(s) (Spitz 2005: 22). Importantly, scriptwriting for television does not in general feature a *unique* author/writer expressing themselves 'poetically' or 'artistically', rather it is both a creative and a commercial team effort (with different writers having different roles, for example, drafting, rewriting), although, as Selby and Cowdery (1995: 90) argue, the writer's voice can nevertheless come through to a certain extent.[5] What this means for the nature of scripted dialogue in terms of differences to naturally occurring conversation will be explored in more detail in Chapter 4. In this section I will only talk about the relation between television producers, the audiovisual text, and its audience.

The relation between a television audience and what they are watching has been described as a particular kind of mediated discourse, *screen-to-face discourse* (Bubel 2006: 46). Like other types of mediated discourse it involves several 'embedded levels' (Short 1981), 'layers' (Clark 1996) or 'orders' (Huisman 2005b: 166) – where characters, the production team and the audience interact as participants in various actions of interpretation. Here I shall adopt Bubel's (2006) model, which takes into account both the layered nature of screen-to-face discourse, its multiple authorship (screenwriters, casting directors, actors, directors, directors of photography, camera operators, composers, sound recordists, mixers and editors), its audience and cognitive processes involved in the construal and interpretation of television dialogue. Her model draws both on cognitive (Clark 1996) and sociological theories (Goffman 1976, 1979), and is represented in Figure 2.1 on page 16.

In this model, the audience are both ratified participants (they are intended to be part of the communicative context) and overhearers (in Goffman's sense).[6] This seems also to be recognized by professional practitioners who suggest that

> The object of television acting . . . is to make the viewer believe that he is watching something that he is **not meant to watch**, that he is, in fact, '**dropping in on** something that was going on before he switched on his set and which will continue after he has left'. (Hayman 1969: 155, quoted in Durham 2002: 82–3; my bold)

So, as Bubel suggests, the television production team designs the dialogue with a target audience (the overhearers) in mind, making educated guesses on its world knowledge and its knowledge of the characters. In so doing, 'the production team and the actors aim for overlap between the characters' common ground and the audience's knowledge in a mediated grounding process' (Bubel 2006: 57).

The 'overhearer design' of television dialogue also entails the intelligibility of television dialogue (compare Chapter 4). On the level of dialogue, actors,

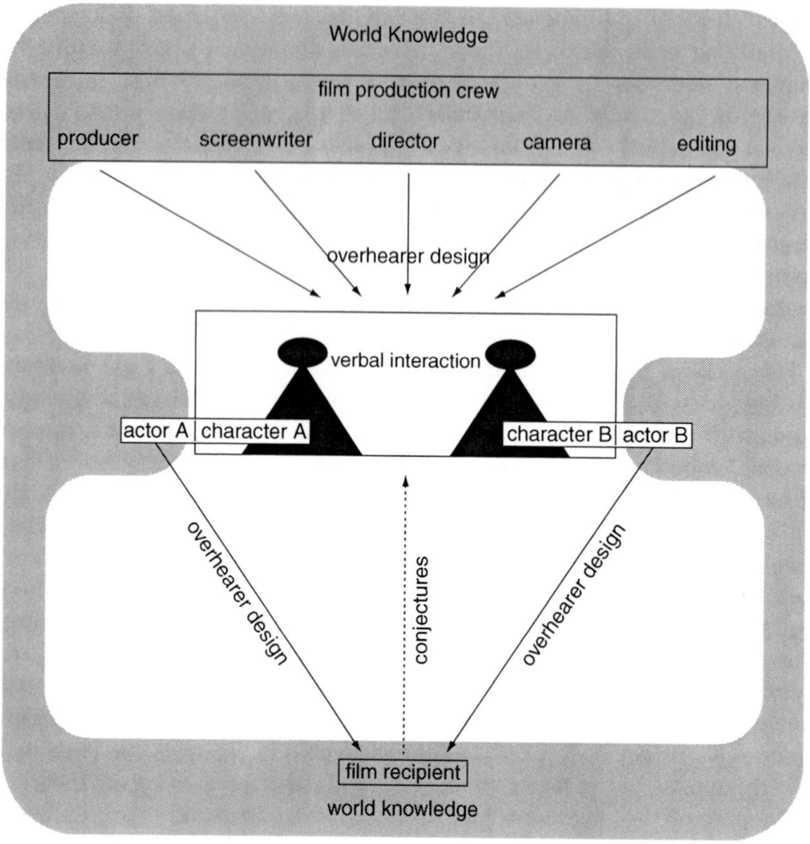

FIGURE 2.1 Screen-to-face discourse (from Bubel 2006: 57).

who are most noticeable to the audience, perform characters' utterances, with the performance being a joint achievement by the production team, with decisive contributions by the camera team, editors, directors and producers. That is, the actor's performance is mediated through technology and depends on the choices made by others (Durham 2002: 82).[7] The audience uses their knowledge to interpret the dialogue and to draw inferences from it. This knowledge is believed to be structured in schemata or frames, and involves various aspects of the world, including knowledge about film or television (e.g. generic patterns or filmic conventions). The audience also engages in *imagination*, imagining what is happening at the level of the television story (Clark 1996), *appreciation*, appreciating the purposes and techniques behind the story (Clark 1996), as well as *character* and *relationship impression formation* (Bubel 2006: 58).[8] We will look more closely at the audience of television series in Chapters 3 and 8.

Implicitly inherent in this model is the distinction between target and actual audience – what Huisman calls 'illocutionary' vs. 'perlocutionary' audience (Huisman 2005b: 155). Target/illocutionary audiences are both envisaged by media producers and construed in the text (see Chapter 3: Section 2). Television is financed by advertising and so needs to attract a large audience, which in turn results in a 'genericizing effect' (Tim Gooding, p.c. 14/10/08), routinization (Ellis 2004), or creative conservatism (the use of established conventions), the segmentation of a television episode and repetitive as well as open-ended stories (Huisman 2005b: 159–60), although the subscription-only cable company HBO (Home Box Office Entertainment) tries for unconventional, surprising and challenging story telling (Akass & McCabe 2007). Creative conservatism also influences dialogue which can be rather conventionalized. In commercial terms, the target audience is 'the audience that is sold to advertisers. Whether or not [this] is then realised as an actual group of consumers who buy the products is one of the great gambles of the free market' (Fulton 2005a: 5). In terms of the media as business, we can make a further distinction between creative agency (scriptwriters, directors, actors etc.), and the agency as television company (Huisman 2005b: 155). Both creative and institutional agencies are listed in the credits at the beginning and end of individual episodes of television series.

Finally, the communicative context, as indicated in Bubel's model above, involves what she calls 'world knowledge', both on the producers' and on the audience's part. This 'knowledge' arguably also includes 'ideology'. In fact, the study of representation, ideology and media texts is a major concern in cultural and media studies (see, for example, Lacey 1998: 98–108, Burton 2000: *passim*, Allen & Hill 2004, O'Shaughnessy & Stadler 2005, Mills 2005: chapter 4, Lancioni 2006, Stokoe 2008: 293). Chapter 8 deals more extensively with the notion of ideology in television series, and more will be said about the complex relationship between ideology, television series and audience there.

3.2 Multimodality

A television series is a multimodal product, involving semiotic modes, or modalities, other than language as well as language:[9] communication 'occurs . . . in tightly bundled clusters of data that bombard the senses' (Esslin 2002: 20), and only some of these data are linguistic. Film and television directors control and stage events as *mise-en-scene* (setting, lighting, costume, action) in space and time (Bordwell & Thompson 2004: 176–228, McIntyre 2008). For instance, characters perform in a particular setting, which 'need not be only a container for human events but can dynamically enter the narrative action' (Bordwell & Thompson 2004: 179). In some television series, for example *Queer as Folk* (Channel 4, UK, 2000–2005), specific objects are associated with particular characters, constituting their 'symbolic domain' (Thornham &

Purvis 2005: 48). More generally, setting can be related to characters and events in narratives in various ways (Toolan 2001: 92–3). Multimodality is also involved in the performance of actors as well as in the control of shots, editing and the construction of the soundtrack. This chapter only lists some aspects of multimodality in the television series; for a more detailed introduction see Bordwell and Thompson (2004) on film and Selby and Cowdery (1995) as well as Lury (2005) on television. We will first look at multimodality in characters and then at multimodality in the product.

3.2.1 Multimodality in characters

Like drama (Short 1998, Sanger 2001: 1), television dialogue is realized in a multimodal performance by actors in a specific setting. This can make all the difference, as the 'body and voice [of the actor] are themselves the medium through which skill is expressed' (Mills 2005: 73):

> [I]n memorizing and speaking the lines, nearly every actor changes the wording. Lines are improvised, cut, repeated, stammered, swallowed, paraphrased; changes may be minor or major, but the results represent the unique alchemy of *that* script in the mouth, mind, and heart of *that* actor. (Kozloff 2000: 92)

In contrast to prose fiction, where characters' internal mental states can be described, in television, as in film (Lothe 2000: 86), such mental states have to be either present in the dialogue or performed by the actors; they need to be 'conveyed externally and visually' (Fulton 2005b: 110) as well as vocally, sometimes in connection with camera techniques (van Leeuwen 1996: 88). The 'dramatic discourse of television drama is heavily dependent upon the close-up shot of the face and the thoughts, emotions and reactions conveyed by that face' (Durham 2002: 87). Other aspects of character identity are also realized in the performance. By restricting our analysis to dialogue only, we thus neglect the meaning potential of other aspects of the performance.

Short (1998: 12) lists the following performance features (compare also Lacey 1998: 11–13) – I have added some relevant references which deal with these features in more detail than is possible in the scope of this section, either in general or with respect to television and film.

Action
What is done on stage (movement, placing of objects and other 'business'),
Gestures
Body position and posture changes
Facial expression
Direction of gaze

(Darwin 1965, Morris 1977, Ekman 1997, 1999, Kozloff 2000: 95–6, Martinec 2001, Kendon 2004, Baldry & Thibault 2006, McNeill 2005, Eisenstein 2008, Hood forthcoming).

Speech
Assignment of general pronunciation features (e.g. non-standard accents, and unusual speech features, like stutters)
Assignment of intonation contours and tonic placement for each line
Paralinguistic phenomena (e.g. tone of voice, loudness, speed of delivery, pauses, breathing etc.)
(Kozloff 2000: 91–5, Chion 1999, van Leeuwen 1999, Baldry & Thibault 2006).

Appearance
Sex, age and physical size of actors
Skin colour, hair colour and other physical features
What the characters wear
(Morris 1977: 213–21, Bruzzi 1997, Bordwell & Thompson 2004: 184–92).

Such multimodal performance features are important for construing character identity in television (Pearson 2007: 44). Performance may also draw our attention to television dialogue: In performance

> the act of communication is put on display, objectified, lifted out to a degree from its contextual surroundings, and opened up to scrutiny by an audience. Performance thus calls forth special attention to and heightened awareness of the act of communication. (Bauman 1992: 44, cited in Pennycook 2007)

In terms of the performing body and its unaltered external features, television characters are 'conflated with the actor who embodies [them]' (Pearson 2007: 44), so that television characters have the same bodily features as the actors who play them. Incidentally, the social sciences have recently seen a 'somatic turn' or 'move towards the body' (see Pennycook 2007 for an overview), with language performance essentially seen as embodied. This is also relevant concerning identity: 'Who you are is partly a matter of how you speak, how you write, as well as a matter of embodiment – how you look, how you hold yourself, how you move, and so forth' (Fairclough 2003: 159). More generally, possible analyses with respect to the body in television include but are not limited to:

- what meanings the body carries in televisual interaction;
- how the body is used by actors in their performance;
- how the body is talked about;
- what bodies are represented (e.g. fat/thin, old/young, dis/abled, 'conventionally beautiful/ugly' etc.).

The bodily multimodal performance of characters in television series can be influential in providing role models to audiences. As Coupland and Gwyn note, following the sociologist Giddens's ideas, 'we can "create" ourselves, to an extent including physically, from all manner of role-models offered to us, particularly via the media' (Coupland & Gwyn 2003: 4). The analysis of multimodality in characters is thus worthy of further research interest, and will be the subject of a more in-depth investigation in Chapter 7.

3.2.2 Multimodality in the product

We can also look at multimodal features in the product, that is, at the meaning potential of the moving image itself, rather than its featured characters' performance. A 'classic' theory of image is Barthes's conceptualization of the denotation and connotation of images (for a discussion see Burton 2000: 29). More recently, social semiotic image analysis has shown ideational (representational), textual (compositional) and interpersonal meaning potential in the still and moving image (e.g. van Leeuwen 1996, Iedema 2001, Kress & van Leeuwen 2006, Caple 2008) and technological, functional and aesthetic aspects of the television image have also been explored (Lury 2005: chapter 1). However, while there are many similarities between the two, the *moving* image differs from the still image in motion (of the camera and depicted participants/entities), sequencing (of shots, scenes etc.), and the addition of speech, music and sound (Turner 1994, van Leeuwen 1996: 82, Iedema 2001). And the image in television differs from the image in film both in technological and other aspects (Lury 2005: chapter 1). Research which has looked at the language of film or technical codes usually considers visual, spatial and temporal aspects (e.g. Selby & Cowdery 1995, Lacey 1998: 23, Huisman 2005b: 169, Lothe 2000), with attention paid to shot size, camera angle, lens type, composition, focus, lighting codes and colour and film stock codes. For example, differences can be made between the kinds of shots used in television – establishing, tracking, long, medium, close-up (e.g. Lury 2005: 26–32). Images are also edited into sequences. Such editing includes the practice of 'continuity editing' (creating continuity from shot to shot), with various conventions of shot sequencing such as eyeline match (one shot shows someone looking at something which is off-screen, the next shot shows the object that is being looked at) or the 180° rule (constructing the action of a scene along a 180° line, with the action taking placing along this line) (Bordwell & Thompson 2004: 310–33). Types of edit between shots and scenes include cut, fade-out, fade-in, dissolve and wipe (Bordwell & Thompson 2004: 294–5). Camera techniques contribute to focalization, narrative voice/position/point of view and narrative development (Fulton 2005b: 108–22), and have an impact on acting (Durham 2002).

Finally, as van Leeuwen (1996) also mentions, moving images combine with sound (see also Chion 1999, Kozloff 2000: 97, Bordwell & Thompson 2004: chapter 9, Baldry & Thibault 2006). Here we can distinguish four dimensions:

1. on-screen dialogue (or monologue);
2. on-screen sound effects whose source is obvious (diegetic);
3. ambient sounds in the background, creating atmosphere;
4. off-screen non-diegetic sounds such as soundtrack music or voice-overs. (Lacey 1998: 52)

An alternative categorization of sound on television distinguishes between types of sound: sound as *voice* (including voice-overs and on-screen dialogue/monologue), sound as *music* (including soundtrack and theme song but also diegetic sound emanating from a seen source such as a radio), sound as *sound* (noises, environmental sounds, sound effects) and sound as *silence* (Lury 2005: chapter 2). Although I will not comment extensively on sound effects, features of on-screen dialogue will be examined more closely in Chapters 4 and 7.

To sum up, performance in film and television is a multimodal one, not simply a linguistic one:

> The simultaneous presentation of all this information [the actors' words, their voices, their intonations; their facial expressions, the look in their eyes, their body posture, their gestures, their costuming; the setting and its use of light and art direction] allows for a tight anchoring of the spectator's identification with the character, but it also permits the viewer to pick up subtle discrepancies and undertones. (Kozloff 2000: 99)

While Chapters 3–6 and 8 of this book focus predominantly on language, Chapter 7 will also take into account multimodality.

3.3 The code of realism

The code of realism is a term that refers to '[t]he imitation of reality' achieved through 'all elements of the film text' (Bubel 2006: 43). This usually occurs in realist television, and includes both techniques described above (e.g. editing conventions such as continuity editing, or the use of diegetic sound or employing hand-held cameras), acting (Durham 2002: 82) as well as the creation of 'convincingly "real" pseudo-human beings' (Pearson 2007: 47), and carefully crafted dialogue (Bubel 2006: 42). With respect to the latter, it needs to be noted that while television dialogue may imitate reality, it is clearly not the same as naturally occurring dialogue, as Chapter 4 will show.

Despite the imitation of reality on television, as in realist novels, there must also be 'a framing assumption shared by [creator and viewer] that they are jointly engaged in the creation of a pleasurable illusion' (Cameron & Kulick 2005: 118). Coleridge famously talked about 'the willing suspension of disbelief' on the part of readers, a concept which can also be applied to the audience of television series and serials. Further, scenes may occur where the realism is broken, for example, through authorial commentary (Kozloff 2000: 57) or through a foregrounding of its constructedness or textuality (Fiske 1994: 253). Television series also often feature characters and actions that are quirky or unusual rather than typical or 'normal' to create drama or humour (e.g. Dr. House played by Hugh Laurie in the series *House* [FOX, 2004–] or the character of Bernard Black played by Dylan Moran in *Black Books* [Channel 4, UK, 2000–2004]). Thus, humour may impact on realism or naturalness to a certain extent (Quaglio 2009). It is useful here to make a distinction between *cultural* and *generic* verisimilitude (Neale 1990, cited in Thornham & Purvis 2005). The former relates to conformity with the commonsense social world, including its norms, expectations and values, whereas the latter refers to conformity with the world of the genre, and allows a play with fantasy, for example, the presence of vampires in *Buffy the Vampire Slayer* (Warner Brothers, 1997–2003) and unexplained phenomena in *The X Files* (FOX, 1993–2002). Ang (1985, cited in Hermes 2005: 107) talks about the *emotional* realism of fictional series. Ontological issues are also of interest to viewers concerning characters, for example, whether someone is true to their character (Matheson 2005: 98). Realism of character is also crucial to enable viewers to form parasocial interactions with them (Giles 2002: 291). For further discussion of the complex notion of realism see Marshall and Werndly (2002: 83–7), Thornham and Purvis (2005: 61–73), and Hermes (2005: 107–08).

3.4 The nature of characters in television

To conclude this chapter, Section 3.4 briefly considers the nature of televisual characters from the point of view of both professional (scriptwriting) practice and media/television studies.

3.4.1 Professional practice

If we consider the nature of characters in television from the perspective of scriptwriting practice, it is clear that great emphasis is placed on characters as part of fictional stories:

> Stories become complex through the influence of **character**. It's character that impinges on the story, dimensionalizes the story, and moves the story in

> new directions. With all the idiosyncrasies and willfulness of character, the story changes. Character makes the story compelling. (Seger 1994: 149, bold face in original)

Similarly, the BBC's guidelines for sitcom place huge emphasis on characters:

> When planning a new idea, the characters should come first and if they are the right characters they will arrive with their world attached . . . Think about the people first, give them histories, test them out in different situations where they are under pressure and see how they react, think about what makes them happy or scared or angry, write monologues for each character in that character's tone of voice . . . Make the people authentic, put them in an authentic world and then find their comic tone. (Quoted in Huisman 2005a: 178)

Scriptwriters are thus advised to research characters' background, for example, their biography, personal/private life, context of culture, historical period, location, occupation, 'inner life', attitudes, language (Field 1984, Seger 1994, Blum 1995). Character, it is pointed out 'is the essence of drama, the primary mechanism from which compelling action arises to hold audiences in thrall' (Atchity in D'Vari 2005: ix).

In terms of scriptwriting advice on how to construe characters, this is therefore often done in terms of the character's relation to the storyline. Thus, writers are encouraged to concentrate on the 'character spine', in terms of thinking about a character's motivation, intention, goals/objectives, mission, actions, obstacles and change (Seger 1994, Blum 1995, Atchity in D'Vari 2005: xii). Similarly, some actors follow questions such as 'Who am I?', 'What do I want?', 'Why do I want it?', 'What must I overcome?' to help them create three-dimensional characters (Cannon 2009). The focus on a character's objectives, actions and circumstances for character development derives from the Stanislavskian (see Note 7) methodology (Durham 2002). These aspects of character are not necessarily just revealed through language as action is also crucial (e.g. Seger 1994). For instance, particular actions at the beginning of a series may be used as 'character keys', 'the small ways a character behaves that tell us about the large ways he'll behave as well' (Vorhaus 1994: 150). In another approach, characters are described in terms of character types such as Mover, Observer, Relater and Energizer (D'Vari 2005).

Both features of the character spine and character types are mostly demonstrated in these books through illustrative descriptions and examples from film/television. While the importance of dialogue (e.g. use of certain phrases, use of regional and social dialects/accents, professional discourse etc.) and multimodal features (e.g. clothes, personal adornments, body) for creating character is noted, there are no systematic comments on what kinds of linguistic devices contribute to construing character. In his comments on scriptwriting manuals, Quaglio (2009: 10) also includes the point that '[v]irtually no linguistic information is provided in these manuals; most "tips" rely on native-speaker intuition'. Indeed, budding screen writers are often encouraged to eavesdrop, practice, read/listen to dialogue, and use their imagination. The aim is to create realistic, credible, complete, consistent and unique characters (Blum 1995: 79). In line with the model of screen-to-face discourse outlined above, television scriptwriters 'model their characters on their culture's conceptions of people, making them person-like' (Pearson 2007: 41). Together with the resulting characterization present in the script, decisions by casting director and costume designer as well as the acting performance contribute to this complex creation of character (Durham 2002).

3.4.2 Media and television studies

If we consider the nature of characters in television from the point of view of media and television studies, fictional characters are similarly attributed a crucial part in the narrative. In sitcoms, plots and theme development can be crucially connected to character identity, and an episode can be more about aspects of a character's personality than about unfolding events (Selby & Cowdery 1995: 97). Similarly, in soap operas 'what we know of the character's past and hopes for the future are all important' (Selby & Cowdery 1995: 175). Viewers 'feel involved and interested' (Livingstone 1998: 119) in soap characters, and they are important for narrative and generic construction (Livingstone 1998: 119). Cohen (1999) reviewing previous studies summarizes as follows: 'In fictional programs, only through involvement with characters do viewers come to care about stories which otherwise lack relevance to viewers' real life'; 'the plot of the serial revolves around a set of characters with which the audience is meant to develop strong relationships'; 'it is the cast of characters, rather than the events, that are the show's main vehicle for influencing audiences' (Cohen 1999: 327).

The nature of television series results in specific characteristics of the televisual in contrast to the filmic or novelistic character. For example, television characters need to be relatively static to sustain a whole series, with room only for some biographical and personal development (Huisman 2005a: 178, Pearson 2007: 50). Although a television character can thus not change drastically,

> the character can be augmented with any number of biographical details, from the narratively trivial . . . to the narratively significant . . . . In television, it's more accurate to talk about character accumulation and depth than it is to talk about character development. The long-running American television

drama can create highly elaborated characters of greater accumulation and depth than any contemporary medium. (Pearson 2007: 56)

The importance of character in long-running television series, which Person mentions in this quote, provides a further reason for focusing the analysis in this book on *television series* in particular. The 'flexi-narrative' structure of television series (see above) is particularly suited to 'celebrate . . . character density' (Creeber 2004: 5). As film and television producer Jerry Bruckheimer says, television allows a fuller exploration of character than film, 'because you have 22 or 23, sometimes 24 one-hour episodes every year to explore them. You not only watch the characters, you get involved in their home life and the dramas within their own personal lives' (Carugati 2005).

As already suggested above, characters are important not only because they contribute to the code of realism, plot and narrative development (Pearson 2007: 49), but also because they allow viewers to emotionally engage and identify with what is portrayed on the screen. Character, as Toolan says, 'is often what most powerfully attracts readers to novels and stories' (Toolan 2001: 80), and no doubt it is also important in attracting viewers to television narratives. Interestingly, audiences can both identify positively and negatively with characters in televisual genres, with 'heroines' not entirely flawless and 'antagonists' not entirely 'evil' (Thornham & Purvis 2005: 47). Certain television genres such as sitcoms present recognizable character types, both social types (e.g. efficient secretary) and stereotypes (e.g. domineering wife) (Selby & Cowdery 1995: 108). It is also a common feature of television programmes that characters are used to carry ideological oppositions (cf. Chapter 8) between different lifestyles (e.g. *Family Ties* [NBC, 1982–1989] and *Dharma and Greg* [ABC/FOX, 1997–2002] as discussed in Feuer 2001b). That is, fictional television characters can stand for attitudes and values (misogyny, homophobia, environmentalism, political ideas), and are frequently contrasted with each other in these terms. Character identity from a linguistic perspective will be discussed in Part Two of this book, where we will look at what previous research in linguistics and media/television studies has said in particular about the *construal* rather than the *nature* of televisual characters.

Summarizing Sections 2 and 3, and extending Huisman's (2005b: 164) list, key features of fictional television involve:

- the design for an audience of overhearers;
- the use of established genres and typical generic make-up;
- the use of established narrative elements (character, action etc.);
- the reflection and construal of social values or ideologies;
- the use of multimodal techniques in the televisual construction (in characters and in the moving image);
- an adherence to the code of realism;

- the construal of highly elaborated but stable characters who are crucial for the fictional narrative.

All of these aspects potentially have an impact on the semiotics (the linguistic and multimodal characteristics) of fictional television, which will be considered in this book particularly with respect to the genre of dramedy (Chapter 3), linguistic characteristics of television dialogue (Chapter 4), and the construal of televisual characters (Chapters 5–8).

Notes

[1] Compare also Pearson (2007) on differences of series and serials with respect to character, and Creeber (2004) for an overview of the main structures of television drama (single play, TV movie, soap opera, series, anthology series, serial and miniseries) and on positive and negative reactions of critics towards the prevalence of series and serials in television.

[2] Other conceptualizations of analytical units in television series include acts, events, beats and story (McKee 1998), frame, shot, scene, sequence, generic stage, work as a whole (Iedema 2001), or shot, phase and macrophase (Baldry & Thibault 2006: 50). Narrative structure will not be discussed in this chapter, as the book focuses on characterization rather than story development. See, for example, Creeber (2004) on characteristics of 'narrative complexity' in television series, such as open narratives with no resolutions and evaded conclusions. For an early, semiotic account of syntagmatic and paradigmatic units in film see Metz (1974); for different conceptualizations of the structure of television see Matheson (2005: 92–93).

[3] There is also a long history of looking at genre in linguistics (see Lee 2001). I am more concerned with the notion of genre in the media industry and in media studies here, though this could profit from a more *linguistic* analysis of different television genres.

[4] By the multidimensional nature of genre Neale means that: 'Genre can mean "category" or "class", generic can mean "constructed or marked for commercial consumption"; genre can mean a "corpus" or "grouping", generic can mean "conventionally comprehensible"; genre can mean "formulaic", generic can mean "those aspects of communication that entail expectation"; and so on.' (Neale 2001: 3). For further discussion of television genres see Burton (2000), Creeber (2001), Davis and Dickinson (2004), Mittell (2004), Thornham and Purvis (2005: 44–61), Mills (2005: chapter 2), Dunn (2005) and Akass and McCabe (2007).

[5] For the global and industrial process of 'making television' involving financing, commissioning, pre-production, shooting, post-production, marketing etc. see, for example, Esslin (2002: 339–41) and Ellis (2004). For processes of scriptwriting see Haddrick (2001), Merriman (2003) and Elliot (2005). For differences between British and American production see Mills (2005: 54–60).

[6] For Goffman (1976, 1979) *overhearers* are unratified participants; *ratified participants* are not specifically addressed by speakers, and *addressees* are addressed

directly. Both Goffman's (1974, 1981) model of speakers, rather than hearers, (the *principal*, whose stance is expressed; the *author*, who generates the form of the content, and the *animator*, the physical sounding box), and Bell's (1991: 39) development in the context of the production of news into four speaker roles with eight sub-roles could also be adapted to fictional television, with manifold roles in producing television dialogue (e.g. film production company, producers, credited writers, scriptwriting team, actors etc.). For instance, the film production company fulfils the role of the principal; writers fulfil the role of the author, and actors fulfil the role of the animator.

7 The actors will perform characters according to their own talents and training such as Stanislavsky's Method Acting, disseminated in the United States by Lee Strasberg (New York Actors' Studio), Elia Kazan, Sanford Meisner and others (see Blum 1995: chapter 6, Collins 2002, Billington 2009), or physical theatre (Hunter 2009). Other theories of acting were developed by Vsevolod Meyerhold in Russia, Bertold Brecht in Germany and Jacques Lecoq in France (Billington 2009). There are manifold practice-oriented handbooks or manuals on acting (e.g. Bruder et al. 1986), with works by Uta Hagen (*Respect for Acting*), Michael Chekhov (*To the Actor: On the Technique of Acting*), Cicely Berry (*Voice and the Actor*), Patsy Rodenburg (*The Actor Speaks: Voice and the Performer*), Jacques Lecoq (*The Moving Body: Teaching Creative Theatre*), Dymphna Callery (*Through the Body: A Practical Guide to Physical Theatre*) or Mel Churcher (*Acting for Film: Truth 24 Times a Second*) being some of the seminal texts in the industry (Sophie Reissner, p.c.). However, as Mills (2005) argues, there is a lack of research on acting and performance (Mills 2005: 68). It is beyond the scope of this book to include the methodology and praxis of acting in television, but see Bordwell and Thompson (2004: 198–207) and *The Guardian*'s *Guide to Performing: Acting* (www.guardian.co.uk/stage/series/guide-to-performing-acting, last accessed 23 July 2009) on acting and different performance styles. Mills (2005: 67–79) also discusses acting, performance and differences between serious and humorous television to some extent, particularly relating to sitcom. From an actor's perspective, Durham (2002) describes differences in acting for theatre and in different categories of television.

8 It should not be assumed that every aspect of the communicative context has the same weight. From a professional point of view, actors and editors have considerable input on dialogue, and marketing to a target audience has a particularly significant influence as well (Tim Gooding, p.c., 14 October 2008). For example, while scriptwriters may be influenced by generic conventions, they may also tailor dialogue to a particular actor.

9 I use the terms *mode* or *modality* to refer to semiotic systems/resources such as language, image and gesture, speaking of *multimodality* when more than one semiotic system is involved. Strictly speaking, we can make a distinction between semiotic resources such as spoken and written language, visual imagery, mathematical symbolism and modalities or channels, for example, visual and aural (Caple 2010, following O'Halloran 2008). In this strict sense, a television series is multi-semiotic (language, image, gesture, facial expression, camera techniques) but bi-modal (visual and aural). However, there is a well-established tradition of speaking of multimodality rather than, say, 'multisemioticity' which I will also follow in this book.

Chapter 3

The Genre of Dramedy and its Audience

This chapter provides a more detailed introduction to one of the prevalent contemporary TV genres – the hybrid 'dramedy', which has elements of (soap) drama and comedy. Some UK and US examples are *Ally McBeal* (FOX, 1997–2002), *Ugly Betty* (ABC, 2006–), *Sex and the City* (HBO, 1998–2004) and *Gilmore Girls* (Warner Brothers, 2000–2007). This chapter also demonstrates how the concepts introduced in Chapter 2 for analysing fictional television can be applied to the analysis of a particular television series using the example of *Gilmore Girls.* (The sub-headings of Section 1 of this chapter thus mirror the headings of Chapter 2.) This is also the first analytical chapter of this book, showing how the advertising discourse of a dramedy construes its audience (Section 2).

1 Introducing *Gilmore Girls*

Gilmore Girls is used in this chapter as a case study to show how the concepts introduced in Chapter 2 can be used to talk about a particular fictional television series. At the same time, this chapter provides a backdrop to the case studies of *Gilmore Girls* that will be used throughout this book to demonstrate aspects and analyses of fictional television series. First, some background will be presented on the programme. *Gilmore Girls* is a contemporary US American television show produced by Amy Sherman-Palladino (seasons 1–6) and David S. Rosenthal (season 7),[1] which ran for seven seasons from 2000 to 2007. At the time of writing it was broadcast in the United States by ABC Family, and was still at N° 58 of *TVguide.com*'s most popular TV shows (www.tvguide.com/top-tv-shows, 12 August 2009). The contemporary nature of the show becomes apparent when considering that at the end of the final season (season 7), one of the protagonists joins journalists in accompanying Barack Obama on his campaign trail. Regarding the topics and storylines of *Gilmore Girls,* here, first, is a short (promotional) description from the official CW network website:

> Set in a storybook Connecticut town (Stars Hollow) populated with an eclectic mix of everyday folks and lovable lunatics, GILMORE GIRLS is a

> humorous multigenerational series about friendship, family and the ties that bind. . . . [T]he series revolves around thirtysomething Lorelai Gilmore and her college-age daughter, and best friend in the world, Rory. Lorelai has made her share of mistakes in life, but she has been doing her best to see that Rory doesn't follow in her footsteps. That may be easier said than done, considering that the two share the same interests, the same intellect, the same coffee addiction and the same eyes.
>
> From the beginning, this unique mother–daughter team has been growing up together. Lorelai was just Rory's age when she became pregnant and made the tough decision to raise her baby alone. This defiant move, along with Lorelai's fiercely independent nature, caused a rift between her and her extremely proper, patrician, old-money parents, Emily and Richard. However, Lorelai was forced to reconcile with them when she found herself in desperate need of money for Rory's tuition.
>
> Continuing to add to the unmistakable style of Stars Hollow is a colorful roster of town characters, including Lorelai's best friend and business partner Sookie St. James, Miss Patty, the local dance teacher and social commentator, Michel Gerard, the haughty concierge of the Dragonfly Inn, and Kirk, the town's jack-of-all-trades and master of none. Rory's two best friends are her intense classmate Paris Geller and childhood pal Lane Kim, who just married fellow musician, Zack, in a typically quirky Stars Hollow celebration. (www.cwtv.com/shows/gilmore-girls/about, last accessed 28 September 2007.)

Secondly, plot keywords for *Gilmore Girls* from *The Internet Movie Database* (www.imdb.com, accessed 26 May 2008) are:

Family	Teen
Fast Talker	Hotel
Yale University	Mother–Daughter Relationship
Shipper	Small Town
Connecticut	Inn
Female Lead	Diner
Female Chef	Prep School
Grandparents	Single Mother
Overbearing Mother	Character Name in Title

Finally, writer, creator and executive producer Amy Sherman-Palladino mentions that she created *Gilmore Girls* to represent a mother–daughter friendship and a studious, sexually not active young female teenager in contemporary society (cited in Calvin 2008a: 5). Coleman (2008) notes that what drives the narrative in *Gilmore Girls* are two 'foundational narrative drives – Lorelai's ongoing conflict with her parents, the two leads [sic] [i.e. Lorelai and Rory] pursuits of romantic fulfillment [sic]' (Coleman 2008: 175). (Table A.1 in Appendix 1 provides a cast list; Calvin 2008b includes further discussion of the series as well as an episode guide but episode recaps and descriptions of the series also abound on the internet.)

1.1 Why *Gilmore Girls*?

There are several reasons for choosing dialogue from *Gilmore Girls* as data throughout this book. In general, the focus on *one* television series has clear advantages in terms of thematic coherence, and we can see how the different analyses can shed light on various aspects of a television series. However, it needs to be pointed out that this book is not about *Gilmore Girls* as such (unlike Calvin 2008b), and thus is not intended as complementary to Quaglio's (2009) analysis of *Friends* or to the *Reading Contemporary Television* book series with individual books targeting television programmes such as *Sex and the City* (Akass & McCabe 2004), *CSI* (Allen 2007) or *Desperate Housewives* (McCabe & Akass 2006). Rather, as mentioned in Chapter 1, I use the data from *Gilmore Girls* primarily for illustrative purposes.

There are also several reasons for choosing *Gilmore Girls* in particular. For instance, it is a very contemporary television series (at the time of writing); all episodes are available on DVD, and transcripts are available online for all seasons. The series has also been very successful in a variety of ways: Commercially, it has attracted as many as 5.2 million viewers in the United States (season 2 and 3) and by season 5, it was the WB channel's second most watched primetime show (www.wikipedia.org;[2] see also Calvin 2008a: 2). *Gilmore Girls* also showed a 120% increase in the cost of an average commercial from 2000 to 2003 (www.nielsenmedia.com). In 2007, there were almost 100 websites dedicated to the series (Calvin 2008a: 2) and more than 10,0000 *Gilmore Girls* fan stories (Smith-Rowsey 2008). Westman (2007) mentions that *Gilmore Girls* enjoys success with 'a wide-ranging demographic – young girls, women 18–34, women over 34, and an increasing number of men' (Westman 2007: 24). Admittedly, however, the target audience of its host network, the CW (see Note 1), are young women between 18 and 34 (Romano 2006), though the median audience of *Gilmore Girls* in 2003 was in fact 32.4 years old (Livsey 2004), and it is 'not necessarily a teen show' (Amy Sherman-Palladino, quoted in 'Welcome to "The Gilmore Girls"' 2003). Culturally, the series has received many awards and award nominations, indicating that the series is recognized in the television industry. Internationally, *Gilmore Girls* was/is broadcast in at least 52 different countries, and academically, papers have been presented on the series in research on popular culture, with two edited volumes dedicated solely to *Gilmore Girls* (Calvin 2008b, Diffrient & Lavery forthcoming). However, it is also true that while there are manifold newspaper or magazine articles and interviews on *Gilmore Girls*, few academic or analytical publications were present before the publication of these two edited volumes, apart from brief mentions in books and journals (Calvin 2008a, email communication). With respect to Calvin's (2008b) edited volume, only a few chapters attend to language use, so there is a clear need for linguistic research on dialogue in the series.

Other reasons for choosing *Gilmore Girls* are, first, the importance of dialogue in the series, and, secondly, its interesting construal of female characters. Both aspects are addressed in more detail below.

Dialogue in Gilmore Girls

Dialogue is a key aspect of *Gilmore Girls,* as actor Yanic Truesdale notes: 'The show is known for the writing. So without that writing you don't have that show' ('The Gilmore Girls Turn 100' 2005). In terms of its realism, humour and dialogue respectively (Westman 2007) *Gilmore Girls* has been compared to other televisions shows like *Roseanne* (ABC, 1988–1997), *Malcolm in the Middle* (FOX, 2000–2006), *Northern Exposure* (CBS, 1990–1995), and *The West Wing* (NBC, 1999–2006). Thus, while multimodal aspects in *Gilmore Girls* as in any other television series are certainly very important, dialogue plays a particularly crucial role in this series, whose script length is 25 pages longer than the industry standard (Westman 2007). As Lauren Graham, who plays Lorelai Gilmore, says with respect to her work as an actress on *Gilmore Girls,* 'This is definitely the most challenging job I've ever had just in terms of how much language I deal with' ('Welcome to the *Gilmore Girls'* 2006). The actors in fact needed a dialogue coach to get their production speech up ('A Best Friend's Peek Inside the Gilmore Girls' 2007), because the dialogue is so fast-paced. This dialogue features manifold references and allusions to pop culture, – especially to film and television as a typical post-modern meta-fictional strategy – politics etc. Westman (2007) talks about 'its attention to intellectual wordplay and to a combination of arcane and current cultural references, all within a realistic setting' (Westman 2007: 23), and mentions intertextual references to classical literature, popular culture, American and European history, celebrity, feminist activism and current events. These are

> scattered liberally throughout the scripts and often appear without contextual cues – as a viewer, you either get the reference or you don't. These references pose a 'puzzle' for the show's audience, according to Lauren Graham and the audience's pleasure resides in sharing the characters' knowledge or in sharing the characters' pleasure in their exchange. (Westman 2007: 24)

Consider extract (1) for instance, with its reference to Kundera's *The Unbearable Lightness of Being*:

(1)

RORY:	Hey. You are not gonna believe it!
LORELAI:	Okay. Hold on. Believe what?
RORY:	Milan Kundera is speaking at our graduation.
LORELAI:	Oh.
RORY:	What? You're not a big Kundera fan?
LORELAI:	Uh, no. I'm unbearably light on him.
RORY:	I see.

(7.21, *Unto the breach*)

The titles of the various episodes themselves are frequently intertextual references, as the above extract from the episode entitled *Unto the breach* also demonstrates with its allusion to Shakespeare ('Once more unto the breach, dear friends, once more, Or close the wall up with our English dead!', *Henry V*).

With respect to intertextual references in a particular news story genre, Caple and Bednarek (forthcoming), following Caple (2008), note that a genre that features such references very frequently

> naturalizes the play, setting up a reading position from which the compliant or 'obliging reader' (Kitis & Milapides 1996: 585) is expected to figure out this play. This is a reader who is not only 'actively involved in the construction of meaning and significance, but also in the intertextual process of activating other texts and discourses which are part of his/her background knowledge in constructing the appropriate myths' (Kitis and Milapides 1996: 585). This is quite a demanding activity, one that requires considerable knowledge on the part of the reader, not only linguistically speaking, but also in terms of the general, popular and cultural knowledge that they must possess in order to participate. (Caple & Bednarek forthcoming)

As is the case with readers of these news stories, viewers of *Gilmore Girls* who 'get' the intertextual references, feel like a part of the community, bonding with the fictional population of Stars Hollow.[3] The references in *Gilmore Girls* work to 'membership the [viewers] into belonging to a community with shared linguistic and cultural values' (Caple & Bednarek forthcoming). As Calvin has put it, 'fans actively participate in unravelling these allusions, and it is one of the ways in which such an interactive viewing experience captivates an audience' (Calvin 2008a: 9). Because of its variety in referencing (both elite/official and popular/mainstream culture) it appeals to a greater range of audiences (Woods 2008: 131), though Scott Patterson (the actor who plays Luke Danes) says: 'It's an educated person's dream to watch that show just to see if they can figure out who that is, what that reference means, cause we sit there on the table reads and all go "huh?"' ('Welcome to the *Gilmore Girls*' 2006). With respect to translating/dubbing *Gilmore Girls* into other languages, references that refer squarely to American culture become a challenge ('International Success' 2004).[4] However, 'getting' these references is only one way of bonding with the series, and not doing so does not prevent viewers from making sense of the story. Further, in the United States, the DVD sets of some of the seasons include 'Gilmore-isms' booklets, where the pop culture references are explained (www.wikipedia.org). The special feature 'Gilmore Girls Goodies and Gossip for "Rory's Dance"' (2000) on the (Australian) DVD set for season 1 has 'on screen factoids' that explain many intertextual references made in this episode. The witty dialogue shown in the special features 'Gilmore-isms' (2000) and 'Who Wants to Talk Gilmore' (2005) include these references as well as other funny lines from season 1 and season 5. From a more critical perspective the allusions affirm viewers' 'status as consumers of and experts on popular culture' (Johns & Smith 2008: 33).

In terms of dialogue, the series is further indebted to earlier genres such as film noir and screwball comedy (see Kozloff 2000 for a description), where viewers were similarly 'asked to admire the witty banter of the script' (Berliner 1999: 6). But whereas in screwball comedies it is lovers who are represented as 'uniquely suited for each other by the way their talk is synchronized' (Kozloff 2000: 174), in *Gilmore Girls* it is a mother (Lorelai) and her daughter (Rory) and their relationship that is thus qualified. They are painted as unique, the only ones to understand their in-jokes, to do the fast-talking, and to get their references, representing a tight and close in-group, which even Lorelai's mother cannot access, often commenting on not understanding them. The references, then, also work 'as a bond between them and to exclude or include others' (Woods 2008: 134). While the analysis of *Gilmore Girls* dialogue in terms of intertextuality is certainly interesting, much research has already focussed on this (Westman 2007, Johns & Smith 2008, Woods 2008). The analyses of dialogue in this book will thus describe other linguistic aspects that contribute to the construal of character identity (Chapters 5–8).

The construal of female characters

With respect to the construal of female characters, *Gilmore Girls* has been praised for changing gender stereotypes and presenting a world where female intelligence is valued:[5]

> All of its characters exemplify, in varying degrees, the obsessive devotion to knowledge associated with the geek, but the characters are also extremely

> sociable and witty. In this combination, they represent only one part of the conventional 'geek' image – intelligence – and dispose of the other parts of the definition: the masculine and the unsociable. . . . In the world of the *Gilmore Girls*, women are brilliant, education is cool, and intelligence is a team sport. Brimming with wide-ranging cultural references delivered with conversational élan, *Gilmore Girls* exceeds the industry standard . . . for female intelligence, offering multiple and recurring images of smart women in a variety of ages and occupations. (Westman 2007: 23)

As such, the construal of female characters in *Gilmore Girls* works contrary to at least one ideology by portraying attractive and intelligent women: 'If a woman was sexually attractive *and* intelligent then there is a likelihood that she would be the dominant partner in any relationship, a role that bourgeois ideology defines as male' (Lacey 1998: 140). At the same time, Whelehan's criticism of *Ally McBeal* (FOX, 1997–2002) and *Sex and the City* (HBO, 1998–2004) also partially applies to *Gilmore Girls*:

> Both *Ally McBeal* and *Sex and the City* focus on the lives of single professional women and both clearly indicate that the primary ambition of these women is to realise themselves through a meaningful and lasting relationship. In both series, female power is celebrated through the depiction of professional success, but this is often undercut by showing the same women spinning out of control emotionally.[6] (Whelehan 2000: 139, quoted in Bubel 2006: 38)

Thus, *Gilmore Girls* does feature scenes where either Rory or Lorelai 'spin out of control emotionally', and romantic relationships with men figure prominently and are clearly seen as highly desirable by the characters. However, *Gilmore Girls* arguably goes further than the above-mentioned series in portraying a single professional *mother* throughout the series rather than just in parts of it, and while the 'quest for Mr Right' does feature in the series, it is not as predominant. As Fleegal puts it,

> *Gilmore Girls* . . . is possibly the first example of a show in which 1) the central character is a single mother who 2) 'got into trouble' at age 16 and 3) resisted the pressure to 'do the right thing' and marry the father, but 4) had the baby and 5) continued on to be a financially and emotionally self-sufficient woman who succeeds at both her chosen career and motherhood. (Fleegal 2008: 144)

In particular for Lorelai's daughter Rory and her friend Paris, education and career is something to be taken into account, while the consequences of being a woman and making career a priority are never just dismissed as irrelevant. Compare the discussion between the two characters in extract (2):

(2)

[Paris explains why she has broken up with her boyfriend Doyle]

PARIS:	It was me, okay? Doyle said to make my decision. He said not to worry about him. He said wherever I went, we'd work it out. So I tried, you know, not to think about him, to take him out of the equation, but I couldn't. Every time I tried to evaluate a school, I'd immediately think about it in relation to Doyle. 'How close is it to him? Is there a good newspaper nearby? What will the commute be like?'
RORY:	Well, those are all valid questions.
PARIS:	No, they're not. This decision is the culmination of everything I've ever worked for, everything. I should choose a school based on its merits, not based on its proximity to some guy.
RORY:	But Doyle's not just some guy.
PARIS:	I know. But I'm only 22. This wasn't supposed to happen yet. I wasn't supposed to meet the guy until I was 30 and clerking for a federal judge or finishing up my residency and when I knew where I'd be when I was ready to settle down.
RORY:	Yeah, but you can't plan everything. I mean, you fell in love. That's a good thing.
PARIS:	Are you willing to make a decision this big based on Logan [Rory's boyfriend]?
RORY:	Well, actually, we talked about it, and we're gonna factor each other in.
PARIS:	What does that mean?
RORY:	Uh, it just means we're gonna take each other into consideration when we make decisions.
PARIS:	Okay. So carry that thought out. Let's say you get The New York Times fellowship and Logan's meetings in San Francisco go incredibly well and he wants to move there. Do you take a job in San Francisco? The Chronicle is a perfectly adequate paper. Or do you go to The New York Times?
RORY:	The New York Times.
PARIS:	Then we're saying the same thing, aren't we?
RORY:	No, not at all.
PARIS:	You're saying your career is your priority over your relationship.
RORY:	They're both priorities.
PARIS:	But your career comes first.

RORY: Well, I didn't say it comes first. I – I'm just not ready to make any sacrifices in that area yet.
PARIS: But you are willing to make sacrifices in your relationship. Hence, your career is more important to you, just like me.
RORY: I wouldn't say 'more important.' I guess I just thought that if Logan and I have to do long-distance again, we'll make it work.
PARIS: Sure. Maybe. Then again, choosing to be apart might be . . . choosing to be apart.
(7.19, *It's just like riding a bike*)

Lorelai for her part 'seems to perfectly embody the values of a third-wave feminist' (McCaffrey 2008: 35), and it is also noticeable that *Gilmore Girls* is one of few shows that focuses on female protagonists (Calvin 2008a), with most sitcoms, for instance, having male characters and content (Mills 2005: 112). Thus, *Gilmore Girls* has been called 'fundamentally feminist' (Calvin 2008a: 2; but see McCaffrey 2008), and has triggered much discussion in terms of gender and ideology (Calvin 2008b). Notions of ideology/representation on television will be discussed in more detail in Chapter 8.

1.2 Form and genre

With respect to the television forms and genres introduced in Chapter 2, *Gilmore Girls* is predominantly a television *series* as opposed to a *serial*. In terms of the distinctions made by Dunn (2005: 132), *Gilmore Girls* falls in fact somewhere between a series and a serial, which, since the 1990s, is common in terms of the 'hybridity' of much televisual fiction (Turner 2001b, Marshall & Werndly 2002: 47, Thornham & Purvis 2005: 16, Matheson 2005: 95). It features the same characters and settings throughout all seasons (the characters' boyfriends change; the setting changes from school to university) and has multiple plotlines, although there are also a few meta-narratives and mini meta-narratives across episodes and/or seasons (Rory's education; Lorelai's relationship with her parents; relationship developments), similar to series such as *Friends* (NBC, 1994–2004) or *Ally McBeal* (FOX, 1997–2002). Each episode is relatively self-contained although there are occasional cliff-hangers across episodes and characters have a memory of (meaning the audience has to know) what has gone on in previous episodes. Even though viewers do not have to watch every single episode in order to follow the story, *Gilmore Girls* does demand some audience loyalty.

As a television product, several units of analysis can be distinguished (see Chapter 2):

- *Gilmore Girls* as a **series**;
- seven **seasons** of the series (one season features 22 episodes and covers one year);

- 153 **episodes** (22 per season, although only 21 in season 1);
- several **segments** within episodes;
- several **scenes** within segments;
- several **shots** within scenes.[7]

In terms of content, as indicated above, *Gilmore Girls* shares some topics with other contemporary television series such as *Sex and the City* (HBO, 1998–2004; Akass & McCabe 2004), for instance the focus on female characters' romantic life, on female friendship, humour and the single woman. In fact, the focus on 'couple-making' (O'Shaughnessy & Stadler 2005: 266) seems to be one that is shared by many television series, where 'the constant unresolved sexual tension or attraction between a couple is a major narrative element' (O'Shaughnessy & Stadler 2005: 266). However, *Gilmore Girls* also features teenagers extensively, and is much more 'family-friendly' than series like *Sex and the City* or *Desperate Housewives* (Touchstone Television/ABC, 2004–), and was in fact funded by the *Family Friendly Programming Forum.*[8]

With respect to genre, *Gilmore Girls* is a drama/comedy hybrid in terms of TV genres as recognized by Roman (2005), a 'recombinant genre' (Weerakkody 2008: 264) that combines elements of comedy and drama. The *Internet Movie Database* describes its genre as both drama and comedy (www.imdb.com, accessed 26 May 2008), Weerakkody (2008) calls it 'comedy-drama' (Weerakkody 2008: 265), and Ross (2004) identifies it explicitly as a 'dramedy' (Ross 2004: 144), similar to other popular series such as *Sex and the City, Ally McBeal, Desperate Housewives,* and *Ugly Betty* (ABC, 2006–), which have also been classified as dramedies (e.g. Creeber 2004, Lancioni 2006). The term 'dramedy' arose in the 1980s and was used with reference to series like *Moonlighting* (ABC, 1985–1989), *The Wonder Years* (ABC, 1988–1993) and *Hooperman* (ABC, 1987–1989) (Lancioni 2006).[9] It refers to a genre that 'fosters the weaving together of comic and dramatic elements across storylines, thus creating a highly complex text – a complexity that lends itself to the articulation of ideological discourse' (Lancioni 2006: 131). Both Neale (2001: 2) and Lancioni (2006: 143) point out that studies of this genre are extremely rare, another reason to focus this book around the discussion of *Gilmore Girls* as a particular instance of this under-researched genre.

Let us briefly look at drama and comedy features in *Gilmore Girls,* then. Marshall and Werndly give the following description of (domestic) TV drama: 'Domestic dramas center on the home, the community, the workplace, and, in particular, are concerned with interpersonal relationships such as those between lovers, family members or groups of friends' (Marshall & Werndly 2002: 45). This is clearly the case with *Gilmore Girls,* which is centred on the home (both Lorelai's and her parents'), the community (Stars Hollow), workplaces (Lorelai's inn, Luke's diner, Rory's school and university) and the interpersonal relationships of the main characters, in particular Lorelai and Rory. Perhaps the series also has some elements of what Marshall and

Werndly identify as a 'new generic strand' (Marshall & Werndly 2002: 49) of female dramas, where

> [k]ey themes are the importance of female friendships, the differences between women and the ability of women to relate to each other as a team. Their narratives assume a 'female' point of view. . . . [They] are concerned with gender, changing gender relations and both masculine and feminine identities. (Marshall & Werndly 2002: 49)

Further, like other shows such as *Friends* (NBC, 1994–2004), *Northern Exposure* (CBS, 1990–1995) and *Sex and the City* (HBO, 1998–2004), the interest of *Gilmore Girls* is in 'small-town life [like *Northern Exposure*] and close-knit communities and friends [like *Friends, Northern Exposure, Sex and the City*] echoing the type of preoccupation with private existence more commonly associated with traditional soap opera' (Creeber 2004: 115). In this respect *Gilmore Girls* appears to have a few elements of what Creeber (2004) calls 'soap drama', a particular mix of television genres, combining elements of soap opera, drama and comedy (see Chapter 2: Section 2):

> [i]n many ways this new type of television drama [soap drama] employs many of the characteristics of soap opera, in particular, its use of close-up (of people's faces) in order to convey intimate conversation and emotion, its concentration on dialogue rather than visual image to impart meaning, and its tendency towards quickly edited scenes as a way of mixing and bringing together a number of varied and multiple storylines. (Creeber 2004: 115)

Examples of soap dramas, according to Creeber, are shows like *Friends, Sex and the City, Cold Feet* (ITV, UK, 1997–2003), *This Life* (BBC, UK, 1996–1997), *Our Friends in the North* (BBC, UK, 1996) and *Queer as Folk* (Channel 4, UK, 2000–2005). In such soap dramas we can find 'an explicit concern with the personal and private "politics" of everyday life rather than concentrating on grand political issues and wider socio-economic debates' (Creeber 2004: 116). However, Creeber argues that

> while 'soap drama' may prioritise the 'personal' over the 'political', it could be argued that it does so in such a way that the political nature of the personal (particularly around issues of identity [*This Life*], sexuality/gender [*Queer as Folk, Sex and the City*] and community/nationhood [*Our Friends in the North*]) is explored and examined more powerfully and thoroughly than ever before. (Creeber 2004: 116)

Example (2) above illustrating Rory's and Paris's thoughts about career and relationships is a prime example of the intertwining of the personal and the social in soap drama. Another example is the conversation in example (3) between Lorelai and her mother, Emily.

(3)

EMILY:	It's like a canoe.
LORELAI:	What's like a canoe?
EMILY:	Life.
LORELAI:	Okay.
EMILY:	You're just paddling along in a canoe.
LORELAI:	Mother, have you ever been in a canoe?
EMILY:	Lorelai.
LORELAI:	Well I just can't picture you in a canoe.
EMILY:	Your father and I have been paddling a canoe together for years. Only now, he's dropped the paddle.
LORELAI:	Ahh!
EMILY:	He just dropped it. Not only that, but now the canoe is going in circles.
LORELAI:	Ah!
EMILY:	Without your father there, I'm paddling on my side and the canoe is spinning in circles, and the harder I paddle, the faster it spins, and it's hard work, and I'm getting tired.
LORELAI:	Dizzy, I would think.
EMILY:	You are in a kayak. You know how to do all of this.
LORELAI:	How does that put me in a kayak?
EMILY:	Kayaks have paddles with things on both ends. You steer it by yourself.
LORELAI:	Mom, you know how to do things by yourself. You are totally capable.
EMILY:	Sure, I went to Smith, and I was a history major, but I never had any plans to be an historian. I was always going to be a wife. I mean, the way I saw it, a woman's job was to run a home, organize the social life of a family, and bolster her husband while he earned a living. It was a good system, and it was working very well all these years. Only when your husband isn't there because he's watching television in a dressing gown, you realize how dependent you are. I didn't even know I owned windmills.
LORELAI:	Mom, now you know, and you know how to right-click.
EMILY:	But you. You provide for yourself. You're not dependent on anyone.
LORELAI:	Hmm.
EMILY:	You're independent.

LORELAI: I am kayak, hear me roar.
EMILY: I mean, look at you. For all these years, you've done very well without a husband.
LORELAI: Maybe so, but I still wanted it to work out.
EMILY: You know, the way I was raised, if a married couple split up, it was a disaster, because it meant the system had fallen apart, and it was particularly bad for the woman because she had to go out and find herself another rich husband, only she was older now. But with you, it's not such a disaster, is it?
LORELAI: I guess not.
EMILY: I mean it's really not such a horrible thing that you're going to get a divorce, not really. Oh, you're gonna be fine.
[Lorelai flinches a little as Emily rubs her shoulder]
LORELAI: Thanks, mom. [very quiet]
EMILY: You may even marry someone else someday. Who knows?
LORELAI: [Snorts] Who knows? [Sighs]
(7.15, *I am kayak, hear me roar*)

This is a good example of how the personal (Lorelai's break-up; Richard's illness) and the social are intertwined in *Gilmore Girls*, and how societal changes are explicitly discussed with respect to their impact on the characters, particularly with respect to gender. It is interesting to note that Creeber (2004) in fact traces the 'personalisation of the political landscape' in soap dramas to the emergence of feminism and 'the realisation that politics can never be satisfactorily disconnected from everyday life, that almost everything in "ordinary life" has elements of the "political" within it' (Creeber 2004: 117–18). Chapter 8 explores the notion of the political in *Gilmore Girls* more critically in terms of ideology, and values that are shared between characters.

While drama and soap drama elements thus are clearly present in *Gilmore Girls*, the series also has many sitcom (Selby & Cowdery 1995, Hartley 2001, Mills 2005) elements, and many similarities with 'domestic comedy', which features a variety of events and people, an emphasis on character interaction, and is often set around a family unit (Huisman 2005a: 175, citing Taflinger 1996). Many sitcoms combine family comportment and workplace in a similar way as *Gilmore Girls* (Hartley 2001). Huisman (2005a) describes sitcom as:

> the most numerous narrative genre on television. The situation is the regular situation in which the permanent characters find themselves; it provides the context in each episode for fresh storylines with visiting characters. As the word 'comedy' implies, the sitcoms should contain humour, should make us laugh . . . . However, the characterisation and setting can vary from cheerfully superficial to a more complex and darker social setting. (Huisman 2005a: 175)

It is important to point out that characters and the interaction of characters are particularly important for sitcoms (Huisman 2005a: 177). The humour of *Gilmore Girls* is similarly mostly character- and dialogue-based, and one particular feature is the quirky and weird small town characters that inhabit Stars Hollow. More generally, genre features of comedy as described by Weerakkody (2008: 265) for *Gilmore Girls* include the already mentioned weird characters whose behaviour is exaggerated and not taken seriously, characters that act as opposites (Lorelai/her mother Emily, Rory's boyfriends Dean and Jess), a (mostly) unmarried lead actress, and stereotyped characters (e.g. Michel, Mrs Kim – compare Chapter 8).

1.3 *Gilmore Girls* as fictional television: communicative context, multimodality, code of realism, character identity

Section 1.3 briefly looks at the characteristics of fictional television (Chapter 2: Section 3) in relation to *Gilmore Girls*, in terms of its communicative context, multimodality, code of realism and character identity.

Gilmore Girls naturally shares the general characteristics of other television series, including their **communicative context**, and I shall only make some brief comments on this here. Featuring screen-to-face discourse the series involves several communication layers and multiple authorship. For instance, creative and institutional agencies of *Gilmore Girls* are listed in the credits for a random episode of *Gilmore Girls* (1.09, *Rory's Dance*) as follows:

At the beginning of the episode:
During title music
Names of eight regular actors
Executive producer Gavin Polone
Created by Amy Sherman-Palladino
During first scene
Names of guest stars
Producer Jenji Kohan
Supervising producer Jed Seidel
Co-executive producer Kimberly Costello
Executive consultant Daniel Palladino
Produced by Mel Efros
Written by Amy Sherman-Palladino
Directed by Lesli LInka Glatter

At the end of the episode:
Executive producer Amy Sherman-Palladino
Associate producer Steve Turner

Story editor Joan Binder Weiss
Director of photography Teresa Medina, A. E. C.
Production designer Sandy Veneziano
Edited by Raúl Dávalos
Music by Sam Phillips
Information on the title song ('Where you Lead')
Unit production manager Burt Burnam
Names of three assistant directors
Executive in charge of casting Barbara Miller, C.S.A.
Casting by Jami Rudofsky and Mara Casey
Names of actors co-starring
Names of costume designer, costume supervisor, set decorator, property master
Wardrobe provided by ALLOY.com, Inc
Names of make-up artist, hairstylist, script supervisor, production coordinator
Names of sound mixer, re-recording mixers, music editor, supervising sound editor
Copyright © 2000 Warner Brothers Television
Dorothy Parker Drank Here Productions
Hofflund Polone in association with
Warner Brothers Television

Similarly, writing the scripted dialogue is a team effort. As with other television series, in writing for *Gilmore Girls* all writers are involved in group conferences on story outlines, with specific dialogue written by different writers. However, as Amy Sherman-Palladino says, 'every draft either I write, or it passes through my hands, or passes through my hands and his [Daniel Palladino] hands, so that there is a consistency of tone' (Sherman-Palladino 2005). In fact, Daniel Palladino and Amy Sherman-Palladino were very involved in the creative process of *Gilmore Girls* dialogue, as this interview illustrates:

> **Dan:** For the six years, we've been working seven days a week, 'cause we knew every aspect of the show. We'd break every story, we'd edit, this last year we directed seven between ourselves, we have written 90-something scripts.
> **Amy:** We also take a pass at all scripts that go out and by the time *our* season ends, by the time I'm done editing and by the time I'm done with sound mixes and everything like that, it's mid-May. We start back June 1. We work through every holiday . . . Christmas, Thanksgiving. It's been quite a load.
> (Sherman-Palladino & Palladino 2006)

With respect to **multimodality**, multimodal features in *Gilmore Girls*, including those listed in Chapter 2, that is, setting and performance features such as action, speech and appearance, provide context in terms of both location and ambience, and also help to construe characters. For instance, Weerakkody (2008: 262) notes that setting plays an important role in *Gilmore Girls*, for example, in differentiating the 'attitudes, values and lifestyles' (Weerakkody 2008: 262) of Lorelai and her parents; in other words, settings provide characterization. Sound, too, works in *Gilmore Girls* to convey ambience and emotional meanings. The music by female singer-songwriter Sam Phillips, has 'connotations of emotional, confessional, female expression' (Woods 2008: 128), and the title song (*Where you Lead* by Carole King) emphasizes friendship and nostalgia (Woods 2008: 129). Incidentally, music is in general important in *Gilmore Girls*: Singer-songwriter Grant-Lee Phillips (formerly of Grant Lee Buffalo) appears repeatedly as the town troubadour (see below), and Sebastian Bach (former member of the band Skid Row) is part of Lane's band. A few groups also have cameos on the show (e.g. The Shins, The Bangles) and there are many conversations about music including Lorelai, Rory and, in particular, Lane, who is a drummer with a band. For explorations of music in the series compare Johns and Smith (2008: 28), and Woods (2008).

While Rory and Lorelai Gilmore share the actresses Alexis Bledel's and Lauren Graham's physical attractiveness, camera shots in fact provide an emphasis on the characters' intellect rather than their attractiveness:

> [T]he camera directs our attention to their rapid-fire exchanges rather than their features – a carefully crafted approach, according to Sherman-Palladino. 'These television shows that have fourteen shots of somebody looking at each other with the wind blowing through their hair drive me crazy,' she tells the interviewer Virginia Heffernan: 'Who's got that kind of time? We got that the girl was pretty when she walked in the door.' Instead of Lorelai and Rory with their hair in the wind, we get 'banter,' exchanges 'consistently peppered with obscure references, often to decades-old pop culture' and to cultural events contemporaneous to the show's initial broadcast. (Westman 2007: 23–4)

With respect to appearance, clothing is also used strategically to construe characters' identity including their attitudinal positioning: 'Lorelai's character was young, fun and hip. She was always willing to do things that were experimental and we just incorporated that into what she put on her body' (costume designer Brenda Maben, quoted in 'Gilmore Fashionistas' 2007), and the characters' clothes change somewhat over the seven years of the series' run, as both characters become more stylish and as Rory changes from a teenager to a young woman ('Gilmore Fashionistas' 2007). Concerning *mise-en-scene* and multimodal performance features, Chapter 7 explores a scene featuring two characters from *Gilmore Girls* in more detail.

Looking at the **code of realism**, *Gilmore Girls* does appear to adhere to this code with some exceptions. Like other television series it features characters and actions that are quirky or unusual rather than typical or 'normal' to create drama or humour. The troubadour in *Gilmore Girls* is a case in point, who provides commentary and draws attention to *Gilmore Girls* as a television series rather than as representing a realistic world, in some sense breaking the code of realism, and 'violat[ing] the suspension of disbelief' (Kozloff 2000: 57). Stars Hollow's town troubadour performs on-and-off in the street, and partially provides the background music in *Gilmore Girls.* For instance, there will be a shot of Lorelai and Rory walking in the street with some background music, and then the camera will pan to show the troubadour actually performing the song on his guitar in the streets. In other words, the song moves from non-diegetic to diegetic sound.

In some scenes, the troubadour actually seems to provide a commentary on the events taking place, as in extract (4).

(4)

[After Lorelai has picked Rory up from prison]

RORY:	I'm so, so sorry.
LORELAI:	I know you are.
RORY:	I was so stupid. I'll never be that stupid again.
LORELAI:	Aw. Sure you will.
RORY:	Oh my god. I got arrested. I have to go to court! I have to go get my car. No – do you have soap at home? Because I have all this ink all over my hands, and –
LORELAI:	Honey. Relax. We will figure it out.

STARS HOLLOW TOWN SQUARE [= next scene]

[The troubadour is singing on a corner.]

TROUBADOR:	I turned twenty-one in prison, doing life without parole. No-one could steer me right, but Mama tried, Mama tried. Mama tried to raise me better but her pleading I denied, leaves only me to blame, 'cause Mama tried. Leaves only me to blame, 'cause Mama tried.

(5.22, *A house is not a home*)

Here, the songs 'match the narrative so well that they almost seem one and the same' (Johns & Smith 2008: 28); however, the fact that the town has a troubadour is of course not 'realistic' as such,[10] but rather another quirky feature of the small community of Stars Hollow (such as its staging of events like the Festival of Living Pictures). Similarly, quirky and 'eccentric' characters abound in *Gilmore Girls*, in particular 'the loony townpeople' (Jackson Douglas, quoted in 'The Gilmore Girls Turn 100' 2005) such as Taylor, Kirk,

Mrs Kim and Lane's band members Zack and Brian, or the comic character Paris. Compare Paris's action in extract (5) below:

(5)

[Rory has written a damning review of a ballet performance and is confronted by one of its dancers]

SANDRA:	I've been dancing three hours a day, seven days a week for fourteen years. I've done two summer sessions with the Miami ballet, and I'm on the waiting list at Juilliard, and now your review is out there for everyone to see!
RORY:	Look, I -
SANDRA:	You're a jerk! I just wanted to come tell you that to your face! You're a jerk, and I hope you die! Bye, jerk. Die, jerk. [Sandra leaves; Paris walks in, goes up to Rory]
PARIS:	The door thing [a note on Paris's and Rory's door saying 'die, jerk'] was about you?
RORY:	Apparently.
PARIS:	[on mobile phone] The strike is off. Stand down. I repeat, stand down.

(4.08, *Die, jerk*)

The humour in this extract arises exactly from Paris's exaggerated and excessive action and the 'militaristic' discourse she uses – perhaps an *imaginable* action (in contrast to, say, animals starting to speak) but not a very 'realistic' or usual reaction to finding an abusive note on a door. However, it is also a *plausible* one in terms of 'the realities of the world created by the programme as opposed to realism in the world of our social experience' (Burton 2000: 151). In other words, the action is plausible in terms of the character of Paris, and in terms of elements of comedy in *Gilmore Girls*, with comic moments relying on exaggeration, 'the wildly inappropriate response' (Vorhaus 1994: 41) and 'on excess, usually physical though sometimes emotional or linguistic' (Mills 2005: 88). In Neale's (1990, cited in Thornham & Purvis 2005) terms, it has 'generic verisimilitude' (see Chapter 2: Section 3.3).

With respect to **character identity** in *Gilmore Girls*, this is treated in more detail in Chapters 5–8 below. However, it is clear that the series is very character-driven:

> without Lauren [the actress playing Lorelai] and Alexis [the actress playing Rory] you don't have a show. You wish you knew them [Lorelai and Rory]. And virtually it carries on all around the show. There, there are people involved that are eccentric and quirky and interesting and you'd like to know them. And that's I think one of the keys to making a successful film, series. (Edward Herrman, quoted in 'The Gilmore Girls Turn 100' 2005)

2 Construing the *Gilmore Girls* Audience

2.1 Construing a target audience

If we consider again the communicative context of a television series such as *Gilmore Girls*, and the model of screen-to-face discourse introduced in Chapter 2, we also have to take into account the audience. As was suggested there, target/illocutionary audiences are both envisaged by media producers and construed in the text:

> [F]rom a theoretical perspective, an audience is called into being by a particular discourse, or 'interpellated' by the text, to use Althusser's term. In other words, an audience doesn't exist until a text addresses it; and by the same token, texts don't simply address a pre-existing and knowable audience. They actually construct a virtual audience . . . As actual individuals who use media products, the extent to which we feel ourselves to be part of an audience depends on whether or not we feel addressed by a media text. Does it speak to us directly? Does it use a language we recognise as ours? Do we feel included in the world view and attitudes articulated by the text? (Fulton 2005a: 5)

One way of analysing how texts construe such a target audience would be through the study of *Gilmore Girls* dialogue, for example, the notion of bonding and including/excluding audience members through the use of intertextual references as described above. However, in addition to analysing the dialogue in *Gilmore Girls* itself, we can analyse the language used purposefully to attract viewers to the series by examining the linguistic text on the back of the covers of the DVD sets for the seven seasons. This is what I will do in this section, that is, provide a short analysis of this particular type of advertising discourse (Goddard 1998, Cook 1992). Bell notes that

> [a]dvertising is, together with news, the principal genre common to all daily media. As well as providing a good case study, it is an important genre in its own right. Its use of language is highly creative. While people may denigrate advertising as a cultural phenomenon, the well-made advertisement appeals to sophisticated linguistic skills. (Bell 1991: 135)

The analysed texts (represented in Appendix 2) are located in a multimodal context, that is, they include semiotic resources other than language (see Figure 3.1) and range in length from 108 to 139 words.

FIGURE 3.1 The texts in their multimodal context.

The purpose of these texts is to persuade potential customers to buy one or more DVDs. This means that the writers of these texts 'must take care to engage with what can be a diverse audience in an appropriate way' (Baker 2006: 50), and they do this through language as well as other semiotic resources (e.g. the pictures on the DVDs, DVD extras, colour schemes etc.). Arguably, the language of these texts is used to 'construe' the target audience for *Gilmore Girls* in the context of buying the DVDs. That is, the texts are 'designed' (Bell 1991) for their readers. This audience design 'informs all levels of a speaker's linguistic choices' (Bell 1991: 105), though I will only look at selected language choices here.

But how can we analyse these texts fruitfully? Throughout this book, explorations of language and television are undertaken using both corpus and discourse analysis. Simplifying greatly, corpus analysis uses computer software to analyse large data sets, whereas discourse analysis manually analyses smaller segments of data. Corpus analysis is more quantitative, and discourse analysis is more qualitative, but there is no one-to-one overlap in that corpus analysis can incorporate qualitative aspects. With respect to the DVD texts, a quantitative analysis using Wordsmith (Scott 2004) software, can, for instance, identify the most frequent content words and proper nouns in these texts (Table 3.1; f >3).

Table 3.1 Frequent words in DVD cover texts

N	Word	Freq.	N	Word	Freq.
1	GILMORE	17	16	DAUGHTER	5
2	LORELAI	12	17	FROM	5
3	YEAR	11	18	HEART	5
4	RORY	10	19	LUKE	5
5	GIRLS	9	20	NEW	5
6	GETS	7	21	ONE	5
7	HOLLOW	7	22	TOWN	5
8	MORE	7	23	EPISODES	4
9	STARS	7	24	INN	4
10	BUT	6	25	LANE	4
11	SEASON	6	26	LIFE	4
12	SERIES	6	27	LORELAI'S	4
13	ALL	5	28	MOTHER	4
14	ARE	5	29	MUCH	4
15	BE	5	30	SURPRISE	4

Not surprisingly, there are many references to characters and setting, including references to relationships between characters: *Gilmore, Girls, Lorelai, Lorelai's, Rory, Luke, Lane, Stars, Hollow, inn, town, daughter, mother.* There are also references to time (*year*) and potential events (*gets, life*). These words are probably related to describing the series and events that are included in the season covered in the DVD set. However, references to the semiotic product (*season, series, episodes*) are also frequent, which, as we will see shortly, are associated with positive evaluations. Similarly, we find expressions of quantity (*more, all, much*),[11] evaluation (including contrast) and emotion (*new, but, surprise, heart*). There thus seem to be two strands in these texts: a focus on the product, its characters and happenings (content, topic; what is evaluated), and an interpersonal appeal using expressions of quantity, emotion, contrast (what the audience get when they buy the DVD).

However, because the number of words in my dataset is limited (858 words), it is possible and more fruitful to look at the language of these texts 'manually'. In so doing I shall use an analysis of evaluative meaning as a starting point, which is part of the interpersonal appeal identified above through the frequency analysis. In fact, such meanings are naturally quite common in certain types of advertising discourse (e.g. Bednarek & Bublitz 2006).

Section 2.2 below introduces the framework used for analysing evaluative language, before section 2.3 reports on the findings, and also briefly considers other linguistic features of these texts.

2.2 Evaluative language, evaluative parameters

Evaluative language is language that expresses some kind of evaluation, attitude, stance or opinion (see Biber et al. 1999, Hunston & Thompson 2000, Martin & White 2005, Bednarek 2006a for introductions). Such language can be studied, inter alia, by considering the kinds of evaluative parameters that are expressed through language. The notion of evaluative parameters derives from my work on evaluative meaning (e.g. Bednarek 2006a, 2008c). This framework takes as a starting point Thompson and Hunston's observation that evaluation 'may relate to certainty or obligation or desirability or any of a number of other sets of values' (Thompson & Hunston 2000: 5), called 'parameters of evaluation' (Thompson & Hunston 2000: 22). In other words, these 'sets of values' can be identified as *evaluative parameters*, covering evaluations of aspects of the world along certain semantic dimensions. For example, writers can evaluate situations as good/bad, expected/unexpected, important/unimportant and so on. The parameter-based framework of evaluation argues that all of these semantic dimensions belong to the complex phenomenon of evaluation. Evaluative parameters thus refer to the standards, norms, values according to which we evaluate something through language. Here I want to look in particular at the parameters of AFFECT, EMOTIVITY, EXPECTEDNESS, IMPORTANCE and POWER.

The parameter of AFFECT relates to the attribution of emotional reactions to the Self or Others (Martin & White 2005, Bednarek 2008a), for instance: *the much-**loved** series* attributes the emotional reaction of 'love' to an unnamed Other, an unnamed **Emoter** (the technical term for the person experiencing the emotion). Affect can relate to several sub-types (Martin & White 2005, Bednarek 2008a) and the emotions can be positive (+), negative (–) or neutral/ambiguous (+/–) **(valence: pos/neg/ambig)**: DESIRE feelings concern wishes, willingness and volition, whereas NON-DESIRE feelings concern reluctance, unwillingness and non-volition. INSECURITY feelings concern anxiety, distrust and embarrassment; SECURITY feelings concern confidence, trust and 'emotional calm'. DISSATISFACTION feelings relate to emotions such as boredom, disinterest, frustration and anger; SATISFACTION feelings relate to emotions such as interest, fascination, admiration, pleasure and gratitude. UNHAPPINESS feelings concern emotions such as sadness and hate; HAPPINESS feelings relate to happiness and love. Finally, SURPRISE feelings simply have to do with the emotion of surprise or its negation. For the rationale for distinguishing between these affect sub-types see Bednarek (2008a: 154–71). Evaluations of AFFECT can be made using a wide range of linguistic items, including the emotion lexicon (e.g. *love, hate, fear, surprise*) and the use of emotive interjections (see Chapter 6).

The parameter of EMOTIVITY is concerned with an **Evaluator's** evaluation of events, things, people, activities or other evaluated entities as good or bad, positive or negative, that is, with the expression of approval or disapproval. Evaluations of EMOTIVITY are expressed by a range of linguistic items which vary enormously in their evaluative force (Bednarek 2006a: 46–8) and are situated on a cline ranging from more or less positive to more or less negative (**valence**), for instance: *the **hit*** [valence: pos] *series known for its **witty*** [valence: pos], *rapid-fire dialogue.* The parameter of EXPECTEDNESS involves an Evaluator's evaluations of aspects of the world (including statements) as more or less expected or unexpected (again, a cline is involved). A useful paraphrase for such evaluations is thus 'how expected or how unexpected does this appear?' For example: *Much of it [a year of change] **is expected** . . . But much of it **is not**.*

The parameter of POWER has to do with how 'powerful' (plus power) or 'powerless' (minus power) Evaluators judge people as being. This includes the notion of incomprehensibility (if something is incomprehensible to us, we are powerless to understand it), richness, stardom, famousness, influence and authority. For instance, in the DVD texts, *Lorelai . . . who's **determined to** help her [Rory] avoid the mistakes that sidetracked Lorelai when she was a teen*, and *Lorelai's **blue-blooded** parents* we could arguably analyse *determined to* and *blue-blooded* as evaluations of power.[12] Table 3.2 gives a summary of the introduced evaluative parameters. Additional parameters will be described in later chapters as they become relevant.

Table 3.2 Evaluative parameters

Evaluative parameter		Definition	Examples from DVD cover texts
AFFECT		attribution of emotional reactions to the Self or Others	see below for examples of AFFECT sub-types
	NON-/DESIRE	reluctance, unwillingness, and non-volition; wishes, willingness, volition	*it seems everyone in town **wants** mother and daughter to reunite*
	IN/SECURITY	anxiety, distrust, embarrassment; confidence, trust, 'emotional calm'	*the **anxiety** of waiting for college acceptance letters*
	DIS/SATISFACTION	boredom, disinterest, frustration, anger; interest, fascination, admiration, pleasure, gratitude	*another **scintillating** . . . year of . . . Gilmore Girls*

(*Continued*)

Table 3.2 (Cont'd)

Evaluative parameter	Definition	Examples from DVD cover texts
UN/HAPPINESS	sadness, hate; happiness, love	*the much-**loved** series*
SURPRISE	surprise	*Lane gets a **surprise***
EMOTIVITY	evaluation of events, things, people, activities or other evaluated entities as more or less good or bad, positive or negative	*the **hit** series known for its **witty**, rapid-fire dialogue*
EXPECTEDNESS	evaluations of aspects of the world (including statements) as more or less expected or unexpected	*Much of it [a year of change] **is expected** . . . But much of it **is not***
POWER	evaluations of aspects of the world (including people) as more or less powerful, e.g. in terms of comprehensibility, stardom, authority	*Lorelai's **blue-blooded** parents*

Importantly, evaluations can be more or less explicit in terms of how evaluative meaning is encoded or 'inscribed' (Martin & White 2005: 61). For instance, there is explicitly evaluative lexis such as *great* (positive EMOTIVITY), *rubbish* (negative EMOTIVITY), *complicated* (minus POWER), but there are also more implicit ways of expressing an evaluation, for example, via negation. Thus, a statement such as *She's not a corpus linguist* can indirectly imply negative or positive EMOTIVITY (Bednarek 2006b), and saying that a relationship causes one to 'not think straight' implies an evaluation of minus POWER. This has been theorized both in cognitive and in semiotic terms (see Martin & White 2005: 67, Bednarek 2006b, 2009d on inscribed/explicit vs. invoked/implicit attitude) and is visualized here in Figure 3.2.

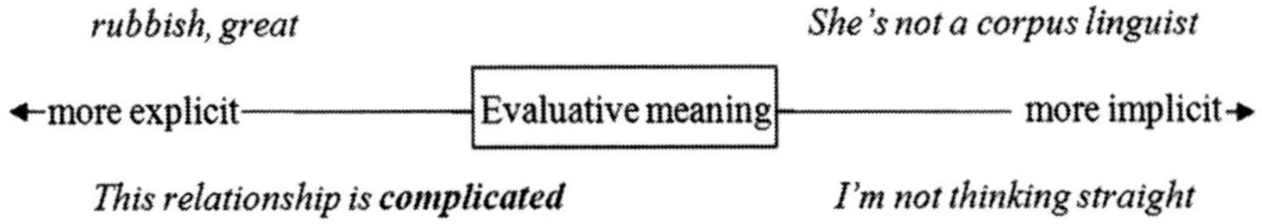

FIGURE 3.2 Explicit vs. implicit evaluative meaning

The analyses of evaluative meaning throughout this book mainly concern more explicit evaluations as they offer a higher degree of inter-rater reliability.

2.3 Evaluative meanings in DVD cover texts

Applying this framework to the DVD cover texts, instances of EMOTIVITY can be found to be most common, followed by AFFECT. Together, evaluative items expressing these two parameters are by far more frequent than evaluations of EXPECTEDNESS, IMPORTANCE and POWER. In fact, evaluations of IMPORTANCE and POWER are not very frequent at all, and no clear tendencies are apparent in their use. The discussion below will thus focus on EMOTIVITY, AFFECT and EXPECTEDNESS only.

Emotivity

First, the texts abound with positive evaluations (EMOTIVITY: POS) of:

- *Gilmore Girls,* the series, and/or the DVD and its semiotic aspects such as dialogue, humour, and storytelling (e.g. *this* ***deluxe*** *6-disc set; its* ***witty*** *. . . dialogue; those* ***acclaimed*** *Gilmore Girls;* ***insightful*** *storytelling; the* ***knowing humour;*** *more* ***fun; deliciously*** *intriguing what's-gonna-happens*);
- Characters/actors, places, things, events in the series (e.g. *a* ***gifted*** *ensemble plays; her* ***super-achieving*** *daughter Rory; the* ***just-gotta-be*** *relationship fans* ***have waited for!;*** *the* ***picture-perfect*** *New England town; the* ***colourful*** *Stars Hollow townies;* ***quick-witted*** *Lorelai; that* ***perfect*** *wedding-dress*).

The only three evaluations with negative valence (EMOTIVITY: NEG) are of Lorelai's parents (*her* ***elitist*** *parents Emily and Richard; the* ***imperious*** *Gilmore père et mere*) – aligning the writer/audience with Lorelai's world rather than that of the senior Gilmores – and of Rory's having two boyfriends (*Rory starts the year with two boyfriends* [*that* ***may be two too many***]), reflecting cultural attitudes.

There are also some evaluations of EMOTIVITY where valence is unclear or ambiguous. These mostly relate to the eccentricity, pace, comedy or drama of *Gilmore Girls* (e.g. *a whole town of* ***dreamers and eccentrics***; *The wit, charm and* ***eccentricity***; *totally* ***off-kilter*** *. . . supporting characters*; ***fast-paced*** *Gilmore dialogue*; ***rapid-fire*** *dialogue*; *a . . . heartbreakingly* ***dramatic*** *Season 5*),[13] and are clearly used to attract viewers/buyers with respect to these particular noteworthy, and interesting aspects of the series as described above.

Affect

AFFECT is also important in these texts. Some occurrences veer towards the descriptive, and simply point out that the audience can expect there to be emotions involved in the series, which, in themselves have the potential to evoke emotional reactions, involvement and engagement in the audience. Examples are: *the knowing* ***humour;*** *a second season of* ***warmth;*** *More fun, more*

***flames**, more flameouts; its . . . balance of life and **laughter.** Oh yes, and **love**; Lorelai **rekindles the flame** with Max; Lorelai has a **romantic fling**; her [Lorelai's] **love affair** with Luke.* These occurrences may be related to emotions of UN/HAPPINESS (e.g. *love affair*) and SATISFACTION (e.g. *humour*).

Other instances of AFFECT construe (a) emotions of the audience and/or the narrator or (b) emotional responses of characters in the series. Where the audience and/or the narrator are Emoters, AFFECT is mainly positive, and the emotions relate to UN/HAPPINESS (6 occurrences); SATISFACTION (5 occ.) and DESIRE (2 occ.). For instance: *the much-**loved*** (HAPPINESS) *series*; *another **scintillating*** (SATISFACTION) *. . . year of . . . Gilmore Girls; all 22 **irresistible*** (DESIRE) *year-two episodes.* These occurrences of AFFECT construe the target audience/buyers as loving and desiring as well as being satisfied by *Gilmore Girls*. Where characters are Emoters, AFFECT sub-types that occur are DESIRE (3), DISSATISFACTION (1), INSECURITY (1), SECURITY (1), HAPPINESS (10), UNHAPPINESS (5), SATISFACTION (8), and SURPRISE (4)/NON-SURPRISE (1), so that valence and types of affect are quite varied. For instance: *it seems everyone in town **wants*** (DESIRE) *mother and daughter to reunite*; *Jess, whose rebelliousness **offends*** (DISSATISFACTION) *the town*; *the **anxiety*** (INSECURITY) *of waiting for college acceptance letters; the once-**confident*** (SECURITY) *golden girl; Hearts **break*** (UNHAPPINESS) ***and mend*** (HAPPINESS); *whose **passion*** (SATISFACTION) *for books; Lane gets a **surprise*** (SURPRISE). It is interesting to compare these descriptions of pos/neg character AFFECT with descriptions of events that are positive or negative for characters. Examples are: ***the mistakes that sidetracked Lorelai** when she was a teen; For Rory, **Cupid** seems to **be on sabbatical**; a surprise that may **send the Luke-and-Lorelai relationship reeling**; after a series of **Mr. Not-Quite-Rights**.* With both positive and negative character affect and these positive and negative events, a 'zig-zag' pattern or 'prosody' (Martin & White 2005: 17–23) of positive and negative occurs – what Zappavigna et al. (forthcoming) call 'alternating' evaluative prosody, which has a 'to-and-fro' structure, moving back and forth between evaluative polarities. This is a pattern where the negative (bold face) and the positive (italics) co-occur in close distance from each other (Figure 3.3).

- Sookie gets a surprise *(a good one)*. And so does the Independence Inn (**not such a good one**).
- Lane gets *a surprise that leaves her reeling with joy*, Luke gets **a surprise that may send the Luke-and-Lorelai relationship reeling**.
- after *buying that perfect wedding dress* and **watching it hang in the closet**
- *Gilmore rising: Lorelai. The Dragonfly Inn is a huge success. And Lorelai's romance with Luke (the just-gotta-be relationship fans have waited for!) steams up Stars Hollow*. **Gilmore going down: Rory. College, boys and career plans crash and burn, leaving the once-confident golden girl reeling**

FIGURE 3.3 The zig-zag prosody

This pattern, which occasionally, like other advertising discourse (Cook 1992: 131–6), features explicit parallelism, can be repeated in the co-text (Figure 3.4).

Hearts break and *mend*, **careers end** and *begin*, **folks stumble** and *pick themselves up*.

FIGURE 3.4 Repeated zig-zag prosody

This zig-zag pattern seems to be related to the creation of drama: if only the positive occurred this might be too boring, and if only the negative occurred this might be too sad – it is the combination of positive and negative that is 'drama-tic'. This to-and-fro of positive and negative indirectly construes *Gilmore Girls* as an exciting and captivating 'dramedy,' even though there are only two explicit references in the texts to the 'dramatic' content of the series: *heart-stopping moments of* ***drama***; *heartbreakingly* ***dramatic*** *season 5*.

EXPECTEDNESS/SURPRISE

Related to this construal of the series as dramatic are evaluations of EXPECTEDNESS (f = 8: unexpected 6; expected 2), and AFFECT: SURPRISE which we can discuss together. Evaluations of EXPECTEDNESS/NON-SURPRISE are either of positive things (***Of course***, *there's much more; What's* ***no surprise*** *is the snappy, wish-I-d said that Gilmore dialogue, knowing humour and insightful storytelling fans adore*), which serve to increase the positive evaluation of the series ('from what we know about *Gilmore Girls* positive things can be expected') or are contrasted with an evaluation of unexpectedness (*Much of it [a year of change]* ***is expected*** *. . . But much of it* ***is not***.). If we look at these contrasts (between the expected and the unexpected) in terms of 'news values' (Galtung & Ruge 1965) which determine what makes events or facts 'newsworthy', this achieves both continuity of expectation (*much of it is expected*) and unexpectedness (*much of it is not*) at the same time. We can relate this back to the point made in Chapter 2 that television series are appealing because they simultaneously provide the viewer with intimacy/continuity/security and suspense/entertainment/novelty.

Evaluations of UNEXPECTEDNESS and of AFFECT: SURPRISE relate to characters or events in the series: for example, ***new*** *faces also come to Stars Hollow; an* ***unexpected*** *out-of-towner; it's a year of* ***change***; *a big* ***new*** *step in her [Lorelai's] love affair with Luke; Sookie gets a* ***surprise***. Clearly these construe the events in *Gilmore Girls* as unexpected, surprising and therefore 'newsworthy', and are aimed at creating the viewers' interest, making them curious to know more and buy the DVDs in order to be able to do so. These evaluations are saying 'things are happening' in the series; it's not the 'same old, same old'. And according to Ortony et al. (1988) one of the global variables that affects the intensity of emotions is unexpectedness, with 'unexpected positive things are evaluated more positively than expected ones, and unexpected negative things, more negatively than expected ones' (Ortony et al. 1988: 64).[14] The references to the unexpected may thus lead viewers to anticipate the experiencing of intense emotional responses in watching the series.

Describing audience response

Going across and beyond evaluative parameters is a tendency to describe audience response with respect to *Gilmore Girls* (a tendency which has already been observed above with respect to AFFECT), including aspects of the DVD and events in the series:

- Audience as *Gilmore* 'fans': *a mother, a daughter, a town and a world that* ***devoted Gilmore groupies*** *have taken as their own; The wit, charm and eccentricity that have created legions of* ***Gilmore Girls devotees;*** *Welcome, Gilmore* ***groupies;*** *the . . . insightful storytelling* ***fans*** *adore;* ***fan****-pleasing DVD extras; the just-gotta-be relationship* ***fans*** *have waited for!; the guy* ***every fan*** *has known was right for her all along;*
- Reputation/fame with audience: *the* ***famed****, fast-paced Gilmore dialogue; the hit series* ***known for . . .*** *; those* ***acclaimed*** *Gilmore Girls; the fourth season of the series* ***acclaimed for****;*[15]
- Positive audience response towards series: *the people* ***you've grown to love;*** *the* ***much-loved*** *series; a mother, a daughter, a town and a world that devoted Gilmore groupies* ***have taken as their own;*** *the snappy, wish-I'd said that Gilmore dialogue, knowing humour and insightful storytelling fans* ***adore;*** *fan-****pleasing*** *DVD extras;*
- Positive audience response towards events/characters in series: *Lorelai's romance with Luke (the just-gotta-be relationship fans* ***have waited for!****); Lorelai . . . ends the year with the guy every fan* ***has known was right for her*** *all along.*

On the one hand, these either help to construe the readership of these texts as 'knowledgeable fans' or point the 'uninitiated' to the fact that *Gilmore Girls* is well known and in fact has many fans, that is, is well worth getting to know. References to fans and fame also background the narrator's own voice, and make it clear that his/her positive evaluations are shared by many. They turn the act of watching *Gilmore Girls* into a communal and social activity rather than an individual experience – for fans, *Gilmore Girls* can become a 'bondicon' (Martin 2008a: 130) around which they can rally.[16] On the other hand, they confirm that it is natural for audience members to form an emotional attachment to a series and its characters, and that this emotional attachment is wholly positive with respect to *Gilmore Girls* (see also above with respect to Affect where the audience is construed as loving/desiring/being satisfied by

Gilmore Girls). Exclamation marks (e.g. *Kirk gets a girlfriend (!), the just-gotta-be relationship fans have waited for*!) also feature frequently, expressing emotion and emphasis. Contributing to the effect of drawing the readership/audience in and making them part of the world of *Gilmore Girls* are direct address, questions and imperatives – again characteristic of ads 'which [attempt] to win us over by very direct address' (Cook 1992: 157), but also characteristic of other media texts that address audiences as if they were personally acquainted with them (Giles 2002: 290). Examples are ***Welcome to** Stars Hollow; **See you** in Stars Hollow; Can it be the Gilmore Girls if the Gilmore girls aren't together**?**; **Get** watching; **fasten** your seat belt*). The same function of making the audience part of the *Gilmore Girls* universe is fulfilled by explicitly conjoining the characters and audience in one sentence (***Lane gets** a life, **Kirk gets** a girlfriend (!) and **you get** a 22-episode vacation in Stars Hollow, plus DVD extras and a mint on the pillow*). There are many other linguistic peculiarities that can be observed in these texts and that have something to do with appealing to the audience. For example, informal or 'eccentric' language is used throughout, which is perhaps supposed to mimic 'Lorelai & Rory' language and make appeal to the presumed youthfulness of the target audience (e.g. *Boola Boola, wish-I-d said that . . . dialogue, Gilmore père et mere*; *oh yes, and love*; use of exclamation marks). Vagueness is used to create mystery, and not to spoil the viewer's entertainment (e.g. *Lorelai . . . ends the year with **the guy every fan has known was right for her all along**; Lorelai finally gets married. Yes, but **to whom**?; deliriously happy with **the big new step** in her love affair with Luke*) where the vagueness is not resolved co-textually, so that, for instance, readers do not know who 'the guy' is that Lorelai ends up with, or what 'the big new step' in Lorelai's love affair with Luke is. In terms of audience design, the texts are designed for a particular audience (which is, presumably, similar to the target audience of *Gilmore Girls* – that is, predominantly but not exclusively young and female), a particular collective, who would appreciate the language of these advertising texts. Others may of course not respond to these texts and feel 'excluded' (see also Chapter 8).

Summing up key tendencies,[17] the DVD cover texts evaluate *Gilmore Girls* as positive and newsworthy, full of emotion and drama, and construe a knowledgeable audience that emotionally and evaluatively interacts and engages with *Gilmore Girls* as well as events and characters in it. They make reference to the suspense, amusement and catharsis audiences get from dramatic television (Esslin 2002: 62), and 'work persuasively . . . to interpellate the audience as coherent and unified individuals empowered to make appropriate choices on their own behalf' (Fulton 2005a: 5–6). More specifically, the texts discursively construe the readership as 'sovereign consumers' (Fulton 2005a: 5) with the power to choose to buy *Gilmore Girls* DVDs and to become/remain *Gilmore Girls* fans. This is a clear example of the business side of television: It must not be forgotten that 'huge business empires . . . run most of the media outlets, geared specifically to creating profits from the commodification of media products' (Fulton 2005a: 4). These texts contribute to the creation of fan cultures (in addition to the series itself, websites, fan forums, by-products such as *Gilmore Girls* books, soundtrack etc.), consisting of like-minded collectivities. Such communities are becoming increasingly important and are often tied to popular cultural products such as TV series:

> Popular cultural texts help us to know who we are, and include us in communities of like-minded viewers and readers. While, formerly, the nation might have been thought to have primarily organized our sense of belonging, our rights, and our duties . . . , it is now facing serious competition from international media conglomerates as well as from fan cultures . . . that invite us into new types of collectivities that stretch far beyond national borders and produce small self-enclosed enclaves within the nation. (Hermes 2005: 1)

Consequently, with respect to an investigation of language and fictional television it sometimes makes sense to go beyond analysing television dialogue to also take into account related language, for example, on DVD covers, on internet websites, in online forums, novels etc. While Section 2 above was hence an excursus away from the language of fictional television into the language of DVD covers, such an excursus can also tell us something about the imagined audience and fan community of fictional television series.

Notes

1 Producers Amy Sherman-Palladino, the creator of the show, and her husband, Daniel Palladino, left after the 6th season because of disagreements with Warner Brothers. David Rosenthal took over the show for its final 7th season (Sherman-Palladino & Palladino 2006). In the United States, the show was hosted by the WB network (www.warnerbros.com/), and the CW television network (www.cwtv.com/). The DVDs are distributed by Warner Brothers.

2 While I shy away from using Wikipedia and other non-academic websites in research in general, websites such as Wikipedia (www.wikipedia.org) and the Internet Movie Database (www.imdb.com) are very useful with respect to up-to-date information on popular culture that is not readily available elsewhere, and will occasionally be referenced in this book.

3 See contributions to Bednarek and Martin (2010) and references therein on the more technical notion of bonding in a Systemic Functional Linguistic framework. Here I am using *bonding* more as a commonsense term.

4 Despite the US-centred nature of some of the intertextual references, *Gilmore Girls* has had significant global success. This is presumably an example of American popular culture having 'become the popular culture of the world at large' (Esslin 2002: xv; compare Chapter 2). In a truly postmodern phenomenon *Gilmore Girls* itself is referenced and alluded to in other television shows such as *Family Guy* (FOX, 1999–), *Six Feet Under* (HBO, 2001–2005), *Scrubs* (NBC,

2001–), *Will & Grace* (NBC, 1998–2006), *Girlfriends* (UPN/CW, 2000–2008), *Joey* (NBC, 2004–2006) and *Veronica Mars* (UPN/CW, 2004–2007) (www.wikipedia.org). Intertextuality in general occurs frequently in contemporary TV series, such as *Dawson's Creek* (Warner Brothers, 1998–2003), see Birchall 2004: 183–5, *The West Wing* (NBC, 1999–2006), see Allen 2004: 21 or *The Simpsons* (FOX, 1989–) to name but a few. In *Lost* (ABC, 2004–), for instance, some character names allude to philosophers (John Locke, Rousseau).

[5] We might thus consider the analysis of *Gilmore Girls* dialogue as an example of positive discourse analysis (PDA) where the analyst is 'positively valuing some aspect of social change' (Martin 2004: 8), and where the focus is on 'discourses that enact a better world' (Martin 2004: 24). However, I shy away from adopting a completely positive stance towards *Gilmore Girls*, as it is still quite mainstream and features a pro-meat-eating ideology which can be viewed critically (see Chapter 8). Another question is whether Lorelai is only allowed to be depicted in the way she is because of elements of comedy in *Gilmore Girls*, joining the set of 'unruly women' in comedy where disruption is allowed to occur because it is distanced from reality (Feuer 2001a, Mills 2005: 114, 140).

[6] These 'postfeminist' series also 'offer women who have made careers but who revel in old-fashioned femininity, and depend on finding the right man for their happiness' (Hermes 2005: 114). *Gilmore Girls* arguably shares some features with other contemporary television drama series (*Buffy the Vampire Slayer*, *Ally McBeal*, *Sex and the City*) which have been classified as *postfeminist*:

> All of these series are generic hybrids, merging elements of soap opera, series drama, comedy, fantasy and, in the case of *Buffy*, horror. All are aimed primarily at a female audience, feature young, independent, usually single women in an urban environment, and engage with issues generated by "second wave" feminism in an ironic, playful and style-conscious manner which might be seen as antithetical to an earlier generation of feminists (Thornham & Purvis 2005: 126)

though I would argue that *Gilmore Girls* does take feminist concerns seriously (as suggested by the explicit discussion of such issues by characters). As the focus of this book is neither on gender nor on sexuality, the complexities of this will not be explored further here but see Hermes (2005: 100–1) on postfeminist television drama and why it is especially worthy of analysis.

[7] While I shall make comments on the series, seasons, episodes, scenes and shots in the course of the analyses in this book, I will not discuss segments. This is because my analyses are not based on watching *Gilmore Girls* 'live' on television, with advertisements, and the 'flow' characterizing television (Thornham & Purvis 2005: 1–11), but rather on watching it on DVD, without advertisements (but with additional information provided in special features). Nevertheless, it has to be acknowledged that segments are important units of analysis; in particular, segments are characteristic for television, with story structure partially determined by commercials.

[8] 'The Family Friendly Programming Forum is a group of over 40 major national advertisers, all members of the Association of National Advertisers and representing approximately 30% of all US television advertising dollars, who are

taking positive steps to increase family friendly programming choices on television. . . . The underlying goal of the Family Friendly Programming Forum is to support and promote content alternatives that adults and children can enjoy together. The definition of family friendly content is purposefully broad. Relevant to today's diverse and complex consumer, it has multi-generational appeal, depicts real life and is appropriate in theme, content and language. Family friendly content also embodies a responsible resolution of issues' (www.ana.net/ffpf, last accessed 17 September 2008).

9 'Dramedies blend the comic and the serious in different ways, some separate comic and dramatic storylines, while others combine drama and comedy together' (Lancioni 2006: 131). Aspects of dramedy also include 'the imaginativeness of the concept, the cleverness of the writing, and the complexity – and quirkiness – of the characters' (Lancioni 2006: 142). Mills (2005: 18) argues that comedy drama will have strong causal narratives, coherent characters and diegesis, but also points out that hybrids like comedy drama are 'notoriously subjective' (Mills 2005: 25) in terms of genre.

10 In fact, criticism of *Gilmore Girls* has centred on the fact that the series is not realistic enough (for a discussion see Calvin 2008a: 15–17). Johns and Smith (2008) describe the Utopian qualities of Stars Hollow.

11 A manual analysis of the texts confirms that intensification and quantification (both types of graduation, see Martin & White 2005) occur frequently throughout, not just with respect to the items identified through the frequency analysis: for example, ***fabulously*** *funny;* ***deliciously*** *intriguing;* ***legions of*** *Gilmore Girls devotees;* ***totally*** *off-kilter,* ***totally*** *engaging;* ***much****-loved;* ***all*** *22 irresistible . . . episodes;* ***super****-achieving; a* ***whole*** *town of;* ***blissfully*** *brilliant;* ***more*** *fun,* ***more*** *flames,* ***more*** *flameouts:* ***more*** *Gilmore;* ***all*** *22 third-year episodes; the guy* ***every*** *fan has known;* ***huge*** *success;* ***heartbreakingly*** *dramatic; adding* ***more*** *sparkle; a townful* ***more;*** ***deliriously*** *happy;* ***big*** *new step;* ***everyone*** *in town; there's* ***much more***. Some of these could also be related to an evaluation of importance (e.g. ***big*** *new step*).

12 Additional evaluative parameters that can be identified are described in Bednarek (2006a, 2008c). Alternative frameworks include different types of evaluative meanings recognized in appraisal theory (Martin & White 2005), and stance (Biber et al. 1999). Various annotation schemes for elements of evaluation, emotion or attitude have been suggested by Hunston (2003), Wiebe et al. (2005), Bednarek (e.g. 2006a, 2008a, c), as well as Wilson (2008) and references therein, working in linguistics and NLP. The diversification of evaluative parameters in my framework to include more than just positive and negative evaluation is supported by findings from computational linguistics: Annotators in a project on annotations of opinion were not comfortable assigning notions of pos/neg to a significant number of instances of evaluative meanings, which 'suggests that simple polarity is not a sufficient notion of attitude type' (Wiebe et al. 2005: 191). It is also noted that 'the most immediate refinement we plan for our annotation scheme involves the *attitude type* attribute' (Wiebe et al. 2005: 205; see Wilson 2008 for this refinement). Chapter 6 deals with emotional/evaluative meanings in more detail.

13 Some of these could have a positive valence depending on reading position (e.g. *fast-paced dialogue*) and depending on co-textual evaluations which surround

them (e.g. *a brilliant array of totally* ***off-kilter****, totally engaging supporting characters*). On the influence of co-text on evaluation see Bednarek (2006a: 209–11).

14 Evaluations of UN/EXPECTEDNESS do not necessarily evaluate events as positive or negative, although co-textually (prospectively or retrospectively) this is possible: *Sooke gets a surprise (a* ***good*** *one.).* For further discussion of surprise/unexpectedness and valence see Bednarek (2008a: 161–5). Contrast (e.g. through conjunction with *but*), which is also related to unexpectedness (Bednarek 2006a), was not analysed in the texts.

15 Some of these could arguably also be construed as evaluations of the importance of *Gilmore Girls* (thus: evaluations of IMPORTANCE: IMPORTANT), which would increase the small number of evaluations of IMPORTANCE in these texts to some extent.

16 Television series in general as well as characters in them have the potential to become both bondicons and anti-bondicons or 'anti-bondies' (Martin 2010), that is, 'hate objects'. Fans engage in a variety of productive practices with respect to their fandom, such as talking with like-minded people, producing their own stories, role-playing etc. (de Kloet & van Zoonen 2007).

17 We could also look at the generic structure of these texts with its combined elements of narrative and commentary/opinion or undertake cross-cultural/cross-linguistic comparisons, that is, analyse the DVD cover texts in various languages and cultures. Most research on advertising discourse in fact seems to be on more 'traditional' ads, for example, commercials on television or advertisements in newspapers/magazines. Future research could design a corpus of DVD cover texts (for more than one series) and explore the linguistic features of this type of advertising discourse in more detail, comparing it with traditional ads as well as book blurbs. Needless to say, the findings reported in this chapter only relate to the *Gilmore Girls* DVDs.

Chapter 4

Television Dialogue

After the excursus into the language of DVD cover texts in Chapter 3, this chapter looks in more detail at the language of fictional television – television dialogue. Dialogue is very important for the genre of dramedy and other fictional television series that incorporate dramatic elements, as drama is 'first and foremost dialogue in action' (Crystal 1997: 75). And television scriptwriters are advised that '[e]xceptional dialogue is your winning ticket to fame and fortune in the writing world' (D'Vari 2005: 189). This chapter first reviews research on language and television, including studies on differences between scripted and 'natural' dialogue/conversation in general. It then shows how corpus stylistic methodology can be used to compare frequent words/phrases in television discourse vs. naturally occurring conversation. A case study of the dramedy *Gilmore Girls* (Chapter 3) will be used for illustrative purposes.

1 Analysing Language and Television

In view of the importance of television outlined in Chapter 2, it is surprising that linguistic and stylistic research has not yet addressed television dialogue in great detail. 'Classic' introductions to narrative (e.g. Bal 1997, Toolan 2001, Rimmon-Kenan 2002) tend not to say too much about television and film dialogue. If narratology deals with this topic, it usually focuses on film, rather than television narrative and, more specifically, on filmic adaptations of literary texts (e.g. Lothe 2000, Sanger 2001: 81–9, Toolan 2001: 103–07). Concerning the analysis of media discourse it is also noteworthy that 'most of the work in media discourse has been on the "factual" genres, and particularly news' (Garrett & Bell 1998: 4). For example, many books on media discourse or on the language of the media (e.g. Bell & Garrett 1998, Bednarek 2006a, O'Keeffe 2006, Johnson & Ensslin 2007, Talbot 2007) focus on various types of non-fictional print items, radio and television broadcasts (ranging from media interviews, chat shows, news magazines to newspapers, radio satires and lifestyle genres to name but a few) but generally do not have much to say about the language of fictional television series. There are however, (at least) three recently published books applying a linguistic framework to television discourse: Marshall and Werndly (2002), Lorenzo-Dus (2009) and Quaglio (2009). Of these, Marshall and Werndly (2002) is a textbook for A-level and undergraduate students focusing on a range of British television genres. As recent as 2009, Lorenzo-Dus suggests that her work is 'the first book-length investigation specifically and thoroughly focused on television talk' (Lorenzo-Dus 2009: 5) but she explicitly excludes all fictional programmes. Quaglio (2009) explores differences between the discourse of *Friends* (NBC, 1994–2004) and natural conversation using Biber's (1988) multidimensional corpus methodology, and is, therefore, rather specialized. Consequently, in terms of research on TV *dialogue*, in particular, linguistic and stylistic research, a lot has yet to be done, although it does appear to be an up-and-coming research topic (e.g. Brock 2004, Tagliamonte & Roberts 2005, Bubel 2006, Bubel & Spitz 2006, Mittmann 2006, Mandala 2007, Paltridge 2007, Stokoe 2008, Wodak 2009), and there is also a growing number of studies on audiovisual translation (e.g. Díaz-Cintas 2009). However, there is much catching up to do before we can begin to reach the wealth of research that has been done on other types of media discourse, in particular the discourse of news media.

Outside linguistics, numerous analyses of media products, including popular culture and television shows, can of course be found in media and cultural studies (e.g. Fine 1981, Creeber 2004, Akass & McCabe 2004, Davis & Dickinson 2004, McCabe & Akass 2006, Allen 2007). Such studies often feature content analysis and similar techniques. Many of the analyses of female-oriented series such as *Sex and the City* (HBO, 1998–2004), *Desperate Housewives* (Touchstone Television/ABC, 2004–), *Buffy the Vampire Slayer* (Warner Brothers, 1997–2003) or *Gilmore Girls* (Warner Brothers, 2000–2007) focus more generally on the representation of gender, female friendship, motherhood, sexuality and romantic love (Bavidge 2004, Akass & McCabe 2004, McCabe & Akass 2006, Calvin 2008b), rather than analysing television dialogue systematically. Even in film studies Kozloff notes that '[w]ith notable exceptions, most of this scholarship has only minimally addressed the most important aspect of film sound – namely, the dialogue' (Kozloff 2000: 6). Further, such studies usually seem to offer little systematic linguistic or semiotic analysis:

> Routinely reduced to such a vague and oversimplified form as to be useless, semiotics, fully realised as the study of linguistic and visual signs positioned in a cultural and historical context, still remains the only systematic approach to explaining how, rather than just what, texts mean. If cultural studies is not to disappear into a vacuum of superficial rhetoric and ambit claims about the hegemonic function of the media, it has to be buttressed by a theorised approach to language, signification and the production of ideology. (Fulton 2005a: 2)

It is also worth pointing out that most television textbooks focus on audience, genre, institution rather than on 'textual' features of television such as image and sound (Lury 2005). Kozloff makes an important point when she says: 'I look forward to the day when analysis of verbal conventions is an expected part of genre study' (Kozloff 2000: 267). Kozloff herself identifies nine functions of dialogue in narrative film, which also seem present in television (see, for example, Field 1984). These functions are: anchorage of the diegesis and characters; character revelation; communication of narrative causality; enactment of narrative events; adherence to the code of realism; control of viewer evaluation and emotions; exploitation of the resources of language (poetic/humor/irony); thematic messages/authorial commentary/allegory and opportunities for 'star turns' (Kozloff 2000: 33–4). Of these, this book looks in particular at the function of dialogue to reveal character (Chapters 5–8), but compare the description of the use of witty dialogue/intertextual references in *Gilmore Girls* in Chapter 3.

A systematic linguistic analysis of television dialogue can provide some input to future investigations of popular culture in media studies and cultural studies, and also focuses attention on a long-neglected type of scripted dialogue. While it goes against the argument that we should study 'real' language, that is, language that is ' "natural", unrehearsed, unscripted' (Pennycook 2007: 61), the analysis of scripted television dialogue advances our understanding of TV writers' internalized beliefs which are transmitted through the created dialogue into a globalized community of TV viewers across the world. As suggested in the model of overhearer design (Chapter 2), scriptwriters 'apply mundane knowledge about normative practices and rely on their audience to do the same in response' (Stokoe 2008: 305). This is mediated by knowledge of genre and scriptwriting conventions. The analysis of such dialogue can thus give us insights into people's cognitive models, or schemata of conversation, as suggested by various researchers (see Spitz 2005: 28, Bubel 2006: 61). In any case, there are clear methodological advantages in analysing television dialogue, for instance that ethnographic details (characters' histories, relationships, personalities etc.) can be considered in the analysis (Bubel 2006: 2). Finally, analysing scripted TV dialogue on its own terms allows us to compare it to other kinds of scripted dialogue (e.g. literary drama) or – the focus of this chapter – to compare it to naturally occurring conversation. Such a comparison allows us to see how conversation is fictionalized and reconstrued in television.

2 Linguistic Features of (Scripted) Fictional Television Dialogue

(Scripted) fictional television dialogue is a particular subtype of scripted/constructed dialogue in general and of scripted dramatic dialogue in particular. Most research in linguistics has in fact focused on the characteristics of dramatic dialogue rather than television dialogue (e.g. Burton 1980) in line with the neglect of the language of television outlined above. There are differences between such dramatic dialogue and 'naturally occurring' conversation, first, with respect to the communicative context (as already described for television dialogue in Chapter 2, Section 3.1).[1] Secondly, dramatic dialogue also has specific linguistic features that characterize it as planned/scripted. Thus, it has been pointed out that '[d]ramatic dialogue, however realistic it may seem, is not identical to naturally occurring conversation' (Spitz 2005: 22). Constructed dialogue in general contains fewer false starts, hesitation phenomena, redundancies, less repetition, deficient syntax, interruption, overlap or simultaneous speech than naturally occurring dialogue. On account of this, dramatic dialogue has been considered a '"pure," "concentrated," "condensed," or "tidied up" version of social intercourse' (Spitz 2005: 25, summarizing relevant research). These points relate to dramatic dialogue but what about *television* dialogue? Comments made on the language of fictional film and television also emphasize that 'the defining characteristics of film dialogue is that *it is never realistic; it is always designed "for us"*' (Kozloff 2000: 121), and it is also designed for specific functions (see page 63). Some general features of television and film dialogue that have been identified – albeit on the basis of at times very limited data – as distinguishing it from naturally occurring dialogue (Sanger 2001, Kozloff 2000, Bubel 2006, Quaglio 2008, 2009) are:

- it exhibits conventions of stage dialogue;
- it comprises certain stock lines;
- it avoids unintelligibility, that is, false starts, overlaps, interruptions, unclear words, abrupt topic shifts etc. to favour intelligibility above acoustic fidelity and naturalism;
- it has a relatively even distribution of (short) turns;
- it has a lower frequency of 'vague' language (e.g. *kind of*; *thing*(*s*), and *stuff*);
- it has a lower frequency of 'narrative' language;
- it has a higher frequency of emotional and emphatic language;
- it has a higher frequency of informal language;
- it is less varied linguistically (e.g. in terms of settings, interaction types, topics);
- it avoids repetitive discourse and fillers, because they do not advance the narrative;
- it contains aesthetic devices, for example, repetition, rhythm and surprise.

Aesthetic devices and conventions also concern the use of voice-over and asides to the audience, for instance in television series such as *Desperate Housewives* (Touchstone Television/ABC, 2004–), *Grey's Anatomy* (ABC, 2005–) (voice-overs) and *Sex and the City* (HBO, 1998–2004), as this example of a direct audience address (in bold face) from Bubel (2006: 49–50) shows:

(1)
[Telephone conversation between Carrie (C) and Charlotte (Ch)]
1 C {*answering the phone*}
hello?
2 Ch hey Carrie.
it's Charlotte.
3 C hey sweetie.
4 Ch hey,
look,
I can't meet you guys for dinner tomorrow night?
because I have an amazing date?
5 C with who?
6 Ch Capote Dunkin.
he's supposedly some big shot in the publishing world,
do you know him?
{*Carrie puts hand over receiver and addresses audience:* ***did I know him? he was one of the city's most notoriously ungettable bachelors.***}
wait wait.
don't . . . even answer that question.
because frankly?
I don't care.
and . . . another thing,
. . . I'm not buying into any of that women having sex like
men crap.
7 C {*Carrie takes receiver down and addresses audience:* ***I didn't want to tell her about my afternoon of cheap and easy sex and how good it felt***}
all right fi:ne.
listen.
have a good time.
and promise to tell me everything.
8 Ch o:h, .
if you're lucky.
bye:
9 C all right.
bye.
(*Sex and the City*, 1.2, *Amazing Date,* transcription according to Bubel 2006, bold face mine)

The above-noted characteristics of TV dialogue are influenced by the communicative context (Chapter 2) of fictional television, primarily in terms of audience (as overhearer) design: television discourse needs to be comprehensible to the audience (avoiding unintelligible and vague language); entertain the audience (including emotional and aesthetic language; avoiding repetition, long monologues or narratives); create characters that the audience finds realistic (featuring informal language); and attract a large audience (featuring conventions of stage dialogue, stock lines; less linguistic variation). For example, differences in the language of the sitcom *Friends* compared to conversation can be linked to the TV series avoiding miscomprehension as well as being interactive/dynamic, and humorous (Quaglio 2009: 147–8). Other differences can be related to narrative and generic structure, with character relationships, settings, topics etc. featured in television series being dependent on respective conventions (see Chapters 2, 3).

On the other hand, a number of linguistic analyses have shown that 'despite obvious differences, dramatic dialogue . . . closely resembles ordinary talk' (Spitz 2005: 532). Bubel notes a similarity of constructed talk to ordinary dialogue, especially in terms of conversational organization (Bubel 2006: 61). Similarly, Tagliamonte and Roberts (2005) find that data from *Friends* show a similar use and patterning of intensification as normal conversation. Rey (2001: 142) shows that scripted language in *Star Trek* series (NBC/Paramount, 1966–1969, 1987–1994, 1993–1999) is similarly 'involved' as face-to-face conversation, and Quaglio (2008: 195) shows the same for sitcom dialogue in *Friends*. And even though frequencies of devices such as repetitions, false starts, fillers and vague language may be lower than in casual conversation, they do occur in scripted television dialogue, as these extracts from *Friends* (NBC, 1994–2004), *Dawson's Creek* (Warner Brothers, 1998–2003) and *Ally McBeal* (FOX, 1997–2002) illustrate:

(2)
Rachel: Hi! Sorry – sorry we're late, we, uh, kinda just, y'know, lost track of time.
(*Friends*, from Quaglio 2009)

(3)
Dawson: No. No. I guess, I'm just a little nervous.
(*Dawson's Creek*, from Mittmann 2006)

(4)
Ally: men can handle it [telling dirty jokes],
women can't we're we're uh
we're not tough enough.
we're we're too we're too (2.0) fragile.
(*Ally McBeal*, from Bubel & Spitz 2006)

When such features do occur they provide realism, comic confusion (Kozloff 2000: 76), show mental states such as emotions (see Chapter 7) or align turn-taking with camera angles (Kobus 1998, quoted in Bubel 2006: 44).

It is further likely that different genres of fictional television have linguistic differences, with more witty, fast-paced dialogue in sitcom and other comedy genres, and more institutional discourse, technical language, criminal cant, jargon or slang in crime series (e.g. *The Wire* [HBO, 2002–2008], *NCIS* [CBS, 2003–], *CSI* [CBS, 2000–]), medical dramas such as *Grey's Anatomy* (ABC, 2005–) or sci-fi series such as *Star Trek* (NBC/Paramount, 1966–1969, 1987–1994, 1993–1999), where examples like the following frequently occur.

(5)

Riker: I've also ordered **a standing yellow alert**. All **Federation allied outposts** have been warned. **Ops** will continue to **monitor** the **long range sensors**. I've assigned Data, LaForge, and Mr Crusher to work with **Commander** Shelby.

(*Star Trek: The Next Generation*, transcription from Rey 2001, my bold)

'Supernatural' television series such as *The X-Files* (FOX, 1993–2002), *Medium* (NBC, 2005–), *Supernatural* (The WB/The CW, 2005–), *Ghost Whisperer* (CBS, 2005–) or *Buffy the Vampire Slayer* (Warner Brothers, 1997–2003) will also have genre-specific vocabulary and discourse:

(6)

Willow I know I'm not the kind of girl **vampires** like to **sink their teeth into**. It's always like ooo you're like a sister to me or ohhh you're such a good friend.

Spike Don't be ridiculous.
I'd **bite** you in a heartbeat.

(*Buffy the Vampire Slayer*, 4.7, *The Initiative*, transcription from Mandala 2007, my bold)

'Teen television' (Davis & Dickinson 2004) such as the above mentioned *Buffy the Vampire Slayer, Beverly Hills 90210* (Fox, 1990–2000), *My so-called Life* (ABC, 1994–1995), *Dawson's Creek* (Warner Brothers, 1998–2003) or *Gossip Girl* (The CW, 2007–) will also feature what can be called 'teen language' (Mandala 2007). For instance, characteristics of the dialogue of teenage characters in *My-so called Life* produced 15 years ago include very frequent uses of *like* as a discourse marker:

(7)

Brian: Um, one of the things we were suppose to do this semester was, uh, this issue of the literary magazine. Ah, **like** we each wrote something, and, ah, but Mayhew, that's our teacher, she, ah, **like** never approved the witting or whatever, cause she, just, she quit. So, well, we just never did it.

(*My So-called Life*, 1.6, *The Substitute*)

Television programmes also differ in the extent to which non-mainstream varieties (e.g. Italian American English or African American Vernacular) are present (compare *The Sopranos*, HBO, 1999–2007, *The Wire*, HBO, 2002–2008). *Gilmore Girls* is very mainstream in this respect, and does not feature such linguistic variety much.

To sum up, it is likely that the language of a fictional television series will feature both aspects particular to the genre it belongs to and aspects unique to its character as a particular popular cultural artifact, while it will also include aspects related to the nature of fictional television series in general. In Section 3 below I will use computer software to investigate in how far *Gilmore Girls* is similar/different to naturally occurring conversation with respect to particularly (in)frequent words and phrases. This is a contribution to studying the characteristics of the dialogue of television series, in particular of a selected dramedy, and of showing how corpus stylistic techniques can be used in the analysis of the language of fictional television.

3 A Corpus Stylistic Analysis of Television Dialogue

As suggested, the analysis of television dialogue is a worthy and fruitful endeavour, but, as with the analysis of DVD cover texts in Chapter 3, the question is how to approach this analysis. This section will introduce a corpus stylistic approach to analysing television dialogue.

3.1 Corpus linguistics and corpus stylistics

Corpus linguistics is an approach to the linguistic analysis of data that uses large computerized collections of text (corpora) and appropriate software to analyse them. The material that is contained in corpora is usually said to be more or less representative for the variety of language that it was designed for, and there are many different types of corpora (see Hunston 2002, Meyer 2002). Depending on the use made of corpora and software, researchers can find out many linguistic features, for instance (1) the frequency with which every word in the corpus occurs, (2) words that are unusually (in)frequent when compared with a reference corpus, (3) all occurrences of a particular word, (4) recurring larger structures (p-frames, n-grams, clusters, phrases), (5) grammatical frames, (6) collocations, (7) occurrences of parts of speech and their combinations, etc. Corpus linguistic applications include discourse analysis, lexicography, stylistics, forensic linguistics, language variation studies and language teaching (Baker 2006).

Particularly relevant to the study of fictional dialogue is *corpus stylistics* (Wynne 2006, Adolphs 2006, Fischer-Starcke 2007, Archer 2007) – corpus linguistic analyses of fictional (usually literary) texts.[2] Stubbs (2005) gives an overview of corpus stylistic investigation and convincingly demonstrates the validity of such research. It is of course, never claimed, that corpus stylistics can show us all aspects of scripted texts or that it is the only way of studying such texts. Rather, as Michael McCarthy says in his introduction to Mahlberg (2007), corpus stylistics offers only a contribution to the 'total sum of linguistic features that characterize a style' (Mahlberg 2007: 19). However, as both Wynne (2006) and Fischer-Starcke (2007) point out, there is in fact relatively little corpus stylistic research yet. Indeed, as far as I am aware, the only corpus linguistic investigations of television series are Rey (2001), Mittmann (2006) and Quaglio (2008, 2009). Instead, corpus stylistic investigations focus on 'classic' literary narrative by authors like Shakespeare, Austen, Dickens, Conrad (e.g. Graves 1999, Hubbard 2002, Culpeper 2002, Stubbs 2005, Fischer-Starcke 2007, Mahlberg 2007, Widdowson 2008, Bednarek 2008d).

Concerning my own corpus stylistic analyses of television dialogue in this book it is useful to consider Adolphs' (2006: 65–9) distinction between intra- and inter-textual analysis. She differentiates between those corpus stylistic analyses that focus on one literary text or text collections ('intra-textual') and those that compare literary texts with other texts ('inter-textual'). The corpus stylistic analyses of this chapter start with an intra-textual frequency analysis but then focus on frequent words and phrases in *Gilmore Girls* versus naturally occurring conversation (inter-textual), allowing a comparison with previous research on television dialogue (Mittmann 2006, Quaglio 2008, 2009). This type of analysis has something in common with corpus stylistic research which uses reference corpora to provide a linguistic norm against which literary language is compared and with whose help literary effects or literary creativity are described (e.g. Louw 1993, Krishnamurthy 1995, Hoey 2005: 172–177; see Wynne 2006 and Adolphs 2006 for further references). However, I am simply interested in similarities and differences between frequent words/phrases in scripted television dialogue as occurring in a particular television series, compared to 'natural' spoken dialogue. Chapters 6 and 8 will then offer an 'intra-textual' analysis of *Gilmore Girls* with respect to characterization.

3.2 Corpora and software

In general, using a corpus for analysing a television series offers the advantage of exploring it as a whole, overcoming the problem of selecting a particular moment for analysis: 'For sitcoms [and other television series, M.B.] with hundreds of episodes, it's almost always possible to find any moment in one particular episode that's capable of supporting any argument, regardless of whether that moment is indicative of the series as a whole' (Mills 2005: 24).

Two corpora comprising data from *Gilmore Girls* were used in the corpus stylistic analyses in this book: (1) TS-GiGi (ca 1.3 million words) and (2) GiGi (ca 1.1 million words). TS-GiGi consists of unprocessed fan transcripts (not the original scripts) of *Gilmore Girls* episodes. These transcripts are available online and are characterized by multiple authorship (e.g. story-board editors, screenwriters, directors – cf. Chapter 2), with the transcribers (the 'fans') being responsible for producing the actual transcript from television. While the transcripts are not 100% accurate, they are much more accurate than the subtitles (which could be automatically extracted as alternative data source), with a much greater number of and more significant mistakes in the subtitles than in the transcripts (five times as many mistakes in a randomly selected 2.24 minute scene; see Table A.2 in Appendix 3). Quaglio (2008, 2009), who also uses such transcripts in his corpus analysis of *Friends* notes that they are 'fairly accurate and very detailed, including several features that scripts are not likely to present: hesitators, pauses, repeats, and contractions' (Quaglio 2008: 191–2). The same applies to the *Gilmore Girls* transcripts. Manual transcription by the researcher may in fact result in similar inaccuracies as are present in the fan transcripts (e.g. typos), and simply was not feasible for a large-scale corpus analysis. However, scenes that are analysed in depth (Chapter 7) were transcribed manually, adding information on verbal and non-verbal behaviour; and all extended examples from *Gilmore Girls* that are quoted in this book were checked against the DVDs.

The TS-GiGi transcripts cover all 153 episodes, consist of word-to-word dialogue as well as some descriptions of setting, action scenes and/or camera movements, and include names of speakers (e.g. Lorelai, Rory, Luke). It can be very useful to the linguist to have this contextual information (Quaglio 2009: 31). The transcripts do not feature linguistic transcription conventions, for example, systematic signalling of emphatic stress, paralinguistic features, lengths of pauses, intonation, overlap etc. TS-GiGi is available both in html- and in txt-file format. In contrast, the GiGi corpus is a processed version of TS-GiGi, which consists of dialogue only and is available solely in txt-file format. For the design of the GiGi corpus the TS-GiGi transcripts were manually edited to delete titles of episodes, descriptions of settings, action sequences, camera movements etc. Both TS-GiGi and GiGi are specialized corpora of scripted dialogue, and are maximally representative of this particular television series (*Gilmore Girls*) but not representative of television dialogue in general. While TS-GiGi will be used in Chapters 5 and 8, GiGi will be used in Chapters 4 and 5. In order not to approach my analyses 'from the position of *tabula rasa*' (Baker 2006: 25) I additionally watched all episodes of *Gilmore Girls* on DVD (rather than reading all of the scripts) so that I was relatively familiar with the corpora.

As far as computer software is concerned, I used Scott's (1999) Wordsmith software package for the analysis of TS-GiGi and GiGi. This software is widely used in corpus linguistics, and is a useful tool for the analysis of large-scale data that cannot be analysed manually. It allows the user to produce frequency lists (lists of words and phrases in the corpus – the *WordList* tool), concordances (occurrences for words or phrases – the *Concord* tool) and key words (words/phrases that are statistically unusual when comparing two corpora – the *KeyWords* tool). The main emphasis in this chapter is on frequency lists for words and phrases/n-grams, but other chapters in this book look at key words (Chapter 5) and concordances (Chapter 8).

3.3 Frequent words in *Gilmore Girls*

Let us look first at a frequency list for the GiGi corpus (dialogue only) in terms of frequent words, as such lists 'are one essential starting point for a systematic textual analysis' (Stubbs 2005: 11).[3] Excluding names, the 20 most frequent words in GiGi are listed in Table 4.1:

Table 4.1 Twenty most frequent word forms in *Gilmore Girls*

N	Word	Freq.
1	I	42,937
2	YOU	40,575
3	THE	31,804
4	TO	27,049
5	A	24,247
6	AND	21,129
7	IT	18,065
8	THAT	13,937
9	OF	12,275
10	IS	10,597
11	IN	10,494
12	WHAT	10,111
13	ME	9026
14	HAVE	8653
15	THIS	8582
16	SO	8363
17	NOT	8356
18	MY	8186
19	FOR	8105
20	JUST	8058

Although this frequency list tells us something about the data in itself, for example, that it might be interesting to look in more detail at questions with *what* (No 12 in the list) or negation with *not* (No 17), we do not yet know which of these frequencies are particular to *Gilmore Girls* and which reflect general language tendencies. In other words, if we analyse the corpus that we are interested in (what Scott & Tribble 2006: 58 call the 'node-text') we need another corpus that works as a standard of comparison, baseline or norm – a 'reference' corpus (Scott & Tribble 2006: 58) – to establish what is special about the node corpus. Consequently, we will now compare ranked frequency lists from *Gilmore Girls* with ranked frequency lists from corpora of spoken American English.

3.4 Frequent words and phrases in *Gilmore Girls* vs. spoken American English

To produce ranked frequency lists, that is, lists of all words/phrases and their rank in terms of frequency (rank 1 = most frequent, rank 2 = second most frequent, etc.) in *Gilmore Girls,* Wordsmith's *WordList* tool was used. The resulting ranked frequency lists were compared with ranked frequency list from two reference corpora: part 1 of the Santa Barbara Corpus of Spoken American English ('SB': ca 140,000 words of spoken American English),[4] and the Longman Spoken American Corpus ('LSAC': ca 4.8 million words). The frequency lists from SB were produced with Wordsmith, whereas word-lists for the LSAC were taken from Mittmann (2004), because I had no direct computational access to the LSAC. The frequency lists were then compared manually, looking at what words occurred in these lists at what position. A position higher up in the list indicates that the word or phrase is more frequent; so if a word form appears as N° 3 in the list from the *Gilmore Girls* corpus, and as N° 50 in the list from a conversation corpus, we can tentatively suggest that the word form is over-represented in the dramedy dialogue with respect to naturally occurring conversation, even though further research and statistical tests would need to confirm this.[5] Such frequencies can tell us about the topic or themes of a corpus – for example, what *Gilmore Girls* dialogue is about, who is talking to whom etc. They can also provide information on linguistic characteristics of the node corpus – for example, how *Gilmore Girls* is different from naturally occurring conversation. Finally, frequent words/phrases can refer to the cultural, historical and social background of the node corpus, for example, to the particular environment in which *Gilmore Girls* is set.

3.4.1 Frequent words in Gilmore Girls *vs. spoken American English*

Concerning individual word forms, *WordList* was used to produce a list of the most frequent words in SB, because Mittmann (2004) does not provide word lists for individual word forms in LSAC. Comparing the lists from GiGi and SB manually (with all names excluded from both lists), it is interesting to observe that number one to nine and other words in the top 20 in both lists are very similar (see Table A.3 in Appendix 5) with more striking differences concerning only some words located between N° 10 and N° 20 on the lists (Table 4.2 on page 73).

For instance, *me* is N° 13 in GiGi but only N° 51 in SB, *not* is N° 17 in GiGi and only N° 55 in SB, and *my* (N° 18 in GiGi) is not among the top 50 word forms in SB. This might indicate that GiGi is more focused on individual speakers than American conversation (*me, my*) or has a higher 'discourse immediacy' (characterized by 1st/2nd person pronouns, Quaglio 2009: 134). With respect to negation (*not*), let us briefly look at three-word clusters in GiGi for *not*

Table 4.2 Top 20 word forms in *Gilmore Girls* vs. SB

No	GiGi	SB
1	I	I
2	you	the
3	the	and
4	to	you
5	a	to
6	and	a
7	it	that
8	that	it
9	of	of
10	is	know
11	in	in
12	what	was
13	me	they
14	have	like
15	this	is
16	so	have
17	not	yeah
18	my	he
19	for	what
20	just	so

Table 4.3 Three-word clusters for *not* in *Gilmore Girls*

N	Cluster	Freq.
1	I M NOT	329
2	NOT GOING TO	236
3	IT S NOT	191
4	THIS IS NOT	151
5	I AM NOT	135
6	I DID NOT	126
7	YOU RE NOT	121
8	I DO NOT	83
9	I'M NOT SURE	74
10	I'M NOT GOING	73
11	IT'S NOT A	69
12	NO I'M NOT	65
13	IS NOT A	65
14	YOU DO NOT	61
15	I'M NOT GONNA	60
16	WHY NOT BECAUSE	57
17	THAT S NOT	56
18	NO IT'S NOT	54
19	YOU ARE NOT	52
20	NOT AT ALL	50

(8356 occurrences) that occur more than 50 times (Table 4.3). While it is beyond the scope of this section to investigate these clusters in more detail, it is noticeable that of these 20 clusters, more than half relate to either the speaker (*I*) or the hearer (*you*), again pointing to the importance of interpersonal interaction (and perhaps conflict) in *Gilmore Girls* (*I'm not, I am not, I did not, I do not, I'm not sure, I'm not going, No I'm not, I'm not gonna, you're not, you do not, you are not*). In fact, *I don't want* is a cluster that is clearly overrepresented in *Gilmore Girls* compared to spoken English (see Section 3.4.2 below). Even those clusters that do not include *I* or *you* explicitly, in particular *this is not, it's not, it's not a, is not a, that's not, no it's not, why not because* seem to be related to an interpersonally loaded interaction between characters, for example, contradicting or questioning.

What is particularly interesting is that the GiGi corpus allows us to observe patterns of interaction *between* characters (since character names have been removed from the corpus); thus, the cluster *why not because* occurs as an *interactive cluster*, which often co-occurs, that is, colligates, with expressions of negated modality (*won't, can't, cannot*). The concordance lines in Figure 4.1 illustrate this interactive cluster.

N	Concordance
8	okay? Paw-paw and Chin Chin cannot come to the test run. Why not? Because they are dogs, Michel. They cannot stay
9	So? So you can't order crispy fries without first ordering fries. Why not? Because you can't make something crispy that doesn't
10	and be surprised. Why don't you tell me what the movie is? No. Why not? Because. Because why? What is the. . .oh no. There is
11	Ok, but if we do think it's Hank - We don't think it's Hank. Why not? Because if we think it's Hank, and then something
12	glow! What do you think? We're not painting my apartment! Heh. Why not? Because we're painting your house! That's why you
13	This is really good. Yeah, what is it? Well, it -. No, don't tell us. Why not? Because every time in my life that I've tasted something
14	are at 6, dinner's at 8. I probably won't be there for cocktails. Why not? Because I have to work. You can't leave work early? No
15	Because I have to work. You can't leave work early? No I can't. Why not? Because it's not in my job description. Well then don't
16	do it. Do what? I'll be your boyfriend. You can't be my boyfriend. Why not? Because you told me that you can't be my boyfriend. If I
17	go through the whole 'the wedding was postponed' explanation. Why not? Because! Then that would lead to the 'what happened?'
18	watch all the men that got away. What? No, you can't do that! Why not? Because! Look, I'm worried about you. Why? Just
19	to be swept. Mom. What? Luke cannot sweep our chimney. Why not? Because you need to be a chimney sweep to sweep a
20	eat there. Ace! I'm just not excited about this particular birthday. Why not? Because, I'm turning twenty-one. Yes? My mom and I
21	me crazy. Well tell Jackson to kick him out. Jackson won't do it. Why not? Because he says it's family and somehow he feels
22	Rory. Fine. Fine. You know, she can't go into the market. Why not? Because you're there. Not on Wednesdays Already
23	first met. You should've just said something. I couldn't do that. Why not? Because then you would've known that I was calling
24	Birthdays aren't a very big deal in the Huntzberger family. Why not? Because birthdays aren't something you achieve. Why
25	May I speak with Rory please? No, you can't speak with Rory. Why not? Because I called you. So what? You don't get to
26	going for us. The crowd'll eat that up. I cannot dance with you. Why not? Because this is Dean's first marathon. We were gonna
27	he just went out. You didn't ask him where he was going? No. Why not? Because he's not two. Yeah, but Luke, he's new in
28	Luke? Yeah, Kirk. What time is it? I'm not saying, Kirk. Why not? Because I just told you 30 seconds ago! More like 45
29	my party. Well what did Lorelai say when you told her? I didn't. Why not? Because of the pudding. Oh, the pudding. Right, I forgot

FIGURE 4.1 Interactive cluster *Why not because*

Inspection of these instances in the TS-GiGi corpus shows that the *why not* and its associated *because* response are of course uttered by different characters, as illustrated in Figure 4.2.

N	Concordance
19	You can't leave work early? LORELAI: No I can't. EMILY: Why not? LORELAI: Because it's not in my job description.
20	boyfriend. RORY: You can't be my boyfriend. LOGAN: Why not? RORY: Because you told me that you can't be
21	whole 'the wedding was postponed' explanation. RORY: Why not? LORELAI: Because! Then that would lead to the

FIGURE 4.2 Three instances of *Why not because* in TS-GiGi

Speech acts with *Why not* are 'demands for explanation' (Spitz 2005: 316) – instances of a speech act that belongs to speakers' 'argumentative resources' (Spitz 2005: 245). Such demands are 'a class of utterances that question the basis for the prior speaker's claim and request that she provide a reason for it' (Spitz 2005: 316). In GiGi (and perhaps in general), they are countered by the interlocutor with some kind of causal explanation/account, which may not be a genuine reason (e.g. *because I say so*; *because I don't want to hear it*; simply *because*), resulting in the observed interactive *why not because* cluster. Not all questions with *why* and negation necessarily result in accounts, as they have different discourse functions. For instance, *why don't you* in the following extract from *The West Wing* (NBC, 1999–2006) works more as a demand or command, and is thus followed by an agreement.

(8)

Bartlett: I've been thinking I'd like to talk about creativity – ah. **Why don't you** get started on some thoughts and I'll join you.

Will: Yes sir.
(*The West Wing*, transcription according to Wodak 2009, bold face mine)

This, incidentally, is also another example of the partially genre-dependent variation of the scripted language of fictional television, with phrases such as *Yes sir* clearly more frequent in those kinds of genres which feature explicit power differences to a great extent.

The analyses of negation with *not* illustrate that it makes sense to move beyond individual words and to look at syntagmatic patterns (clusters, n-grams) such as *why not because*. Stubbs has suggested that 'one gains a much better impression of both the content and of the . . . nature of the discourse, via longer recurrent expressions' (Stubbs 2008: 5). Thus, the next section analyses frequent clusters in *Gilmore Girls* compared with spoken American English.

3.4.2 Frequent n-grams/phrases/clusters in Gilmore Girls *vs. spoken American English*

Longer syntagmatic structures have been investigated in recent corpus studies by Biber et al. (1999), Stubbs and Barth (2003), Stubbs (2005: 17–18), Mittmann (2004, 2006), O'Keeffe et al. (2007), Mahlberg (2007) and Römer (2008). They have been shown to have discourse structuring functions (O'Keeffe et al. 2007: 61), to distinguish text-types (Stubbs & Barth 2003: 76), to be register/genre sensitive (O'Keeffe et al. 2007: 61) and to allow an automatic identification of evaluation (Römer 2008). Researchers use various names for these structures:

> There are no standard terms for such strings, which are called 'dyads', 'tryads', etc by Piotrowski (1984: 93), 'clusters' by Scott (1997a), 'recurrent word-combinations' by Altenberg (1998), 'statistical phrases' by Strzalkowski (1998: xiv), 'lexical bundles' by Biber et al. (1999), or simply n-grams. We call them 'chains'. (Stubbs & Barth 2003: 62)

I shall use the terms *n-gram, phrase* or *cluster* for such 'multi-word strings of two or more uninterrupted word-forms' (Stubbs & Barth 2003: 62), with *n* referring to the number of word-forms making up the cluster, and follow corpus linguists such as Biber et al. (1999) in identifying them on a purely automatic, quantitative basis, that is, without taking into consideration grammaticality, semantics or idiomaticity (Wray 2002). Note that this has both advantages and disadvantages:

> The advantage is that the process is objective, and can pick up frequent chunks not easily brought to light merely by introspection or intuition. But it also means that a bundle might consist of (a) fragmentary strings which

> nonetheless are highly frequent such as *are to my, this one for,* (b) frequent, syntactically incomplete but meaningful strings such as *to be able to* or *a lot of the*. . ., and (c) more obviously semantically and pragmatically 'whole' expressions such as *on the other hand* and *as a result.* (O'Keeffe et al. 2007: 61)

In order to compare n-grams, lists of n-grams from GiGi (produced using Wordsmith) were compared with lists of n-grams from the LSAC provided in Mittmann (2004). See Tables A.4–A.6 in Appendix 5 for the top twenty 2-grams, 3-grams and 4-grams in GiGi and LSAC and their rank in these corpora. This comparison shows that there is some overlap between the lists, indicating that the spoken discourse in GiGi has been relatively well designed to mirror 'natural' spoken American English, and is in line with the code of realism (Chapter 2: Section 3.3) as well as previous analyses that have shown some similarities between dialogue from television series and face-to-face conversation (Tagliamonte & Roberts 2005, Rey 2001, Quaglio 2008, 2009). In Bednarek (in preparation) I explore how n-grams in scripted and unscripted spoken corpora (GiGi, LSAC and a television dialogue corpus) differ from general language corpora (American National Corpus, British National Corpus) in order to show in more detail what results depend on general language tendencies. Preliminary findings suggest that word frequencies in *Gilmore Girls* are indeed much closer to spoken corpora than to general language corpora, and that word frequencies in *Gilmore Girls* are also closer to frequencies in a corpus containing scripted TV dialogue than to frequencies in corpora with 'natural' dialogue. This would suggest that there is indeed something like a register of fictional TV dialogue.

On the other hand, there are also certain differences between the two lists, particularly with respect to 4-grams. More specifically, there are 11 instances where the differences between 2-grams in the two lists is lower than five (*I don't, you know, in the, and I, have to, going to, do you, to be, of the, want to, on the*); in a further two instances the difference is lower than ten (*I was, don't know*). Six 2-grams are over-represented in *Gilmore Girls* (*are you* [27]; *I just* [20]; *a little* [16], *I have* [15], *I know* [12], *this is* [11]), and six are under-represented (*uh-huh* [>81], *and then* [38], *I think* [18], *to do* [13], *I mean* [11], *it was* [11]). The number in brackets refers to the difference between the lists, for example, *I was* occurs at rank 13 in GiGi and at number 9 in LSAC and thus has a difference of only 6; *uh-huh* is not in the top 100 of 2-grams in Gigi but occurs at rank 19 in LSAC and thus has a difference higher than 81.

Moving on to 3-grams, in seven instances the difference between the two lists is </= five (*I don't know, I'm going to, you know what, you want to, going to be, I want to, don't want to*); in a further five instances the difference is lower than ten (*I have a, I have to, a lot of, you have to, what do you*). Seven 3-grams are over-represented in *Gilmore Girls* (*are you doing* [>95], *oh my god* [>84], *this is a* [56], *have to go* [50], *what are you* [28], *do you think* [17], *I don't want* [12]); eight are under-represented in *Gilmore Girls,* of which four are not even in the top 100 in GiGi (*a little bit* [>88], *you know I* [>83], *I mean I* [>82], *to do it* [>81], *one of the* [65], *do you have* [30], *I don't think* [15], *do you want* [12]).

Finally, concerning 4-grams, only in four instances is the difference between the two lists lower than ten (*you don't have to, I don't want to, I don't know what, you want me to*). Thirteen 4-grams are over-represented in *Gilmore Girls* of which six are not in the top 100 in GiGi (*what are you talking* [>93], *are you doing here* [>90], *nice to meet you* [>89], *I'll be right back* [>87], *to talk to you* [>83], *where are you going* [>81], *are you talking about* [95]; *I just wanted to* [58], *I have to go* [41], *I want you to* [36], *what do you mean* [31], *what are you doing* [16], *what do you think* [15]); fifteen are under-represented in *Gilmore Girls* of which four are not in the top 100 in LSAC (*I don't know why* [>85], *but I don't know* [>82], *and I was like* [>84], *or something like that* [>92]; *I thought it was* [63], *do you want me* [46], *I was going to* [40], *if you want to* [29], *I don't know how* [29], *are you going to* [25], *I don't think so* [21], *I don't know if* [21], *in the middle of* [15], *you know what I* [12], *do you want to* [12]).

We will now look more closely at those n-grams that are actually over- and under-represented in GiGi with respect to spoken North American English. Table A.7 in Appendix 5 lists these according to 2-grams, 3-grams, 4-grams, but I will discuss them together here.

3.4.2.1 Under-represented n-grams

Table 4.4 lists n-grams that are under-represented in GiGi to various degrees according to possible discourse classifications. Some of these classifications are taken from Mittmann's (2006) and O'Keeffe et al.'s (2007) classification of n-grams, but note that we would have to look at the n-grams in context to see if they actually fulfil these functions and that alternative classifications are possible (e.g. Quaglio 2009, Bednarek in preparation).

Table 4.4 Under-represented n-grams

	Under-represented in GiGi
Possible hedging; interpersonal function; discourse marking; (in)direct; politeness; face	*I think, I don't think, I mean, I mean I, you know I, you know what I, a little bit, do you want, do you want me, I don't know if, if you want to, do you want to*
Possible narrative function/quoting/ response marker	*and then, and I was like, it was, uh huh*
Vague language	*or something like that*
Mental processes *know/think*	*but I don't know, I don't know how, I don't know why, I don't think so, I thought it was*
Going to (future/locative)	*I was going to, are you going to*
Question with *have*	*do you have*
Other	*to do, to do it, one of the, in the middle of*

First, it seems as if interpersonal uses of language (e.g. hedging, politeness) and vague language either present a challenge to *Gilmore Girls* scriptwriters or that they are avoided because they introduce 'clutter', unintelligibility or repetition and do not advance the narrative. Mittmann (2006) notes that *you know, kind of, sort of, like, I mean, I think,* which are also related to interpersonal functions and vagueness, are underrepresented in her television data (from *Friends* [NBC, 1994–2004], *Dawson's Creek* [Warner Brothers, 1998–2003] and *Golden Girls* [NBC, 1985–1992]). While my corpus does not produce the exact same results as hers, the fact that n-grams such as *you know I, I think, I mean* and *I mean I* are underrepresented in GiGi is very much in line with her findings. Mental processes with *know* and *think* might also fulfil similar interpersonal functions and could be cross-classified. Quaglio (2008) also mentions that features associated with vague language (e.g. *or something like that, you know*) are less frequent in the sitcom *Friends* than in natural conversation, which is similar to the findings for *Gilmore Girls* (e.g. *or something like that, you know I*). The similarities of findings for various television series might point to this being a general characteristic of television dialogue.

Secondly, it is noticeable that n-grams that point to a possible narrative function (including quotation and response markers) such as *and then, and I was like, it was, uh-huh* are underrepresented in *Gilmore Girls*.[6] In fact, there are only 16 occurrences of *I was like* in *Gilmore Girls,* of which the majority are used as quotation markers (introducing the speaker's speech or thought), while others occur as discourse marker (Figure 4.3).

N	Concordance
1	do you want with one meatball?' And I was like 'It's a mother/daughter thing.'
2	LUKE: Nope. LORELAI: Okay, so I was like, "Are you crazy? Isak Dinesen
3	you. LORELAI: Like today I got up and I was like, left side cool, right side not so
4	like this happened to me when I was like ten. I was so into Leif Garrett
5	it, the minute the cigar was finished, I was like, "What the hell are you doing?
6	in - the TV, the stereo speakers. And I was like - LORELAI: Oh my God, will
7	about? LANE: You told me when I was like six that this was my special
8	and then, oh, when it started to snow, I was like, somebody's telling me
9	What's going on? LORELAI: Oh, wow. I was like in a Zen trance, I was totally
10	Beach. Last time I was at the beach, I was like eighteen. LORELAI: Oh, I was
11	LORELAI: Cars, they drift. RORY: And I was like, "I said no to 1 and I said no to
12	happened, I just called Logan and I was like, "yeah, yeah. "Oh, I love the
13	then one day, I just -- I woke up, and I was like, "olive? I don't like olive. Not to
14	forward to filling in for Lane deal. So I was like oh no! and she's like, "it's
15	day picnic, I dropped my sandwich, and I was like, "oh, great, now I've got to
16	Yeah and my old man ran off when I was like 10 -- no note, no nothing. So I

FIGURE 4.3 Occurrences of *I was like* in *Gilmore Girls*

The decision not to use *be like* as a quotation marker might have been a conscious one, since Rory, for instance, while being a young woman is also construed as very intelligent, and in some people's minds *be like* is associated with American teenage girls of a particular variety, quite dissimilar to Rory.

Concerning n-grams that point to a possible structuring function within a narrative (*and then, and I was like, it was*) it seems as if narratives, in particular, extended ones occur less frequently in *Gilmore Girls* than in ordinary conversation. This is not surprising: Kozloff (2000: 71–3) notes that monologues are rare in film whereas duologues are most frequent. While narratives are jointly constructed, they do mean that one character is allowed to hold the floor for longer than his/her interlocutor, and that momentum may be lost. *Gilmore Girls* in particular, is characterized by the witty dialogue between characters, and extended narratives might not fit within this framework (see Chapter 3). Again, this is also in line with findings by Quaglio (2009), who notes that extended topics and narrative features are less frequent in *Friends* than in natural conversation, and points to this as another general register characteristic of television dialogue.

With respect to the remaining under-represented n-grams (*going to, do you have* and others), it is possible that *Gilmore Girls* either does not use as much talk about going to a place or *going to* for future or that *gonna* takes over the future function. In fact, there are 2261 occurrences of *gonna* compared to only 1775 occurrences of *going to* + verb in *Gilmore Girls,* but it is not clear if the transcription is entirely reliable. In any case, more in-depth research is necessary to say more about the use and function of these and other n-grams both in *Gilmore Girls* dialogue and in casual conversation. While it would have been possible to do so for GiGi, I had no access to the LSAC, so no comparison of usage and meanings could be undertaken.

3.4.2.2 Over-represented n-grams

Moving on to over-represented n-grams in GiGi now, Table 4.5 on page 80 lists them according to possible discourse classifications (questions with *talk** are doubly classified).

Just a few comments on these n-grams: again, there are some similarities to Mittmann's and Quaglio's findings. Mittmann (2006) notes that 'more routine formulae that are tied to specific communicative situations' (Mittmann 2006: 577) occur in dialogue from *Friends, Dawson's Creek* and *Golden Girls.* Quaglio (2009) mentions that the cluster *thank you so much* occurs more frequently in the sitcom *Friends* than in natural conversation as well as greetings and leave-takings (*hi, hey, bye*). These observations also apply to the over-represented GiGi 4-grams *I'll be right back* and *nice to meet you.* The latter might have to do with the nature of recording conversations for corpus design purposes, where it would not normally be ethical to record strangers and, consequently, *nice to meet*

Table 4.5 Over-represented n-grams

Over-represented in GiGi	
Expletives/interjections	*oh my god*
Possible hedging; interpersonal function; discourse marking; (in)direct; politeness; face	*I know, I just, I just wanted to, I want you to, do you think, I don't want, a little*
Routine formulae tied to specific communicative situation	*nice to meet you, I'll be right back*
Wh- and *are you* questions	*what are you, what are you talking, what do you mean, where are you going, what are you doing, what do you think, are you talking about, are you doing, are you, are you doing here*
cluster with *talk**	*what are you talking, are you talking about, to talk to you*
cluster with *have*	*I have, have to go, I have to go*
Other	*this is, this is a*

you may not be represented much in a corpus of spoken English. It also reflects a further situational difference between conversation and television data: 'conversations are usually recorded in particular places without much "movement" of speakers. In other words, speakers do not keep arriving and leaving as frequently as in the television show' (Quaglio 2009: 135). Concerning the over-representation of *oh my god*, this is also similar to Mittmann's (2006) data where *god* is more frequent in TV than in spoken AE, and similar to Quaglio's (2008, 2009) *Friends* data which has higher frequencies of emotional and empathic language. In order to say more about the other over-represented n-grams (e.g. the ones with potential interpersonal functions, clusters with *have (to)* – linked to informal language by Quaglio 2009: 109 – *are you* questions), more detailed analyses would be needed. Since a comparison of scripted with 'naturally occurring' conversation is not the sole focus of this book and for reasons of scope, I will limit further discussion of over-represented n-grams to *are you/wh*-questions, clusters with *talk** and the usage of *god* in interjections (*god, oh god, for the love of god, dear god, good god, thank god, for god's sake*).

Are you questions are in fact closely tied to *wh*-questions and n-grams with *talking*, as shall be seen. Using Wordsmith (*Concord*) for looking at clusters with *are you* gives us more information on the kind of questions that might be interesting to analyse further. Table 4.6 on page 81 lists 4-word clusters for *are you* that occur more than 50 times in GiGi. I shall focus first on the most frequent cluster, *what are you doing*. Extending the pattern to include possible insertions between *what* and *are you doing* (e.g. *what* **the hell** *are you doing*), there are 415 occurrences of this cluster: *What are you doing* (403), *What the hell are you doing* (10), *What on earth are you doing* (2). The fact that *on earth* and *the hell* occur within the cluster points to the evaluative/emotional 'loadedness' of

Table 4.6 Four-word clusters for *are you*

N	Cluster	Freq.
1	WHAT ARE YOU DOING	402
2	ARE YOU TALKING ABOUT	169
3	WHAT ARE YOU TALKING	160
4	ARE YOU DOING HERE	138
5	WHERE ARE YOU GOING	82
6	ARE YOU GOING TO	69

this question. In fact, *what . . . are you doing* clusters can be sub-divided into the following major groups:[7]

- *what are you doing?* (181)
- with explicit evaluative/emotional signal:
  - *What* ***the hell/on earth*** *are you doing . . .* (12)
  - *What . . . are you doing* ***X-ing*** (7)
  - *What . . . are you doing* ***with*** X (6)
  - *What . . . are you doing,* **Vocative** (4)
  - **Vocative,** *what . . . are you doing?* (26)
  - **Interjection**, *what . . . are you doing?* (9)

- locative (164):
  - *What . . . are you doing* ***here?*** (137)
  - *What . . . are you doing* **LOCATION** (27)

- temporal (14):
  - *What . . . are you doing* **TIME**

- action (4)
  - *What are you doing* ***back from the dead****?/What are you doing* ***up****?*

It would be possible to sub-classify these further. For example, *what are you doing* can be used either neutrally (*Hi. What are you doing?*) – similarly to temporal usages (implying *what are you doing* ***at the moment***) and perhaps another instance of a greeting routine formula – or more negatively as a demand for explanation (*Hey, what are you doing? I told him never to come sniffing around here again!*). In some cases this may be signalled by the immediate co-text (e.g. ***Hey****, what are you doing?;* ***wait****, what are you doing?;* ***Stop****. What are you doing?*); in other cases more co-text and context is necessary to determine the discourse function of *what are you doing*. Some important evaluative/emotional signals in the immediate co-text include the use of interjections and vocatives as well as the syntagms *What . . . are you doing with X* and *What . . . are you doing X-ing.* Another possible sub-group of such signals might consist of attention getters such as *hey,* and 'alerts' (Mittmann 2006) such as *wait/ stop.* The evaluative phrase *What are you doing* X-*ing*, which is grammatically 'unusual', as the '*ing* ending . . . does not appear to carry progressive meaning' (Kay & Fillmore 1999: 22) is particularly interesting in as far as the whole phrase *what . . . are you doing* works to evaluate the following non-finite clause negatively, as shown by some examples from the corpus:

- and what are you doing **agreeing to come over here all the time?**
- what the hell are you doing **calling Christopher;**
- what are you doing **talking to him about stuff like that;**
- what are you doing **yelling 'Fire';**
- what are you doing **telling my daughter to lie**.

With respect to the semantics of the 'what's x doing y' (WXDY) construction Kay and Fillmore (1999: 4) note that 'we have an overall scene (frame) in which a JUDGMENT OF INCONGRUITY is attributed by a JUDGE (prag) to some STATE OF AFFAIRS' (Kay & Fillmore 1999: 21). It seems to me that this judgement of incongruity expresses both unexpectedness and negative evaluation or emotion on the part of speakers, in particular when combined with *the hell* (e.g. *What the hell are you doing calling Christopher*). Such instances can again be classified as demands for explanation.

As also becomes apparent, many *what are you doing* questions are locative, especially in the form *What are you doing here?* indicating character surprise at the presence of other characters. Interestingly, it achieves this without using any explicitly emotional language. A corpus-driven approach[8] such as the analysis of frequent *n*-grams can thus come up with new insights into evaluative/emotional language without making many theoretical *a priori* assumptions. This presence of the emotion of surprise in *Gilmore Girls* may be the result of the putative intent of the TV series' creators to capture the interest of viewers by having unexpected things happen to characters in the series.

Clusters N° 2 (*are you talking about,* 169 occurrences) and N° 3 (*what are you talking,* 160 occurrences) in Table 4.6 above both involve *talking.* There is of course overlap between these two clusters; thus *are you talking about* occurs in these forms:

- *Are you talking about* PERSON? (5)
- *Are you talking about* ACTION? (2)
- *Are you talking about* PLACE? (2)
- *What on earth are you talking about?* (3)
- *What are you talking about* ? (158)

The important 5-gram is hence *What are you talking about,* which, again is a demand for explanation that may be associated with argumentative discourse or interpersonal conflict, expressing an evaluation of incomprehensibility (Bednarek 2006a) on the part of the speaker. Remember that three n-grams in Table 4.5 above also relate to *talk**: *what are you talking, are you talking about, to talk to you.* To complement the analysis of TALK let us briefly look at 7-grams in *Gilmore Girls* (see Table A.8 in Appendix 5). The most important 7-grams (f > 7) are:[9]

- *can I **talk** to you for a* (13 occurrences) – followed by either *sec/second/minute* or *moment*;
- *I don't want to **talk** about this* (10 occurrences);
- *I don't know what you're **talking** about* (8 occurrences);
- *I don't want to **talk** about it* (8 occurrences);
- *I just want you to know that* (8 occurrences);
- *I wanted to **talk** to you about* (8 occurrences);
- *What do you want me to do* (8 occurrences).

Five of these 7-grams again include *talk**. Thus, talking emerges as a central action in GiGi, where the normal expectation is that issues and problems are talked about and 'talked through', though characters may refuse to obey this expectation. This might be related to the genre of *Gilmore Girls* as a 'female' dramedy – reflecting social action that is, perhaps stereotypically, associated with women. Arguably, it might be suggested that *Gilmore Girls* thus belongs to the long tradition of associating 'trivial talkativeness with femininity' (Kozloff 2000: 11). Mehl et al. (2007) mention that the 'stereotype of female talkativeness is deeply engrained in Western folklore and often considered a scientific fact' (Mehl et al. 2007: 82), while their own research did not reveal significant sex differences in the number of words uttered per day. However, while talkativeness may indeed be associated with the main female protagonists in the series, their dialogue is intelligent and witty, and neither Rory nor Lorelai are in general 'being silenced or ridiculed for blathering' (Kozloff 2000: 268). In other words, while *Gilmore Girls* perhaps does confirm the stereotype of 'talkative women', the portrayal of these women is sympathetic and there are strong female characters in the series. *Gilmore Girls* certainly goes against the prevalent tendency that Kozloff identifies for American films, which, she says, 'offer evidence of a deep distrust of verbal proficiency: articulate, polished speakers . . . are almost always villains' (Kozloff 2000: 78).

Talking things over is also related to drama:

> The drama of melodramas lies primarily in the development of interpersonal relationship – there are few, if any, scenes of silent physical action. On-screen

> time is devoted to discussing the characters' feelings or decisions – melodramas convey the sense of a 'debating society' where the action lies in the thrashing out of contesting viewpoints, or even in philosophical discussions of the nature of love or duty. (Kozloff 2000: 241)

This is clearly the case in *Gilmore Girls*, where Lorelai and her mother Emily frequently 'thrash out contesting viewpoints', and where character's dialogues also concern the discussion of social issues (compare Chapter 3).

Additional 7-grams with *talk* or *tell* which occur further below in the wordlist confirm the importance of talking in *Gilmore Girls*: *I want to* ***talk*** *to you about* (7), *don't want to* ***talk*** *about this anymore* (6), *have no idea what you're* ***talking*** *about* (6), *I have to* ***talk*** *to you about* (6), *I* ***talk*** *to you for a sec* (6), *have to* ***talk*** *to you about something* (5), *I just wanted to* ***tell*** *you that* (5), *I need to* ***talk*** *to you about* (5). Moreover, similar to the n-grams *What are you talking about* and *What on earth are you talking about* these phrases point to confrontational or at least problematic issues, in particular:

I don't want to talk about this
I don't want to talk about it
I don't know what you're talking about

Further, *I wanted to talk to you about, I have to talk to you about* and *I need to talk to you about* often seem to be used to introduce confrontational or problematic issues, such as in the following examples:

- I wanted to talk to you about Rory **and this ridiculous accusation of her being a loner and how that's somehow something bad**;
- I have to talk to you about **how it's all feeling wrong**;
- I need to talk to you about **something serious**.

Again, this seems to be the result of what we might call a 'dramatic' element in *Gilmore Girls* that is used to capture the viewers' interest.[10] The importance of talking in *Gilmore Girls* is also part of a more general tendency for certain television series to feature people who 'spend time together (*hang out*) and *talk*' (Quaglio 2009: 113) – compare, for example, the well-known characterization of *Seinfeld* (NBC, 1989–1998) as 'a show about nothing', that is, of course, nothing but talk.

3.4.2.3 Excursus: emotive interjections

Following the findings above that *oh my god* is over-represented in *Gilmore Girls*, and the presence of character surprise indicated by the n-gram *What are you doing here?* as well as Quaglio's (2008, 2009) findings on the importance of emotional/emphatic language in *Friends*, it was decided to explore emotionality in the series further and to complement the corpus-driven frequency analyses with a corpus-based analysis of a selection of common emotive interjections. First, the TS-GiGi corpus was searched for occurrences of the following interjections:

Jesus	*rats*
Christ	*crap*
Geez/jeez (including *oh geez* etc)	*dangit*
hell	*bummer*
damn/damn it	*yikes*
shit	*oh dear*
fuck	*drat*
shoot	*my goodness*
yuck	*wow*
god	*whoa*
oh god	*whew*
for the love of god	*ugh*
dear god	*ah/aw/oh man*
good god	*ew*
(oh) thank god	*argh*
for X's sake (*for heaven's sake, for Pete's sake, for god's sake, for goodness sake*)	*yay*
	aw (excluding *aw man*)

Some of these were analysed in a previous study (Bednarek 2008b), with a focus on characterization (see also Chapter 6) and gender. For the present study, an additional 17 interjections were analysed, whose occurrence in *Gilmore Girls* dialogue was noticed while watching episodes on DVD. In Ameka's (1992) terms, these interjections include both primary interjections (*yuck*), secondary interjections (*damn*) and interjectional phrases (*oh thank god; for the love of god*), which are predominantly, though not exclusively emotive rather than cognitive (if surprise is regarded as emotive).[11] Importantly, interjections 'are all produced in reaction to a linguistic or extra-linguistic context, and can only be interpreted relative to the context in which they are produced' (Ameka 1992: 108). For example, looking at occurrences of *oh my god* in its context in GiGi (not reproduced here for copyright reasons), this can be associated with emotions of

- positive or negative surprise;
- annoyance/exasperation, panic, disgust;
- pleasure/happiness, admiration.[12]

There are also other, more bleached meanings where *oh my god* indicates involvement, or marks a sudden realization. This means that the meaning of interjections becomes clear only by looking at the context and gesture/facial expression/tone of voice etc. Counting interjections will only tell us about emotionality/involvement but not about the particular emotions involved. Nevertheless, a corpus analysis does show a number of interesting things, which I will only briefly summarize here.

For example, there is a clear difference in the frequency of emotive interjections, with the most frequent interjections (raw frequency > 50; includes use as non-minimal response) being: *wow* (756), *oh my god* (504), *whoa* (242), *ugh* (214), *god* (213), *aw* (175), *geez/jeez* (149), *oh god* (102), (*oh*) *thank god* (96), *ah/aw/oh man* (85), *for X's* (*heaven's/Pete's/god's/goodness*) *sake* (55), *my god* (54). Less frequent are: *damn* (*it*) (47), *ew* (38), *shoot* (31), *yay* (28), (*oh*) *my goodness* (25), *crap* (23), *bummer* (20), *hell* (20), *yikes* (17), *rats* (16), *yuck* (9), *whew* (8), *oh dear* (7), *drat* (7), *dear god* (6), *good god* (6), *for the love of god* (5), *argh* (4). This can be compared to frequencies from the American English conversation part of the Longman Spoken and Written English Corpus (LSWEC – 2,480,800 words) reported by Norrick (2008). In this corpus, the most frequent primary and secondary interjections are in descending order: *yeah* > *oh* > *well* > *uh-huh* > *mhm* > *mm* > *um* > *uh* > *huh* > *hey* > *hm* > *wow* > *ah* > *ooh* > *boy* > *god* > *man* > *shit* > *damn* > *whoa* > *fuck* > *gosh* > *gee* > *jesus* > *hell* > *jeez* > *yuck* > *holy shit* > *goly* > *dammit* > *fucking A*. Even though different interjections were examined and different methodologies used, and a direct comparison is thus not possible, some apparent differences become clear. For instance, *wow* seems more important in *Gilmore Girls* than in everyday AE conversation – this is supported by Quaglio's (2009: 94) analysis which found that *wow* (as interjection but not as non-minimal response) was 2.6 times more frequent in *Friends* than in the LSAC. Further there are no occurrences for (*Jesus*) *Christ*, *jesus*, (*holy*) *shit* or *fuck* in *Gilmore Girls*, although there is one humorous occurrence of *Jesus, Mary, Joseph and a camel*. This reflects the 'family-friendly' character of the show – a clear influence of external factors. As noted, *Gilmore Girls* was funded by *the Family Friendly Programming Forum*, which requires ' "a responsible resolution of issues" and a show that parents and kids can watch together' (Burke Erickson 2008: 64). In this sense, no unbiased reflection or construal of reality is possible in the series. Quaglio (2008) similarly finds that *shit*, *fuck* (and variations) do not occur in the sitcom *Friends* because of external restrictions, and that the overuse of other expletives compensates for this. We can also compare this with findings by Mittmann (2006) for the American TV series *Friends* (NBC, 1994–2004), *Golden Girls* (*NBC, 1985–1992*) and *Dawson's Creek* (Warner Brothers, 1998–2003). She observes that *god* and *hell* occur frequently in these TV series (in contrast to the f-word), with *god* '[taking] over the functions of many other swear words. It is interesting to note in this context that in the films the word *hell* occurs predominantly as part of the sequence WH- + *the hell* (mostly *what/who/how the hell*)' (Mittmann 2006: 577). The latter finding is also confirmed by the analysis of *what the hell* in Bednarek (2008b), which may point to these features being characteristic of certain television genres in general not just the *Gilmore Girls*. Bednarek (in preparation) finds that other television series have even more occurrences of the n-grams *what the hell, the hell* and *the hell are* than *Gilmore Girls*. However, it is also highly likely that the non-use of strong expletives and taboo words (such as *fuck, shit* etc.) in *Gilmore Girls, Friends, Dawson's Creek* and *Golden Girls* differs greatly from their use in programmes that do *not* aim to be 'family-friendly', and that *do* feature a high frequency of such language (e.g. *The Wire* [HBO, 2002–2008], *The Sopranos* [HBO, 1999–2007], *Sex and the City* [HBO, 1998–2004]). That is, while TV dialogue may well in general be more 'emotional' than naturally occurring conversation, different series and genres are distinguished in *how* they express such emotionality.

Figure 4.4 again shows the most frequent emotive interjections in TS-GiGi.

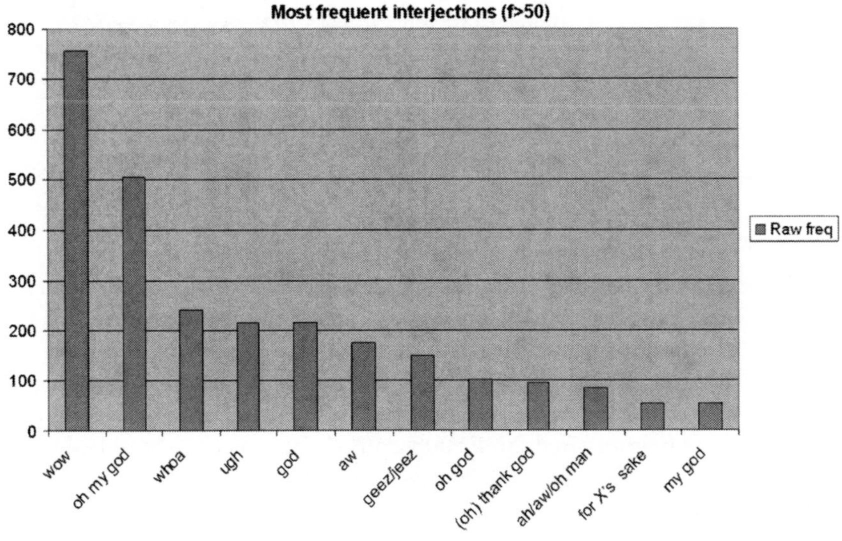

Figure 4.4 Most frequent emotive interjections

As said, I have not analysed meanings in more detail as I would have needed to take into account the multimodal context for 2645 occurrences even if the analysis was restricted to these 12 frequent interjections, though I did exclude uses that were not interjections (e.g. use of *wow* as verb: 'to wow someone' or *damn* as adjective: *damn woman*). However, let us look at the dictionary meanings listed in OALD and Collins Cobuild for these interjections (for a critique of such definitions see Wierzbicka 2003: 286–7), and what these definitions tells us about emotionality in the series (Table 4.7 on page 88).

Table 4.7 Dictionary definitions of emotive interjections

	OALD	Collins Cobuild
wow	great surprise or admiration	very impressed, surprised, or pleased
god, good god, my god, oh god, oh my god	surprised, shocked or annoyed	surprise, fear, or excitement
geez/jeez	anger, surprise, etc.	shocked or surprised about something
for x's sake	emphasize that it is important to do sth or when you are annoyed about sth	to express annoyance or impatience, or to add force to a question or request
whoa	–	you think they are talking too fast or assuming things that may not be true
thank god/goodness	pleased about	very relieved
ugh	think that sth is disgusting or unpleasant	think something is unpleasant, horrible, or disgusting
aw	disapproval, protest, sympathy	–
man	surprise, anger, etc.	angry or impatient

With respect to these potential emotional meanings of frequently occurring interjections, both 'positive' (admiration, pleasure, sympathy, relief), 'neutral' (surprise) and 'negative' (shock, annoyance, anger, disgust, disapproval, fear, impatience) emotions occur. Negative emotions are important and point to conflict, with *geez, for x's sake, whoa, ugh, aw, man* and interjections with *god* all potentially signalling negative emotionality. Surprise, which can be positive, negative or neutral (Bednarek 2008a: 161–5) also seems relatively significant with *wow, geez/jeez, man* and interjections with *god* potentially signalling surprise, confirming some of the assumptions made above about the language of dramedy. Note also that the cluster *I can't believe,* and the inserts *oh* and *wow* which similarly indicate surprise and/or indignation are also over-represented in the sitcom *Friends* (Quaglio 2008, 2009). Surprise may turn out to be one of the important emotions for TV series in general. Emotionality further reflects the close relationships between characters in *Gilmore Girls,* which is also the case in a number of other genres such as domestic sitcom (see Quaglio 2009 on *Friends*). However, without looking at the context these claims relate only to types, not to tokens, and we can only make hypotheses as to associations of interjections with emotions: that is, Table 4.7 tells us which interjections can potentially signal which emotions, but not how often each emotion is in fact signalled. Emotive interjections will be explored in more detail with respect to characterization in Chapter 6.

4 Conclusion and Comparison with Other Research

To conclude, in this chapter I have looked at words and n-grams that are under- and over-represented in *Gilmore Girls* compared with spoken American English. This led to a more detailed investigation of the n-grams *why not because* (identified as interactive cluster and demand for explanation), *what are you doing* (with different discourse functions, including demand for explanation and with *what are you doing here* expressing character surprise), *what are you talking about* (another demand for explanation) and some clusters involving *talk* (pointing to the construal of femininity, drama and confrontation). The occurrence of phraseologies that point to argumentation or confrontation is not surprising. After all, *Gilmore Girls* is a series that 'gains its narrative momentum from intergenerational bonding and conflict' (Woods 2008: 127); see also the special feature 'Who Wants to Argue' (2001/2002). Arguably, dramedy in general involves some kind of conflict. In this it is similar to traditional drama dialogue (Burton 1980: 116): 'the interactants [in drama] – fictitious as they are – argue, try to assert themselves, insult each other, ignore each other, refuse to do what they are asked to do, don't bother to be polite, create unnecessary obstacles and so on' (Burton 1980: 116). Conflict, as a screenwriting handbook advises is 'the lifeblood of drama' (Seger 1994: 163), and conflict between characters is also crucial to a comic narrative (Vorhaus 1994: 51). The analyses also illustrated how corpus linguistic techniques can be used to investigate a particular cultural product (here *Gilmore Girls*). By comparing findings from *Gilmore Girls* with findings from *Friends*, *Dawson's Creek* and *Golden Girls* (Mittmann 2006, Quaglio 2008, 2009) – reported throughout this chapter, and summarized in Table 4.8 on pages 90–91 – the analyses also suggest that some findings may be true for certain genres of fictional television discourse in general while individual series are clearly linguistically distinguished from each other, too (Bednarek in preparation). It is also reasonable to assume that phrases pointing to argumentation or confrontation, which were found in *Gilmore Girls*, will occur across dramedies, as scriptwriters are aware of the need to heighten drama, and one way of doing this is through the creation of such character dialogue.[13] Emotional/emphatic language in general contributes to this '"dramatic" effect' (Quaglio 2009: 105). The analysis of emotive interjections showed that emotionality is relatively varied (positive, negative and neutral emotions occur), while the occurrence of negative emotions and emotions of surprise indicates the importance of conflict and surprise for dramedy but also points to the nature of relationships between characters.

At the same time, a mixed picture emerges, with certain expletives, hedges, discourse markers, interpersonal features more frequent in television dialogue, and others more frequent in naturally occurring conversation. Much more linguistic research is needed, using larger and more varied corpora of television dialogue (including different genres) and diverse research methodologies

Table 4.8 Comparison of corpus analyses of scripted television dialogue

Author	Methodology	Corpora	Over-represented in TV data	Under-represented in TV data
Mittmann (2006)	Cluster analysis	50,000 word corpus of dialogue from *Friends, Dawson's Creek, Golden Girls* (mix of TV genres) vs. 4-million-word Longman Spoken American Corpus	routine formulae (e.g. *hi, I'll see you*); interactive features (e.g. *please, thanks*); alerts expressed as imperatives (e.g. *wait, look, listen, come on*); apologizing expressions (*I'm sorry*); certain expletives (*god/hell*)	certain expletives (especially the 'f-word'); discourse features/vague language (*you know, kind of, sort of, like, I mean, I think*, and *or something*)
Quaglio (2008, 2009)	Multidimensional analysis	600,000 word corpus of *Friends* dialogue (sitcom) vs. 590,000-word American English conversation sub-corpus of the *Longman Grammar Corpus* (comprising casual conversation, task-related dialogue, phone conversations, work conversations)	emotional/emphatic language; informal language e.g. greetings/leave-takings *hi, hey, bye*; stance markers *perhaps* and *maybe*; selected intensifiers (*so, really, totally*); inserts (*oh, wow*); the stance marker *of course*; some non-minimal responses (*sure, fine*); certain expletives (*damn, bastard, bitch, son of a bitch, suck, screw(ed) up, ass, crappy*), innovations with *all, so, totally*, lexical bundles (*I can't believe, thank you so much*), emphatic *do* and copular verbs (*look, feel, sound*)	vague language; narrative language e.g. hedges (*kind of, sort of*), coordination tags (*or something* (*like that*), or *anything* (*like that*), (*and*) *stuff* (*like that*)), vague reference (*thing*(*s*), *shit*), the discourse marker *you know*, the stance marker *probably*, the modal verb *might*, utterance final *so*, the non-minimal response *wow*, and selected expletives (*shit*(*ty*), *fuck* and variations, *piss*(*ed*) (*off*)); past tense, 3rd person pronouns, perfect aspect, past perfect, non minimal responses

This chapter	Ranked frequency lists for words/ n-grams	1.1 million word corpus of *Gilmore Girls* dialogue (dramedy) vs. 140,000-word Santa Barbara Corpus of Spoken American English and lists derived from 4-million word Longman Spoken American Corpus	first person pronouns (*me, my*); negation with *not;* interjection (*oh my god*); certain hedges, discourse markers, interpersonal features (*I know, I just, I just wanted to, I want you to, do you think*); routine formula (*nice to meet you, I'll be right back*); *wh-* and *are you* questions (*what are you, what are you talking, what do you mean, where are you going, what are you doing, what do you think, are you talking about, are you doing, are you, are you doing here; I don't want*); clusters with *I have* (*I have, have to go, I have to go*); clusters with *talk** (*what are you talking, are you talking about, to talk to you*), other (*this is (a)*)	certain hedges, discourse markers, interpersonal features (*I think, I don't think, I mean, I mean I, you know I, you know what I, a little bit, do you want, do you want me, I don't know if, if you want to, do you want to*); narrative features (*and then, and I was like, it was, uh-huh*); vague language (*or something like that*); mental processes *know/think* (*but I don't know, I don't know how, I don't know why, I don't think so, I thought it was*); *going to* (future/locative: *I was going to, are you going to*); question with *have* (*do you have*); other (*to do (it), one of the, in the middle of*)

(not just quantitative), before we can draw a more sophisticated picture of the language of fictional television series. Bednarek (in preparation) analyses a corpus comprising 50 episodes from 10 different fictional TV programmes belonging to a variety of genres to explore the characteristics of fictional TV dialogue in more detail and to show how dialogue in *Gilmore Girls* is similar/different from it. Preliminary findings suggest that other genres differ from the series both in the use of particular n-grams (e.g. less *nice to meet you* than in *Gilmore Girls* and more *what the hell*) and, more generally, in the degree of informal, vague, narrative and formulaic language and in the presence of genre-related vocabulary.

Part I of this book, *Fictional Television: Dialogue and Drama*, has provided a general introduction to the analysis of fictional television (Chapter 2), to dramedy and the language used to promote it on DVD (Chapter 3) and to the analysis of the language of fictional television/dramedy (Chapter 4). It also introduced the series (*Gilmore Girls*) that is used in this book to illustrate points about methodology, about fictional television, and about the genre of dramedy. Part II now moves on to investigate how dialogue and other resources construe character. D'Vari (2005) notes that 'what makes stories interesting is discovering the complexity within characters, and waiting with anticipation for the fireworks that have been building between characters via plot conflict and personality style to begin' (D'Vari 2005: 45). Similarly, character is considered both by media practitioners and academics as important for drama, plot, narrative development and engagement with the audience. The following chapters offer some first insights into the linguistic and multimodal construal of characters in fictional television series.

Notes

[1] On theatrical talk vs. face-to-face talk see also Goffman (1974: 139–44) – only some features of theatrical talk also occur in television talk; there are systematic differences between the theatrical and the television 'frame'. See also Fine (1981) on conversational participants, topics and conversational styles in soap opera vs. 'real world' conversations.

[2] In a narrow definition, stylistics concerns 'the study of the language of literature' (Wynne 2006: 223), and most stylistic research concerns literary texts (Crystal 1997: 71). However, I would like to broaden the notion to include the study of the language of fictional artefacts, including film and television broadcasts (see also Leech & Short 1981: 11 on a broad definition of *style*). I would thus see this book as a contribution to stylistics in general, and to corpus stylistics (Wynne 2006) in particular. For an overview of contemporary approaches to stylistics see Lambrou and Stockwell (2007); for an overview of corpus and computational stylistics see Wynne (2006), Fischer-Starcke 2007, Archer (2007).

[3] Note that the analyses focus on word forms rather than lemmas. WordList settings for all queries were as follows:

Word length: 1–14
Word frequency: 1– maximum
Type/token basis: 1000
numbers not included
case sensitivity not activated

Queries were undertaken for words (clusters deactivated) and n-grams (clusters activated with different cluster sizes ranging from 2–4 and 7).

[4] 'The Santa Barbara Corpus of Spoken American English is based on a large body of recordings of naturally occurring spoken interaction from all over the United States. The Santa Barbara Corpus represents a wide variety of people of different regional origins, ages, occupations, genders, and ethnic and social backgrounds. The predominant form of language use represented is face-to-face conversation, but the corpus also documents many other ways that that people use language in their everyday lives: telephone conversations, card games, food preparation, on-the-job talk, classroom lectures, sermons, story-telling, town hall meetings, tour-guide spiels, and more.' (www.linguistics.ucsb.edu/research/sbcorpus.html, last accessed 9 September 2008). Appendix 4 lists the conversations included in the subset of 140,000 words that I used for the analyses in this chapter.

[5] An alternative to manually comparing ranked frequency lists is a computational key words analysis (see Chapter 5). This allows to pinpoint words and phrases that are *statistically speaking* more/less frequent in the node corpus than in the reference corpus. The results are less dependent on high frequency words/phrases. However, this alternative was not possible, as I had no access to the LSAC, and as the SB is not big enough to act as a reference corpus in Wordsmith: According to research mentioned by Scott and Tribble (2006: 65), a reference corpus should be around five times bigger than the node corpus. Note that the results described below differ slightly from those mentioned in Bednarek (2008b) because this was a preliminary study and used a less sophisticated methodology.

[6] There are only 229 occurrences for *uh-huh, huh-huh, uh huh* in GiGi, but it is possible that not all occurrences were transcribed by the 'fan' transcriber. However, dispersion shows that there is at least one occurrence in each episode, signalling awareness on the part of fan transcriber(s) of these phrases.

[7] The total number of occurrences makes up more than 415, as some instances were counted twice, for example, some 'locative' ones include an explicit evaluative/emotional signal (*what the hell are you doing here?*), so were counted both as evaluative and as locative.

[8] Talking about large-scale corpus linguistics, Tognini-Bonelli (2001) makes a distinction between *corpus-driven* and *corpus-based* linguistics. The term *corpus-based* is employed 'to refer to a methodology that avails itself of the corpus mainly to expound, test or exemplify theories and descriptions that were formulated before large corpora became available to inform language study'

(Tognini-Bonelli 2001: 65), and the term *corpus-driven* refers to an approach where 'the commitment of the linguist is to the integrity of the data as a whole, and descriptions aim to be comprehensive with respect to corpus evidence' (2001: 84). However, the two approaches represent a continuum rather than a strict dichotomy, and much research is situated somewhere in between (Halliday 2004: 24).

9 Note that 7-grams from GiGi could not be compared to lists of 7-grams from either the LSAC or the SB because they are not provided by Mittmann (2004), and because the SB is too small to yield many occurrences of 7-grams. Frequency is inverse to cluster size: as cluster size goes up, the raw frequency of occurrence goes down, but differences between corpora appear to become more pronounced: 'If turned into a *reductio ad absurdum*, then our claim that longer chains discriminate between text-types is self-evident, since if a chain is long enough it will uniquely identify an individual text. In other words, there is clearly a limit to the length of chains which recur in normal texts. For example, a 40-word chain would be unlikely to occur frequently in a single text, or to be repeated in independent texts by different authors (and if it was, it might well be evidence of plagiarism)' (Stubbs & Barth 2003: 76).

10 Other 7-grams reflect the emotionality in the series, which fulfils similar functions as well as construing character relations (*I just want you to be happy* (7); *if it makes you feel any better* (7); *what the hell is wrong with you* (7)). Still others relate to characters in relation to locations (e.g. *have to get back to the inn, than go to the club with you*) or to organizations (*of the Daughters of the American Revolution*).

11 Wierzbicka (2003) distinguishes between emotive, volitive and cognitive interjections but notes that there are close links between these, in that, for example, the same form may express different meanings. Thus, some of the occurrences of the emotive interjections investigated here may not primarily be used emotively.

12 Wierzbicka (e.g. 2003) would argue that the meaning of interjections should be 'captured in rigorous semantic formulae' (Wierzbicka 2003: 337), using 'a language-independent semantic metalanguage' (Wierzbicka 2003: 338) rather than English emotion terms. Since I am not interested here in cross-cultural or cross-linguistic comparisons, I will continue to use the English terms for reasons of simplicity and naturalness.

13 In a University of Technology, Sydney (UTS) workshop for budding scriptwriters on editing and improving their scenes (*Writing for Television*, 21 October 2008) convenor Tim Gooding, a scriptwriter himself, made many suggestions relating explicitly to the heightening of drama through the creation of more obstacles, more resistance between characters, increased pressure, more conflict, more mystery, increased suspense, build-up of stress, pressure, urgency, thus resulting in more impact on the audience. This is sometimes referred to with respect to sense of urgency in writing handbooks: 'A rule of thumb: *the greater the sense of urgency, the greater the dramatic conflict.* If a character desperately wants to achieve a goal, and some obstacle is thrown in the way, the dramatic tension heightens in direct proportion to that emotional intensity' (Blum 1995: 82, italics in original).

Part II

Fictional Television: Character Identity

Chapter 5

Dialogue and Character Identity

This chapter is the first of the four chapters in Part II to look at television dialogue and characterization – linking back to one of the key functions of television dialogue: the revelation of character (see page 63). As we have seen in Chapter 2 (Section 3.4), both media practitioners and academics observe how important character is for televisual narrative. Vorhaus (1994) summarizes as follows:

> Story structure experts will tell you that it's vital for an audience to care. The central character or hero of any successful story, they'll tell you, must arouse in the . . . viewer's mind both sympathy and empathy. That is, you're supposed to like the hero and he's supposed to be like you. If that happens, you engage emotionally with the hero and gladly undertake his quest with him; you care. (Vorhaus 1994: 33)

From the point of view of Media Psychology, characters 'help to mediate a range of television effects, through the processes of imitation, identification, role modeling and parasocial interaction' (Livingstone 1998: 119). A linguistic analysis of how dialogue can reveal character is thus very worthwhile. After a brief review of existing research on the construal of character identity through language, the chapter uses corpus-stylistic methodology (see Chapter 4) in order to explore the idiolect or individual style of fictional characters, looking at their 'total, individual linguistic thumbprint' (Culpeper 2001: 166) with respect to an analysis of key words and n-grams.[1]

1 Approaching Character Identity

Surprisingly, little research has been undertaken on character identity, let alone televisual character identity. In fact, there is a wealth of linguistic research on language and identity, but this focuses on the identity of 'real', 'alive' people rather than the identity of scripted characters or what I would like to call 'character identities'– that is, the identities of characters in fictional genres.

Thus, for the analysis of character identity, we need to look at research in literary studies, stylistics, narratology and media studies (e.g. Bal 1997, Bennison 1998, Rimmon-Kenan 2002, Culpeper 2001, Toolan 2001, Bubel 2006), where the terms *character* and *characterization* are used to describe how writers imbue the 'people' in their texts with certain characteristics, personalities or identities – how characters are construed in discourse or how readers infer certain characteristics from discourse. While there are a number of individual studies on character/personality in literary texts (e.g. Bennison 1998, Taavitsainen 1999, Hubbard 2002), Rimmon-Kenan (2002) suggests that 'the elaboration of a systematic, non-reductive but also non-impressionistic theory of character remains one of the challenges poetics has not yet met' (Rimmon-Kenan 2002: 29). Bal (1997) also states that there is 'no satisfying, coherent theory of character' (Bal 1997: 115) available in narratology, and Toolan (2001) mentions that character 'is the element in narratives that seems least amenable to systematic analysis. As a result it remains relatively neglected within narratological studies' (Toolan 2001: 80). Hubbard (2002) notes that even special issues on characterization of *Poetics Today* (1986) and *Style* (1990) do not 'provide or suggest a systematic linguistic account of features of characters' dialogue as a way either to a better understanding of readers' responses to them or to a fuller appreciation of the craft of the writer' (Hubbard 2002: 69). Both Crystal (1997: 75) and Culpeper (2001) further note that research on characterization in recent years has focused on prose rather than drama. Culpeper (2001) explains that

> [t]his is surprising, since it is in drama that characters are particularly salient. Unlike typical prose fiction, in drama there is usually no narrator who intervenes and guides our perception of a character: we are exposed in a direct way to their words and actions, and, of course, on stage we are exposed to their very physical presence. (Culpeper 2001: 2)

Research that does attend to dramatic dialogue tends to focus on conventional drama, which only has some similarities with television drama. With respect to televisual characterization, character identity is also a much neglected aspect in film and television studies (Pearson 2007: 41), although general remarks concerning the nature of the televisual character have been made there, as already outlined in Chapter 2 (Section 3.4).

Literary studies/stylistics/narratology

Research in literary studies that does focus on character can be summarized as attempts to categorize characters. Semantic approaches try to elaborate lists of features ('semes') such as 'good/bad', 'male/female' that distinguish characters from each other (Toolan 2001: 88–90). Attempts have been made to establish different semantic axes along which characters can be classified (e.g. social roles such as father, farmer or personality traits such as diligence, flexibility) (Bal 1997: 126–9). Other approaches have looked at character roles (Greimas 1966, Propp 1968), where 'actant roles' such as 'hero' and 'villain' are distinguished. For a recent analysis of a *West Wing* (NBC, 1999–2006) episode along these lines see Wodak (2009). Frye (1957) also focuses on character types such as 'impostor' and 'buffoon', and this can be compared to the character types distinguished in scriptwriting books (Chapter 2: Section 3.4). Finally, research influenced by Forster (1987) distinguishes 'flat' (rather simple) and 'round' (more elaborated) characters. Since such literary studies focus on character typologies rather than the linguistics of characterization, they are not immediately relevant, but Toolan (2001) and Culpeper (2001) give a good overview of these approaches. More relevant to this book are attempts in literary studies to provide lists of features that play an important role in characterization (Rimmon-Kenan 1983, Pfister 1988). These have been systematized and elaborated by Culpeper (2001), and will be discussed below with respect to his cognitive linguistic approach to characterization. Bal's (1997: 125–6) important point that there are different principles which 'work together to construct the image of a character' (Bal 1997: 126), including repetition (repeated characteristics), accumulation (of different characteristics), character relations and transformation (changes in character) will be seen at various points in the book.

More generally, Culpeper (2001: 5–9) summarizes research on characterization in literary criticism as belonging to either of two camps (see also Rimmon-Kenan 2002: 31–2): (1) the 'humanizing approach' which assumes that characters have much in common with real people in that they imitate or 'are' very much like them, and (2) the 'de-humanizing approach' which argues that characters 'have a purely textual existence' (Culpeper 2001: 7). However, the two positions are not necessarily incompatible:

> [T]he two extreme positions can be thought of as relating to different aspects of narrative fiction. In the text characters are nodes in the verbal design; in the story they are – by definition – non (or pre-) verbal abstractions, constructs. Although these constructs are by no means human beings in the literal sense of the word, they are partly modelled on the reader's conception of people and in this they are person-like. (Rimmon-Kenan 2002: 33)

In this book my theoretical stance follows Culpeper's own mixed approach which assumes that while we interpret character from discourse, we apply cognitive mechanisms in this interpretation that are modifications of the processes we use in our interpretation of character or identity in everyday life:

> [T]he cognitive structures and inferential mechanisms that readers have already developed for real-life people might be used in their comprehension

> of characters. However, an awareness that character stems from a fictional text means that we might modify our interpretative procedures. For example, we may attribute particular significance to the words or actions of a character, because we know they have been selected for a particular reason by the author; or we may make particular predictions about a character (for example whether they get happily married or killed), because we assume them to belong to a particular fictional role (such as hero, villain). (Culpeper 2001: 10–11)

We will come back to this notion of inferring character below when considering cognitive linguistic approaches to characterization.

Media studies and cognitive stylistics

The research undertaken in literary studies/narratology does not usually consider televisual narratives. Looking at research on televisual characterization we need to turn to media studies (see Chapter 2 for the scriptwriting perspective on characters). In general, analytical frameworks for exploring character identity are not much discussed there, but one approach within television studies is similar to the structural approach noted for narratology above, where character traits are put on a chart to see where on a continuum a character falls with respect to variables such as intelligent, sociable, pleasure oriented, excitable and warm (Selby & Cowdery 1995: 177). Selby and Cowdery (1995: 176) also analyse character biography in terms of social variables such as age, ethnicity, class, marital status, parental status, domestic situation and work. In another take on character identity, Pearson (2007), elaborating on Bordwell (1985), suggests that there are six elements of character identity. These are psychological traits/habitual behaviours; physical characteristics/appearance; speech patterns; interactions with other characters; environment and biography (Pearson 2007: 43). However, rather than looking at these aspects with the help of textual analysis, she sees them as 'abstracted from the design of the text and existing in the story, that is, in the minds of producers and audience, rather than conducting a close textual analysis of individual scenes/episodes/codes' (Pearson 2007: 43). While this approach does not tell us what linguistic and multimodal features in the text construe character identities, it does have some similarities with approaches to characterization in cognitive stylistics. The interest here is in cognitive processes of character impression formation (Culpeper 2001) or relationship impression formation (Bubel 2006) – how character identity and relationships between characters (e.g. friendship) are inferred by readers. For instance, Culpeper's (2001) interest lies predominantly in 'how we form impressions of characters in our minds – not just characters themselves or their personalities' (Culpeper 2001: 2), although his model also includes a 'surface structure' of 'the particular linguistic choices attributed to characters' (Culpeper 2001: 37) – choices which represent 'textual cues' (Culpeper 2001: 163–234) as far as character identity is concerned.

This is in fact the level of analysis that I focus on – the textual rather than the cognitive. This focus on the linguistic analysis of dialogue means that we are interested in searching for *what* in the text tells us (the viewers/readers) something about character and identity – Culpeper's 'textual cues'. Esslin (2002: 20–2) argues that the characters in TV drama are primarily perceived as images and that what they say, the verbal, is secondary. However, note the importance of dialogue in series such as *The Simpsons* (FOX, 1989–), *The West Wing* (NBC, 1999–2006), *House* (FOX, 2004–) or indeed *Gilmore Girls* (Warner Brothers, 2000–2007). His statement seems no longer true in the sophisticated world of contemporary television which has seen so many high-quality productions emerging in recent years. It must not be forgotten that in television 'dialogue lines are explicitly designed to reveal character' (Kozloff 2000: 44). As briefly mentioned in Chapter 4, one of the functions of dialogue is the revelation of character, telling viewers something about characters' mental states and personality. Dialogues 'make characters substantial, . . . hint at their inner life' (Kozloff 2000: 43), and differentiate characters from one another (Pearson 2007: 44). In television, as in film it is mainly dialogue which construes relations between characters as well as their attitudes towards each other (Fulton 2005b: 108). Following Barthes we can say that 'the character and the discourse are each other's accomplices' (Barthes 1974: 178, quoted in Lothe 2000: 80). Thus, focusing on the textual (linguistic and multimodal) level is a worthwhile endeavour.

Drawing on research on the identity of 'real' people as well as literary research (Rimmon-Kenan 1983, Pfister 1988), Culpeper lists a number of features in the text that 'give rise to information about character' (Culpeper 2001: 163). These include explicit cues, where 'a character . . . provides explicit information about him or herself [or] . . . about someone else' (Culpeper 2001: 167), implicit cues – 'cues that are important in conveying . . . character information which has to be derived by inference' (Culpeper 2001: 172), and authorial cues ('cues over which the character notionally has no power of choice' [Culpeper 2001: 229]).[2] Textual features listed by Culpeper (2001) include:

- explicit cues
  - self-presentation (character gives explicit information about self)
  - other-presentation (character gives explicit information about other character(s))

- implicit cues
  - conversational structure (e.g. turn length, turn-taking, turn allocation, topic shift, topic control, incomplete turns/hesitations, interruptions)

  - (non)adherence to conversational maxims; conversational implicature
  - lexis (Germanic vs. Latinate, lexical richness/diversity, surge features/affective language, terms of address, key words)
  - syntactic structure
  - accent and dialect
  - verse and prose
  - paralinguistic features (e.g. tempo, pitch range/variation, loudness, voice quality)
  - visual features: kinesic features and appearance (e.g. stature, clothing, facial expression, posture)
  - context: a character's company and setting
  - (im)politeness strategies (see also Spitz 2005 on disputes in plays) or features

- authorial cues
  - proper names
  - stage directions.

We can see from this list that manifold devices may be used by the authors of dramatic texts to create character identities, not all of which are relevant to television series (e.g. verse and prose). With respect to film dialogue in particular, Kozloff (2000: 73–84) also mentions the significance of conversational structure, the degree of a character's verbal competence, and the use of foreign languages, dialect, and jargon as well as the importance of character voice (pace, intonation, volume). Bubel and Spitz (2006) show how verbal humor is an important means in *Ally McBeal* (Fox, 1997–2002) of characterizing televisual characters, and Mandala (2007) demonstrates how marked *-y* suffix adjectives in *Buffy the Vampire Slayer* (Warner Brothers, 1997–2003) work in the construal of televisual friendship groups. Bubel (2006) explores how alignment patterns, terms of address and questions contribute to the linguistic construal of character relations in *Sex and the City* (HBO, 1998–2004). Similarities with language devices identified in identity research on 'real' people also become apparent, where a certain feature 'stands for (connotes, implicates, signals, evokes, indexes) being a member of [a] social group' (Coupland 2007: 21).[3] While comments on other features relevant to characterization (e.g. conversational structure, paralinguistic features, visual features) will be made in later Chapters (6–7) the section below focuses on key words and key n-grams as part of lexicogrammar. There are several reasons for this: on the one hand, this is a methodological decision, limiting the scope of the analyses; on the other hand, as Culpeper points out, 'research undertaken to examine the relationship between lexis and personality or character is patchy' (Culpeper 2001: 183), and there is thus a need for linguistic analysis in this area. While lexical and grammatical features of dialogue play a significant role in characterization, 'what the relevant . . . dimensions are and how one goes about revealing them in an analysis has been largely overlooked' (Culpeper 2002: 11). Again, corpus stylistic methodology will be used, with *Gilmore Girls* dialogue as data.

2 Analysing Character Identity Using Corpus Stylistics

2.1 The corpora

For the analyses in this chapter the GiGi corpus (described in Chapter 4) was automatically split into separate files, and the speaker names removed, with each file containing the dialogue of specific characters only:[4]

- all.txt (dialogue of all characters);
- Chris.txt (Chris's dialogue only);
- Emily.txt (Emily's dialogue only);
- Lorelai.txt (Lorelai's dialogue only);
- Luke.txt (Luke's dialogue only);
- Richard.txt (Richard's dialogue only);
- Rory.txt (Rory's dialogue only);
- Sookie.txt (Sookie's dialogue only);
- Not_Lorelai.txt (dialogue of all characters except Lorelai).

With these sub-corpora of the GiGi corpus, we have access to self-contained texts which represent a whole 'universe': everything a particular character has produced in his/her fictional lifetime (i.e. his/her 'total, individual linguistic thumbprint' [Culpeper 2001: 166]), and everything all characters have uttered in the fictional world of *Gilmore Girls*. This is a huge advantage of using fictional data to study identity: 'by reading the whole text we have access to that character's whole life – complete and finite' (Culpeper 2001: 145), whereas in the real world, this is of course not possible. In a way, these sub-corpora are also diachronic corpora as they allow us to track changes in the language of *Gilmore Girls* characters from season 1 to season 7 (Bednarek forthcoming). Again, we are looking at the series as a whole rather than at a particular moment or a particular episode in a long-running television series where, as said, 'it's almost always possible to find any moment in one particular episode that's capable of supporting any argument, regardless of whether that moment is indicative of the series as a whole' (Mills 2005: 24).

2.2 Frequency of character names and turns

Again, as in the corpus investigations in Chapter 4 let us start with a frequency list, this time using TS-GiGi without excluding the names of characters as speakers and as addressees. Consequently, the frequency list for this corpus will naturally have many character names in it. This tells us not only about the characters who are allocated frequent turns but also about the characters about whom other characters talk or that other characters address in the series. The following names turn up among the 200 most frequent words in TS-GiGi (Table 5.1).

Table 5.1 Character names in TS-GiGi

N	Word	Freq.
4	LORELAI	37,777
6	RORY	29,035
13	LUKE	12,994
28	EMILY	7969
48	SOOKIE	5554
60	LANE	4360
62	PARIS	4271
63	RICHARD	4253
80	LOGAN	3188
84	DEAN	2950
90	JESS	2733
99	KIRK	2409
114	CHRISTOPHER	2117
121	MICHEL	2012
138	TAYLOR	1855
155	JACKSON	1522
156	ZACH	1521

These are the major and minor characters in the series, both in terms of talking, being talked to and being talked about. A number of important social relationships are enacted by them, such as:

- Mother–daughter (Lorelai–Rory; Emily–Lorelai; Lane–Mrs Kim);
- father–daughter (Lorelai–Richard; Rory–Christopher);
- friendships (Lorelai–Rory, Lorelai–Sookie; Lorelai–Luke; Rory–Lane; Rory–Paris);
- partners (Lorelai–Luke/Christopher/Max . . . ; Rory–Dean/Jess/Logan . . .; Sookie–Jackson; Lane–Zach);
- other (employer–employee; seller–consumer; etc.).

The list also demonstrates that the 'quirky' small town characters of Stars Hollow, the setting of *Gilmore Girls*, are quite important (Michel, Kirk, Taylor), with Kirk higher up in the list than Christopher (Rory's father and Lorelai's on-and-off partner) – compare the description of *Gilmore Girls* in Chapter 3. Note that this list does not show us the number of turns for each character.

Table 5.2 Speaker turns and number of tokens in TS-GiGi and GiGi

	TS-GiGi	**GiGi**
Speaker	**Turns**	**Tokens**
Lorelai	32,497	323,456
Rory	23,024	184,893
Luke	9,757	85,209
Emily	6,659	76,803
Sookie	4,379	41,928
Richard	3,297	36,712

This can be investigated through a *Concord* search for the speaker name in capitals followed by a colon, since this is how speakers are marked in TS-GiGi. Table 5.2 above shows that the main speakers in *Gilmore Girls* are Lorelai and Rory followed by Luke and Emily, Sookie and Richard. Table 5.2 also gives the numbers of tokens for these characters' dialogue in the GiGi sub-corpora. Thus, the analysis will predominantly centre on Lorelai, as she is arguably the main character in *Gilmore Girls*, both in terms of turns and in terms of tokens, as far as dialogue is concerned.

2.3 Key words/-n-gram analysis: a corpus stylistic case study

In the following sections I demonstrate how key words/n-grams analysis can be used to explore televisual characters in a particular series. Section 2.3.1 discusses key words and characterization; Section 2.3.2 describes the findings of the case study.

2.3.1 Using key words/n-grams analysis in studying characterization

In corpus linguistic terms, a *key word* refers to a word that occurs with unusual frequency in a given text or collection of texts when this is compared with a reference corpus of some kind (but see Stubbs 2008 for three different ways in which the term *key words* has been used). This means that a key word can be unusually frequent or infrequent (Scott 1997). *Keyness* is defined in terms of statistical 'unusuality'. How exactly does this work? We need two corpora: the node corpus and a reference corpus, which provides the standard of comparison. After choosing a reference corpus, we produce word-lists of the two corpora (with the help of Wordsmith's *WordList*), that is, lists of all words and their frequency in the two corpora. Wordsmith's *KeyWords* software then compares these two word lists, and identifies key words with the help of tests of statistical significance (log likelihood or chi-square). The same procedure can be followed for larger structures, that is, n-grams/clusters (see Chapter 4: Section 3.4.3).[5] This chapter will show how key word/n-gram analysis can be used to study the contribution of lexicogrammatical key words and n-grams to the construal of televisual character identity. Drawing on Enkvist's (1964, 1973) research, Culpeper (2002) suggests that the study of characterization 'can benefit from an empirical approach, specifically, a methodology for identifying what might be the "key" words of a text' (Culpeper 2002: 12), and uses *Keywords* analysis for exploring characterization with respect to six Shakespearean characters. Similarly, Culpeper (2001) suggests *Keywords* analysis can be used 'to help reveal what the salient lexical features of a particular character are' (Culpeper 2001: 183).[6] My analyses differ from Culpeper's (2001, 2002) in three ways: I look at clusters/n-grams in addition to single key words; my data is from contemporary television; and my sub-corpora for individual characters' dialogue are bigger than Culpeper's. While Bednarek (forthcoming) investigates the 'stability' of televisual characters as hypothesized in Media Studies (see Chapter 2: Section 3.4) using *Keywords*, the analyses in this chapter will concern characters' unique voices or scripted idiolects. The following questions can be asked in this respect: Given that characters interact with other characters but that their dialogue is scripted, how similar and different are characters from each other? Given the team-effort of scriptwriting how variable is one character's voice and how different from other characters (scripted by the same writer)? For instance, does Lorelai closely resemble other *Gilmore Girls* characters or does she have a unique voice?

2.3.2 Lorelai as unique character

It might be expected that there is variability within a character's voice, as different writers are involved at various stages of the production process (Chapter 2: Section 3.1), or that different characters have similar patterns of language use, as the same scriptwriter may create the dialogue of various characters. However, there is clearly a need for consistency of voice in terms of characterization and identification. Further, media studies research suggests that dialogue does differentiate characters from one another (Pearson 2007: 44), and scriptwriters advise that '[e]ach character in your novel or script should speak with a different rhythm and unique choice of words' (D'Vari 2005: 155). Thus, my hypothesis is that a given character does in fact have a unique voice and that the character can be distinguished from other characters through language use. In order to test this assumption and to analyse the uniqueness of Lorelai's voice, Lorelai's dialogue (with all other characters in all seasons) was compared to that of other characters. Since the reference corpus needs to be bigger than the node corpus (Scott & Tribble 2006), Lorelai's dialogue corpus was used as node corpus only when compared with the dialogue of all other characters, and as reference corpus when compared with the

Table 5.3 Key words/n-grams of *Gilmore Girls* characters

Character comparison	Key words/n-grams
Lorelai vs. all other characters	more: *mom, dad, um, oh, honey, uh, ugh, no, okay, inn, hon, hey, aw, gran, hi, ooh, wow, cause, hm, huh, ok, know, god, bye, hmm, and, kid, ha, coffee, yes, well, ah, mm, weird; my mother, the inn, my parents, you know, my god, oh no, oh my, oh my god* less: *issue, editor, mama, wonderful, grandpa, this, I've, nope, to, your, I, grandma, I've got, my mom, your father, your mother*
Chris vs. Lorelai	more: *I, she,* less: *um, mom, he, oh*
Emily vs. Lorelai	more: *your, wonderful, father, certainly, course, to, her, dinner, isn't, would, very, at, sit, woman, she, next, is, week, you, this, your father, your mother, would you, of course, you like, all right* less: *hm, ah, inn, coffee, I'm, mean, ugh, pretty, sorry, big, bye, got, good, know, ok, oh, cause, huh, thanks, great, no, dad, hi, uh, mom, okay, yeah, I know, I mean, you know, my mother*
Luke vs. Lorelai	more: *yeah, diner, hell, what, here, doing, got, I, you, right, I'll, this, fine; the hell, the diner, what the, what are, I don't, what are you* less: *wow, inn, very, please, mother, bye, hello, dad, yes, and, god, our, hi, love, we, oh, um, om, oh my, I love, my god, my mother; oh my god*
Richard vs. Lorelai	more: *very, well, business, as, to, your, of, her, is, a, man, this; your mother, all right* less: *inn, you're, great, guy, bye, but, and, huh, cause, so, just, mean, thanks, wow, no, know, god, really, um, yeah, okay; my god, come on, I mean*
Rory vs. Lorelai	more: *grandma, grandpa, I, I'm, school, class, mean, book, paper; my mom, I don't, I have, I just, I have to* less: *diner, mother, huh, cause, dad, her, aw, oh, daughter, ah, ooh, kid, ugh, the, inn, honey, uh; all right, you know, the inn, my parents*
Sookie vs. Lorelai	more: *he, ooh, his, and* less: *her, please, um, mom; all right*

dialogue of individual characters (since she is the character with the most dialogue). Table 5.3 shows the results (speaker names and *going to/gonna, want/wanna* removed – see Note 5) for key words/n-grams that occur at least 50 times (to ensure dispersion). Looking at Table 5.3 we can make a number of comments. First, Lorelai does clearly have a unique voice and is distinguished from other characters. We can also see that Lorelai is distinguished more from some characters (Emily, Luke, Richard, Rory) than from others (Chris, Sookie), perhaps construing relationships between characters or resulting from the scriptwriting process. Her uniqueness clearly contributes to viewer identification. This may reflect a deliberate attempt on the part of the creators to provide consistency of character voice despite multiple authorship and the exertion of a degree of control by agencies. Creator/producer of the *Gilmore Girls* Amy Sherman-Palladino has said that 'every draft either I write, or it passes through my hands, or passes through my hands and his [Dan Palladino] hands, so that there is a consistency of tone' (Sherman-Palladino 2005).

Looking at Lorelai's more frequent key words she is on the one hand characterized through her relationship with her family (*mom, dad, hon, kid, honey, gran, my parents, my mother*), her workplace (*inn, the inn*), her individual tastes (*coffee*) – which, incidentally, are already set up in the very first scene of the first episode of *Gilmore Girls* when Lorelai begs Luke for more coffee, and are often explicitly referred to in the series – and a great emotionality (e.g. *oh no, oh my god, god, wow, ooh*) which she shares with Sookie (see analyses of emotive interjections in Chapter 6). With respect to Barker and Galasiński's point that within popular Western notions of identity 'identity is an essence signified through signs of taste, beliefs, attitudes and lifestyles' (Barker & Galasiński 2001: 28), the 'essence' of Lorelai is in fact partially shown through signs of taste, interpersonal relationships, personality and 'lifestyle' (Machin & van Leeuwen 2007: 44). The importance of tastes (e.g. food, music, films) for defining the personalities of Lorelai and Rory is also evident in their use of intertextual references (see Woods 2008: 134, and Chapter 3) and in their attitudes towards food (Chapter 8).[7]

In order to show in more detail what distinguishes characters from each other we can classify all key words/n-grams according to potential discourse functions (Table 5.4).

Table 5.4 Potential discourse functions of key words/n-grams

	Key words/ n-grams
Potentially evaluative/ emotional	*honey, hon, okay, ok, weird, wonderful, great, fine, good, all right, right, certainly, very, really, of course, course, cause, pretty, big, well, ah, aw, oh, uh, ugh, ooh, wow, oh no, ha, god, my god, oh my, oh my god, hell, what the, the hell, thanks, please, sorry, would, would you, you like, love, I love, but, just, I just, I have to*
Relationship-oriented	*mom, dad, gran, my parents, father, your father, your mother, grandma, mama, grandpa, my mom, my mother, mother, daughter, kid*
Response and discourse markers	*no, yes, yeah, nope, um, well, ah, mm, hm, huh, hmm, om, you know, know, I mean, mean, I know*
Greetings	*hello, hey, hi, bye*
Content key words	*inn, coffee, the inn, issue, editor, dinner, next, week, diner, the diner, business, school, class, book, paper*
Pronouns or involving pronouns	*he, she, I, your, her, you, this, our, we, his, I've, I've got, I'm, I don't, I have, I'll, you're, what are you*
Other	*guy, man, woman* *what, what are, here* *is, isn't, sit, got, doing, come on* *and, of, the, to, as, at, a, so*

Without investigating these in further detail, we can say that characters are distinguished by references to their significant relationships (terms of address/expressions of family relationships: for example, *mom, dad, kid*); by references to their environment (work/home: *inn, editor, dinner, the diner, business, school, class*), through differences in the use of response and discourse markers (e.g. *yes, nope, you know*) and greetings (*hi, hello*), through differences in pronoun use relating to who characters are talking to and who they are talking about (e.g. *he, she, I, we*) and, most crucially, through differences in emotional and evaluative language (e.g. *wow, great, wonderful*).[8] With some of these, level of formality rather than discourse function may play a role: for instance, Emily and Richard (the parents) have significantly fewer occurrences of *hi, yeah, I know, I mean, guy, wow* than Lorelai. Example (2) demonstrates that scriptwriters are – at least intuitively – aware of the power of language to differentiate characters, here levels of linguistic (in)formality, and that they make use of this explicitly in distinguishing characters, and in construing relationships between them:

(2)

LORELAI: Hi Dad.
RICHARD: Lorelai.
LORELAI: Swell party.
RICHARD: Uh, yes, it's mostly your mother's doing.
LORELAI: [laughs] So, um, **what just went down there**?
RICHARD: **Down where**?
LORELAI: Just now, the handshake with the man in the gray flannel suit – did you **score a deal**?
RICHARD: Well, **one doesn't score deals** in the insurance business, Lorelai. **One builds relationships** based on trust and fulfilling the client's needs.
LORELAI: Sorry.
RICHARD: Mr. Lundquist and I, uh, just
LORELAI: Uh, Mr. Lundquist?
RICHARD: Yes.
LORELAI: Lundquist from Aero International?
RICHARD: Yes.
LORELAI: You **bagged** the Swede?
RICHARD: Well, just as **I didn't score a deal, I also haven't bagged the Swede**. We simply talked, we came to an agreement, we shook hands.
LORELAI: You shook hands, that means –
RICHARD: I'm sending him the contracts in the morning.
LORELAI: Dad, that's big!
RICHARD: Yes, I suppose it is big.
LORELAI: Ha, that's gigantic! It's a whole new market for you. It opens up all of Scandinavia, doesn't it?

RICHARD: Beyond that. Lundquist is his company's rep for Russia as well.
LORELAI: Russia!
RICHARD: Da!
LORELAI: Look who's taking over the world.
RICHARD: I suppose that would be me.
LORELAI: [smiles] I see that you hired Karen.
RICHARD: Uh, yes, well, I had to get someone in here.
LORELAI: She seems to be working out well.
RICHARD: Well, she's no . . . Margie, but we'll see. Now, if you'll excuse me, **I have several more 'deals to score' now that I have finished 'bagging' the Swede.**
[Richard walks away and Emily walks over]
(2.20, *Help wanted*)

Episode 2.20, from which Example 2 is taken, is in a sense very much about the relationship between Lorelai and her father Richard, involving conflict when Lorelai stops helping her father out in his office because of her own job. While this particular scene still begins with conflict – played out in terms of Lorelai's and her father's contrasting use of levels of informality ('score a deal', 'bag the Swede'), it ends with Richard showing that he has accepted Lorelai's stopping to help him by mimicking her language, and thereby, to a certain extent, her interpersonal identity. The scene ends with reconciliation.

When considering key words/n-grams we are talking about statistical preferences, however, and individual instances can go against these statistical preferences or norms. This norm-breaking can be discussed in stylistic terminology with respect to foregrounding (Mukařovský 1970, quoted in Culpeper 2001; see also Fowler 1986: 71ff). Foregrounding involves 'intentional divergence from what usually happens' (Culpeper 2001: 129), a departure from an established norm, in this case a 'text-internal' (Culpeper 2001: 131) norm for an individual character, concerning 'target-based expectancies' (Culpeper 2001: 120) in cognitive parlance. With respect to the breaking of text-internal linguistic norms and the construal of character relationships, it is evident that scriptwriters make use of its effects. Consider the following extract from Episode 1.3, which is about Rory bonding with her grandfather Richard, and Lorelai struggling to come to grips with this, as her own relationship with her father is very strained.

(1)
LORELAI: Y-You had a big lunch at the club?
RORY: Yeah, it was quite good.
LORELAI: Quite? What's with the quite?
RORY: What do you mean?
LORELAI: You don't ever say quite.

RORY: I've said quite plenty of times.
LORELAI: Whatever. So besides the 'quite good' lunch you had, what else happened?
[. . .]
(Some scenes later; Lorelai's house. She and Rory are sitting outside. Rory is looking in a handheld mirror while Lorelai is reading.)
LORELAI: Should I leave you two alone?
RORY: I think I wanna change my hair.
LORELAI: Really? I think it looks quite good.
RORY: You're funny.
(1.3, *Kill me now*)

The dialogue here revolves around Rory's unusual use of the modulator (diminisher/downtowner) *quite*. In this episode its use is clearly connected to Richard, who is in fact the only character in this episode to use *quite* before this scene (he uses the word five times). It is also associated with Richard more generally, as *quite* is one of Richard's key words across episodes (compare list on page 113). Text-internally, then, there is a norm that associates Richard with the use of *quite* (fulfilling a similar function as a 'signature interjection', see Chapter 6), a norm which is then broken by Rory, and consequently taken up as significant by Lorelai. For her, the linguistic mimicking signifies much more; it signifies Rory bonding with her grandfather, siding with Lorelai's parents rather than Lorelai in the conflict between them. Again, the use of evaluative language, here a particular linguistic item (*quite*), is stylistically and interpersonally significant. We can relate this to the notion of salience/noticeability and to Eckert's (2008) point about style: 'Once the agent isolates and attributes significance to a feature, that feature becomes a resource that he or she can incorporate or not into his or her own style' (Eckert 2008: 457). In this case, Lorelai isolates and attributes significance to the feature 'quite' and interprets it as a style belonging to Richard but now incorporated by Rory, attaching interpersonal significance to this incorporation, along the lines of 'first you adopt their language, then their values'. That the conflict between Rory and Lorelai is resolved is demonstrated by the humour in the later scene. A corpus linguistic analysis here gives some empirical grounding to comments such as the following:

> Anxious that Rory will enjoy an afternoon of golf with her father at the Stars Hollow country club and, in my view, jealous of the potential emotional access she will have to her taciturn father, Lorelai is keen to disparage her daughter's bonding in 'Kill Me Now' (1.03). Eager to trash the experience over Luke's diner food she asks her daughter what she would like to order. Rory replies, 'I had a big lunch at the club' – she then adds with a gentile accent which annoys her mother – 'which was *quite* good.' Lorelai

immediately assumes her daughter's lack of appetite, coupled with her new absorption of the patter of . . . the élite, is effectively a kind of repudiation of the life she has created for her daughter. (Coleman 2008: 183)

In Bal's (1997) terms a corpus stylistic analysis, when combined with the analysis of norm-breaking, can potentially illuminate all of the four principles 'which work together to construct the image of a character' (Bal 1997: 126), namely the principles of repetition (repeated characteristics), accumulation (of different characteristics), character-relations and transformation (changes in character). Thus, key words/n-grams analysis was used above to investigate the repeated linguistic behaviour of characters (repetition), and the different linguistic key words/phrases that distinguish characters (accumulation). While character relations and changes in character (transformation) were not analysed here (but see Bednarek forthcoming), it was shown how a corpus analysis can provide information on the norms that are set up in texts, and how the breaking of such norms can be interpreted by characters as a change in interpersonal relationships.

2.3.3 The significance of evaluative/emotional preferences

Let us briefly return to the finding that evaluative/emotional preferences seem to differentiate characters, as shown in Section 2.3.2. The significance of these evaluative/emotional key words and n-grams is confirmed when complementing the key word analysis above (where $f > 49$) with a look at selected examples for character key words/n-grams where $f < 50$ (with numbers in brackets referring to occurrences):

- Emily (Lorelai's mother, stay-at-home wife): **potentially evaluative/emotional**: *lovely* (44), *a lovely* (17), *a wonderful* (21), *ridiculous* (33), *simply* (27), *on earth* (23), *what on earth* (17), *goodness* (20), *my goodness* (13), *absurd* (11), *dear* (22), *young* (44), *sake* (18), *hardly* (14), *nonsense* (12); **relationship-oriented**: *father and* (30), *my granddaughter* (17), *your grandfather* (25), *your father's* (8), *your father and* (29), *father and I* (24), *the two of* (26), *two of you* (23), *you two* (37), *the two* (28), *two of* (29); **environment or role-related**: *come in* (47), *would you like* (39), *the living room* (22);
- Luke (Lorelai's friend/partner, diner owner): **potentially evaluative/emotional**: *jeez* (17), *damn* (36), *hell is* (22), *what the hell* (38), *the hell is* (22); **relationship-oriented**: *my sister* (13), *my dad* (24); **environment or role-related**: *my diner* (24), *coming right up* (15), *can I get* (21), *I get you* (16), *to the diner* (16), *my truck* (12), *a diner* (17); **informal**: *nope* (28), *nah* (17);
- Richard (Lorelai's father, in insurance): **potentially evaluative/emotional**: *wonderful* (46), *young* (44), *lovely* (16), *proper* (13), *dear* (13), *a very* (44), *a fine*

(8), *a proper* (6), including modality: *suppose* (16), *I suppose* (16), *perhaps* (19), *certainly* (20), *quite* (27), *simply* (12); **relationship-oriented**: *my granddaughter* (14), *your grandmother* (15), *my wife* (6), *your father* (13); **environment-related**: *office* (29), *my office* (11), *company* (29), *insurance* (18), *golf* (15);

- Rory (Lorelai's daughter, at school/university): **relationship-oriented**: *hi grandma* (19), *and grandpa* (29), *my grandparents* (16), *grandma and* (29), *and grandma* (12), *grandma and grandpa* (21), *my boyfriend* (31); **environment-related**: *professor* (29), *campus* (31), *editor* (26), *notes* (32), *studying* (37), *study* (45), *the paper* (44); **informal**: *nope* (49), *yep* (43);
- Sookie (chef): **environment-related**: *sauce* (24), *onions* (10), *vegetables* (12), *lemon* (13), *cake* (24), *vegetable* (7), *the sauce* (7), *tasted it* (6).

Thus, it does look as if main characters in general are distinguished from each other through their environment and relationships, levels of informality in their language (potentially indicating age as well as other characteristics), and, most crucially, evaluative/emotional preferences. This partially relates to Pearson's (2007) list of character features – psychological traits/habitual behaviours; physical characteristics/appearance; speech patterns; interactions with other characters; environment; and biography (Pearson 2007: 43) – and shows that textual/linguistic analysis *can* give valuable cues about character identity, as character features such as the environment and character interactions are in fact linguistically (and multimodally, see Chapter 7) construed. Concerning *Gilmore Girls* in particular, producer, creator and writer Amy Sherman-Palladino has stated that '[i]t's very important that it feel like the same show every week, because it is so verbal. It's not about car crashes or vampires or monsters or suspense. It's really **about people talking to each other and the way they talk to each other**, which is very specific. It's a little bit more work' (Sherman-Palladino 2005, my bold).

In order to show what kinds of evaluative/emotional meanings distinguish characters we can look at these in more detail classifying them according to the framework of evaluative parameters already introduced in Chapter 3: AFFECT, EMOTIVITY, UN/EXPECTEDNESS and POWER. Additional evaluative parameters that have not yet been introduced are RELIABILITY and CAUSALITY. Evaluations of RELIABILITY are connected to what is generally described as epistemic modality or modalization in linguistics, that is, to matters of reliability, certainty, confidence and likelihood. They relate to evaluations of how likely it is that future events will happen. Evaluations of CAUSALITY concern evaluations of the causes and consequences of events and happening. A useful paraphrase for such evaluations is 'what are causes/reasons – what are effects/consequences? Who was/is responsible for this happening/event'? The force of evaluations can also be modulated, that is, increased/up-scaled or decreased/down-scaled (Martin & White 2005: 135ff, Bednarek 2006a: 44). Modulation is not an evaluative parameter as such but rather operates across parameters

(Bednarek 2006a: 44), and is therefore not in small caps. Taking this into account, the potential evaluative/emotional linguistic items listed above can roughly be classified as:

- AFFECT: *would, would you, you like, love, I love;* interjections etc. (outbursts of affect): *ah, aw, oh, uh, ugh, ooh, wow, oh no, ha, god, my god, oh my, oh my god, hell, what the, the hell;* terms of endearment: *honey, hon;* conventionalized: *thanks, please, sorry*;
- EMOTIVITY: *wonderful, great, fine, good, all right, right, okay, ok, well, big, pretty*;
- UNEXPECTEDNESS: *weird, but*;
- EXPECTEDNESS: *of course, course*;
- POWER: *I have to*;
- RELIABILITY: *certainly*;
- CAUSALITY: *cause*;
- Modulation: *just, I just, very, really, pretty.*

The significance of this finding, namely, that different types of evaluative/emotional language (AFFECT, EMOTIVITY, EXPECTEDNESS, RELIABILITY, CAUSALITY, POWER, modulation) distinguish characters from each other, and thus construe character identity is very high. As said, *Keywords* analysis is a corpus- (or data-) driven methodology (cf. Chapter 4, Note 8) which does not make many theoretical *a-priori* assumptions other than that the recurrence of words/n-grams in a corpus is relevant, and has thrown up evaluative/emotional style as significant in characterization. This finding will be taken as a springboard for further analyses of character identity in Chapters 6–8 and the establishment of the concept of 'expressive identity' (Chapter 6).

In summary, we have seen that Lorelai is construed as a unique character through repeated linguistic patterning, allowing viewers to engage with her as a specific character. It is hypothesized that this is the case for many contemporary television characters, even though further investigations with more varied data are needed to confirm this, and series and serials will need to be analysed comparatively. However, this hypothesis would make sense since unique characters allow viewers to emotionally engage and identify with who is portrayed on the screen, and since one of the explicit aims of scriptwriters is to create *consistent* and *unique* characters (Blum 1995: 79, Tim Gooding, p.c.). Further, characters attract viewers to television narratives, and are a way of creating the engagement of viewers, which is crucial in the contemporary television landscape. Australia's Channel Ten chief programmer David Mott says: 'If you don't create viewer engagement, they just won't be bothered.' (Idato 2009: 3). Contemporary television series are in fact frequently character-driven, like *Gilmore Girls*. In how far the corpus findings presented in this chapter are the result of conscious planning on the part of scriptwriters is a matter for future research. Concerning n-grams, researchers have argued that the contribution of chunks 'to language use is subliminal and not immediately accessible to the intuition of the native speaker' (O'Keeffe et al. 2007: 64) – although this may not be true with respect to all chunks/n-grams. This does suggest that key words/n-grams are not necessarily the result of conscious planning on the part of scriptwriters. This is also confirmed by the fact that there are no systematic comments in scriptwriting publications on what kinds of linguistic devices contribute to construing character (Chapter 2: Section 3.4). While so-called 'show bibles' are frequently given to new writers as part of the television production process to give them information about characters (e.g. in terms of favourite places, attitudes etc.), there is some evidence that 'the bulk of the process [of scriptwriting] occurs below the level of conscious awareness' (Mandala 2007: 67).

Notes

1 The notions of 'idiolect' and of 'individual style' both refer to the same concept but belong to the different sub-disciplines of literary studies/linguistics (Hänlein 1999). The concept of key words/n-grams will be explained below.

2 Culpeper (2001: 164) explicitly notes that he follows Pfister (1988) in his organization of textual features. His classification of explicit/implicit cues also has similarities with suggestions made by other researchers such as Ewen (1971, cited in Rimmon-Kenan 2002: 59–60), Bal (1997: 131), Lothe (2000: 81–5) and Toolan (2001). The distinction between Self- and Other-presentation appears similar to Bal's (1997: 130) distinction between characters talking about themselves, characters talking about others, and narrators talking about characters.

3 Examples are: membership categorization devices (Sacks 1992, Schegloff 2006), person-referencing practices (Tracy 2002: chapter 3), identity-based nouns and adjectives (Baker 2003), social actor categories (Machin & van Leeuwen 2007: 44–8), explicit dis/claiming of identity (Cameron & Culick 2005: 112), conversation/interaction sequence and structures (Antaki & Widdicombe 1998, Tracy 2002: chapter 7, Benwell & Stokoe 2006: chapter 2), pragmatic/interactional features (Holmes 1997), vocabulary and metaphor (Fairclough 2003), evaluative and emotional language (Fairclough 2003, Martin 2008b, Knight 2010, Tracy 2002: chapter 10), stylistic range (Holmes 1997), code switching (Tracy 2002: chapter 6, Auer 2007a), phonological and morphological variables (Holmes 1997, Fairclough 2003, Eckert 2008), paralinguistic devices (Tracy 2002: chapter 5), contextualization cues (Gumperz & Cook-Gumperz 2007), politeness and face features (Brown & Levinson 1987, Tracy 2002: chapter 4, Spencer-Oatey 2007), and narratives (Benwell & Stokoe 2006: chapter 4, Tracy 2002: chapter 9, Martin 2008b). These features or clustering of some of these features ('style') can be considered as 'indexes of identity' (Gumperz & Cook-Gumperz 2007: 479). However, what Bubel (2006) points out with respect to language and social relationships is also true with respect to

language and identity: there is no one-to-one relation between a specific textual cue and a specific aspect of identity; rather, 'all language and paralanguage structures are ambiguous and their metacommunicative meaning is jointly accomplished' (Bubel 2006: 32). There is not just one stable social meaning for one feature. Further, all these textual cues can be said to 'influence one another through the ways in which they are combined, and their characterizing effect is enhanced through narrative variation and repetition' (Lothe 2000: 84). Finally, how do we know that 'such-and-such a thing . . . is indeed an identity category, or the associated characteristic of an identity category?' (Antaki & Widdicombe 1998a: 9). The complexity of identity becomes apparent: for example, is a particular person on a particular occasion 'doing GENDER', 'doing AGE', 'doing BEING AN ACADEMIC', 'doing BEING A FRIEND' or 'doing HIM/HERSELF'? How do we know which identity aspects are relevant? For discussion of these issues see, for example, Benwell and Stokoe (2006), Auer (2007c: 32).

4 The splitting of the files into sub-corpora was undertaken by computational linguist Mark Assad on the basis of the speaker identification provided in the corpus (speaker name in capitals followed by colon), as shown in this example:

LORELAI: Hi, Drella, hi. I was just wondering, um, could you be, uh, nicer to the guests?
DRELLA: I'm sorry. Did you not want a harp player?

On account of the amount of data, neither these sub-corpora nor TS-GiGi or GiGi were manually checked by me for correctness so that 100% accuracy of the transcripts is not guaranteed.

5 This is how the software identifies clusters according to WordsmithTools help: Suppose your text begins like this:

Once upon a time, there was a beautiful princess. She snored. But the prince didn't.
If you've chosen two-word clusters, the text will be split up as follows:
Once upon
upon a
a time
. . .

With a three-word cluster setting, it would send
Once upon a
upon a time
. . .

Keywords settings for all queries were as follows (for *WordList* settings see Chapter 4):

log-likelihood
max *p* value: 0.000001
max wanted: 500
minimum frequency: 3
minimum frequency: 1
associate minimum frequency: 5

Note that the analyses focus on word forms rather than lemmas. Further, no dispersion analysis was undertaken, that is, an analysis of where particular words/phrases occur (Culpeper 2001: 200, Stubbs 2005: 12–13, Baker 2006: 60), since this was beyond the scope of the analysis. However, only those key words/n-grams are listed that occur more than 50 times in total, so that some consistency and balance is ensured. Another problematic issue is related to possible spelling variants in the corpus (e.g. *mum/mom*) or inconsistent transcriptions (e.g. *gonna/going to, ok/okay*) that cannot automatically or reliably be identified. Further key words/n-grams may be found if the p value is changed.

6 On other key words studies see Scott (1997), Stubbs (2002), Scott and Tribble (2006), Archer (2007), Bednarek (2008d), and Mike Scott's website (www.lexically.net/wordsmith/index.html, last accessed 8 August 2008).

7 There may be other factors that create Lorelai's character, for example, her tendency for joking remarks and intertextual references described in Chapter 3, which will not be picked up by a key word/n-gram analysis, or indeed, other quantitative analyses. Corpus analyses are limited to investigating formally defined features and key words/n-gram analysis studies them in terms of statistical tendencies only. Compare, for example, Johnstone and Bean (1997) for a more qualitative, ethnographic investigation of various factors tied to 'individuals' creation of distinct voices that express changeable, idiosyncratic identities' (Johnstone & Bean 1997: 224).

8 In fact, if we look at character outlines as used in the television industry, characters are often described in terms of personality features (exuberant, uninhibited, courageous), emotion (loving, grief, desperate), job (menswear business) and interpersonal relations (daughter, father). For example, in this outline of *Mortified* (Nine network Australia, 2006–2007):

> Don is an exuberant, uninhibited and loving father who runs a menswear business in the local mall. He's known locally as 'The Underpant King', an epithet in which he revels, but fails to see causes grief to his younger daughter. Having inherited a menswear shop from his late father, Don is launching a desperate mid-life mission to expand the business into something bigger and better. Like Taylor, he's one of life's doers, and also naturally courageous – he once dropped his trousers, dived into the ocean and rescued a drowning backpacker. This might have won him a medal for bravery, but caused his eleven year old daughter unspeakable embarrassment. (Webber 2005)

Chapter 6

Expressive Character Identity and Emotive Interjections

The findings of the last chapter have suggested that evaluative and emotional language is particularly relevant in the construal of character identity, showing that key words/n-grams realizing the evaluative parameters of AFFECT, EMOTIVITY, UN/EXPECTEDNESS, POWER, RELIABILITY, CAUSALITY as well as key words/n-grams acting as intensifiers/modulators distinguish characters from each other. These are linguistic features that can indicate a variety of identity aspects, for instance degrees of emotionality or attitudes and values. It looks like these aspects of identity are particularly important in televisual characterization. This chapter explores them under the notion of 'expressive character identity' and investigates characterization through the use of emotive interjections. The concept of expressive character identity will also be taken up in Chapters 7 and 8.

1 Analysing Expressive Character Identity

1.1 The concept of expressive character identity

I use the term *expressive character identity* to refer to a kind of scripted identity that is related to the emotionality and the attitudes/values/ideologies of characters in fictional television genres.[1] I call this type of identity 'expressive' (rather than calling it 'affective' or 'evaluative' identity) to capture the fact that it concerns various kinds of expressive aspects, including emotions, values and ideologies. In other words, expressive identity can be used as a cover term to include 'emotional identity', 'attitudinal identity', 'ideological identity' etc. Note that I do not take 'expressive' here to necessarily refer to some kind of 'spontaneous', involuntary expression or a mirroring of some kind of internal mental state. Rather, when actors perform expressive character identity they make use of scripted linguistic resources and multimodal performance features (Chapter 2: Section 3.2.1), using what can be called expressive features (see below). I am not concerned with notions such as the sincerity, veracity, intentionality, spontaneity of expressivity, etc. in this book; nor am I concerned with the semiotic status of such expressions (e.g. signs or symptoms).

To repeat, *expressive identity* is used in a broad sense to include emotions, evaluations, attitudes, values and ideologies. Examples of linguistic resources that construe expressive identity quite explicitly would be emotive interjections (e.g. *Oh my god!* – compare Section 2 below), evaluative statements (e.g. *That was a great kiss* – compare Chapter 7) or announcements of ideological beliefs (*I don't see how anybody can resist eating meat* – compare Chapter 8), but other, less explicit resources and multimodal performance features are also relevant. We will look into what kinds of verbal and non-verbal behaviour can construe expressive character identity in more detail in Section 1.2 below as well as in Chapters 7 and 8. It is important to point out that I do not consider expressive identity as the only aspect of identity to be considered in characterization: other personal, social role and group membership categories (see Culpeper 2001 for this distinction) also play a role.

Why, then, is it worthwhile to focus on expressive character identity? On the one hand, it is in itself interesting to look at how expressive aspects of identity are performed and represented on television. For instance, there is a long history of research on *ideology* and television (cf. Chapter 8). As pointed out in Chapter 2, television characters frequently stand for attitudes and values (Selby & Cowdery 1995: 116), and it is therefore worthwhile investigating what kinds of ideologies/attitudes are expressed by characters in fictional television. If we consider *emotional* aspects of expressivity, the cultural aspect of emotions is clearly significant. Cultural psychologists suggest that emotions are 'socially and culturally shaped and maintained, especially by means of collective knowledge that is represented in linguistic convention, everyday practice, and social structure' (Kitayama & Markus 1994: 10). Thus, while some aspects of emotion do seem to be biological/universal, emotional experience and our attitudes towards as well as feelings about it (what has been called *emotion ideology*; Turner & Stets 2005: 36) are clearly influenced by culture (Ellsworth 1994). For instance, van Meel talks about emotions as 'shaped by art', including 'visual forms like movies and TV in modern times' (van Meel 1994: 163). A significant body of research has investigated emotion and art (van Meel 1994, Oatley 2003, Robinson 2005), but without systematically exploring the role of cultural artefacts such as TV series in the socialization of emotion. It is in this respect that the analysis of emotional expressive identities in television is well worthwhile.

Moreover, the empirical findings described in Chapter 5 have shown that linguistic features construing expressivity (emotional/evaluative key words/n-grams) are particularly relevant in the construal of televisual character identity and distinguish characters from each other. From a qualitative perspective, Bubel (2006: 150) shows that characters differ in their frequency of terms of endearment (*sweetie, sweetheart, honey*) in *Sex and the City*. Taavitsainen

(1999) and Martin (e.g. 2008b) also look at how differences in personal affect/evaluative language construe characters/identities in fictional texts. Taavitsainen finds that 'personal affect features play a role in defining personalities' (Taavitsainen 1999: 231) in *The Canterbury Tales,* and Martin's (2008b) analysis demonstrates how differences in appraisal construe 'authoritative' vs. 'unassuming' identities of two characters in an Alexander McCall Smith novel. Hubbard's (2002) corpus linguistic study of involvement features shows different patterns of use by two characters in Jane Austen's *Sense and Sensibility*. This research, then, shows that emotional/evaluative language differentiates fictional characters.

Another indicator of the importance of expressive meaning for characterization is that the vast majority of the descriptors that Culpeper's (2001) informants use to describe characters in a John Osborne play seem what he calls 'personal' (e.g. *grumpy, impatient, loving, racist, dislikes surprises, cheerful, impulsive*); while 'emotional state' ones (*frustrated, cheerful*) also occur. Both of these groups would be included as descriptions of expressive character identity, as they concern attitudes, ideologies, emotional dispositions and emotional reactions (the other descriptors his informants use concern social roles, age, appearance, health). This indicates the importance audiences attribute to expressive features in interpreting characters. Descriptions of characters used in the television industry also include expressive character features, for example, Don in *Mortified* (Nine network, Australia, 2006–2007) 'is an exuberant, uninhibited and loving father who runs a menswear business in the local mall' (Webber 2005) or Patty in *My So-called Life* (ABC, 1994–1995) 'was being this tight-ass over-grinning, smiling tense person but she was ultimately protecting her daughter' (Claudia Weill, quoted in 'My So-called Life Story' 2007). Similarly, character types recognized in guides for scriptwriting include expressive characteristics such as 'brash', 'insecure', 'aloof', 'confident' (D'Vary 2005: 3), and emotion is one of the components of the personality chart used in this approach to creating characters (D'Vary 2005: 19). How viewers/practitioners describe/view characters may depend on the genre of the particular fictional television narrative. Concerning three selected soap operas (*Dallas* [CBS, 1978–1991], *Coronation Street* [ITV, UK, 1960–], *EastEnders* [BBC, UK, 1985–]) Livingstone (1998) notes that themes of morality, potency and gender were important for audience representations of characters in distinct ways, and that evaluative dimensions are partially relevant to perceiving and classifying television characters: 'social evaluation (sociable, warm, likeable), potency (dominant, hard, values power), morality, and approach to life are generally important to representations of all three programmes studied' (Livingstone 1998: 127). As she says, '[c]ertain dimensions are beginning to emerge as central to the genre of soap opera, such as values, family, modern/traditional approach to life, centrality to the community and morality as a specific version of evaluation' (Livingstone 1998: 136). This ties in with the aforementioned comments that televisual characters are used to carry ideological oppositions between different lifestyles (Feuer 2001b).

Finally, with respect to relationships between viewers and fictional characters, aspects of expressive identity arguably play a key role in parasocial interaction, identification and affinity. Parasocial interaction concerns imaginary social relationships between media user and media figure (e.g. friendship); identification concerns similarity between media user and media figure where a salient feature in the media figure is shared by the media user (e.g. attitudes); affinity simply concerns the media user's liking of a media figure (Giles 2002: 289–90). Giles (2002) notes that 'the expression of an opinion [by the media figure] may chime with the opinion of the user and create a positive judgment based on attitude homophily' (Giles 2002: 296), one of the stages of developing a parasocial relationship. Similarly, the affinity or liking that we feel towards a character is influenced by personality features or attributes of characters such as (though not limited to) emotional reactions (Cohen 1999: 330). It can be argued that the expressive identity of characters plays a big part in the formation of parasocial relationships (e.g. on the basis of attitude homophily), in contributing to identification with characters (e.g. on the basis of similar opinions/attitudes), and in developing affinity towards characters (e.g. on the basis of their emotional reactions). Chapter 8 looks at this in more detail in terms of viewers bonding, affiliating and identifying with characters.[2]

1.2 Analysing linguistic resources that construe expressivity

As the focus of this book is on the textual level – on characterization through television dialogue and other performance features – we need to consider the kinds of features that can potentially construe expressive character identity, what we may call *expressive features* or *resources*. Crucially, these are *functionally* defined, that is an 'expressive feature' is one that functions to contribute to the construal of expressive identity (construing emotionality or values or evaluations or ideologies etc.) in a given context. Since they are functionally defined, there is no pre-defined set of expressive resources. In other words, talking about expressive features does not imply that such a feature necessarily always carries ideological, evaluative or emotional meaning. However, it is likely that those features that have been associated with evaluative or emotional meaning in linguistics can function as expressive resources even if they are not the *only* linguistic features to do so. Table A.9 in Appendix 6 gives an overview of selected resources that can be classified as potentially expressive according to previous research.[3] On the level of speech acts/functions, these involve acts such as apologizing, congratulating, complimenting, complaining, praising, boasting and others (Norrick 1978, Marten-Cleef 1991), although it is more fruitful to look at these in terms of *expressive sequences* (see Chapter 7).[4] Particular linguistic resources that have been linked to emotion, affect, evaluation, stance, appraisal, subjectivity in a variety of approaches in linguistics include: prosodic signals (e.g. rhythm, pitch, loudness), evaluative lexis, the emotion lexicon, connotative meanings of lexis, modal adverbs/adjectives/verbs/nouns, hedges, intensifiers, emphatics, exclamation, swearing/expletives, style markers, evidential markers, negation, conjunction (in particular concessive/contrastive), repetition, metaphor, interjections, affective morphology, vocatives and more (see Selting 1994, Caffi & Janney 1994, Bednarek 2006a, 2008a, Wilce 2009 for recent overviews).[5] In written language, typographical features like multiple punctuation (!!!), eccentric spelling, capital letters or emoticons represent emotions (Claudel 2009). Paralinguistic and nonverbal features such as facial expressions, vocal cues, gestures, body posture, body movement and physiological cues have also been connected to emotion (see, for example, Planalp 1999: 44ff, Goodwin & Goodwin 2000). Obvious examples are crying, kissing, embracing, laughter, applause. Multimodal performance features (Chapter 2) are clearly important for construing expressive character identity: 'When performed, dialogue not only conveys semantic meaning but also the emotional state of the speaker, even the beat-by-beat fluctuation of his or her feelings' (Kozloff 2000: 95).

Such expressive features have mainly been considered in terms of 'real' people. With respect to characterization in particular, Culpeper (2001: 191) proposes that the use of *bloody* and *hell* contributed to informants' describing characters as 'frustrated', 'miserable', 'unsatisfied' and that the repeated occurrence of the speech acts of complaint/apology led them to describe characters as 'irritable' vs. 'apologetic' respectively – hence construing aspects of what I call expressive character identity. In fact, we can find expressive resources on almost all the levels that Culpeper (2001) mentions as relevant for characterization (see Chapter 5: Section 1).

- Explicit cues
  - self-presentation (character gives explicit information about self), for example, *I'm a feminist* (ideological expressive identity); *I'm angry* (emotional expressive identity);
  - other-presentation (character gives explicit information about other character(s)), for example, *She's a feminist; He's angry.*

- Implicit cues
  - conversational structure, for example, hesitations, interruptions signalling nervousness, emotional turmoil, anger;
  - lexis, for example, surge features/affective language (*Oh my god*!);
  - syntactic structure, for example, inversion in exclamations (*How dare he*!);

  - paralinguistic features, for example, tempo, pitch range/variation, voice quality, loudness;
  - visual features, for example, facial expression, posture;
  - (im)politeness strategies/face/image/relational-work.

- Authorial cues
  - stage/script directions, for example, *spoken nervously.*

It is important to note that these resources are only potentially expressive, and that we always need to look at their use in a given co- and context to relate them to the construal of a particular expressive identity. Further, as suggested above, some expressive resources do not necessarily carry explicit evaluative or emotional meaning but can nevertheless be tied to expressive identity (see analyses of ideology in Chapter 8). It is therefore not possible to give an exhaustive, context-free list of resources construing expressive identity. For example, a high frequency of commands may reflect a character's social role or their expressive tendency to be aggressive (Culpeper 2001: 235–6). However, the analysis of emotional/evaluative resources is a good starting point to study the construal of expressive identity.

When we look at verbal and nonverbal expressive resources we consider how expressive identities are construed in the performance (e.g. through the dialogue). We can consider the occurrence of such behaviour in various ways:

- We can look at the types, kinds and range of expressive resources (e.g. what types of emotions and what parameters of evaluation are expressed; what is the semiotic status (index/symbol/icon) of the signs involved; in what mode (*pur/vécu*) is the resource expressed);[6]
- We can look at the intensity of the expressive resources (see, for example, Morris 1977: 116–19 on 'shortfall' and 'overkill' signals);[7]
- We can look at the frequency and patterning of selected expressive resources;
- We can look at what resources cluster to form an expressive style (cf. Tallman 1979, cited in Fine 1981, on personal and intimate style; Tannen 1984 on conversational involvement styles, Selting 1994 on emphatic speech style).

The choice of what expressive features to analyse also depends on the methodology. For instance, in a large-scale corpus analysis, we can consider selected resources that are formally definable (e.g. interjections), whereas in a qualitative discourse analysis we can consider a much larger number of expressive resources, that need not necessarily be formally definable.[8] At the next stage we need to relate these resources to expressive identity, that is, we need to consider how the occurrence of expressive features construes a particular type of expressive identity, for example, an identity of being 'emotional', 'a whinger', 'determined', 'upset' or 'harmony-seeking'. Semiotically speaking, the text construes potential expressive identities; cognitively speaking, it can give rise to the audience's formation of character impressions (see Culpeper 2001 for the role of bottom-up/top-down processing, including the role of prior knowledge). Compare Figure 6.1.

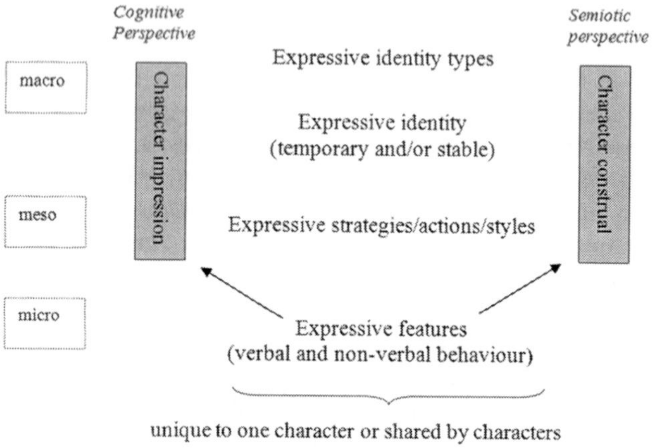

FIGURE 6.1 Modelling expressive identity

As becomes apparent, this model of expressive character identity is influenced both by cognitive models of characterization (Culpeper 2001), by semiotic models of individuation (Martin 2007: 294) and by image research that takes into account different levels (micro/meso/macro) of analysis (Behn 2007), even though I do not necessarily adopt the concepts taken from these models on a one-to-one basis. In particular, Figure 6.1 suggests that we can consider the relation between expressive features and expressive identity from a cognitive or a semiotic perspective. From a cognitive perspective, expressive features function as cues in the dialogue (including verbal and non-verbal behaviour) that give rise to the audience's impressions of expressive character identity for instance in terms of emotionality, attitudes, ideology. Other factors such as prior knowledge play a role in character impression too (Culpeper 2001: 34) but are not represented in this figure. From a semiotic perspective – the one primarily taken in this book – expressive features potentially construe expressive character identity. From this perspective we are interested only in the meaning potential of the relevant verbal and non-verbal dialogue cues.

Further, as suggested by the three boxes (macro/meso/micro) on the left-hand side of Figure 6.1, we can consider dialogue cues and expressive identity on different levels. We can look at expressive features as micro cues, that is, at the individual occurrence of features or we can consider how they function as a particular expressive strategy or action (such as a particular ideological strategy) or how they form an expressive style on the meso level. Finally, on the macro level we can consider the expressive identities (both temporary and/or stable) that are construed/that arise and see if they are related to a finite (?) number of expressive identity types such as 'Worrier', or 'Pessimist'.

How do such expressive identities relate to personal and shared aspects of identity? I would suggest that, like lifestyles (Machin & van Leeuwen 2007: 50), expressive identity combines individual and social identity – it is both a way of expressing a character's unique identity and simultaneously aligning one character with other characters who share similar expressive identities (e.g. in terms of values, ideologies; see Chapter 8). As Figure 6.1 illustrates, expressive features can be unique to one character (individual identity) or shared by a group of characters (social identity). In analogy to the notion of 'community of practice' (e.g. Wenger 2007), we could use the terms 'community of ideology', 'community of attitude', 'community of affect' or 'community of desire' to refer to groups of people with shared expressive identities.

Concerning the model visualized in Figure 6.1, it is also important to emphasize that expressive features are seen to construe aspects of expressive identity *both* dynamically/temporarily (at one particular instance in time; localized and situated) and repeatedly (as patterns, creating a relatively stable expressive identity that spans different instances and contexts).[9] For instance, a character can be emotional in one particular instance or exhibit a general tendency to be emotional across instances. We could then argue that the occurrence of verbal and non-verbal features gives rise to audience 'impressions' (Culpeper 2001: 190) of expressive character identity that are either tied to a particular situation or seen to apply more generally. One can either infer that particular behaviour corresponds to a general disposition (stable expressive identity) or explain it through contextual and other factors. Various factors influence the interpretation of behaviour such as a plausible external stimuli (a trigger/a circumstance) and in/consistency of behaviour (see Culpeper 2001: 115–29 for further discussion). So expressive features can both be used 'as a conventional way of signalling that a character has a particular emotion or attitude' (Culpeper 2001: 193) at a particular point in time and more generally. That is, an audience can interpret behaviour as indicating a character's expressive identity as far as a particular scene is concerned, but could still consider this as an exceptional behaviour as far as this character's *general* expressive identity is concerned. The more the behaviour is repeated across instances, the more likely it seems that a stable expressive identity is attributed by the audience. Figure 6.2 on page 126 visualizes this relationship. This assumption is in line with the notions of high consistency and low distinctiveness in Attribution theory, concerning degrees to which a character reacts in the same way to different stimuli across situations (Culpeper 2001: 128). The higher the consistency and the lower the distinctiveness the more likely it is that a behaviour is attributed to a person's disposition rather than other factors.

To illustrate the model introduced above in the ensuing chapters, I first look at the frequency and patterning of selected expressive resources. Specifically I consider the linguistic construal of emotionality at the micro-level through emotive interjections (this chapter, below) and I consider the linguistic construal of an ideology shared by characters, primarily through evaluative language (Chapter 8). In both cases, linguistic features are repeated across instances construing a relatively stable expressive (emotional/ideological) identity. These analyses make use of a large corpus and are hence limited to studying *selected* expressive resources. In contrast, Chapter 7 considers expressive style as cluster of verbal and nonverbal resources and relates this to the meso-level performance of unique expressive identities in a particular instance, hence construing temporary expressive identity. This analysis is only of one scene, and can therefore take into account a considerable number of expressive resources. Reference will be made throughout to the types, range and intensity of expressive resources used, micro-, meso- and macro-levels of analysis and the expressive identities construed. However, I will not consider cognitive/psychological (Livingstone 1998, Culpeper 2001) aspects of audience impression formation (as this would require audience research) or relate expressive identities to established identity/personality types (as this is beyond the scope of this book).

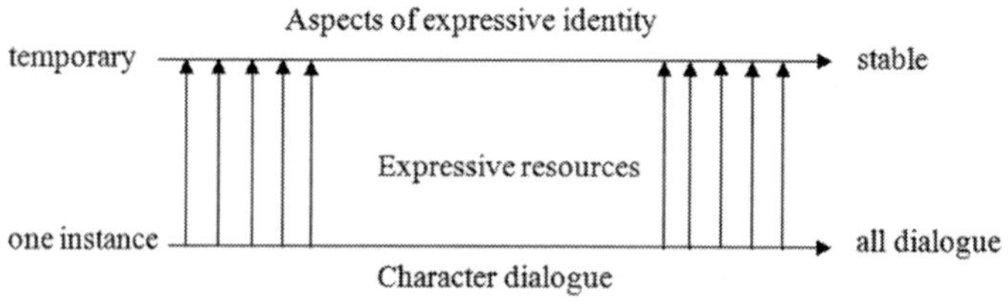

FIGURE 6.2 Construing expressive identity

2 Analysing Emotionality with Respect to Characterization

The following sections investigate the use of emotive interjections by characters, analysing expressive character identity with respect to emotionality and, as before, using the dramedy *Gilmore Girls* (Warner Brothers, 2000–2007) to provide data for a case study. Interjections were chosen because they form a relatively closed set and are formally defined, that is, they can be used as search terms in a large-scale corpus analysis, without there being any need to manually annotate the corpus beforehand. Moreover, the decision to focus on interjections follows the finding of the importance of *oh my god* in the analysis of 3-grams in *Gilmore Girls* in Chapter 4 above. Further, interjections are very clearly and unequivocally related to expressivity, as they have been linked to affect or emotion in a variety of approaches in linguistics. They have been defined as 'relatively conventionalised vocal gestures . . . which express a speaker's mental state, action or attitude or reaction to a situation' (Ameka 1992: 106) and have been referred to as 'outbursts' of emotion (Taavitsainen 1999; Martin & White 2005: 68). Hübler (1998) following Bally (1965) lists an emotive interjection (*damn it*) as an example of expressive language used in the *mode vécu,* that is, in 'a global, holistic mode involving the whole person with all her/his senses and feelings' (Hübler 1998: 5; see Note 6). Bednarek (2008a) groups them with 'emotional talk', that is, linguistic features that do not denote but (conventionally) signal emotion. Finally, interjections are clearly part of 'surge features' (Taavitsainen 1999: 219) that work as implicit cues to characterization (Culpeper 2001: 190). These 'are frequently used by authors . . . as a conventional way of signalling that a character has a particular emotion or attitude' (Culpeper 2001: 192–3).

2.1 Interjections and character construal in *Gilmore Girls*

In my first case study of the construal of expressive character identity, I analysed emotive interjections, and considered them in connection with character construal. In essence, this involved looking at the frequency of the previously analysed interjections (described in Chapter 4, Section 3.4.3.3) according to character, a micro-level feature of their expressive (emotional) style or idiolect. The six characters with the most turns/tokens in *Gilmore Girls* are Lorelai, Rory, Luke, Emily, Richard and Sookie (as seen in Chapter 5), and looking at the co-text of all interjections (= 2964 occurrences) in TS-GiGi allows us to identify them as speakers of different interjections. With respect to the analysed interjections and looking only at these main characters, the following observations can be made. First, some characters are construed as more emotional than others. Indeed, Lorelai has the most interjections per 10,000 words (37.9), followed very closely by Sookie (36.5), and then by Rory (27.8), Luke (19.2), Emily (12) and Richard (5.7).[10] Figure 6.3 on page 128 visualizes this.

Interestingly, both Lorelai and Sookie are almost equally emotional, and though adults, they are more emotional than the more 'rational' intellectual teenager Rory (Lorelai's daughter), in line with their general expressive character identity: 'The boisterous Lorelai is 32 going on 16; the serious Rory is 16 going on 32' (Millman 2000). Which is not to say that Lorelai cannot be 'rational' at times or that Rory is not capable of emotional behaviour, as evidenced by scenes in episodes 4.11 (*In the clamor and the clangor*) or 4.14 (*The incredible shrinking Lorelais*) to name but two examples. Remember that the

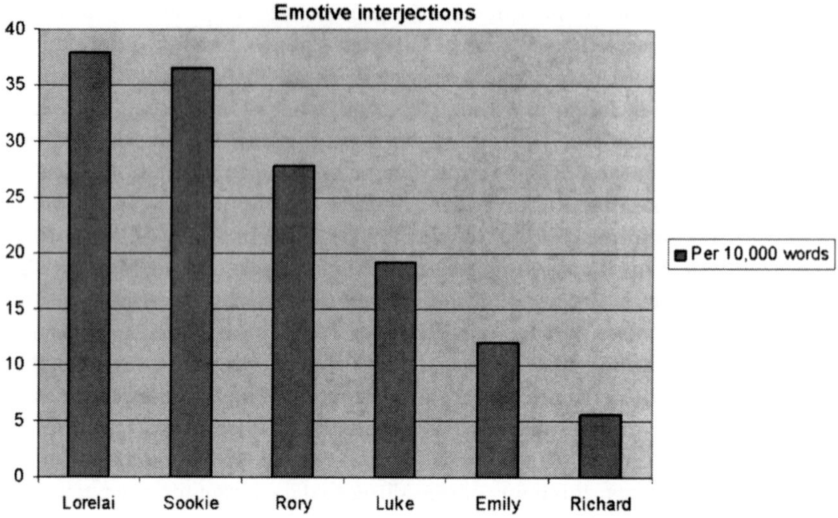

FIGURE 6.3 Occurrences for emotive interjections across characters

corpus linguistic analysis focuses on repeated tendencies of selected expressive features only. It is also noteworthy that Lorelai's parents – Emily and, in particular, Richard – are far behind in terms of interjections used to signal emotionality. However, this just relates to interjections and it is in fact reasonable to assume that Emily and Richard use other expressive resources. The key words/n-grams analyses in Chapter 5 seem to indicate that they both like to use particular evaluative language (e.g. adjectives, adverbs): for Emily some expressive key words/n-grams were *lovely, wonderful, ridiculous, simply, absurd, dear, young, hardly, nonsense*; for Richard they were *wonderful, young, lovely, proper, a very, a fine, a proper*. Perhaps interjections in general are too unequivocally expressive, emotional and involved for these characters, belonging to the 'mode vécu' (Hübler 1998: 8). Wierzbicka (2003: 339) notes that the use of interjection may be linked to the 'spontaneous and uninhibited show of emotions' (2003: 339), which neither Emily nor Richard would approve of. Remember that these characters are described as 'extremely proper' (see Chapter 3). Example (1) illustrates that it is part of Richard's character, and a source of conflict between him and Lorelai, that he does not approve of involved expressions of emotionality (here an expletive not an emotive interjection).

(1)
LORELAI: [answers phone]
Um, hello, the Gilmore Group. Mr. Hensen . . . why, yes, he
RICHARD: [gestures that he doesn't want to talk]

LORELAI:	just walked out. May I take a message? Uh huh . . . [looks through the drawers for a pen] Um, how are you spelling, uh, Larry? [Richard hands her a pen] Oh, traditionally, great. Okay, uh, thank you for calling . . . bye bye. [hangs up] **Where the hell** are your pens?
RICHARD:	Uh, **watch your language, young lady**. What did Larry want?
LORELAI:	He wanted to know **where the hell** your pens are.
RICHARD:	**Lorelai.**
LORELAI:	He just wants you to call him, Dad. Where are all the office supplies?

(2.20, *Help wanted*)

Since Lorelai is the most expressive in terms of interjection usage (confirming the n-gram analysis in Chapter 5 where Lorelai was distinguished from other characters partially through emotionality), it might be expected that it is Lorelai who uses *all* interjections most frequently. However, this is not the case. First, there are differences with respect to each character regarding the interjections they most frequently produce, and secondly, characters are associated with specific interjections. Table 6.1 below lists the most frequent interjections for each character.

On the one hand, there are distinctive frequency profiles for each character with respect to frequency scales such that no two characters have identical distributions of interjections. On the other hand, disregarding scaling and just looking at which interjections are produced frequently by characters, groupings do become possible. Two main groupings become apparent from Table 6.1: While Lorelai's, Rory's, Luke's and Sookie's most frequent

Table 6.1 Most frequent emotive interjections for six characters

Character	Most frequent interjections per 10,000 words (raw frequency >2; rounded to 2 digits)
Lorelai	*wow* (9.86), *oh my god* (6.12), *ugh* (4,67), *aw* (3.65), *god* (2.81), *whoa* (2.32)
Rory	*wow* (10.11), *oh my god* (5.41), *whoa* (2.33), *god* (1.95), *geez/jeez* (1.4), *aw/oh man* (0.92)
Luke	*wow* (5.15), *geez/jeez* (4.3), *whoa* (2.23), *aw/oh man* (1.29), *oh my god* (1.17), *aw* (0.94)
Sookie	*oh my god* (11.69), *wow* (6.68), *ugh* (4.05), *oh god* (3.1), *god* (3.1)
Emily	*oh my god* (4.17), *for X's sake* (2.08), *(oh) my goodness* (1.59), *(oh) thank god* (0.91)
Richard	*for x's sake* (1.63), *oh my goodness* (1.09), *my god* (0.82), *oh my god* (0.54)

interjections overlap quite considerably, husband and wife Richard and Emily (who share three interjections) are distinguished from these four younger characters by their frequent use of *for x's sake* and *(oh) my goodness*. On the one hand, this could construe more closeness between characters, and contribute to establish relations such as mother–daughter (Lorelai, Rory), friendship (Lorelai, Luke/Sookie), romantic love (Lorelai, Luke) and husband–wife (Richard, Emily). This would be in line with findings by Mandala on *Buffy the Vampire Slayer* (Warner Brothers, 1997–2003) where close friends had similar frequencies of marked *-y* adjectives. This usage also has to do with age and generation. Interjections such as *wow* and *geez/jeez* seem 'hipper', more informal and younger (and therefore inappropriate for Richard and Emily, who hardly ever use them) than *for x's sake* and *(oh) my goodness*, which Richard and Emily both like. Generally speaking, it appears as if similar characters are related by their usage and non-usage of interjections; for instance, Richard uses hardly any interjections but when he does, he tends to use the same ones as Emily. Both Luke and his nephew Jess like to use *geez/jeez*. This clearly is significant for the construal of expressive character identities in terms of repeated patterning, intersubjectivity and the sharing of expressive identities.

Now let us look briefly at which character uses which interjection most frequently compared to other main characters. While Table A.10 in Appendix 7 lists interjections plus associated most frequent speakers, Table 6.2 below only gives a summary (where raw frequency > 2).

It becomes apparent that Lorelai's interjections are informal/young (*rats, yay*) and, according to their OALD definitions, potentially signal emotions of annoyance (*rats*), pleasure (*yay, (oh) thank god*), disapproval, protest, sympathy (*aw*), anger/impatience (*for the love of god*), surprise/relief (*whew*) and disgust (*ugh*). Thus, she is quite varied emotionally. This might tie in with discourses on gender and emotion, for instance with men less emotional, more 'logical', 'stronger' than women, and excess of emotionality evaluated as negative (Burton 2000: 176). From a critical perspective and with a focus on gender (rather than on identity in general), this construes a particular construction of femininity.

Table 6.2 Interjections associated with particular characters

Interjections (f>2)	Character associated with interjections
aw, for the love of god, (oh) thank god, rats, ugh, whew, whoa, yay	Lorelai
aw/oh man, crap, geez/jeez, damn (it)	Luke
bummer, wow, whoa, yuck, yikes	Rory
ew, god, oh god, oh my god, (oh) thank god	Sookie
for x's sake, (oh) my goodness	Emily
my god	Richard

> Females are constructed in terms of an **emotional reading**. In their various representations they are expected to be bitchy, passionate, jealous, vindictive, affectionate, and so on. A generous palette of emotional colours is ascribed to females, attached to stereotypes and tied to a simplistic notion that women are, simply, emotional (that is, again, more than men!). (Burton 2000: 181)

In contrast to Lorelai, Luke's interjections seem more negative, stronger, more expletive, and perhaps more 'male' (Bednarek 2008b: 107):[11] *man, geez* (surprise/anger), *damn* (*it*) (annoyance/disappointment), *crap* (not in OALD but reasonably associated with displeasure). In spoken American conversation, 'men's expletive frequencies were significantly higher than women's' (Precht 2006: 24) so that Luke's expletives arguably construe him as 'male'. Compare also his expressive key words *damn* and *hell* listed in Chapter 5. In both Lorelai and Luke gendered assumptions on emotional practices thus seem to be illustrated. However, these findings refer just to selected expressive features and to statistical tendencies – for instance, there is an episode in *Gilmore Girls* (3.22, *Those are strings, Pinocchio*) which has both men (Luke, Jackson) and women (Lorelai, Sookie) crying, though the fact that the men are also crying seems to create a humorous effect. While *Gilmore Girls* largely appears to conform to traditional gendered discourses on emotionality it *is* possible for television series to go against the predominant trend of following cultural discourses on emotionality. The television series *The X-Files* (FOX, 1993–2002) was exceptionable in terms of portraying a female protagonist (Dana Scully) as skeptical/rational and a male protagonist (Fox Mulder) as intuitive and emotional (Hermes 2005: 55).

Continuing with the other characters, Rory's interjections are informal/young (*bummer, whoa, wow, yuck, yikes*), and can construe emotions such as disappointment (*bummer*), surprise/admiration (*whoa, wow*), disgust (*yuck*), and surprise/fear (*yikes*) – again relatively varied emotionally. Sookie's interjections predominantly involve *god* (surprise, shock, annoyance), and indicate her not being construed as very varied or sophisticated emotionally. Finally, Emily's interjection are more formal/'older' and related to emotions of annoyance/impatience (*for x sake*) and surprise (*my goodness*). (Richard's interjection (*my god*) only occurs three times so will not be discussed here.) Patterns of interjection usage thus seem related to the construal of unique expressive character identity. This is also the case for what can be called 'signature' interjections. My definition of a signature interjection is as follows:

a) the interjection is produced by one speaker most frequently compared to other characters;
b) among the group of interjections thus identified, the signature interjection is the one that is most frequent for that character.

For example, for Lorelai *aw, for the love of god, rats, shoot, ugh, whew*, and *yay* satisfy criterion (a), but among this group *ugh* is most frequent (4.67 per 10,000 words), and is thus defined as Lorelai's signature interjection. Apart from *damn (it)*, *(oh) thank god* and *whoa*, which are almost equally produced by two or more characters, for other interjections it is possible to identify one speaker as most frequent. Among those, signature interjections for the main characters are: Rory: *wow* (10.11 per 10,000 words), Luke: *geez/jeez* (4.3), Emily: *for X sake* (2.08), Sookie: *oh my god* (11.69). If frequency is used as criterion for salience (but see Stubbs 2005: 11) these can be seen (together with the multimodal context in which they are produced, such as a particular tone of voice) as markers of identification, character differentiation and expressive character identity, as they are repeatedly and frequently associated with one character. Esslin (2002) argues that in drama, as in the 'real' world,

> we are constantly confronted with people and situations we have to view, recognize and interpret; we are compelled to select the information we need by concentrating on a few significant features and rejecting the bulk of data that continuously bombard our senses. (Esslin 2002: 19)

Signature interjections may well belong to these 'few significant' features that are selectively interpreted by viewers in their construal of character identity. In Eckert's (2008) words, they are linguistic features that can be attributed significance and then become a stylistic resource – here one that is associated with the style of individual characters, their expressive idiolect.

2.2 Character identity, performativity and 'breaking the norm'

The focus above was on expressive character identity as repeated, patterned semiotic behaviour but what happens if these patterns get disrupted? What happens when a character's one-off use of an interjection breaks the norm that has been set up in the series?

When characters use an interjection they normally would not use, the situation where they use it is marked as particularly emotional. Compare the metalinguistic comments and explicit descriptions of situations as markedly emotional in the following two extracts:

(2)

LORELAI:	Rory called.
LUKE:	I know! She called and yelled at me.
LORELAI:	No, she called and yelled at me!
LUKE:	Yeah, but I'm the one who had to hear it, and she was loud! And she said – **'hell'. I never heard her say 'hell'. I didn't even know she knew how to say 'hell'.** [Flustered.] She was mad and she yelled and she said '**hell**'.

LORELAI: Yeah, but she called.
(6.07, *Twenty-one is the loneliest number*)

(3)
[Lorelai enters.]
LUKE: Hey!
LORELAI: You ready?
LUKE: For what?
LORELAI: For this! The moment you've all been waiting for! [She vibrates her tongue.] Brrrr!
LUKE: What's that?
LORELAI: It's a drum roll.
LUKE: It sounded more like a helicopter.
LORELAI: Well, it's a drum roll, go with it, okay?
LUKE: I'm with it. [murmuring]
LORELAI: Ladies and gentlemen, Rory Gilmore! [She opens the door. Rory is entering]
RORY: Hi Luke!
LUKE: Hey, Rory, you're back! [They hug.]
RORY: I'm back!
LUKE: Good! You look good. Healthy, happy. Huh, here with your mom, both of you here. It's great, you know! **Yay**! [Awkward pause.] **I don't think I've ever said 'yay' before. Sounded weird.**
LORELAI: A little.
LUKE: Come, sit, sit.
(6.10, *He's slippin' 'em bread, dig?*)

In both situations, the usage of interjections by characters goes against their individual norm, the stable language patterns that have been set up with respect to the characters of Rory and Luke. For instance, Rory tends not to use stronger expletives such as *hell* (which can but need not be an interjection), in line with her expressive identity. And Luke would not use an interjection such as 'yay', which is associated mainly with Lorelai and Rory. As in Chapter 5, we can consider this as foregrounded, a departure from a text-internal norm or target-based expectancy set up for an individual character in terms of their expressive character identity, resulting in a construal of strong emotionality. Culpeper (2001: 133) notes that norm-breaking behaviour is particularly interpretable and informative. The norm-breaking, 'weirdness' and 'emotionality' are explicitly referred to in these examples, as such frequency norms are not necessarily salient to the audience.

A different but no less interesting example of norm-breaking is Paris Geller, a female character who uses the expletives *damn it* and *hell* which are predominantly associated with male characters in *Gilmore Girls* (Bednarek 2008b).

In other words, she breaks text-internal norms that apply to more than one character and that appear gender-related. We can discuss this with respect to Butler's notion of performativity (Butler 1999, Salih 2006, Jagger 2008). According to Butler, gender identity is not in any sense pre-given, but rather performatively construed:

> [T]he substantive effect of gender is performatively produced and compelled by the regulatory practices of gender coherence. Hence, within the inherited discourse of the metaphysics of substance, gender proves to be performative – that is, constituting the identity it is purported to be. In this sense, gender is always a doing, thought not a doing by a subject who might be said to pre-exist the deed. . . . There is no gender identity behind the expressions of gender; that identity is performatively constituted by the very 'expressions' that are said to be its results. (Butler 1999: 34)

Importantly, performativity is characterized by its *repetitive and ritual* character (Butler 1999: xv); it requires

> a performance that is *repeated*. This repetition is at once a reenactment and reexperiencing of a set of meanings already socially established; and it is the mundane and ritualized form of their legitimation. Although there are individual bodies that enact these significations by becoming stylized into gendered modes, this 'action' is a public action. There are temporal and collective dimensions to these actions . . . (Butler 1999: 191)

This notion of performativity 'opens up the space to explore how sedimentation occurs (and **can be opposed**)' (Pennycook 2004: 15, my bold). If identity is seen as repeated patterning, it is not wholly stable and open to change: 'Indeed, it is this instability that enables the possibility of **resistance and change**' (Jagger 2008: 3, my bold). Arguably, then, the character of Paris represents an attempt to oppose a particular kind of sedimentation of gender identity in popular culture (one, where women do not use 'strong' interjections/expletives like *hell* and *damn*). However, the impact of this attempt depends on how she is evaluated by the audience. Paris is partially construed as harsh, insensitive, undiplomatical and blunt. In fact, the observations that Culpeper (2001) makes with respect to Katherina in *The Taming of the Shrew* also hold for Paris, who breaks 'normative expectations at a variety of behavioural levels, both linguistic and non linguistic. . . . The importance of this behavioural pattern is that it allows us to infer that the cause of her behaviour lies not in external phenomena, but in her personality' (Culpeper 2001: 272). However, Ridinger-Dotterman argues that '[w]ithout ignoring the excess of her perfectionism, and certainly without failing to acknowledge her bitchiness, we begin to see Paris as more than just a villain and embrace her as a strong, albeit imperfect, woman' (Ridinger-Dotterman 2008: 62). Ultimately, audience research would be needed to investigate the potential relations between media users and the media figure Paris. In any case, a corpus stylistic analysis of performativity, the analysis of norms concerning identity and their breaking can arguably demonstrate that, indeed, 'Butler's abstract philosophical arguments can be used to some effect in empirical social sciences' (Cameron 2005: 492).

2.3 Expressive identities in fictional television

This chapter has introduced the notion of expressive character identity and has made use of corpus stylistic methodology to analyse the use of emotive interjections within this framework. A case study of *Gilmore Girls* has demonstrated how emotive interjections contribute to construing different expressive character identities: For instance, if we just consider their use of emotive interjections (micro-level), the characters Lorelai and Sookie are prone to emotional outbursts of various kinds (both positive and negative) (meso-level), construing what we might call a varied emotional expressive identity (macro-level). Luke uses 'strong' and 'negative' interjections, construing perhaps a stereotypically male and negative emotional expressive identity. His character is in fact quite gruff, and a bit of a misanthrope. Finally, Emily and Richard tend not to show their emotions through the 'spontaneous' use of emotive interjections; they are relative non-performers of emotional outbursts, construing a 'non-emotional/reserved' expressive identity. Table 6.3 uses these selected characters to illustrate how this analysis can be related to the model for expressive identity introduced above.

If we had access to large corpora containing individual character's dialogue from other fictional television series we could investigate if and how emotive interjections differentiate between characters in other series. While I had no access to a proper corpus of another series, I used a transcript database search (available at www.losthatch.com/transcripts.aspx, last accessed 5 June 2009)

Table 6.3 Expressive identity through emotive interjections

Macro	Stable (repeated) expressive identity: emotionality	Lorelai and Sookie: varied emotional expressive identity Luke: male negative emotional expressive identity Emily and Richard: non-emotional/reserved expressive identity
Meso	expressive style expressive strategies/actions	more or fewer emotional outbursts pos vs. neg emotion 'strong' vs. 'weak' expletive vs. non-expletive
Micro	expressive feature (verbal)	emotive interjections

to briefly consider the use of three interjections (*damn/damn it, son of a bitch, hell*) by four male characters in the 'mystery drama' series *Lost* (ABC, 2004–) (Table 6.4). This search engine allowed me to search for word forms and phrases in individual character's dialogue in 86 episodes across four seasons, but did not allow me to calculate normalized frequencies (e.g. per turns/tokens). I also had to manually exclude non-interjection usages (e.g. *damn island, give a damn, you son of a bitch, hell of a, x the hell* etc.) of these word forms and phrases.

Table 6.4 Frequencies for three expletive interjections in *Lost*

	Male characters in *Lost*			
Interjection	**Hurley Reyes**	**John Locke**	**Jack Shepard**	**Sawyer**
damn/damn it	3	1	12	7 (but many other uses of *damn* than the others – 59 occurrences of the word form *damn* vs. Jack Shepard's 14 occurrences)
son of a bitch	1	–	–	19 (sometimes co-text lacking so unclear if addressed to someone or not (i.e. meaning *You're a son of a bitch*, which is not an interjection use), but note that Sawyer is responsible for 27 occurrences of 32 for all usages of *son of a bitch* by male characters)
hell	–	1	1	24
Total	**4**	**2**	**13**	**50**

Table 6.4 shows that it is clearly the character of Sawyer who is distinguished from the other male characters through his frequent use of these expletive interjections, and perhaps expletives in general – suggesting that 'expletiveness' may be a key dimension in expressive styles, rather than or in addition to interjection usage. The following example shows a clustering of expletives in Sawyer's speech.

(3)

Sawyer C'mon. C'mon! Impact velocity. Physics **my ass**. Alright . . . **Son of a bitch**. Unbelievable! Hey! Hey! Don't even think about it. Hey! **Damn it**. **Hell**, Freckles, I knew you wanted it. I just didn't know how bad. Whoa-hoa, you're going to have to come up with a new move. Ow. God. Okay. Okay. Okay, this is just silly. C'mon. Hold on. Got a proposition for you. You tell me what's inside and I'll give it to you.

(*Lost*, 1.12, www.losthatch.com/transcripts.aspx, bold face mine)

Considering the frequencies in Table 6.4 is also possible that 'son of a bitch' is an expressive 'signature' phrase for Sawyer, as he is responsible for 27 of 32 occurrences of the word form 'son of a bitch' by all male characters.

With respect to the investigation of signature interjections, there are also other television series where characters have emotive signature interjections, such as Homer Simpson's *d'oh* (*The Simpsons*, FOX, 1989–). In general, such features are related to 'catchphrases' or 'dialogue tags' (D'Vary 2005) that are used to distinguish characters from each other. Catchphrases, however, are very clearly psychologically salient, for example, Sidney Charles 'Pop' Larkin's *perfick* (*The Darling Buds of May*, ITV, UK, 1991–1993), Marilyn Whirlwind's *uh-uh* (*Northern Exposure*, CBS, 1990–1995), Nelson Muntz's *haw-haw* (*The Simpsons*, FOX, 1989–), Dr Sam Becket's *oh boy* (*Quantum Leap*, NBC, 1989–1993) or Gatsby's *old sport* to give an example from prose fiction (*The Great Gatsby*). D'Vary's (2005) 'dialogue tags' distinguish characters from each other and can concern catchphrases, sentence structure, tone, in/directness, paralinguistic features. Signature interjections can thus be seen as part of dialogue tags and, if psychologically salient, as similar to catchphrases. For a discussion of statistical and psychological salience see also Leech & Short (1981). While I hypothesize that it is often expressive resources (e.g. *d'oh, perfick, oh boy, son of a bitch*) that are used as catchphrases, signature phrases or dialogue tags, further research needs to be done to bear out this hypothesis.

These combined findings support the assumption that a number of linguistic resources, including emotive interjections, are used to build up different expressive identities of characters in fictional television series in general rather than just in the analysed series and genre (dramedy). Whether the genres of dramedy and other hybrid drama genres are particularly prone to this on account of the importance of emotionality in these genres will need to be investigated further. Future research will also need to connect the notion of performativity and the breaking of norms to concepts such as individuation, instantiation and structuration (see Note 9). Finally, it is important to point to a number of limitations of the corpus study of emotive interjections other than those already mentioned. As said, interjections are not the only resource to construe expressive identity so we need to look at other expressive resources too, to get a fuller picture. Further, the analysis above did not really consider the multimodal performance of expressivity (resources such as gesture and facial expression) or the discursive, localized, dynamic and intersubjective construal of expressive character identities (e.g. facework, turn-taking). An analysis of emotive interjections (or other selected expressive features) is thus ideally accompanied by additional analyses of other expressive resources and character interaction. This is the aim of Chapters 7 and 8.

Notes

[1] A note on terminology: The relation between evaluation (attitude, value) and emotion (affect, emotionality) is very complex, and depends on how each of

these terms is defined. If we define affect very broadly, we can list a wide range of resources (Bednarek 2009b) that express affect discursively, including certain types of evaluative language (e.g. *Fantastic*!). But well-established definitions of evaluative language (e.g. Biber et al. 1999, Martin & White 2005) also include references to emotion (*I love this shirt*!). In such approaches the emphasis is on different sorts of evaluative language, including epistemic stance (modality, evidentiality). With regard to how the terms are used in this book, as a rule of thumb *evaluation/evaluative language* refers to evaluative language along a number of parameters (see Chapter 3), including both EMOTIVITY (*fantastic*; *rubbish*) and AFFECT (attribution of emotional reactions to Self/Other). The terms *emotion/affect/emotionality* are used to refer only to expressions of emotion, including evaluations along the parameter of AFFECT, such as explicit emotion labels (*love*), conventionalized affect (*I'm sorry*) and 'outbursts' of affect (*oh my god*) as well as nonverbal behaviour (e.g. facial expression). But I often talk about emotional/evaluative language to discuss the two without distinguishing clearly between them. I am not too much concerned in this book with distinguishing strictly between evaluative and emotional language, as there are fuzzy boundaries between them, as any distinction would be purely a result of particular definitions and perspectives on them, and as both are clearly related to the expression of positive/negative stance. Finally, *expressivity* is seen as a cover term including evaluation and affect alongside other notions such as ideology. Misleadingly, I have elsewhere called 'expressive identity' 'interpersonal identity' (Bednarek 2010). However, in Halliday's (e.g. Halliday & Matthiessen 2004) approach, the interpersonal function, which is concerned with meanings that can be considered as 'enacting our personal and social relationships with the other people around us' (Halliday & Matthiessen 2004: 29) intrinsically includes all speech functions and other systems such as mood, whereas I am only interested in those resources that function to construe expressive identity. Even though I have borrowed the term 'expressive' from previous research in linguistics, my use of it is not identical to the way it is used in functional theories of language (Bühler 1934, Jakobson 1960, Leech 1974) or in speech act theory (Levinson 1983, Bublitz 2001, Adolphs 2008). Looking at speech act theory first, some researchers in fact argue against seeing expressives as speech acts in their own right but rather suggest that expressive meaning is part of every type of speech act (see Marten-Cleef 1991: 26–7; 29). Where a distinct class of expressive acts *is* recognized, definitions differ widely, but are all rather too narrow for my purposes. For instance, threats are not an expressive but a commissive speech act in Searle's classification, while they could also functionally construe expressive character identity. Searle's definition of expressives seems further limited to utterances with particular syntactic structures (Marten-Cleef 1991: 18), Austin's *behabitives* (apologies, thanks, sympathy, attitudes, greetings, wishes, challenges) do not include the expression of the speaker's own emotions (Marten-Cleef 1991: 31); Norrick (1978) excludes expressions of intention and emotions directed at future states; Marten-Cleef (1991: 86, 87) limits expressive acts to spontaneous and momentary reactions to concrete events. She also excludes evaluations ('Bewertungen'), although she notes that the borders between evaluative and expressive acts are fuzzy (Marten-Cleef 1991: 89).

Considering functions of language, various resources that have been classified as relating both to expressive (interjections) and to conceptualizing (emotion lexicon) functions of language (Foolen 1997: 16, Wierzbicka 2003: 288) could both be used to construe expressive identity (see Table A.9 in Appendix 6). Only if expressive meaning/function is defined in a way as to include all resources that concern expressive identity, that is, expressive aspects of identity such as opinions, judgements, desires, ideologies, emotions, emotional dispositions, etc., *and* only if expressive meaning is defined pragmatically/functionally rather than semantically would there be overlap.

[2] While I am concerned with scripted character identities as construed in fictional television, and only claim here that expressive character identity is crucial in this context, it may be relevant for other scripted identities (as suggested by Taavitsainen's 1999 and Martin's 2008b research), and perhaps we could even add 'expressive identity' to the different kinds of identity mentioned in identity research (Crystal 1997, Zimmerman 1998, Tracy 2002, Fairclough 2003: 160–1, Machin & van Leeuwen 2007: 49–50). Several researchers have indeed tied the use of expressive language features to the construal of identity. Without going into detail, modality and evaluative language in particular have been linked to the analysis of persona, identity and style in linguistics (e.g. Fairclough 2003, Martin 2008b). DeFina et al. (2006: 7) also note that identity involves, *inter alia*, the construction of evaluative and epistemic stance and relationships to ideology, and Tracy (2002: 173) states that features of involvement can work as discursive practices implying personal and relational identities. Eckert (2008) makes a distinction between social types which includes stances such as 'formal', 'polite', 'careful', 'annoyed'. Martin and White (2005) talk about 'syndromes of evaluation which characterise an individual' (Martin & White 2005: 203). Finally, Bamberg (2009) argues for considering emotions in the management of situated identity activity, suggesting that emotion displays are employed in the service of identity construction, become styles and part of selves. It is thus probable that the notion of expressive identity can also be fruitfully applied to analysing the construal and negotiation of individual and social identities of 'real' people.

[3] Camera angle, shot size, editing, lighting and sound (multimodality in the product: authorial cues in Culpeper's 2001 terms) are also associated with expressive meanings of various kinds (Turner 1994, Carroll 1996, Iedema 2001, Fulton 2005b: 122, Lury 2005: 16, 39, Lorenzo-Dus 2009), although these expressive meanings do not always relate clearly to expressive character identity but may also be targeted at viewers, for instance trying to make them empathize with characters. My analyses are interested in character cues (dialogue and performance by actors), rather than authorial cues so no more will be said about these aspects.

[4] We may also include certain strategies of politeness, relational work, face-work (Spencer-Oatey 2007), image-work (Behn 2007, 2009), and strategies for bonding, solidarity and affiliation (Stivers 2006, Martin 2008b, Knight 2010, Bednarek 2010). Behavioural differences which can be described in terms of these frameworks (e.g. face) clearly contribute to construing characters on television (see Chapter 7, and Culpeper 2001: 235–62).

[5] The challenge here is that the 'emotionale Wende' (Schwarz-Friesel 2007: 15) – the affective turn – in the social and cognitive sciences has resulted in emotion research being a very vibrant, huge interdisciplinary field with publications in disciplines as varied as philosophy, psychology, neuroscience, anthropology, sociology, communication studies, linguistics, media studies, literary theory, computer science, conversation analysis, discursive psychology etc. Within linguistics, too, many sub-disciplines are interested in relevant issues, for example, within cross-cultural/linguistic research, translation studies, anthropological linguistics, second language acquisition/teaching, sociolinguistics, conversation analysis, pragmatics, and cognitive linguistics to name but a few. What is lacking is an attempt to systematize the findings from these disciplines into a unified framework. Relatively recent overviews of research on evaluation are given in Thompson & Hunston (2000), Bednarek (2006a), and of research on emotion in Schwarz-Friesel (2007), Bednarek (2008a), Wilce (2009). Wiebe et al. (2005) mention research in literary theory, artificial intelligence (AI), formal linguistics, natural language processing (NLP) and computer science. Computational research generally focuses on automatic sentiment classification (Wiebe et al. 2005) or on emotional/expressive behaviour for the purposes of creating embodied conversational agents (www.tsi.enst.fr/~pelachau/, last accessed 28 July 2009). Corpus linguistic research also tries to identify evaluative meaning automatically, while noting the limits of this methodology (Hunston 2004, Bednarek 2006a: 8, Römer 2008). Research in conversation analysis and discursive psychology is generally interested in the interactional role of assessments, evaluative practices and stance (e.g. Pomerantz 1984, Wiggins & Potter 2003, Stivers 2006, Maynard 2003, cited in Schegloff 2007). More recent research in linguistics includes Tracy (2002), Kärkkäinen (2003), Fairclough (2003: chapter 10), Biber (2006), Englebretson (2007) on stance/stancetaking; Mushin (2001) on evidentiality; (Edwards 2007) on subjectivity; Thomson and White (2008) on appraisal, and Wilce (2009) on emotion. A bibliography of research on evaluative meaning can be downloaded from www.MonikaBednarek.com/10.html.

[6] Expressive resources have different semiotic status; those that carry emotional or evaluative meaning can be indexical (interjections), symbolic (e.g. emotion lexicon) or symbolic-indexical (words with pos/neg connotations) (Konstantinidou 1997: 94–8). Expressive behaviour can be performed in the *mode pur* or the *mode vécu*: Hübler, following Bally (1965), talks about the *mode vécu*, as 'a global, holistic mode involving the whole person with all her/his senses and feelings' (Hübler 1998: 5), and the *mode pur* as 'a particularistic, isolating, analytic mode' (Hübler 1998: 5). Examples of the former are interjections (*damn it*) and of the latter descriptions of emotional reactions (*I am getting mad*). Related to distinctions in semiotic status and in mode is the distinction that is made in most emotion research between emotion talk and emotional talk (see Bednarek 2008a: 11 for an overview of relevant research) where 'emotion talk' refers to expressions that denote affect/emotion, and 'emotional talk' refers to verbal and non-verbal features that conventionally signal or imply affect/emotion, including the use of evaluative language (Bednarek 2008a: 11; Bednarek

2009b). (In this approach 'emotion' is used in a broad sense to include certain kinds of evaluative meaning.)

7 It is here that we can include resources that modify (boost or attenuate) the illocutionary force of speech acts (Holmes 1984), evaluations of evidentiality and reliability as well as modulation (Bednarek 2006a), intensity markers (Labov 1984), and the appraisal system of graduation (Martin & White 2005).

8 These two methodologies represent two of the three methodological 'prongs' proposed by Bednarek (2008b, 2009a). A large-scale corpus study (Chapters 6 and 8) allows us to make quantitative and qualitative comments about a number of selected expressive resources in a large amount of data; a manual study of one scene (Chapter 7) enables an in-depth analysis of a large number of selected expressive resources in a small amount of data. The third proposed prong concerns the analysis of a corpus which is small enough to be annotated for semantic-pragmatic and multimodal features but large enough to allow some generalization. Because of the time-consuming nature of annotation, this kind of analysis was not undertaken for this book. At present only some expressive features can be identified automatically, although '[t]here has been a recent swell of interest in the automatic identification, and extraction of opinions, emotions, and sentiments in text' (Wiebe et al. 2005: 165) in computer science. This means that much of this annotation would need to be done manually or semi-automatically at present. Ideally, a team of researchers would annotate a large corpus for multimodal expressive features, apply statistical tests to find significant clusters of expressive features, and check if these clusters can be interpreted as expressive identities or identity types. It would be useful at this stage to take into account further research in psychology and narratology on personality and character types. Concerning expressive identity, a three-pronged quantitative–qualitative approach would then allow us to see how it is discursively produced and performed in localized and situated contexts (the 'doing' of identity at particular points in time), how it is dynamically performed across contexts, and how it is repeatedly performed, creating a perceived coherence and stability of identity (as sedimented through repeated behaviour).

9 The relation between individual instances and the creation of a relatively stable identity can be theorized with respect to notions such as instantiation (Halliday & Matthiessen 2004: 26), individuation (Martin 2007) or structuration (Giddens 1984). In these related views an instance simultaneously reflects, is influenced by and construes and potentially transforms the underlying system – this system can be language (Halliday & Matthiessen 2004), the reservoir of cultural meaning (Martin 2007), social structure (Giddens 1984) or expressive identity. Crucially, this means that expressive identity is both seen as temporary, localized, discursive (instance) and as more stable (system). The way we can access both is through looking at discursive behaviour (the use of expressive resources).

10 Assuming a binomial distribution, differences between all characters are statistically significant (95% confidence) apart from the difference between Lorelai and Sookie. Statistical calculations were done for me by Abigail Brown (University of Technology, Sydney).

[11] Bednarek (2008b) found that in *Gilmore Girls* the interjection *oh my god/god* is perhaps more female, whereas *geez, damn* and *damn it* (perhaps also *for X's sake/ my god*) are more male. This partially reflected Precht's (2006) findings that *damn* is significantly higher in men and *god* significantly higher in women in American conversation (Precht 2006: 25). That strong expletives are associated with male characters in television is also supported by an analysis of *Lost* (ABC, 2004–) transcripts using the transcript database search available at www.losthatch.com/transcripts.aspx (last accessed 5 June 2009). Looking at 86 episodes, this search found that the word form *damn* is uttered 125 times by male characters and only 9 times by female characters, and the word form *son of a bitch* is uttered 32 times by male and only twice by female characters (see below for further detail on which male characters utter these word forms). However, if we compared individual characters with each other, rather than genders, it is theoretically possible that a particular female character has more occurrences of expletives (and other features) than a particular male character. Or that a particular male and female character (e.g. Luke and Lorelai) share more than a particular female and female character (e.g. Lorelai and Emily), as other contextual and situational factors such as ethnicity, age, status/power are entwined with gender, and as there may be gender-internal variation. Sophisticated statistical tests may need to be applied to entangle these various factors. Further, there is an inherent danger in committing 'sociological essentialism' (Coupland 2007: 76) by analysing gender in such a quantitative way. Therefore, the focus of this chapter is not solely on factors such as class, gender, age, though reference will be made to them (in particular, to gender), but rather on expressive character identity.

Chapter 7

The Multimodal Performance

This chapter deals with the multimodal performance of expressive identities. Whereas Chapter 6 only looked at the construal of expressive identity through language, this chapter considers both verbal and non-verbal behaviour that functions to construe diverging expressive identities. In a further case study of *Gilmore Girls* (Warner Brothers, 2000–2007), a 'break-up' scene – classified as particularly emotional – is analysed in detail to show how different expressive character identities are construed in a situated context. Where Chapter 6 was more concerned with repeated performances across texts, this chapter looks at the multimodal performance in one particular instance allowing us insights into 'temporary' rather than 'stable' aspects of expressive identity.

1 Analysing Expressive Character Identity in Depth

In contrast to Chapter 6, where corpus linguistic methodology was employed and the focus was on emotive interjections, this chapter investigates verbal and nonverbal behaviour of characters in one scene, drawing on various studies of nonverbal behaviour (e.g. Ekman & Friesen 1975, Morris 1977, Baldry & Thibault 2006). Looking at multimodal performance allows us to explore another aspect of expressive identity – how it is co-construed across different modes and how it is construed in character interaction. In line with the focus on expressivity, the chapter sets out to examine the behaviour of two characters in a particular 'emotional' scene in *Gilmore Girls*. While it is difficult to outline exact criteria as to how an 'emotional' scene can be defined, we can use culturally accepted views as to what kinds of events are likely to impact on us emotionally: loss, death, illness, conflict, break-up. In this chapter, we will look at a scene that involves the break-up of a romantic relationship between two characters (see Bednarek 2008b for analysis of a 'conflict' scene).

The in-depth analysis will show how expressive character identities are construed intersubjectively in character interaction in localized contexts and enables us to take into account multimodal resources. However, it will only allow us to make comments as to the temporary, one-off construal of expressive identities – in contrast to the corpus study of Chapter 6 where analyses of repeated patterns were possible, but where character interaction and multimodality were left aside.

Crucially, the discourse analytical perspective of this chapter allows for an investigation of expressive identity that takes more adequately into account that '[s]peaking . . . is ultimately an interactive phenomenon, grounded in dialogically organized discursive exchanges' (Gumperz & Cook-Gumperz 2007: 498). The inclusion of multimodal resources also takes into consideration that expressive identity can be construed through modes other than language, and that, theoretically, there may be instances where verbal behaviour does not explicitly construe expressive identity but nonverbal behaviour does. With respect to emotionality, this has been emphasized, inter alia, by Goodwin and Goodwin, who argue for an '**embodied performance** of affect' (Goodwin & Goodwin 2000: 26, bold face in original), and by Wilce (2009), who underlines that 'it is moving, mindful bodies – vocalizing words with a particular quality, gesturing, etc. – that perform emotion' (Wilce 2009: 49). While linguistic cues exist that help us to identify the emotional content of utterances even without access to audio- or audio-visual files (Quaglio 2009: 88), its full complexity only becomes apparent when analysing it multimodally.

2 Expressive Identities in a Break-Up Scene

2.1 'Maybe we need to take a little time away from each other' – introduction to the scene

The *Gilmore Girls* scene (from season 1, episode 11) that will be analysed is about the break-up between one of the main characters (Lorelai – see Chapter 5) and Rory's school teacher, Max Medina, and ends the first romantic relationship in the series. Before looking at the scene in detail, here is a short description of the episode in terms of relevant events before the scene.

> As Lorelai and Max grow closer, Rory begins to get attached to the idea of Max in their lives, which worries Lorelai. Sookie and Lorelai have a frank discussion about relationships. Lorelai tries to ease out of her relationship with Max during Parent's Day at Chilton, but ends up passionately kissing him in his classroom just as Paris walks by. Stung by the details in the newspapers about her parents' messy divorce, Paris tells everyone in the lunchroom about Max and Lorelai to deflect gossip away from her and towards Rory. Rory dashes out to speak to her mother. She asks Lorelai if it is true. Lorelai is horrified to find out that her liaison with Max is now common knowledge. She apologizes to Rory but the damage is done. A few days later, Lorelai meets Max at a coffee shop.
> (1.11, *Paris is Burning:* edited extracts fromwww.tv.com/Gilmore+Girls/Paris+is+Burning/episode/5081/recap.html; last accessed 19 June 2009)

The scene that will be analysed is the meeting between Lorelai and Max at the coffee shop that is referred to at the end of this summary. This scene was chosen because it occurs in the first season of the series; it is the first break-up scene, and as a scene that occurs early on in a television series it is important in establishing characters (Bubel 2006: 63); and 'tagging' them with verbal and nonverbal behaviour that will define them (Pearson 2007: 42).

A transcript of the scene, including detailed information on the characters' nonverbal behaviour, is provided in Table A.11 in Appendix 8. I will also make considerable use of multimodal transcription (Norris 2002), that is, employing images (illustrations of screenshots) and text,[1] when talking about individual instances of verbal and nonverbal behaviour. For ease of reading, a simplified transcript showing shots and verbal behaviour only is provided in Table 7.1 (transcription conventions are described in Appendix 8). Where dialogue spans two rows, this means that there is a change in camera shots that happens mid-turn, that is, while one of the characters is talking.

(1)

Table 7.1 Transcript of break-up scene, 1.11, *Paris is burning*; length: 3 minutes, 28 seconds

Long shot with Max in foreground (shot 1a), camera movement from right to left, following barista's action and then resting on Max and Lorelai 	*Coffee shop in Hartford, Max sitting at the counter* *We see barista pouring coffee into mug and handing it to Max sitting at the counter. Lorelai can be seen in the background entering the coffee shop and walking towards Max; other customers are visible in the background* M Thanks (to barista) (Pause: 7 seconds – Lorelai walking in) L Hey Mister wanna buy a really nice copy of Proust. M How ya doing? L <Hmm> <well> you know. You? M Ah hmm you know it also. L Yeah. (Pause: 4 seconds)
Medium shot with focus on Lorelai (shot 2a) 	L So that parent's day is fun. M A:h it was a big hit this year (.) L Look (.) the other day, (.) we were going skating and Rory said "why don't we invite Max to come along with us" and that was a little wei:rd for me. M Me

(Continued)

Table 7.1 (Cont'd)

Medium shot with focus on Max (shot 2b) 		too, I don't skate. (.)
Shot 2a (L)	L	She's never really referred to anyone I've dated by their first name before. I-I always kept her out of that part of my life, so it was like "=the=mustache guy"= "the=earring=guy" the: (.) "peg leg guy".
	M	Oh,
Shot 2b (M)		so you have a thing for pirates (.)
Shot 2a (L)	L	She never called anyone by their na:me before. (.) She likes you. (.) She likes us, and so my mind instantly went to "oh my god =what=if=we=break=up=she'll=be=crushed", and then my next thought was "oh my go:d what if we break up I'll be crushed".
Shot 2b (M)		And then as you know all hell broke loose.
	M	I understand.
Shot 2a (L)	L	I freaked out. I'm so sorry. I-I never meant to treat you like that. I'm-I'm not very good at this. (.) Ask Skippy.
	M	Skippy?
	L	I'm so so sorry.
Shot 2b (M)	M	I was called into headmaster Charleston's office today.
Shot 2a (L)	L	Let=me=guess, he=put=his=arm=around=you=and=said"=I=don't=understand=why=you=crazy=kids=can't=work=this=out".
Shot 2b (M)	M	He said I was jeopardizing my career and my future at Chilton,

Shot 2a (L)	L	Oh ↓
	M	And at first I was incensed, outraged and "how da:re he" (.)
Shot 2b (M)		and then I realized that he was right. What happened the other day was completely <unprofessional>. I never in my life would have considered pulling off something like this. (.) He should've fired me.
Shot 2a (L)	L	But he didn't
Shot 2b (M)	M	Not yet, but the word probation was tossed around quite a bit though.
Shot 2a (L)	L	I'm sorry.
Shot 2b (M)	M	I was the one who started the kiss.
Shot 2a (L)	L	And I'm the one who knocked it up to NC- Seventee:n
Shot 2b (M)	M	I-I honestly did not think that this was gonna be so complicated.
	L	I know.
	M	I mean you told me it would be. I didn't listen. I didn't want to.
Medium to medium close-up shot with focus on Lorelai (shot 3a) 	L	It's not your fault. If I hadn't acted like a two year old and tried to run away and pretend that you weren't what you are to me then we wouldn't have fought, we wouldn't have kissed, I wouldn't have humiliated my daughter, and the (.) whole thing would've been fine.
Medium to medium close-up shot with focus on Max (shot 3b) 		(Pause: 4 sec)
	M	I-I do not know what to do here.

(Continued)

Table 7.1 (Cont'd)

Medium close-up shot on Lorelai (shot 4a) 		I-(pause: 2 sec) I've never been in a relationship like this before, I-
Shot 3b (M)		I'm not thinking straight.
Shot 4a (L)	L	I know. Me either.
Shot 3b (M)	M	That was a great kiss.
Shot 4a (L)	L	Beyond great (Pause: 3 sec)
Shot 3b (M)	M	Maybe we need to take a little time away from each other.
Shot 4a (L)		(Pause: 5 sec)
	L	Okay,
Shot 2b (M)	M	You know just to figure out how to do this so it's not so hard.
Shot 2a (L)	L	Su:re, that makes sense.
Shot 2b (M)	M	I just-I don't have any other answers right now.
Shot 2a (L)	L	No. You're right. You're-you're absolutely right.
Shot 2b (M)	(Pause: 3 sec)	
Shot 4a (L)		<I really really like you Max Medina.>
Shot 3b (M)	M	(.) <I really really like you Lorelai Gilmore.>
Shot 4a (L)	L	Well, as long as we have that straightened out.
		(Pause: 3 sec)
Shot 3b (M)	M	Goodbye Lorelai.
Shot 4a (L)		(Pause: 4 sec)
	L	°°Bye°°

Long shot with Lorelai in foreground (shot 1b) 	L (non-verbal behavior only)

As the transcript shows, Lorelai and Max break up in this scene;[2] however, we re-encounter Max in episode 1.17 where the characters recommence seeing each other. In 1.21 Max proposes to Lorelai, and they break it off again in season 2.

2.2 Analysis of mise-en-scène

With respect to analysing multimodality (Chapter 2: Section 3.2) and to provide necessary background information on this scene, let us start with a general description of the mise-en-scène (setting, props, costumes, codes of dress, movement, spatial relations, placement of objects etc,) and sound. The setting where this scene takes place is in a modern American coffee shop/café, mainly at the counter where Max and later Lorelai are sitting when this exchange happens. Apart from the beginning when we have a short exchange between Max and the barista, there are only two participants talking. The dialogue is therefore classifiable as a 'duologue' –

> the most fundamental structure of screen speech, because they [duologues] are a dramatic necessity. Two characters in conversation provide . . . 'action,' . . . suspense, . . . give-and-take . . ., because new information or emotional shadings can be exchanged, questioned, reacted to. (Kozloff 2000: 72)

During the duration of the scene we can see various elements in the background associated with the setting, for example, barista and customers, counter, espresso/coffee maker, chalk boards with 'cappuccino' written on them, tables and chairs, coffee accessories, silver jugs etc. As a coffee shop, this setting is a public place yet associated with a crucial aspect of Lorelai's expressive identity – her extreme liking of coffee (see Chapter 5). Concerning the two protagonists, Lorelai and Max are 'Caucasian', in their early to mid-thirties; both have dark hair, and are, arguably, very attractive (photos of Scott Cohen, the actor who plays Max Medina, can be accessed at www.imdb.com/name/nm0169753/

mediaindex, last accessed 1 April 2009 and photos of Lauren Graham, who plays Lorelai Gilmore, can be accessed at www.imdb.com/name/nm0334179/mediaindex, last accessed 1 April 2009). Lorelai is wearing smart grey trousers, a light-blue turtleneck sweater underneath a tank top/vest, and a brownish trench coat as well as black leather gloves (when entering); she is also carrying a brown leather bag and wearing understated make-up (red lipstick and some light eye shadow). She looks 'professional' at some level, and seems to be in a job where appearance is important (which is indeed the case). Max in contrast, is wearing a shirt and tie (which we can barely see) underneath what is possibly a brown woollen jumper or tank top/vest and a brown corduroy jacket on top. His appearance signifies 'teacher'. Their clothes thus tell viewers that they are both meeting in this place on their way from/to work or in a lunch break. Some of the actions that are performed in this scene are: The barista pours some coffee and hands it to a customer who is sitting at the counter and who we then recognize as Max. Lorelai enters the coffee shop, walks towards Max who is drinking coffee, and greets him, thus being transformed from an aspect of the 'ground' to a 'dominant figure' (see Baldry & Thibault 2006: 189 for these terms). He sets his coffee cup down and greets her. She puts down her bag on the seat next to her and sits down next to him (to his right, but viewers see Max on the right hand side and Lorelai on the left-hand side in the shot). For most of the scene Max is sitting with both of his elbows on the counter, his right hand or both hands holding on to the coffee mug – unless he is gesturing with his arms and hands (which he does not do much – see Section 2.3.4). Lorelai is at first sitting behind the counter with her arms by her side (so we can't see her hands unless she is gesturing) and still wearing her leather gloves, which she takes off after talking to Max for a while, and sometimes rests her elbows and/or hands on the counter, occasionally on top of the leather gloves or with her finger tips touching each other. Neither of them gets up during the exchange. After the duologue ends, Max gets up and walks out of the coffee shop, looking back at Lorelai who remains sitting at the counter by herself.

With respect to sound, we have diegetic on-screen dialogue between Lorelai and Max, very low volume on-screen background noise (murmuring etc. of customers in coffee shop), whose source is obvious and which contributes to creating ambience and atmosphere, and off-screen non-diegetic soundtrack music at the beginning of the scene. The soundtrack music is by female singer-songwriter Sam Phillips, a music generally 'dominated by an acoustic guitar and a sung refrain, the melody composed of "la-la-la"s' (Woods 2008: 128), although here the melody is actually made up of 'ah-ah-ah's. It starts at the end of the previous scene, which features two other characters (Jackson and Sookie) talking to each other and continues to the beginning of this scene, starting to fade out when Lorelai starts talking and being inaudible by the end of her first sentence (. . . *Proust*). It thus seems to have a clear textual function, providing a link between two scenes featuring different characters. At the same time, it functions as 'contextual ground' (Baldry & Thibault 2006: 51) to the scene, providing mood and ambience. However, there is no further soundtrack music after the first sentence, and although ambient sounds feature in the background, the 'acoustic focus' (Baldry & Thibault 2006: 52) is clearly on the voices of Lorelai and Max.

2.3 Performing expressive identities multimodally

2.3.1 Introductory remarks

So far I have described only some aspects of the mise-en-scène in terms of multimodality. For reasons of scope, more detailed multimodal analyses in this chapter will be restricted to the investigation of expressive identity, and, therefore, multimodality in the characters rather than the product (see Chapter 2: Section 3.2 for this distinction).[3] That is, not much will be said about technical codes such as camera angle, lens type, focus, lighting etc. This is not to downplay the importance of multimodality in the product in the performance of expressive identity, rather, it is a restriction necessitated by the scope of this chapter. Shots are shown in Table 7.1 above.

For practical reasons, I focus on selected aspects of verbal behaviour (evaluative and emotional language, speech act sequences) and nonverbal behaviour (hand/arm gestures; head movements/gaze; facial affect) and discuss these separately. Further expressive resources (e.g. stuttering/repetition, interruption, pauses, sighs) will be mentioned but not discussed separately, while it was not possible to analyse others at all (e.g. pitch range, voice quality; see Selting 1994, Hancil 2009 on prosody in emphatic/affective speech). However, all resources were interpreted in the complex multimodal ensemble; that is, transcription and functional interpretation was done in relation to watching the scene on DVD. This is important because kinesic units (e.g. smiling) have no stable meaning; rather, we have to look at their co-patterning with other modes to interpret them (Baldry & Thibault 2006: 178). In the following, I will show how these various aspects contribute to construing two diverging expressive identities:

- Max: less emotional, more serious, in control, following a hard decision through.
- Lorelai: more emotional, optimistic, harmonious/supportive, upset (in a controlled way).

2.3.2 Verbal behaviour: evaluative and emotional language

If we look first at those elements of language that express evaluation or emotional reactions, we can see which characters are more strongly associated with this kind of explicit expressivity. We can classify these according to the

Table 7.2 Evaluative parameters: Lorelai vs. Max

Evaluative parameter	Lorelai	Max
EMOTIVITY (POS/NEG)	12	8
EXPECTED: KNOWN	4	1
+/− POWER	7	8
AFFECT	14	5
Other	–	1
Total	**38**	**23**

evaluative parameters introduced in Chapter 3 and already used in Chapters 3 and 5, namely AFFECT, EMOTIVITY, EXPECTEDNESS, IMPORTANCE, and POWER. As Table 7.2 shows, Lorelai uses more evaluative and emotional language overall than Max.[4]

The overall affect is that there is a stronger association of Lorelai with such language than of Max.[5] However, it must be pointed out that Table 7.2 includes all uses of evaluative and emotional language, whether or not Lorelai and Max are the Emoters and Evaluators or not. In other words, all instances were counted, whether or not they were attributed to another person (***He*** [Charleston] ***said*** *that I was jeopardizing my career and future at Chilton* [EMOTIVITY: NEG]; ***He*** [Charleston] *put his arm around you and* ***said*** *'I don't understand why* [minus POWER] *you crazy kids* [EMOTIVITY: NEG] *can't work this out* [minus POWER]?'). It is thus more useful to focus the discussion on instances of where the Emoter and the Evaluator is the Self (Lorelai/Max respectively). Table A.12 in Appendix 9 shows all instances for Lorelai and Max, including Triggers of AFFECT and Targets of other evaluations. There are a few categories in Table A.12 where differences in frequency appear particularly pronounced and interesting. For instance, Lorelai has more instances of AFFECT overall than Max (10 vs. 4), more AFFECT outbursts (3 vs. 0), more conventionalized AFFECT (3 vs. 0), and more different types of AFFECT (6 vs. 3), which makes her a lot more emotionally involved and varied than Max in this scene. Incidentally, Lorelai's speech also features more repetition (*I'm so so sorry*; *I really really like you*), which further points to great emotional involvement. Affect outbursts such as *oh* (here pronounced with a tone that indicates negative surprise) can occur as reactions to events (here: Max's statement), and are 'one systematic practice for making a precisely placed and appropriate display of emotion with minimal lexical resources.' (Goodwin & Goodwin 2000: 16; when used as discourse marker *oh* was not counted as expressive). Further, Lorelai has more instances of POSITIVE EMOTIVITY (6 vs. 3) and more instances of EXPECTED: KNOWN (4 vs. 1) than Max, whereas Max has more instances of minus POWER than Lorelai. The former contributes to construing Lorelai very much as other-oriented, understanding and harmonious, with Lorelai agreeing with Max, telling him that he is right, that she knows what he is saying, that what he is saying makes sense etc (see Section 2.4.4). The latter has to do with Max using 'powerlessness' as justification of the break-up (see Section 2.4.4). A picture thus emerges where the expressive identities that are temporally and linguistically construed in this scene diverge in terms of a scale of emotionality, with Lorelai being more emotionally involved than Max. Additionally, Lorelai is also optimistic, harmonious/supportive whereas Max feels 'powerless' regarding their relationship and its (emotional) impact on him, contributing to his less emotional expressive identity. This will be discussed in more detail in Section 2.4. But let us first consider the contribution of nonverbal behaviour.

2.3.3 Nonverbal behaviour and acting

Looking at nonverbal behaviour as expressive resource in general Ekman and Friesen (1975) argue that '[e]motions are shown primarily in the face, not in the body. The body instead shows how people are *coping* with emotion. . . . Body movement reveals, of course, not just how someone copes with emotion, but also what a person's attitudes, interpersonal orientations, etc., might be' (Ekman & Friesen 1975: 7).[6] Both the face and the body can thus be used by actors to construe different aspects of expressive identity. Actors can perform a variety of nonverbal expressive resources ranging from facial affect (e.g. smile) to gaze behaviour (e.g. looking downwards) to various kinds of gesturing. For instance, 'emblems' (Ekman 1997) such as the 'OK' or 'thumbs-up' sign express an individual's evaluation of a target, whereas 'tie-signs' (Morris 1977: 86) such as walking arm in arm express intersubjective emotional relationships. Movement can indicate a performer's evaluation of a situation, an affective disposition towards a performed action or a more general emotional state of mind (Baldry & Thibault 2006: 207). With respect to the performance of nonverbal expressive resources, actors need to be skilful to avoid over- or under-acting, and how nonverbal resources are performed or 'controlled' by them also depends on acting techniques, styles of acting, training and television forms and genres (Chapter 2: Section 2).[7] However, for the point of the analyses below it is irrelevant in how far the investigated performance features are 'controlled' by the actors or arise automatically as a 'by-product' of the acting, and no hypotheses will be made as to this. As said above, I am not concerned with notions such as the sincerity, veracity, intentionality, spontaneity of expressivity, etc. in this book.

There are a variety of different functions of such expressive behaviour. As these are not so much our concern here because the focus is on the function to construe character, some general remarks will suffice. What becomes apparent in looking at the break-up scene is that actors' expressive behaviour fulfils narrative functions and manages audience expectations. For instance, Max's behaviour at the very beginning of the scene (observing his hand and sighing) foreshadows, if you will, what is to follow in the scene. His gaze

Table 7.3 Extract from transcript

	Other modes	Language
M	*Max is predominantly looking down in front of him, shaking head slightly as speaking*	I-(pause: 2 sec) I've never been in a relationship like this before, I- I'm not thinking straight.
L	. . .	I know. Me either.
M	*Max breathes out 'puh', shaking head very slightly [sort of 'unbelievably great'] predominantly looking down in front of him*	That was a great kiss.
L	. . .	Beyond great (Pause: 3 sec)
M	*Max turns to look Lorelai in the eye, has lowered eyebrows (crease)*	Maybe we need to take a little time away from each other.

behaviour later on in the scene (looking down) also creates credibility. This becomes apparent when considering an extract from the transcript (Table 7.3 above), which includes a description of Max's nonverbal behaviour. If we just look at the language we have some ambiguity at first – the emotional impact of being in the relationship in terms of 'irrationality' and 'powerlessness' (*I'm not thinking straight*) can be evaluated both as positive or as negative, as evidenced by love songs such as Alanis Morissette's *Head over Feet* with co-textually positively evaluated lines like *I've never wanted something rational.* This ambiguous statement is then followed by a positive evaluation (*That was a great kiss)* before the break-up statement. In terms of language, then, the break-up statement comes as a surprise to both Lorelai and the audience as it follows an ambiguous (but potentially positive) statement and an explicit positive evaluation, but it is made believable because Max's gaze behaviour sets up some negativity throughout. And, therefore, if one watched the scene without sound, one would still be able to tell to some extent what is happening.

Let us briefly look at another example (Image 7.1 on page 155). While demonstrating Max's downwards gaze, these images simultaneously show Lorelai's rather negative emotional reaction (facial affect). This tells us that Max's statement has the potential to be evaluated negatively, and that further negative statements may come – specifically, that this may already be the beginning of a breaking-up sequence (see Section 2.4.4 below).

At this stage it needs to be emphasized again that although I describe both verbal and other behaviour separately, it is typically performed and interpreted as a cluster (simultaneously across modes), sequentially (temporally), and in interaction between characters (e.g. as a reaction to what another character said). An example of an 'angry' emotion cluster is described by Ekman as follows: 'a person looking directly at you, with her head thrust slightly forward, brows lowered and pulled together, eyes glaring, and whose

IMAGE 7.1 'I do not know what to do here'

lips are tightly pressed' (Ekman 1997: 333). Selting (1994) notes the *clustering* of prosodic (e.g. marked pitch), syntactic (e.g. ellipsis) and lexicosemantic (e.g. intensifiers, evaluative lexis) features in emphatic speech style and Weatherall and Stubbe's (2009) analyses of telephone complaint calls also show the clustering of resources (explicit reference to emotional states; emotive formulations and extreme case formulations; prosody and paralanguage) in displays of affectivity. As we will see below, paralanguage, head movement and gaze cluster in character's behaviour. Facial affect and gestures can also express different meanings simultaneously and meaningfully. For example, in Image 7.2 we see part of Lorelai's reaction to Max's break-up statement.

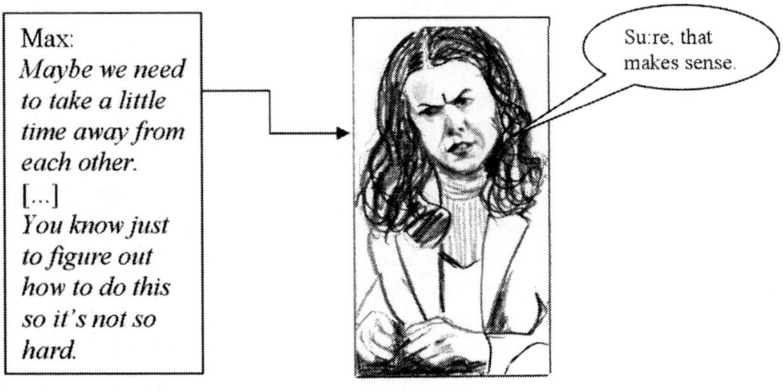

IMAGE 7.2 'Sure, that makes sense'

Max: 'Maybe we need to take a little time away from each other.'
a.
b.
c.
d.
Lorelai: 'Okay'
e.
f.

Images 7.3 a–f Lorelai reacting to break-up statement

In her language, Lorelai expresses comprehensibility and agreement (*Sure, that makes sense*), ostensibly being harmonious and supportive. However, we can see in her negative facial affect and her fidgety fingers/restless hands that she is upset, even though she is not crying or openly expressing negative emotion through language. Ekman and Friesen point out that where affect in words and affect in the face differ, it is usually the facial expression that matters more (Ekman & Friesen 1975: 137), indicating quite clearly to the viewer that the break-up in fact does *not* make sense to Lorelai. We can interpret this contradiction as showing that Lorelai is upset but tries to control her emotions to a certain extent in front of Max (see Section 2.4.4 for further discussion).

To demonstrate the importance of sequentiality and interaction, Images 7.3 a–f above show Lorelai's immediate reaction to the break-up statement. We can see here how facial affect and head movement combine sequentially and dynamically to perform an emotional reaction, how this is plainly a reaction to what another character said and how camera shots manage whose face we get to see as viewers. All the above points need to be borne in mind regarding the descriptions of expressive behaviour below, which are somewhat static, fragmented and simplified in comparison to what is actually happening on screen. For instance, images used in the chapter only show us one phase (McNeill 2005: 31–3) of what may be a complex gesture.

2.3.4 Hand/arm gestures

Considering first gesturing by the characters with hands and arms, both characters are clearly restricted, as they are sitting behind a counter (see mise-en-scène description above). Lorelai is at first sitting with her arms beside her and behind the counter, and it is only later in the scene that we can see any arm and hand movements. Max's arms and hands on the other hand are in view throughout. If we look at Max's and Lorelai's gestures contrastively in terms of frequency and type, differences become apparent. Max is not gesturing much overall. Rather, he is clutching his coffee mug, with his hands mostly resting on the mug, and occasionally his thumb stroking the top of the mug or fingers tapping on it. There are only very few exceptions where Max freely gestures with his hands/arms (see Appendix 8 for where they occur). The movements are:

- scratching his neck;
- moving his hand to his forehead;
- putting both hands upwards;
- putting a hand above his eyes to his furrowed forehead, then scratching nose with the side of his hand.

Image 7.4 illustrates the 'hand to forehead' movement. Together with facial expression (here: furrowed forehead) such movements may either be read as

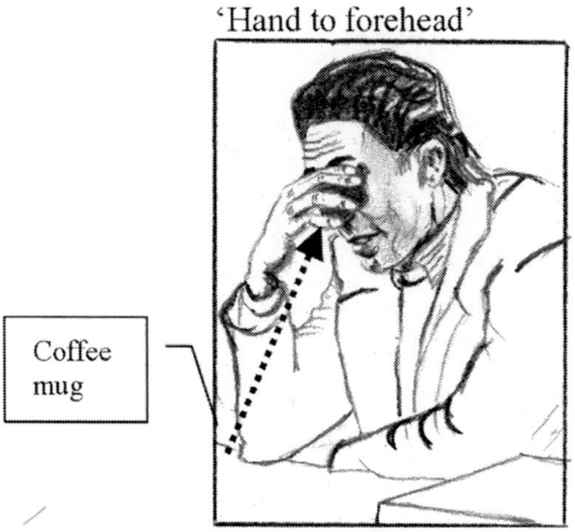

Image 7.4 Max's 'head to forehead' movement

straightforward indications of negative affect, or as 'displacement' activities – 'small, seemingly irrelevant movements made during moments of inner conflict of frustration' (Morris 1977: 179).

In any case, Max's hand/arm gestures are rare, and mostly appear to indicate negative affect. In contrast, Lorelai gestures more freely more frequently, and her gesturing is more varied. Lorelai's main movements in this scene are:

- touching Max affectionately on the back (at greeting; both salutation display and tie-sign in Morris's 1977 terms);
- lifting both arms and letting them fall on her knees;
- gesturing with hands to accompany speech (various types: raising hands, circular movements, waving movement, opening hands up, pointing hands upward, forming square, forming triangle, moving up-and-down, pointing gesture, specifying gesture, 'stop' gesture);
- pushing hair behind ear (possibly a displacement gesture);
- 'wringing' hands and 'fidgety' fingers.

Images 7.5 a–e illustrate some of these movements schematically. What we can see is that Lorelai is on the one hand more 'lively' gesturally than Max (in terms of frequency), and on the other hand more varied (in terms of types), although the 'fidgety fingers', indicating negative affect, are prominent

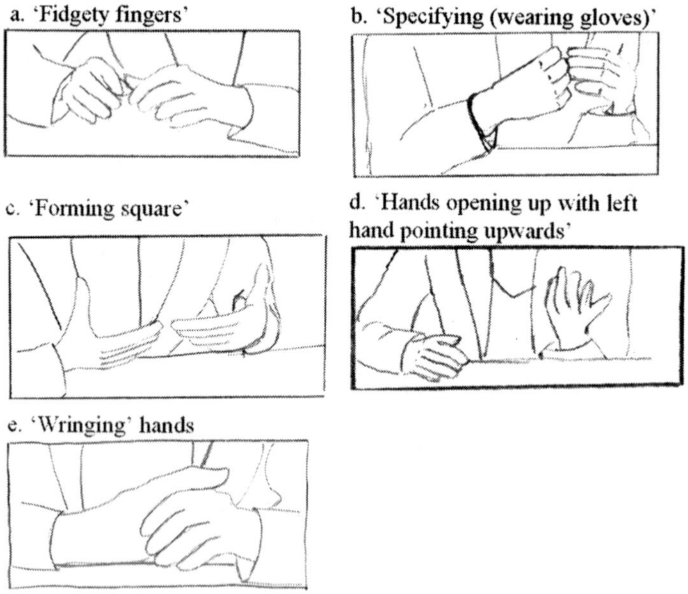

Images 7.5 a–e Selected hand movements by Lorelai

and persistent later in the scene (see transcript for when movements occur). The two characters clearly exhibit different expressive behaviour and construe diverging expressive character identities, although the emotional character of the scene (break-up) has some implications for the prevalence of negative affect in both characters.

2.3.5 Head movements/gaze

Considering head movement/gaze, both characters generally look at each other when talking, with some down/front/sideways movements in-between, for instance to signal turn-taking (Kendon 1967, cited in Coulthard 1985: 66–7). For example, when Max speaks, he may start by looking at Lorelai, then look down and then look at her again at the end of the sentence. This appears similar to what happens in unscripted conversations, and is

> a highly characteristic 'dance' of gaze shifts. The speaker starts his statement with a glance at his companion. Then, as he gains momentum of thought and word, he looks away. As he is coming to the end of his comment, he glances back again to check the impact of what he has said. While he has been doing this, his companion has been watching him, but now, as the listener takes over the talk and becomes the speaker, he, in turn, looks away, glancing back only to check the effect of his words. In this way, the talk and the eyes go back and forth, in a remarkably predictable pattern. (Morris 1977: 75)

Gaze movement, therefore only becomes particularly noteworthy and expressive when characters do not follow this pattern. In fact, as Max is breaking up with Lorelai (starting with *I honestly did not think . . .*), there is a repeated pattern of him looking down or away from her (although he may at times shift the gaze to her at the end of his turn, and does look directly at her when uttering the important break-up statement *Maybe . . .*). This potentially indicates negative affect, with downwards gaze commonly associated with sadness (Ekman & Friesen 1975: 119). Headshakes are another interesting pattern for Max. Shaking one's head can express 'a wide range of NOs, from "I cannot" and "I will not" to "I disagree" and "do not know". It can also signal disapproval or bewilderment' (Morris 1977: 68). Taking into account their accompanying (indicated by double arrow) or preceding (indicated by arrow) verbal co-text, Max's head shakes can potentially be classified as shown in Table 7.4 on page 160, if we interpret them in their multimodal co-text. Note in particular Max's rather negative reaction to Lorelai's expression of positive affect (*I really really like you Max Medina*), indicating that he thinks this is inappropriate or does not make things easier, that her expression of emotion does not offer a real solution to the 'problem' (see Section 2.4.4). By way of comparison, Table 7.5 on page 160 shows Lorelai's head shakes in more detail (bold face signals that the head shake co-occurs relatively clearly with a particular lexical item).

Table 7.4 Max's head shakes

Max's head shakes			
Speaker	**Accompanying or preceding co-text**		**Potential meaning**
Max	*A:h it was a big hit this year*	←→	expressing disbelief? indicating irony?
	That was a great kiss	←→	expressing disbelief
	I-I honestly did not think that this was gonna be so complicated *I-I do not know what to do here* *I'm not thinking straight* *I just - I don't have any other answers right now*	←→	reinforcing negation (expressing bewilderment?)
Lorelai	*<I really really like you Max Medina>*	— followed by head shake →	indicating disapproval

While Max's head shakes are more strongly associated with reinforcement of negation and disbelief (because they accompany his frequent evaluations of the relationship in terms of 'powerlessness') and Lorelai's perhaps more with negative affect, it is unclear if these differences would be strong enough to have an impact on their own – however, they do contribute to the construal of expressive character identities in connection with other modes. In fact, there seems to be a cluster that is quite strongly associated with Max, which involves him shaking his head, sighing, and having a serious expression (lowered brows). This cluster expresses disbelief or negative affect (see Appendix 8 for co-text and position).

Table 7.5 Lorelai's head shakes

Lorelai's head shakes			
Speaker	**Accompanying or preceding co-text**		**Potential meaning**
Lorelai	*… and that was a little* ***wei:rd*** *for me*	←→	Unexpectedness
	… and then my next thought was **"oh my go:d** *what if we break up I'll be crushed".*	←→	Negative affect?
	I'm sorry *You're-you're absolutely right*	←→	Negative affect? Expressing disbelief?
	It's not your fault	←→	Reinforcing negation
Max	*Skippy?*	— followed by head shake →	Irrelevance/'Never mind'/unimportance

There are also no strong differences between Max's and Lorelai's usage of downward/sideways gaze. Like Max's, Lorelai's looking away seems to indicate negative affect, as it occurs when she apologizes, when she takes responsibility, and as a reaction to Max's break-up statement (see Images 7.3 a–f on page 156) both while he is present and after he has left (also pressing her lips together, perhaps a particular type of 'lip biting' which frequently occurs with averted gaze [Bamberg 2009]), showing how upset she is. Like Max, she looks directly at her conversational interlocutor when making an important point (*I really really like you Max Medina*) – this expression of positive affect is further emphasized through the medium close-up shot on her. Thus, while there are no strong differences in terms of frequency and function, there do seem to be some qualitative differences in discursive usage construing the emotional reactions of the characters differently. Again, we also find a strong impact of the negative emotionality of the events discussed and happening in the scene, which results in negative affect for both characters.

2.3.6 Facial affect

In terms of the face as expressive resource we are interested in facial movements that indicate evaluative stance or emotion, whether or not they are emblems (symbolic gestures such as a wink), referential expressions (referring to past/future emotions), emotional role playing actions (enacting another person's emotions) or facial expressions of emotion (involuntary movements) (Ekman 1997).[8] Since we are dealing with television, we are interested in performed facial movements (whether actively controlled or automatically arising from the emotional state the actors deliberately and strategically put themselves in – as indicated above). This resembles but is physically different from the involuntary facial 'expression' of emotion (Ekman 1997 – incidentally, certain involuntary facial expressions are referred to by Ekman as 'micro-expressions', as recently popularized in the television series *Lie to Me*, FOX, 2009–).

Considering Max's facial movements, what is apparent is that he displays a serious face for most of the talk, indicated by lowered eyebrows resulting in vertical wrinkles (a 'crease') between the eyebrows (compare Image 7.6 on page 162), which clearly expresses negative affect, and probably indicates 'a serious mood' (Ekman & Friesen 1975: 83). In fact, Max only has some positive affect at the beginning of the scene, when he smiles when Lorelai comes in, as part of a salutation display (Morris 1977). Even when indicating positive affect verbally, his face expresses negative affect, as illustrated in Image 7.8 on page 163. Overall, Max's facial expression does not vary greatly, and 'seriousness' predominates throughout the scene.

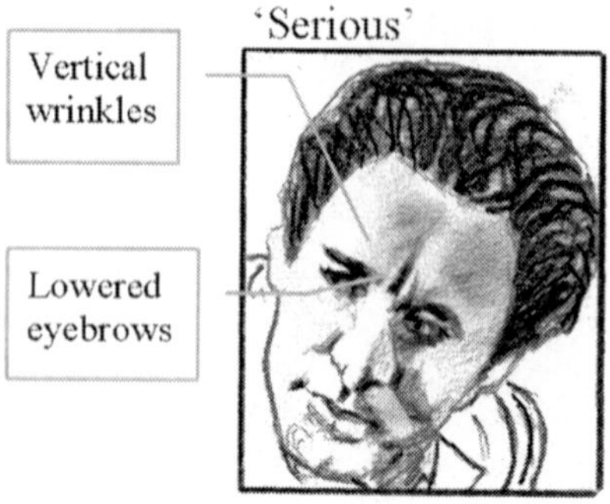

IMAGE 7.6 Max's facial expression

In contrast, Lorelai, shows a variety of smiles, construing different intensities (see Ekman & Friesen 1975: 103–07) and types (Ekman 1999) of positive affect, ranging from a sexy smile to a sad-affectionate smile (interpreted by taking into account other facial movement, for example, eyes), as illustrated in Images 7.7 a–f.

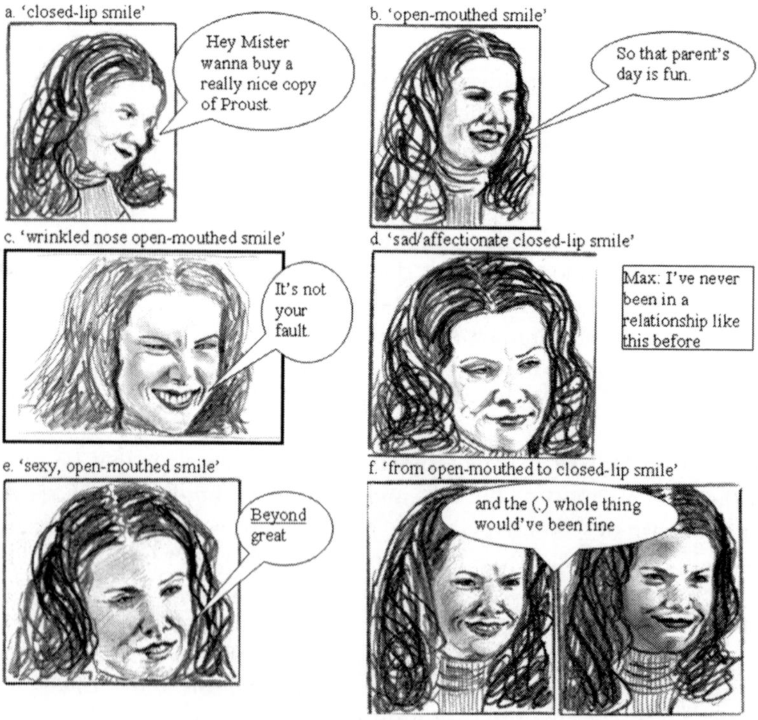

IMAGES 7.7 a–f Selected smiles by Lorelai

Overall, Lorelai has more positive affect than Max, probably because her character does not know that a break-up is coming, whereas Max has presumably made this decision before their meeting. Her smiles, as seen, are quite varied and occur throughout until the break-up statement (*Maybe we need to*. . .). It is also interesting to compare her facial affect with Max's when expressing their reciprocal affection (Image 7.8) (no furrowed forehead).

Image 7.8 Facial affect and reciprocal affection

However, Lorelai also has much negative affect, first when she apologies (see Section 2.4.1.2), but especially as a reaction to Max's statements (e.g. *I've never been in a relationship* . . .) and after the break-up statement. As Images 7.9 a–d show, these appear mainly related to facial expressions associated with sadness, where the corners of the lips are down and eyebrows drawn together (Ekman & Friesen 1975: 117) – also note Lorelai's downward gaze in some instances.

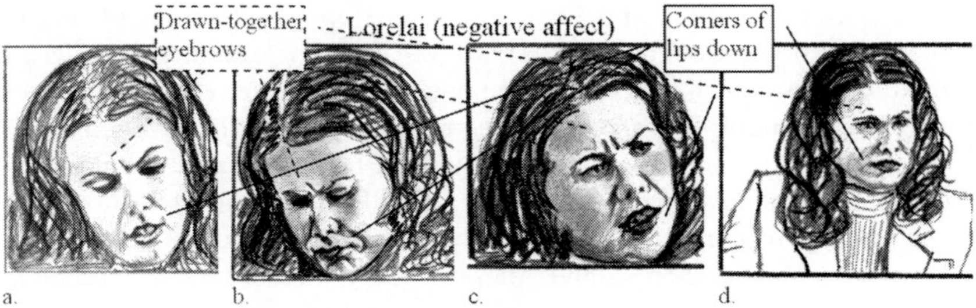

Images 7.9 a–d Selected expressions of negative affect for Lorelai

In total, Lorelai's facial affect in this scene is more varied than Max's because of differences in character's knowledge and because of differences in terms of decision-making – it is Max who has made the decision to break up. Lorelai therefore exhibits both more positive affect and seems more upset (negative affect). However, Lorelai is still relatively controlled emotionally in this scene, compared to the scene that follows, where Rory finds Lorelai at home lying on her bed crying, and comforts her by stroking her hair, lying down with her and hugging her. That is, Lorelai is emotional and upset albeit in a controlled way in this scene, as we have already seen above.

2.4 Expressive identity in interaction

2.4.1 Expressive sequences

While the above descriptions of nonverbal behaviour have to some extent taken into account interactions between the two characters, the analysis of evaluative language as an expressive resource in Section 2.3.2 only involved quantitative aspects and a rather synoptic perspective. It thus makes sense to return to verbal behaviour in speech act sequences involving both characters, where a more sequential perspective is needed. As Goodwin and Goodwin argue, 'a single participant's display of emotion must be analyzed by embedding it within a larger sequence of action' (Goodwin & Goodwin 2000: 6). As we will see, the way characters behave socially (e.g. in terms of preference organization, image/face work, im/politeness, affiliation/solidarity) contributes to the construal of expressive identities. See also Bennison (1998), Culpeper (2001) and work cited therein for how conversational structure, and (im)politeness contribute to characterization, and Stokoe (2008) on how dispreferred behaviour and other normative breaches function to elicit laughter from television audiences (Stokoe 2008).

The notion of expressive sequences that is applied below is influenced by the conversation analytical (CA) conceptualization of sequences such as *adjacency pairs* and *sequences of sequences* (see Levinson 1983, Schegloff 2007), and follows recent research on image-related sequences. Behn (2007, 2009, following Goffman 1971 and Holly 1979) develops the concept of image-related sequences to refer to 'patterned exchanges' or 'interactive patterns' related to participants' negotiation of images. Such image-related sequences are made up of moves (e.g. acceptance, compliment, justification – Behn 2007) and come in different classes (fixed pattern of turns vs. unbound and continuous). Importantly, sequences are not formally or structurally defined but functionally determined, as they 'can be realized by an infinite range of different speech acts' (Behn 2009). Adopting this notion of *sequences* and relating it to expressive identity, *expressive* sequences are interactive patterns of speech acts between participants that can be associated with expressive meanings (e.g. emotions, evaluations, ideologies). Examples of expressive sequences are joking sequences, apology sequences, blame sequences, and breaking-up sequences (see below). These can all clearly be related to positive (joking) or negative emotion (apology, break-up) as well as evaluation (negotiation of blame).[9] In the analysis of such sequences, the main focus is on the construal of expressive identity rather than on the negotiation of face/image. That is, in contrast to image-related sequences they are not defined by reference to relational face/image-work, but according to whether or not they express a speaker's emotions, attitudes, ideologies etc – although it is very likely that such sequences will have an impact on the negotiation of face/image. For instance, an apology sequence may be part of a 'remedial sequence' used to provide a remedy to offending a participant's image, as apologies are a type of 'offense-remedial-related action[.]' (Robinson 2004: 293), and impacts on relationship negotiation (compare Bubel 2006: 158–61 on *Sex and the City* [HBO, 1998–2004]). Expressive speech acts in general have been linked to social functions and rituals (Norrick 1978, Marten-Cleef 1991: 33), and *can* but need not be explored in these terms. And rather than analysing the break-up scene in its entirety, we will only look at certain sequences: joking sequences (2.4.2), blame sequences (2.4.3), and the breaking-up sequence (2.4.4).[10] Sequencing in conversation is a dynamic and intertwined process, and different expressive sequences may not always be clearly and easily segmented (as becomes apparent in the discussion below).The description and labeling of these sequences is influenced by CA research, in particular on preference organization, while it is clearly *not* an instance of CA research in terms of type of data, methodology, and level of descriptive detail and technicality. This is because while I find the CA notion of preference organization (Pomerantz 1984, Robinson 2004) helpful in describing characterization, my own background is not in CA and my focus in this section is not on sequence organization as such but on expressive identity in interaction.

2.4.2 Joking sequences

Joking sequences are sequences of speech acts that include a (witty) joking remark and its uptake or development. Joking remarks are distinguished from narrative jokes in not having a particular format with explicit preface, build-up and punchline (Bubel & Spitz 2006), and may include teasing, wordplay or punning (see Norrick 1993 on these and other kinds of conversational humour). They also seem to be inserted into other sequences (see below). In the *Gilmore Girls* scene, they seem to have an 'adjacency pair' (Schegloff 2007: 13–21)-like format, in that a joking remark is followed by take-up in the form of another joking remark or laughter (preferred response), although joking sequences can also be started and then abandoned. Norrick (1993) also argues that 'joking and laughter are linked as two parts of an adjacency pair' (Norrick 1993: 23), with laughter the preferred response. The joking sequences in the scene occur up to Max's statement about jeopardizing his career, with a change in mood from then on. The presence of these joking sequences relate to the genre and the nature of the dramedy *Gilmore Girls* (Chapter 3). At the same time, they arguably contribute to the construal of expressive identities, presenting initiators of jokes as non-serious. While Max initiates two joking remarks (*Me too. I don't skate/Oh so you have a thing for pirates*), Lorelai initiates four (*Hey Mister, wanna buy a really nice copy of Proust?/So that parent's day is fun./– ask Skippy/Let me guess . . .*).[11] As far as reactions to interlocutor's jokes are concerned, crucially, Max construes a negative affective reaction to Lorelai's final joking remark (Table 7.6), whereas Lorelai laughs at all of Max's jokes, even when they interrupt her apologizing sequence (see Appendix 8).

Table 7.6 Extract from transcript

M	I was called into headmaster Charleston's office today.	*Max's brows visibly lowered – 'crease' above nose between eyebrows*
L	Let=me=guess, he=put=his=arm=around =you=and=said"=I=don't=understand= why=you=crazy=kids=can't=work=this= out".	*Max sighs* [starting mid Lorelai's turn]
M	He said I was jeopardizing my career and my future at Chilton,	*Max's brows visibly lowered – 'crease' above nose between eyebrows*

Here Max's failure to laugh at Lorelai's remark, and his other expressive behaviour indicate his negative affective reaction towards Lorelai's joke, treating it as inappropriate, and show his serious stance towards the introduced topic. Norrick (1993: 8) remarks that the absence of laughing may trigger inferences, since '[j]okes and puns call for laughter upon completion; they build a slot for laughter into the structure of the ongoing conversation, which makes us expect laughter and notice its absence'(Norrick 1993: 7). Max's sigh substitutes for the preferred response of a laugh and is clearly noticeable, or marked. This is also the last joking remark in this scene.

2.4.3 Blame sequences

Blame sequences are sequences of speech acts that revolve around the attribution of responsibility or blame for a negatively evaluated event. Such sequences can but need not include an embedded apology sequence/adjacency pair, which consists of an explicit apology with illocutionary force indicating devices such as *(I'm) sorry, I must apologize, our apologies* (Robinson 2004: 319) and its uptake. There are several sequences in this scene that revolve around the negotiation of responsibility/blame. They feature embedded accounts, or explanations, for negative behaviour (which can be in form of a story telling), explicit apologies, assessments (which can be in form of a story telling), explicit acceptance of blame, and displays of cognitive, evaluative or affective stance.[12]

Considering the analysed scene, in the first blame sequence (Table 7.7), Lorelai accepts responsibility for what happened (her withdrawal from Max resulting in the kiss at Lorelai's school) and apologizes explicitly – note that some joking sequences are inserted here too, which will not be discussed again.

Table 7.7 Blame sequence I

	BLAME SEQUENCE	
L	Look (.) the other day, (.) we were going skating and Rory said "why don't we invite Max to come along with us" and that was a little wei:rd for me.	*account for (negative) behaviour (in form of a story telling sequence)*
M	Me too, I don't skate.	*joking*
L	(.) (laughs at joke)	*sequence*
L	She's never really referred to anyone I've dated by their first name before. I-I always kept her out of that part of my life, so it was like "=the=mustache guy"= "the=earring=guy" the: (.) "peg leg guy".	*account for (negative) behaviour continued*
M	Oh, so you have a thing for pirates	*joking*
L	(.) (laughs at joke)	*sequence*
L	She never called anyone by their na:me before. (.) She likes you. (.) She likes us, and so my mind instantly went to "oh my god =what=if=we =break=up=she'll=be=crushed", and then my next thought was "oh my go:d what if we break up I'll be crushed".	*account for (negative) behaviour continued*
	And then as you know all hell broke loose.	*mentioning negative consequences of behaviour (part of story)*
M	I understand.	*displaying cognitive/evaluative stance*
L	I freaked out	*account for (negative) behaviour continued*
	I'm so sorry.	*explicit apology*
	I-I never meant to treat you like that.	*expressing non-intentionality*
	I'm-I'm not very good at this. (.)	*account for (negative) behaviour continued*
	Ask Skippy.	*joking sequence*
M	Skippy?	*repair (clarification question)*
L	(indicates non-verbally that irrelevant/not important)	*indicating irrelevance; abandoning joking sequence*
L	I'm so so sorry.	*explicit apology*
M	I was called into headmaster Charleston's office today.	*dispreferred response (topic shift; see below)*

We can see from Table 7.7 that Lorelai partially explains or accounts for her negative behaviour through telling a story. The story includes evaluating an utterance by her daughter explicitly as *weird* and mentioning that this has never happened before, indicating her consequent inference of her daughter's affective reaction causing her, Lorelai, to have an emotional 'freak out'. This emotional reaction – the 'freak-out' – and a general disposition (generally not being *very good at this*) are also used as accounts (excuses) for her negative behaviour. Her acknowledgement of blame is also framed in terms of non-intentionality or non-volition (*I never meant to treat you like that*), and Lorelai explicitly apologies for 'treating you like that' (*I'm so sorry, I'm so so sorry*). In acknowledging blame, Lorelai offers at least two strategies (Benoit 1995: 74–95): evading responsibility (e.g. *I freaked out*; *I never meant to treat you like that, I'm not very good at this*) and mortification (e.g. *I'm so sorry*).[13] Both of these strategies, however, imply that it is Lorelai who is responsible for what happened – in contrast to the alternative strategy of denial (Benoit 1995). So it is her who takes the blame for the situation she and Max are in. Interestingly, while Max's reaction includes one explicit expression of understanding, a display of cognitive/evaluative stance, which can be construed as a partial acceptance of Lorelai's apology or account (*I understand*), he does not react to her 'intense' explicit apology (*I'm so so sorry*) with an 'absolution' (*That's alright/That's okay*) or a 'disagreement with the need to have apologised', that is, preferred responses to an apology (Robinson 2004). This means that the exchange is not closed and the behaviour not forgiven (Edmondson 1981). Rather, Max opens up a related blame sequence with a mention of the negative consequences of their behaviour (Table 7.8 on page 169).

The sequence represented in Table 7.8 essentially features Max's negative assessment, or evaluation, of his own behaviour as unprofessional and deserving of severe negative consequences (again in form of a story – an exception to the tendency of a low degree of narrativity in television dialogue, compare Chapter 4). At the same time, while this sequence partially negotiates joint responsibility, responsibility is primarily attributed to Lorelai. Again, this sequence features the use of strategies by Lorelai which imply that she is responsible for the situation: reducing offensiveness (*But he didn't* [fire Max]), and, crucially, mortification. The latter occurs both in the form of an explicit apology (*I'm sorry* – which could be treated as an expression of sympathy but is clearly taken up by Max as apology), and in the form of an explicit indication of her responsibility. While this is at first contradicted by Max's accepting blame himself (*I was the one who started the kiss*) – a preferred response to an apology ('*disagreeing with the need to have apologized*' (Robinson 2004: 302; italics in original) – when Lorelai indicates her responsibility, or accepts blame, a second time (*I'm the one who knocked it up to NC-17*), he does not contradict her. This is a dispreferred response, as it seems reasonable to assume that a preferred response to self-blame would be a contradiction, just like

Table 7.8 Blame sequence II

	BLAME SEQUENCE	
M	I was called into headmaster Charleston's office today.	*topic-opener beginning story telling sequence concerning the negative consequences of their behaviour (working as negative assessment)*
L	Let=me=guess, he=put=his=arm= around=you=and= said"=I=don't= understand=why=you=crazy=kids= can't=work=this=out".	*joking*
M	(sighs, starting mid Lorelai's turn)	*sequence*
M	He said I was jeopardizing my career and my future at Chilton,	*assessment/telling continued*
L	Oh ↓	*displaying cognitive/affective stance*
M	And at first I was incensed, outraged and "how da:re he" (.) and then I realized that he was right. What happened the other day was completely <unprofessional>. I never in my life would have considered pulling off something like this. (.) He should've fired me.	*assessment/telling continued*
L	But he didn't	*mitigating negative consequences*
M	Not yet, but the word probation was tossed around quite a bit though.	*mentioning negative consequences of behaviour*
L	I'm sorry.	*explicit apology*
M	I was the one who started the kiss.	*preferred response (accepting blame = disagreeing with need to apologize)*
L	And I'm the one who knocked it up to NC-Seventee:n	*accepting blame*
M	I-I honestly did not think that this was gonna be so complicated.	*dispreferred response (expressing ignorance and negative assessment of relationship)*
L	I know.	*displaying cognitive stance; accepting expression of ignorance*
M	I mean you told me it would be. I didn't listen. I didn't want to.	*accepting blame*
L	It's not your fault. If I hadn't acted like a two year old and tried to run away and pretend that you weren't what you are to me then we wouldn't have fought, we wouldn't have kissed, I wouldn't have humiliated my daughter, and the (.) whole thing would've been fine.	*accepting blame*
M	Pause: 4 sec	

the preferred response to a self-deprecation is disagreement (Pomerantz 1984: 77). Instead of a contradiction, Max continues with an assessment of their relationship as *so complicated,* foreshadowing the subsequent breaking-up sequence (see below). Although this is followed by Max's accepting blame as not having wanted to listen to Lorelai, Lorelai's explicit statement that it is not his fault, and her own acceptance of blame is not contradicted by him but followed by a four-second pause, suggesting that this is a dispreferred response (see Pomerantz 1984).

What we can say with respect to the blame sequences in this scene, then, is that they do involve some joint negotiation of blame, with both Max and Lorelai alternatively accepting responsibility. On the other hand, only Lorelai explicitly expresses apologies (*I'm sorry* × 3) and explicitly denies Max's fault (*It's not your fault*), and at several occasions her taking of responsibility remains uncontradicted. Further, she initiates this voluntarily, without responding to a reproach or a 'request for repair' (Benoit 1995: 39), but rather, in rhetorical terms, offers a 'preemptive *apologia*' (Benoit 1995: 85). This effectively construes Lorelai as more responsible than Max, but also construes her as *willing* to take the blame, as harmonious, as seeking to apologize and thereby make it right again. Max, on the other hand, may not be overtly concerned with establishing responsibility for the event, as he has already made his decision and is trying to break up with Lorelai.

2.4.4 The breaking up sequence

A breaking-up sequence is a sequence of speech acts that revolve around statements that end or put a halt to a relationship (e.g. *We need to take a little time away for each other*). While it is difficult to say where exactly the 'preparation' on Max's part for his break-up statement begins, it makes sense to regard the breaking-up sequence as starting after the four-second pause, that is, where he first expresses an evaluation or assessment of their relationship (*I honestly did not think that this was gonna be so complicated*) – which means that the sequence has an embedded blame sequence, which will not be discussed again. The sequence further comprises assessments of their relationship (including 'affective' assessments, and assessments of the impact of the relationship and/ or aspects of the relationship, for example, kissing), an explicit break-up statement, displays of cognitive/affective stance, and accounts for the break-up (Table 7.9 on page 171).

We can see that Max, who initiates the break-up, prepares and performs the break-up by continually evaluating or assessing the relationship rather negatively in terms of 'powerlessness', and that he uses this to justify or account for the break-up, in addition to the negative consequences it has for his job. That is, the relationship is evaluated as too complicated or difficult and its

Table 7.9 The breaking-up sequence

	The breaking-up sequence	
M	I-I honestly did not think that this was gonna be so complicated.	*expressing ignorance and negative assessment of relationship*
L	I know.	*displaying cognitive stance; accepting expression of ignorance*
M	I mean you told me it would be. I didn't listen. I didn't want to.	*accepting blame*
L	It's not your fault. If I hadn't acted like a two year old and tried to run away and pretend that you weren't what you are to me then we wouldn't have fought, we wouldn't have kissed, I wouldn't have humiliated my daughter, and the (.) whole thing would've been fine.	*accepting blame*
M	Pause: 4 sec	
M	I-I do not know what to do here. I-(pause: 2 sec) I've never been in a relationship like this before, I-I'm not thinking straight.	*assessment of relationship (impact on self)*
L	I know. Me either.	*assessment of relationship*
M	That was a great kiss.	*assessment of relationship*
L	Beyond great. (Pause: 3 sec)	*assessment of relationship*
M	Maybe we need to take a little time away from each other.	*assessment/break-up statement*
L	(Pause: 5 sec) (non-verbal neg affect) Okay,	*displaying affective stance; agreeing*
M	You know just to figure out how to do this so it's not so hard.	*account for break-up and assessment of relationship*
L	Su:re, that makes sense. (non-verbal neg affect)	*displaying cognitive/affective stance*
M	I just-I don't have any other answers right now.	*assessment of relationship*
L	No. You're right. You're-you're absolutely right. (non-verbal neg affect)	*assessment; display of affective stance*
	(Pause: 3 sec)	
	<I really really like you Max Medina.>	*(affective) assessment*
M	(.) <I really really like you Lorelai Gilmore.>	*(affective) assessment*
L	Well, as long as we have that straightened out.	*summarizing assessment/ 'post-completion musing' (Schegloff 2007: 142)*
	(Pause: 3 sec, followed by good-byes)	

impact on Max as rendering him rationally incapacitated to some extent. Compare:

- *so complicated*;
- *I do not know what to do*;
- *I'm not thinking straight*;
- *to figure out how to do this*;
- *so hard*;
- *I don't have any other answers.*

While Lorelai agrees with his evaluation of the relationship to some extent (*me either*), it does not seem to be as problematic for her as for him. As noted in Section 2.3.2, it is Max who feels 'powerless' regarding their relationship and its (emotional) impact on him.

Further, we can assume that Lorelai does not really want the break-up to happen, which is also indicated nonverbally as seen above. But neither does she try to convince Max otherwise, and she is very harmonious verbally in her reaction to his break-up statement (*Okay*; *Sure, that makes sense*; *No you're right. You're, you're absolutely right*), largely agreeing with him. This may be an attempt on her part to protect her image, to save face and not to show how much it affects her emotionally, that is, controlling her emotional reaction at least verbally. Note also the fact that the interaction takes place in a public setting (see above). There is, perhaps, one attempt to influence Max otherwise in her explicit affective assessment (*I really really like you Max Madina*), but otherwise she is not trying to be difficult, dramatic, or a 'diva' but to accept his decision in a mature way. The tendency to harmony and support ties in with other observations already made above and can be seen in Lorelai's reactive turns in general. On the one hand, we have seen above (page 152) that Lorelai makes frequent use of evaluations of expectedness such as *I know*. These and other lexico-grammatical devices seem to be used to express a sort of harmonious other-centredness and agreement. If we consider Lorelai's responses to Max, they are predominantly supportive, apart from one joking interruption, and one contrastive statement (*But he didn't*):

- laughing at Max's jokes;
- apologizing/taking blame;
- expressing belief, agreement or understanding;
- sharing Max's emotions/evaluations.

In fact, throughout the scene Lorelai gives preferred responses (laughing at joke, agreeing with assessment [Pomerantz 1984], disagreeing with self-blame), and also makes many 'supportive moves' (Behn 2009), including expressing appreciation for her interactant (*I really really like you*; agreeing, laughing, smiling), expressing appreciation of interactant's extentions (*You're right*), appreciating an interactant's role in the conversation (adhering to principles of communication, for example, in giving preferred responses).[14]

Although Max's reactive turns are also quite harmonious and supportive, as the scene does not feature a conflict-rich break-up, they are not so to quite the same extent. While in some of his responses to Lorelai he shares her evaluations (e.g. in his jokes) and ostensibly reciprocates her affect (*I really really like you Lorelai Gilmore*), nonverbally his disapproval is made clear. We can see him turning away from Lorelai and shaking his head (as already discussed above) before he replies. He also breathes in and out quite loudly as he utters the affective statement and has negative facial affect, all together creating the impression of regarding Lorelai's statement as either somewhat inappropriate, unhelpful or childish. He also has more dispreferred reactions (sighs rather than laughs at Lorelai's joke, does not contradict her taking blame) – which are cognitively foregrounded (Culpeper 2001: 174) – thus has fewer supportive moves (one expression of understanding, one of taking blame, one reference to her knowledge), does not smile at her and offers no explicit apologies. Other reactive turns include joking, contrast and asking for clarification.

In summary, although featuring a break-up, the scene is rather non-conflicting in nature. Apart from the discussed features, frequent nodding by both participants, which can be an 'acknowledging' ('I am still listening'), encouraging ('how fascinating'), understanding ('I see what you mean'), agreement ('Yes, I will') and factual ('that is correct') nod (Morris 1977: 68; see Carter & Adolphs 2008 on head-nods as backchanneling), also works supportively, though perhaps it can also indicate resignation. It can be argued that the harmonious nature of the scene makes the break-up even more tragic and 'drama-tic', as the characters are breaking up *despite* how well they get along and *despite* their reciprocal feelings for each other, as explicitly stated in the last turns. Non-fluency features such as hesitations, incomplete turns, repetitions and re-starts can indicate lack of control and affective reactions (Bennison 1998: 73, Culpeper 2001: 217). In this scene, the noteworthy clustering of pauses indicates dispreferred turns but also emotional turmoil on the part of *both* participants, as do prosodic features as well as interrupted sentence structure (*I just – I don't have any other answers right now*) and repetitions (*I-I do not know what to do here*; *You're, you're absolutely right*). Max is clearly finding it emotionally difficult to break up with Lorelai. However, as indicated by an in-depth analysis of this scene, expressive resources are used to construe Lorelai's expressive identity as more upset and more emotional than Max as well as more apologetic and supportive.

3 Conclusion

In the description of verbal and nonverbal expressive behaviour we have seen how they work together to construe two diverging expressive identities. At times, the different modes reinforce the same expressive meaning (e.g. head shake accompanying negation), at others they contradict each other (e.g. verbal vs. nonverbal behaviour) to create complex expressive meanings. The former is common when speech and gesture occur, as they are usually co-expressive, that is, expressing in distinctive ways 'a single underlying idea in speech and gesture *simultaneously*' (McNeill 2005: 22). The latter are particularly interesting from a meaning-making point of view (e.g. using emotional language in 'unemotional' voice or using non-emotional language but using emotional gesturing/intense facial affect; or expressing positive affect in language but negative affect in the face or hand gestures expressing affect but the face being neutral etc.), as they can construe complex meanings such as irony or 'controlled/involuntary distress'. Ultimately, future descriptions need to go beyond separating approaches that fragment the body and need to focus even more on clustering, sequencing and simultaneities, both with respect to verbal and nonverbal behaviour (Theo van Leeuwen, p.c.). This could only be done to some extent in this chapter. Further, multimodality in the product (Chapter 2: Section 3.2.2) also needs to be incorporated when looking at this behaviour in the context of film and television performance, as it influences what audiences can see (cf. Table 7.1 above).

The above analyses can be related to the model for expressive identity introduced in Chapter 6 – compare Table 7.10.

Table 7.10 Expressive identity: the multimodal performance

Macro	temporary/situational expressive identity: attitudinal and emotional	Max: less emotional, more serious, in control, determined, following a hard decision through; emotionality of relationship as threatening Lorelai: partly optimistic, harmonious/supportive, upset in a controlled way, emotionally varied/lively
Meso	expressive style expressive actions/strategies	Frequency and variety of gestured emotion Frequency and variety of facial affect More or less Affect in language Variety of evaluative parameters in language More or less supporting/harmonious
Micro	expressive features (verbal and non-verbal)	Facial affect, gesture, gaze, evaluative language; turn-taking behaviour

While multimodality in the product (e.g. shots) were not analysed in detail, it is interesting to note that shot size works to emphasize Lorelai's emotions rather than Max's, as we only get medium close-up shots on her, not on Max. These shots also emphasize certain of her emotions, predominantly negative affect (sad/upset).

As we have seen in this scene, affective and evaluative meanings are expressed in dynamic interaction between participants through a combination of language, paralanguage, speech act sequences, gesture, etc. and can respond to particular events. Just looking at this one scene, then, may only tell us about temporary, localized and situated expressive identities. But from what we know of Lorelai's more stable expressive identity (Chapter 6), it seems that Lorelai's gestural liveliness, emotional variety and emotional outbursts instantiate a more general (stable) emotional expressive identity. However, it is unclear whether her initial tendency to optimism, her harmonious/supportive moves, and her tendency to control her emotions in a break-up scene recur across the series or whether they reflect only a temporary expressive identity. Further detailed analyses (e.g. of all break-up scenes) would need to be done to ascertain this. One factor that may have an influence on expressive behaviour is whose choice the break-up is, so that expressive behaviour in such scenes may well fluctuate within the series. For instance, Max seems more emotional earlier on in this episode, when Lorelai tries to break up with him, and conforms less to gender stereotypes there than he does in this scene. See also Chapter 6 on factors that impact on whether behaviour is seen by the audience as corresponding to a general disposition (here: stable expressive identity) or not. While we have no information on Max's general (stable) expressive identity, note that in another episode (3.19, *Keg! Max*!) he performs a much more 'emotional' expressive identity.

Even though the analysis of character behaviour in only one scene does not allow us to relate this behaviour to a more stable expressive identity, it must be emphasized that the analysis of one-off occurrences – construing temporary/situated identities – can be highly significant in characterization:

> One-time actions tend to evoke the dynamic aspects of the character, often playing a part in a turning point in the narrative. . . . Although a one-time action does not reflect *constant* qualities, it is not less characteristic of the character. On the contrary, its dramatic impact often suggest that the traits it reveals are qualitatively more crucial than the numerous habits which represent the character's routine. (Rimmon-Kenan 2002: 61)

This chapter offered a case study of a *Gilmore Girls* scene to show how different expressive character identities are construed multimodally and in a situated context. The analysed resources (language, gesture, facial expression) are also available to other actors/actresses and used by them to construe expressive character identities in different series. For instance, the character of Gregory House in *House* (FOX, 2004–), is partially characterized through his anti-social behaviour, and his lack of bedside manner (www.fox.com/house/showInfo/, last accessed 2 June 2009). Another example is the anti-social character of Bernard Black played by Dylan Moran in *Black Books* (Channel 4, UK, 2000–2004). Differences in expressive behaviour clearly contribute to construing characters on television beyond *Gilmore Girls*.

Notes

1 All illustrations in this chapter were kindly done for me by Helen Caple.

2 In this chapter I will talk about 'Max' and 'Lorelai' as if I was talking about people interacting in natural conversation – this is, however, to be understood as a shorthand to referring to televisual characters as they are construed and performed in the television production process rather than as an attempt to fully 'humanize' them (see Chapter 5: Section 1).

3 This chapter will not deal with multimodal co-occurrence relations (Kendon 2004, Martinec & Salway 2005, Baldry & Thibault 2006, Caple 2010, Zhao 2010, Zappavigna et al. 2010) as such since my interest is in characterization. In analysing a televisual scene such relations can be quite complex, as relations between shots, sound (e.g. dialogue or voice-over), facial affect, gestures and actions as well as different linguistic levels are concerned:

> Film is a complex of systems of signification and its meanings are the product of the combination of these systems. The combination may be achieved through systems either complementing or conflicting with each other. No one system is responsible for the total effect of a film. (Turner 1994: 135)

For instance, the relation between participants and sound in the moving image can be analysed in terms of text-image relations (Martinec & Salway 2005) as projection of locutions (on-screen dialogue) or as projection of ideas (voice-over with participant on-screen). But often, voice-overs occur without any participant visible on-screen, and the relation between what is seen and heard on screen becomes more complex. Both multimodality in characters and multimodality in the product (Chapter 2: Section 3.2) need to be taken into account in such analysis: 'meaning-making resources that belong to the production and editing of video texts . . . interact in patterned ways with the meaning-making resources of the human body' (Baldry & Thibault 2006: 173).

4 Remember that the evaluative parameter of (+/-) POWER includes evaluations of in/comprehensibility (Chapter 3). The category of 'other' classifies Max's use of *honestly* – this can be classified as an evaluation of STYLE (Bednarek 2006a) and intensification.

5 On account of the small numbers, no tests for statistical significance were applied. Note also that Lorelai utters more words in this scene than Max (299 vs. 220) and that we could therefore consider relative frequencies. However,

even then the tendencies remain the same, although they are less pronounced. It is unclear whether the small difference in the characters' number of words in this scene would be perceived by the audience.

6 It should be mentioned that my view of expressivity (including emotion), as previously outlined in Chapter 6, may differ from the authors that I draw on in describing nonverbal behaviour. While a detailed comparison of my views with theirs is beyond the scope of this chapter, note in particular that I do not take 'expressive' to necessarily refer to some kind of 'spontaneous', involuntary symptom of an internal state of mind. In the context of acting, actors make use of resources that are associated with expressive meanings, but for the purposes of my descriptions I am not concerned with their sincerity, veracity, intentionality or spontaneity.

7 It also depends on the nature of the expressive feature, for example, some kinds of gestures are not easily controllable; some aspects of voice are more easily manipulated than others, although '[a] good actor . . . can become capable of changing his voice and giving it all kinds of inflections and dimensions merely with the means nature has given him' (Chion 1999: 169). One handbook suggests that portraying emotion is beyond the actor's control and will arise naturally from physical action (Bruder et al. 1986: 71–93). For further references on acting see Chapter 2: Note 7.

8 Generally, I assume that 'conversational signals' (usually single facial movements accenting/underlining speech; Ekman 1997), are expressive only to a low degree, and as their analysis is very time-consuming, I have disregarded them in the transcript.

9 Norrick (1993) talks about 'the speaker's presentation of a **personality** through the joke performance' (Norrick 1993: 16, my bold), with different kinds of humour (funny personal anecdotes, wordplay, puns, sarcastic comments) relating differently to self-presentation (Norrick 1993: 44). Humour is also crucial in 'interpersonal semantics' (Eggins & Slade 1997: 124) and important for solidarity, affiliation and characterization (Norrick 1993, Bubel 2006, Knight 2010, in preparation). Apologies have been classified as 'expressive' speech acts in Searle's terms (Norrick 1978, Levinson 1983: 240, Marten-Cleef 1991).

10 The whole scene could be analysed with respect to sequence organization in CA (Schegloff 2007) terms. It includes at least the following sequences:

- action type sequence (of 'howaryou' [sic] greeting sequences);
- assessment adjacency pair with first pair part working as topic opener; the pair simultaneously works as joking adjacency pair;
- reciprocal or exchange sequence of telling sequences by Lorelai (a telling that works as an account and is interrupted by joking inserts on Max's part) and Max (a telling that works as an assessment; interrupted by joking inserts and display of cognitive/affective stance on Lorelai's part; the telling makes up an assessment first pair part, and ends with some negotiation of blame, including an apology adjacency pair);
- action type sequences (of assessment adjacency pairs, initiated by Max), interrupted by blame sequence; last assessment first pair part works as breaking-up statement;

- affective assessment adjacency pair (initiated by Lorelai and closed by Lorelai with a summarizing assessment);
- greeting adjacency pair.

The scene could also fruitfully be analysed in terms of other frameworks such as discourse structure (Coulthard 1985), exchange structure (Martin & Rose 2007b) or genre (Eggins & Slade 1997, Martin & Rose 2007a). Such analyses would give us varying perspectives on the structure of the scene as a whole; but, as mentioned, this is not the aim of my analyses in this chapter and no such analysis will be undertaken. Further, as also stated above, the approach taken to expressive speech sequences in this chapter follows functional rather than formal definitions. Ultimately, it may be possible to identify explicit criteria for different kinds of expressive speech acts, 'drawing principally on the systems of interpersonal meaning' (Eggins & Slade 1997: 192). However, this would only be possible on the basis of more data analysis, and it is not clear whether there are, for example, linguistic criteria for unequivocally identifying, say, all joking sequences. It is also doubtful whether it is always easily possible to draw a clear distinction between 'fact' and 'opinion' as implied in Eggins and Slade's network of speech functions (1997: 193) – see Chapter 3 for references concerning the theorizing of explicit (inscribed) vs. implicit (invoked) opinion.

[11] The first joking remark (*Hey, mister...*) also works as greeting, and is an in-joke, referring to Lorelai's earlier failed attempts to return a Proust book borrowed from Max. The last joking remark (*ask Skippy*) is an intertextual reference to a conversation taking place at the beginning of the scene between Luke, Lorelai and Rory, where Max was not present. It thus excludes Max to a certain extent while including the audience. The conversation is about how Lorelai maltreated her hamster, Skippy.

[12] Whether or not blame sequences always include these moves is unclear, as no other data were consulted, and as these data are scripted. However, research has shown that apologies frequently co-occur with and are part of sequences such as accounts and remedial episodes/cycles (Robinson 2004: 293, Note 7). In fact, depending on how 'account' is defined, blame sequences may be very similar to account sequences. However, there is no consensus on how to define 'account', what it includes, and what its phases or moves are (Benoit 1995: 39). See Benoit (1994) and Robinson (2004) for overviews of research on apologies, accounts (excuses and justifications) and accepting blame. In some cases, this research treats accounts or acceptances of blame themselves as apology so that one open question is 'whether or not the sorry-based unit and offers of apology are merely "explicit" methods of apologizing, or whether the action of apologizing is essentially constituted by such "explicit" methods' (Robinson 2004: 322). In other approaches apologies and related acts such as admission of guilt are treated as accounts themselves (Benoit 1995: 32–9). Accounts can further be sub-divided into different types (Benoit 1995: 51–61). Both accounts and explicit apologies participate in their own sequences (e.g. are preceded/followed by particular moves).

[13] Benoit (1995: 74–82) suggests five categories of image restoration strategies: denial (denying the act), evading responsibility (evading or reducing the

person's responsibility for the act, for instance in terms of lack of control or ability), reducing offensiveness (reducing the offense, for instance minimizing its negative effects), corrective action (promising to improve the situation) and mortification (admitting blame, apologizing, asking for forgiveness).

[14] These could also be discussed as 'alignment practices' from a conversation analytical perspective (see Bubel 2006: 91–138 for an overview of relevant research and an analysis of *Sex and the City*).

Chapter 8

Expressive Character Identity and Ideology: Shared Attitudes

This chapter deals with a further aspect of expressive identity: ideology. Whereas Chapters 6 and 7 were primarily concerned with resources of emotionality and evaluation, and how they *differentiate* characters from each other, this chapter looks primarily at (ideological) attitudes that are *shared* between characters. Even though Chapter 6 also showed similarities between characters in terms of emotive interjection usage (e.g. Lorelai and Sookie, Emily and Richard, Luke and Jess) we can say that both Chapters 6 and 7 were mainly concerned with the 'individual' aspect of expressive identity. In contrast, while this chapter also describes differences between characters it is mainly concerned with the 'social' aspect of expressive identity (in terms of shared values, attitudes and beliefs). In another case study of *Gilmore Girls*, corpus linguistic frequency and concordance analysis as well as some qualitative discourse analysis is used to show how characters that we are asked to identify with share particular mainstream normative values, in contrast to those that are portrayed negatively. The chapter also links the analysis to broader concerns about ideology and representation in fictional television.

1 Ideology and Expressive Identity

1.1 Ideology and television

The notion of ideology is one that has many definitions and that has been studied from many perspectives (see, for example, Williams 1983: 153–7, van Dijk 1998b, Eagleton 1991, Norval 2000, Scollon & Scollon 2001, Decker 2004). Eagleton (1991: 1–2) lists 16 definitions of ideology, and van Dijk argues that ideology 'is one of the most elusive notions in the social sciences' (van Dijk 1998a: 23). However, a considerable number of definitions see ideology as having to do with perspectives, values, attitudes, worldviews, tacit assumptions and belief systems that are shared by social agents or social groups (e.g. Fowler 1986: 130, Scollon & Scollon 2001: 108, Huisman 2005a: 172, Adolphs 2006: 84), that is, '*social belief systems*' (van Dijk 1998b: 29). For instance, ideology can be seen as encompassing 'the perspectives that a person takes up towards his or her *Umwelt,* the ethical values that seem unproblematic, unarguable, objectively "natural" in her or his world' (Huisman 2005a: 172). Van Dijk (1998b) notes that '[m]any authors would agree that an ideology is something like a shared framework of social beliefs that organize and coordinate the social interpretations and practices of groups and their members, and in particular also power and other relations between groups' (van Dijk 1998b: 8). And Scollon and Scollon (2001: 183) propose that ideology includes, *inter alia,* the worldview, beliefs and values of a group. Similarly, I want to talk about ideology in this chapter as encompassing the shared values and belief systems of characters. This is a working definition where the important notion of power, which is frequently connected to ideology, is at first put aside in an approach where we analyse shared values as such before deciding whether or not an analysis in terms of power is adequate. In this chapter, a discussion of ideology in terms of power will be deferred to Sections 2.4.3 and 3.1. Eagleton (1991) suggests that '[n]obody has yet come up with a single adequate definition of ideology' (Eagleton 1991: 1), and this is no doubt true also of the conception of ideology taken up here (see, for example, van Dijk 1998b: 3, 49 for criticism but Adolphs 2006: 81 for an endorsement). However, as a working definition it allows us to investigate a particular belief system or, in stylistic terminology, a certain *mind style*[1] (Fowler 1986) shared among characters in a television series (in the case study below: *Gilmore Girls* characters). For reasons outlined below I focus just on their attitudes towards 'meat-eating' excluding many other value and belief systems (e.g. towards/about marriage, gender roles, family structure, class, ethnicity).

In fact, much research in Media and Television studies has considered the relationship between television and ideology. Most researchers seem to argue that television genres can be seen to reflect and construe social change in terms of ideology:

> In the relationship between genre and ideology it can be argued that genres adapt to hegemonic changes – the way a dominant ideology secures consent to its world view, but has to keep on securing it in the face of oppositional forces. So if the dominant representation of the police force gets out of step with the consensual view of it, then the genre must adapt. At the industry level this is called giving the viewing public what it wants or what will be popular with audiences. At the level of ideology it is interpreted as helping to create a new consensus or dominant ideology. In this way, genres act to articulate, in a very powerful way, what Roland Barthes calls the 'myths' of society. (Dunn 2005:138)

Genre, as Hermes (2005: 41) suggests can also be a site for debating and negotiating cultural norms, for example, with respect to gender. The characters and events in television series reflect aspects of culture and occur 'against a backdrop of social and moral issues' (Quaglio 2009: 17). For example, the dramedy *Gilmore Girls* portrays a single, unmarried mother and her daughter as the 'nuclear family', as well as featuring singledom, break-ups, separations and divorce. This is in line with similar changes in the genre-related domestic sitcom that have been happening in the United States since the 1990s (Feuer 2001b, Huisman 2005a: 176, Mills 2005: 44). Feuer (2001b: 70) in fact argues that the sitcom is so successful and popular because of its 'ideological flexibility', allowing it to both illustrate contemporary ideological conflicts and provide simultaneous entertainment. The construal of character identity can also be part of the negotiation of cultural ideology (Pearson 2007: 48). It is interesting, too, to compare Paltridge's comments on the dramedy *Sex and the City* (HBO, 1998–2004; for a discussion of this show with respect to feminism see Creeber 2004):

> A further presupposition underlying the *Sex and the City* conversation is the issue of who will propose to whom; that is, the agency of the action being discussed in the conversation. It is a clear assumption here that the man will propose to the woman, not the other way round. As independent as Carrie and her friends are, it is less likely that they would propose to a man (or that they would refuse him, should he ask). (Paltridge 2006: 47)

Incidentally, *Gilmore Girls* contrasts with *Sex and the City* in featuring a woman (Lorelai) proposing to a man (Luke) with him subsequently accepting her proposal. At the same time the dramedy acknowledges and thematizes cultural assumptions about marriage proposals in character dialogue:

(1)
PATTY: Well, enough about us, honey. Come on, Luke, tell us, how'd you do it?
LUKE: Well, actually, I didn't . . . Lorelai proposed to me.
[Patty and Babette's expressions change.]
BABETTE and PATTY: Oh.
PATTY [disappointed]: You went modern.
[Luke nods.]
BABETTE: Well, that's still okay, sugar. The important thing is, you're getting married!
PATTY [monotone]: We're very happy for you, Luke.
[Babette elbows her.]
BABETTE: Yes, we are.
PATTY: Yeah.
LUKE: Uh-huh, thanks. Well, I-I've got some work to do. I'll talk to you guys later.
[He gets up and leaves them.]

PATTY: She proposed.
BABETTE: Yeah, well, thank god he's got a good ass.
(6.01, *New and improved Lorelai*)

As can also be seen in this dialogue, marriage is the only imaginable and desirable teleological endpoint for a relationship for the two characters of Babette and Patty (two rather elderly women): 'The important thing is, you're getting married!' (this attitude is also expressed by other characters, though not by all. A crucial point of conflict in the series is that Lorelai refused to marry her daughter's father, Christopher, when she became pregnant as a teenager.) As Williams has suggested, texts can include 'residual' discourse (older values that are still accepted by some), 'dominant' discourse (contemporary values that are accepted by most) and 'emergent' discourse (new values that are gradually accepted by society) (Williams 1977, cited in O'Shaughnessy & Stadler 2005: 180). The fictional TV show *Mad Men* (AMC, 2007–) portrays ideologies prevalent in the 1960s such as sexism, anti-Semitism and homophobia – hopefully only very marginal 'residual' discourse in contemporary society. An example of how scripted television dialogue changes over time, as society also changes, is described by Rey (2001), whose analysis of *Star Trek* (NBC/Paramount, 1966–1969, 1987–1994, 1993–1999) finds that 'traditional differences between female and male language . . . appear to be breaking down' (Rey 2001: 155), with more current series showing new linguistic behaviour and gender roles. Other examples of TV reflecting social change are the existence of series featuring gay protagonists (e.g. *Will & Grace* [NBC, 1998–2006], *Queer as Folk* [Channel 4, UK, 2000–2005], *The L-Word* [Showtime, 2004–2009]) and the increasing inclusion of gay and bisexual characters (at least in some episodes of) contemporary television series (e.g. *My So-called Life* [ABC, 1994–1995], *Dawson's Creek* [Warner Brothers, 1998–2003], *Grey's Anatomy* [ABC, 2005–], *House* [FOX, 2004–], *The Wire* [HBO, 2002–2008]). Concerning ethnicity, British soaps have been featuring central black or gay characters since the 1980s (Marshall & Werndly 2002: 9), while well-known US sitcoms featuring African-American characters include *The Cosby Show* (NBC, 1984–1992), *The Fresh Prince of Bel Air* (NBC, 1990–1996), and, more recently, *Everybody Hates Chris* (UPN/The CW, 2005–2009).[2] Much research in television and film studies considers social change (see Hermes 2005: 16, and Mills 2005: 8 for brief overviews), and characters in television series other than *Gilmore Girls* also explicitly thematize cultural assumptions, for instance with respect to gender. Consider this extract from *Ally McBeal* (FOX, 1997–2002):

(2)
Ally . . . because you know what?
One of the last vestiges of gender bias [is the dirty joke=]

> Men can handle it,
> [women can't we're we'er uh]
> we're not tough enough.
> we're we're too we're too (2.0) fragile.
> (*Ally McBeal*, transcription from Bubel & Spitz 2006)

As an instance of the genre of dramedy (related to both sitcom and soap, see Chapter 3) and as a particular television series, *Gilmore Girls* can thus be seen as both reflecting, construing and negotiating different cultural ideologies (residual/dominant/emerging). Conflicting ideologies are represented by different characters (e.g. Lorelai and her mother, Emily Gilmore), and are the source of much conflict (Calvin 2008a: 14). This is a common feature of television programmes where characters are used to carry ideological oppositions between different lifestyles (Livingstone 1998, Feuer 2001b). For analyses of *Gilmore Girls* and cultural stereotypes or ideological positions, particularly with respect to gender see Westman (2007) and Calvin (2008b). The focus of my own analysis will be on shared attitudes towards food, in particular the eating of meat. On the one hand, we can consider this as part of a general research interest into whether and how mainstream attitudes/ideologies are reproduced in fictional television, where we zoom in on attitudes towards one particular aspect of contemporary society. On the other hand, the choice of analysing attitudes towards meat-eating, as a sub-category of the general ideology of food in *Gilmore Girls*, was inspired by several factors.

First, it was inspired by the relative neglect of the ideology of food in television, media studies and critical discourse analysis (CDA) where the majority of analyses of television and ideology/representation, identity and power seem to concentrate on more obviously significant notions such as gender, class, ethnicity, capitalism and institutional power. A similar focus is apparent in studies of ideology outside television and in studies of identity, but see, for example, Cook (2004, cited in Adolphs 2006) on ideology in the context of genetically modified food, Lakoff (2006) on food and identity in American society, Coupland (2007: 119–21) on identity, style and talk about food/dieting, and the many readings on food, identity and the body across disciplines.

Second, it was motivated by the important ethical dimensions involved in attitudes towards eating meat, where resulting eating practices have an impact on other living beings, on the environment and on developing nations. Food is not value-free. It is clear that our attitudes towards food and resulting practices have an obvious evaluative and ethical dimension (Singer & Mason 2007), with food choices impacting on the treatment and killing of animals and environmental damage. Eating only certain kinds of food can hence become 'an act of civic virtue' (Lakoff 2006: 152). However, note that I am not taking an explicit CDA stance in this chapter.

Third, even though not quite as apparent as gender, age, ethnicity etc., attitudes towards food play a crucial role in terms of identity: '"minor identities" like culinary preferences . . . contribute significantly to our sense of ourselves: who we are, how competent we are, who our friends are or should be, whom we admire or disdain' (Lakoff 2006: 165). We can thus relate attitudes towards eating meat both to the individual ('sense of ourselves: who we are') and to the social ('who our friends are or should be, whom we admire or disdain') aspects of expressive identity.

Fourth, food is an important aspect in *Gilmore Girls* – the series that will be used as case study – as outlined by Coleman (2008) and Haupt (2008), focusing, respectively, on narrative and gender roles. Coleman (2008) notes that 'the incidence of consumption and preparation of food occupies, in most instances, numerous points of an episode's running time' (Coleman 2008: 177), for example relating to dinners at Emily and Richard's, visits to Luke's diner, and conversations with chef Sookie, and concludes that 'food enjoys an unusual degree of narrative space' (Coleman 2008: 178) in this particular dramedy. Eating practices and attitudes towards food probably also play a big part in many other series that feature domestic settings and interactions, so that we can take the analysis of *Gilmore Girls* as a springboard for further analysis of other television series and serials.

1.2 The ideology of food and expressive identity

How does ideology relate to the notion of expressive identity? In Chapter 6 it was proposed to use the notion of *expressive character identity* to refer to a kind of scripted identity that encompasses expressive aspects such as emotions, emotional dispositions, values, attitudes, stances and evaluations. Ideology – referring to characters' values and attitudes – is thus but one part of expressive character identity. Ideology is also closely tied to individual and social identities in 'real' life:

> On the one hand, ideology is no mere set of abstract doctrines but the stuff which makes us uniquely what we are, constitutive of our very identities; on the other hand, it presents itself as an 'Everybody knows that', a kind of anonymous universal truth. (Eagleton 1991: 20)

The ideology of food, too, relates crucially to our identity. In Lakoff's (2006) words, 'we are what we eat', and in relation to expressive character identity, characters are partially construed by how they evaluate eating. Speaking with Eagleton, we can say that ideology 'is certainly subjective in the sense of being subject-centred: its utterances are to be deciphered as expressive of a speaker's attitudes or lived relations to the world' (Eagleton 1991: 19) so that ideological utterances about meat-eating are expressive of characters' attitudes towards and relations to meat-eating and thus part of their expressive identity.

According to Lakoff (2006) our feelings about food are an aspect of identity that is subtle and not likely to be problematized, while being linked to both individual and group identity (like expressive identity in general; see Chapter 6):

> What we can and cannot eat, what kinds of edibles carry prestige, how much we are expected to know about what we eat – all of these are aspects of individual and group identity that may remain stable in a society for long periods of time, or may go through abrupt shifts. In this arena, as in others, socially competent individuals learn to bring their self-presentation into conformity with the ethos of the group in which they live. Those who wish to maintain their standing as competent persons learn to change their behaviour with the times, in eating as in sexual or conversational style. Thus the attitudes and behaviours of individual both mirror those of the larger society, and create them in microcosm. (Lakoff 2006: 143)

In *Gilmore Girls*, shared and unshared attitudes towards food certainly contribute to bonding and the creation of solidarity between characters. Consider extracts 3 and 4 below:

(3)

EMILY:	The roast looks perfect. Oh, Jess, you eat meat, **I hope**. I forgot to ask.
JESS:	**I'm a carnivore**.
EMILY:	**Good. I don't see how anybody can resist eating meat.**
JESS:	**It's why we have teeth.**
EMILY:	**That's how I feel**. Dinner parties used to be simple. Now every time we give one, I have to run my menu down with every person on the list. It's tiring. This one [pointing with head at Rory] eats just about anything.

(3.14, *Swan song*, my bold)

(4)

LORELAI:	I smell meat, is that meat?
VALET:	Why, yes, miss, it is meat.
LORELAI:	Oh, he called me miss. There's meat and a miss, I'm happy.
RORY:	What's the occasion?
RICHARD:	Well, I thought we might like some appetizers with our cocktails tonight.
LORELAI:	Would we ever.
VALET:	The first batch is ready, sir.
RICHARD:	Wonderful, on the table please.
LORELAI:	Mm, **god it smells good**.

RORY: **I love** a good steak on a stick.
RICHARD: **Me, too.**
RORY: *We should form a club.*
LORELAI: *Steak-On-A-Stick club.*
(5.08, *The party's over,* my bold and italics)

In both examples (3) and (4) the characters share positive attitudes towards meat (in bold) – either towards the eating of meat in general (3) or towards particular types of meat (4), creating their own discursively construed in-groups, implicitly excluding Vegetarians and others. These are instances of what Knight (2010) calls 'communing affiliation' (Knight 2010: 49), where conversational participants commune around shared attitudes. This is also an example of how expressive identity (here: held attitudes/values) combines individual and social identity, and is both a way of expressing a character's unique identity and simultaneously aligning one character with other characters who share similar expressive identities (Chapter 6).

Vice versa, attitudes towards food can become a site for discord and conflict, as in example (5) below:

(5)
AURORA: Here's your plate, sir. I hope it's not too hot . . . the plate, not the food. [very quietly; turns into unintelligible whispering]
RICHARD: **Oh, well. It's fish again.**
EMILY: It's sea bass.
RICHARD: And sea bass is a fish . . . hence my comment **'surprise, surprise . . . it's fish again.'**
RORY: It **tastes good.**
RICHARD: **Tastes like fish.**
EMILY: **I don't think it tastes fishy.** Sea bash is not a fishy fish. Mackerel is a fishy fish. Trout can be a fishy fish. But sea bass is not really a fishy fish.
RICHARD: **I didn't say it tasted fishy. I said it tasted like fish.**
RORY: I think it tastes **good.**
[4 turns]
RICHARD: This fish is **bland.**
EMILY: Would you like some more lemon-dill sauce?
RICHARD: No.
EMILY: Okay.
LORELAI: The sauce is **good,** mum.
EMILY: It's **nice, isn't it?**
LORELAI: **Tart, but not too tart.**
EMILY: Stefan, the chef that we stole from the Lowells, is doing a **marvelous** job incorporating the dietary recommendations . . .

RICHARD: **Enough.** If **forced**, I may eat this fish, but **I absolutely refuse** to **waste my time** having a conversation about it.

(7.15, *I am kayak, hear me roar*, my bold)

In this extract, Richard consistently evaluates the served fish negatively as something undesirable and tasteless, creating a conflict between him and his wife Emily – note, for example, the negations (*don't think, didn't say, No*) and absolutes (*I absolutely refuse*) which commonly occur in conflict/disagreement (Lorenzo-Dus 2009: 106). Lorelai and Rory try to defuse this conflict by showing their appreciation of the dish, and sharing a positive evaluation with Emily (e.g. *The sauce is good/It's nice, isn't it*) with the joint goal of providing a 'remedy' to Emily's offended image (in Behn's 2009 terms, following Goffman 1967, 1971), thus mitigating her image loss and establishing harmony.

The language the participants use in the above examples to talk about food illustrates how 'the language people use in interaction can join them together – or, indeed, keep them apart – in particular social ways' (Day 1998: 151). The sharing and non-sharing of attitudes towards and evaluations of food thus contributes to the creation of bonding and solidarity between characters or put it at risk, and attitudes towards food are part of expressive character identity.

Section 2 below focuses predominantly on those attitudes towards meat-eating that occur repeatedly across *Gilmore Girls* and are thus shared by most characters, especially by the protagonists who are portrayed positively and who we as viewers are asked to identify with. First I will introduce the study of language and ideology, particularly using corpus linguistics.

2 The Ideology of Eating Meat in *Gilmore Girls*

2.1 Ideology and corpus linguistics

Considering the study of ideology, we can look at ideology from at least three perspectives: the social functions of ideologies; the cognitive structure of ideologies; and the expression of ideology in discourse (van Dijk 1998a: 23–4). The focus of this chapter is on the latter. While it is beyond the scope of this chapter to discuss possible relations between language and ideology in detail, language has been connected to ideology in many approaches, for example, as playing a crucial part in both changing and reproducing ideology (Fowler 1986: 130). According to Foucault, discursive formations, which have much to do with the notion of ideology (see Note 1), 'are built bottom up from disparate micro-instances' (Mittell 2004: 174). Ideological strategies such as positive self- and negative other-presentation are implemented through language (van Dijk 1998b: 317–18). The media play a crucial role in this, as some argue (see also discussion below in Section 3), as ideological values are presumably circulated through social institutions like the media (Thornham & Purvis 2005: 74).

In novels, we can look for ideology in either the narrative voice or in the voice of characters (Fowler 1986: 13); similarly in fictional television we can look for ideology in the narrative voice as construed, for example, through camera techniques (see Chapter 2: Section 3.2.2) or in the dialogue of televisual characters. With respect to the latter – the focus of my analyses here – we need to consider also whether or not viewers are invited to bond with characters or not. Arguably, if a sympathetic character, a protagonist who is clearly portrayed positively and invites identification, embodies a certain ideology we can assume that we are also invited to share this particular ideology (but see Section 3.2 below). On the other hand, if a character is portrayed negatively and embodies a certain ideology we can assume that we are not invited to share this ideology. One way of studying ideology in dramedy, then, is through an analysis of the ideology expressed by characters that are portrayed positively/negatively. Another way of studying ideology in dramedy is through an analysis of the ideologies that are shared by many characters and are spread throughout the text. Both ways of studying ideology will play a role in the analyses of this chapter, and quantitative (frequency and concordance) as well as qualitative (discourse) analysis will be used in this endeavour using corpus linguistic concordance analysis.

Baker (2006) and Adolphs (2006) as well as other corpus-based discourse analysts have convincingly demonstrated that analysing frequency and patterns of meaning around particular lexical items with the help of a concordance analysis can reveal ideology as discursively construed attitudes for example towards refugees (Baker 2006) or towards Europe (Mautner 2000). A corpus analysis is powerful in the way in which it allows us to see all instances at the same time and to 'uncover hidden patterns of language' (Baker 2006: 19) of which we may not necessarily be aware. However, studying ideology using large corpora and corpus linguistic methodology is still very much in its infancy (Adolphs 2006: 81) as are corpus-based discourse analyses in general (Baker 2006: 6, but see Partington et al. 2004). At the same time, a corpus analysis that focuses on repeated patterns allows the researcher to get at the 'stable', 'sedimented' and 'decontested' nature of ideologies (Norval 2000: 316).

In this chapter I analyse frequencies of and concordances for lexical items concerning meat-eating such as *Vegetarian, meat, burger*. Unlike Chapter 6 where the expressive resource analysed was formally definable (emotive interjections), what is formally definable here are the entities (lexical items concerning meat-eating) towards which attitudes are taken. The concordances were produced using corpus linguistic software, in my case Wordsmith (Scott 2004). Wordsmith's Concord programme produces lists of all instances of a search term in the corpus, including its co-text (words occurring to the right or to the left of it). Baker (2006) gives a very accessible overview of using concordances in discourse analysis. By way of exemplification Figure 8.1 below shows concordances for *Vegetarian** displayed in the KWIC format where the search term is presented with its immediate co-text to the right and to the left.

N	Concordance
1	I've never eaten this healthy. So, "vegan" doesn't just mean "vegetarian." SUSAN: No -- no animal products of any kind. No
2	Did you not get it? He's having the chicken? The Dalai Lama's a vegetarian, so obviously he's not having the chicken. Sorry.
3	EMILY: Roast beef. Oh, I hope Logan's not some kind of vegetarian. RICHARD: Well, his grandfather owned ten thousand
4	EMILY: Lorelai, it's your mother, I – SOOKIE: Hey, we've got vegetarians in April! What, were you hiding them? LORELAI: Yes,
5	it every day. I mean, one minute you could be. . .oh, let's say a vegetarian, and the next minute you could accidentally have a bite
6	eight o'clock. SOOKIE: I thought you said you weren't gonna let vegetarians in here anymore. LORELAI: No, you said you weren't
7	And we're off. SOOKIE: Okay, I just got a message that a vegetarian menu was requested for tonight. LORELAI: Yeah,
8	in here anymore. LORELAI: No, you said you weren't gonna let vegetarians in here anymore. SOOKIE: But I'm making my baked
9	then we will never again be able to get any produce and all our vegetarian clients will die. SOOKIE: I'm scared. LORELAI: I know.

co-text | search term | co-text

FIGURE 8.1 Concordances for *Vegetarian**

The star (*) is used as a 'wildcard' so this includes occurrences for *Vegetarians* as well as *Vegetarian*.

Looking at concordances in this format allows us to see repeated co-textual patterns for selected search terms such as *Vegetarian**. It allows us to see exactly in what co-text and how these search terms are used, for example whether or not a selected term is surrounded by positive or negative evaluation – a phenomenon variously called semantic prosody, semantic preference or semantic association (see Bednarek 2008e for an overview of research in this area). We can also see other patterns of usage, which may be phraseological and/or semantic-pragmatic and need not necessarily include explicitly evaluative language in order to express attitudes towards meat-eating. In fact, even though the main focus below is on explicitly evaluative language we will also see examples where linguistic features that do not carry any explicit evaluative meaning function as expressive resource (compare Chapter 6).

An analysis of concordances goes beyond the kind of more quantitative information apparent in frequency lists or automatic collocation analysis in allowing us to view semantic/pragmatic meanings such as evaluation. However, many search terms have no clear evaluations surrounding them within a span of a few words, and if we only considered their immediate co-text (as shown in Figure 8.1) we would miss much about the discursive construal of ideology:

> Analysing individual concordance lines without reference to the text from which they originate, or indeed, the particular passage of text that surrounds them, may affect our analysis in a way that makes it difficult to make statements about traces of ideology in a language. (Adolphs 2006: 81)

It thus makes sense to either 'grow' the co-text so that we can see more of the text surrounding the search term, or to directly access the text. Both options are available with Concord and were frequently made use of in my analyses. There are at least two advantages of doing a concordance analysis that takes into account the wider co-text: looking at concordances allows the researcher to identify patterns that are not formally identifiable such as evaluative or

Table 8.1 Within turn and across turn evaluations in *Gilmore Girls*

Evaluation	Examples (bold face mine in all)
Within turn	I **love** lamb chops with Sicilian olives, rosemary and garlic, and a warm potato and chorizo salad. (3.11, *I solemnly swear*) **Who the hell** made chicken and dumplings? (6.09, *The prodigal daughter returns)* This roast beef is **delicious**. (2.20, *Help wanted*)
Across turns	RORY: Thanks, Caesar. Since we were short on time, I had them make us something to go. My Yale **special**. LORELAI: Oh, share, share. RORY: Sausage wrapped in a pancake tied together with bacon. (4.02, *The Lorelais' first day at Yale*)
	LUKE: Lamb and artichoke stew, penne with pesto and potatoes, roasted garlic with rosemary focaccia, tomatoes stuffed with bread crumbs and goat cheese, and ricotta cheesecake with amaretto cookies to go with your coffee. LORELAI: **You're the perfect man**. (5.08, *The party's over*)
	LORELAI: Okay. Peas are out. What smells **so good**? LUKE: Fried chicken. LORELAI: Luke, **will you marry me**? (6.07, *Twenty-one is the loneliest number*)
	LUKE: So, I see you had the pot roast. JASON: Yeah. LUKE: **Good**, huh? JASON: Yeah, **very good.** (4.22, *Raincoats and recipes*)

ideological patterns, which automatic collocation analysis may miss, and looking at the wider co-text allows the analysis of patterns that stretch across turns and are complex. This is particularly important with respect to evaluation in spoken discourse, as evaluation can both occur within and across turns, as exemplified in Table 8.1.

For instance, what evaluations refer to sometimes only become apparent when looking at several turns, as in example (6):

(6)

(6a) Concordance in KWIC format

N	Concordance
13	and spend some time apart. RORY: May I have some more roast, please, Grandma? EMILY: Of course you may.

(6b) Occurrence in text

RORY: May I have some more **roast**, please, Grandma?

EMILY: Of course you may.
LORELAI: It's really **good** tonight, Mom.
(4.09, *Ted Koppel's big night out*)

Here we need to either 'grow' the view or go directly to the text in order to see that the evaluation that Lorelai expresses in (6b) relates to the roast that the characters are eating and that is mentioned by Rory – in other words, the *it* carries both endophoric (anaphoric) and exophoric reference. Evaluation has a textual (Bednarek 2006a: 8) and prosodic nature (Martin & White 2005), and frequently works retro- or prospectively across clauses or sentences (Lemke 1998), as indicated in the following examples (search term in **bold**, evaluation underlined):

- Oh, suddenly life's fun, suddenly there's a reason to get up in the morning – it's called **bacon**! (3.02, *Haunted leg*);
- **Pork** is bred leaner these days. It has a different taste. Less fat equals less flavor. (3.05, *Eight o'clock at the oasis*);
- I need real food, peasant food. Hearty bread, **meat**, cheese, a little pickle chips, a sauce, a special sauce. This is the food that sustains me . . . (2.20, *Help wanted*);
- **Meat** loaf, mashed potatoes, stuffing. Comfort food, huh? (2.08, *The ins and outs of inns*);
- It should be fun. There'll be **turkey** legs. (4.20, *Luke can see her face*);
- You, me, and raw **fish**? Is that safe? (7.02, *That's what you get folks, for makin' whoopee*).

The manual examination of concordance lines is also necessitated by the fact that evaluation can be implied very indirectly:

(7)
SOOKIE: I mean, one minute you could be oh, let's say a vegetarian, and the next minute you could accidentally have a bite of a stuffed **pork** chop that changes your entire way of thinking.
Implied evaluation → the stuffed pork chop is so good it makes vegetarians not be vegetarian any more
(3.02, *Haunted leg*)

(8)
BABETTE: Patty, you wanna try my fish?
MISS PATTY: Fish has too much mercury
BABETTE: For this **fish**, you'll eat the mercury

Implied evaluation → the fish is so good you don't care about the mercury
(4.22, *Raincoats and recipes*)

(9)
LORELAI: It's raw **fish**. Dip it in Soya sauce and swallow it real quick.
Implied evaluation → the fish tastes so bad you have to eat it quickly
(6.07, *Twenty-one is the loneliest number*)

(10)
CHRISTOPHER: Then once we've been treated for frostbite and had our stomachs pumped of reindeer **meat**, we'll go defrost on a beach somewhere.
Implied evaluation → reindeer meat is so terrible you have to have your stomach pumped
(7.05, *The great stink*)

In Sections 2.3–2.4 below I describe evaluative or ideological patterns concerning the eating of meat and Vegetarianism. Hence, I do not list phraseological patterns per se (such as *side of bacon*, *piece of chicken*) but rather discuss patterns that are ideologically significant in terms of expressing attitudes towards (the eating of) meat. So rather than studying the *phraseology* of eating meat, I study the *ideology* of eating meat. The discussion of evaluations of food in this chapter will be limited to ideology, and I will proceeded via 'making strange the otherwise too-familiar' (Burton 1980: 102), in this case the naturalization of eating meat. This, however, means, that I am disregarding the actual discourse functions of such evaluations, for example, their use in the ordering of food, in commenting on food, in praising the cook etc. (see Wiggins & Potter 2003 on uses of evaluations of food during family mealtimes). Neither will I look at evaluations of food in terms of status, power or solidarity, for example, who evaluates whose food and how, how is this responded to, what is the effect in terms of negotiating power, solidarity and face/image and so on. The focus is on showing how the use of language around the respective search terms construes character attitudes towards meat-eating, Veganism, and Vegetarianism, and to relate this to expressive character identity. Sections 2.3–2.4 below describe the results of analysing the frequency and co-textual patterning of the search terms *vegetarian**, *vegan**, *veggie*,[3] *vegetable**, *tofu**, *soy*, *meat*, *roast*, *turkey*, *beef*, *pork*, *lamb*, *veal*, *chicken*, and *burger**. This analysis will be complemented by qualitative studies of relevant scenes and characters. The corpus linguistic methodology made use of in this chapter can be regarded as an alternative methodology complementary to those widely used in Media and Television studies at present (such as content and framing analysis; see Entman 1993, Bonfiglioli et al. 2007).

2.2 Results I: Frequency

First, consider the raw frequency with which the respective search terms occur (Table 8.2).[4]

Table 8.2 Raw frequency of search terms in *Gilmore Girls*

Search term	Raw frequency
*burger**	98
chicken	82
fish	65 (but 16 in one episode; 10 in another)
*vegetable**	46
meat	40
bacon	39
turkey	39 (but 11 in one episode)
roast	38
lamb	32
beef	27
pork	25
*tofu**	13 (but 7 in one episode)
*vegetarian**	9
soy	8
veal	5 (but 3 in one episode)
*vegan**	2
veggie	1

We can compare these frequencies to the 'real world' consumption of meat in the United States. Figures for 2005 show that red meat (beef, veal, lamb, mutton, pork) is consumed ahead of poultry (chicken, turkey) and fish, as listed in Table 8.3.

Table 8.3 Per capita consumption of meat in US

Per Capita Consumption in US in 2005	
Red meat, poultry, fish	201.8 pounds per person (= 100%)
Red meat (beef, veal, lamb, mutton, pork)	54% of 201.8 ppp
Poultry	36.8% of 201.8 ppp
Fish	8.1% of 201.8 ppp

Source: Figures listed in American Meat Institute 2007

Comparing Table 8.3 with mentions relating to red meat, poultry and fish, we can see that while the exact figures are not reproduced, the proportions of mention in *Gilmore Girls* are similar to the proportions of consumption in the United States (Table 8.4).[5]

Table 8.4 Mentions of meat in *Gilmore Girls*

Mentions of meat in *Gilmore Girls*		
Total instances	490	100%
beef, veal, lamb, pork, burger, bacon, meat, roast*	304	62%
chicken, turkey	121	24.7%
fish	65	13.3%

In other words, the dramedy seems to reflect or reproduce current meat consumption practices in the United States, at least to a certain extent. Whether or not this also serves to reinforce these practices will be discussed in more detail in Section 3 below. Other comments can also be made concerning the raw frequency of search times. As a reminder and to facilitate interpretation let us look at the respective frequencies again, represented as graph in Figure 8.3.

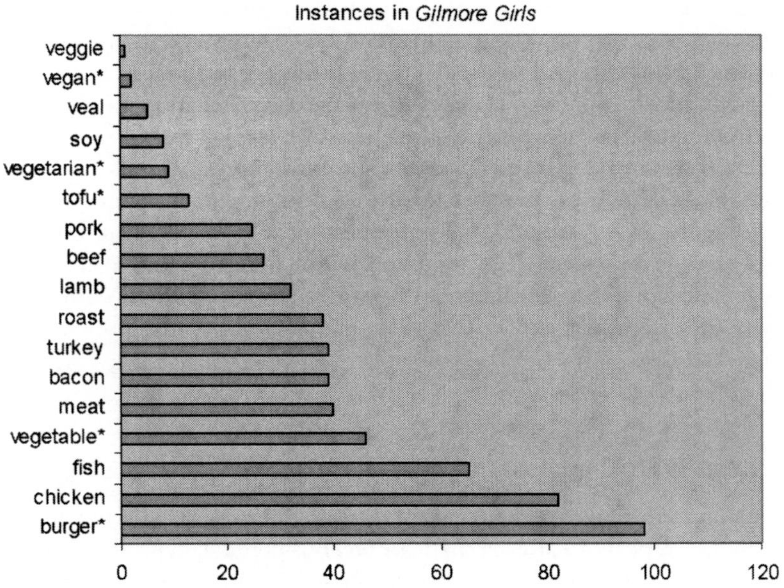

Figure 8.3 Instances of meat-related search terms in *Gilmore Girls*

First, the occurrences for search terms relating to the eating of meat are by far more frequent than occurrences for search terms relating to Vegetarians and Vegetarian eating practices, with the exception of *vegetable**, which, however, is not as strongly associated with Vegetarian eating as are *soy* and *tofu* and is often part of a 'meat 'n veg' dish as well. The other exception is *veal* which is less frequent than *soy, tofu* and *vegetarian**. In fact, eating veal is much less accepted in the United States and other countries than the eating of other animals, because of the widely publicized inhumane raising conditions of calves (using veal and gestation crates is banned by the European Union) and campaigns by organizations such as The Humane Society of the United States. Several states in the United States (Florida, Arizona, Oregon, Colorado, California) have banned either gestation crates and/or veal crates (www.hsus.org/farm/camp/totc/, accessed 1 April 2009).

Nevertheless, in terms of frequency we can arguably detect a tendency of silencing the Other (the Vegetarian/Vegan), and a tendency to naturalize the eating of meat. There are only two occurrences of *Vegan** and only nine of *Vegetarian**: in general, Vegans/Vegetarians are not mentioned, not talked about, not discussed; they are not part of the *Gilmore Girls* universe, are invisible, more or less written out of existence (apart from Mrs Kim, see below).[6] However, it might be argued that 'meat-eaters' are even more invisible; they are not talked about and not discussed either. In fact, there is not even a word for them – we can only 'creatively' call them *meat-eaters* or *non-Vegetarians* or, humorously, *carnivores*. But there is no doubt that almost all characters in *Gilmore Girls* are in fact meat-eaters. However, there is a crucial difference in that the 'meat-eaters' are the unmarked, 'normal' case, so we would not expect a particular term referring to them or an at-length discussion of why someone chooses to eat meat (rather, Vegetarians usually encounter questions concerning their reasons for *not* eating meat). Meat-eaters and meat-eating is the US norm, similar to heterosexuals, and female nurses/male detectives. In other words, we do not expect people to specify that someone is *hetero*sexual, a *female* nurse or a *male* detective, but we do except people to specify that someone is not heterosexual, a male nurse or a female detective. Similarly, if Vegetarians existed in the universe of *Gilmore Girls* we would expect this to be mentioned because they would be the marked case.

2.3 Results II: Concordance analysis

Moving on to the co-textual analysis of the search terms, the discussion below is limited to repeated patterns that can be considered as typical and general tendencies; I will generally not discuss one-off occurrences or occurrences that cannot be grouped into a more general repeated pattern.

2.3.1 Vegetarian/Vegan eating practices

The discussion will start with the patterns for *vegetarian** and *vegan**. Considering the nine occurrences of *vegetarian**, several of these occur in the co-text of negative attitudes towards vegetarians. This is particularly the case with chef Sookie as demonstrated by extract (11).

(11)

SOOKIE:	Okay, I just got a message that a **vegetarian** menu was requested for tonight.
LORELAI:	Yeah, Lasanos, party of five at eight o'clock.
SOOKIE:	I thought you said you weren't gonna let **vegetarians** in here anymore.
LORELAI:	[laughs] No, you said you weren't gonna let **vegetarians** in here anymore.
SOOKIE:	But I'm making my baked stuffed pork chops for tonight.
LORELAI:	Well, make 'em for the other guests and make something else for the Lasanos.
SOOKIE:	Like what?
LORELAI:	I don't know. Pasta, you make great pasta.
SOOKIE:	But that's boring, anyone can make pasta. I'm an artist. You don't dictate to an artist, you don't tell him what to do. I mean, no one ever walked up to Degas and said, 'Hey, pal, easy with the dancers, enough already. Draw a nice fruit bowl once in awhile, will ya?'
LORELAI:	A great artist can make art out of anything, including pasta.
SOOKIE:	Fine, pasta, whoo.
[13 turns]	
SOOKIE:	People change, you know. They do it every day. I mean, one minute you could be oh, let's say a **vegetarian**, and the next minute you could accidentally have a bite of a stuffed pork chop that changes your entire way of thinking.
LORELAI:	Sookie.
SOOKIE:	Oh, suddenly life's fun, suddenly there's a reason to get up in the morning – it's called bacon!
LORELAI:	Forget it.
SOOKIE:	Come on!
LORELAI:	Pasta.
SOOKIE:	Let the people grow, dammit!

(3.02, *Haunted Leg*)

It becomes apparent, then, that one of the main characters in *Gilmore Girls*, Lorelai's best friend and business partner Sookie, exhibits a clearly negative attitude towards Vegetarians. This is quite obviously the case in this extract, but occurs again in another episode (SOOKIE: *Hey, we've got vegetarians in April! What, were you hiding them?* LORELAI: *Yes, I'm evil that way.*) Here negative evaluation seems mainly based on the assumption that Vegetarian cooking is not as sophisticated or exciting as non-Vegetarian cooking and consequently does not allow Sookie the same way of expressing her talent as chef. Lorelai's attitude in this extract is less clear. As a professional, she treats Vegetarians as guests whose wishes have to be respected, just as you have to put up with other clients' special desires. This is also confirmed by Lorelai's words in another episode, where Sookie is about to go on a date with her 'produce guy', Jackson, and is scared that if it goes wrong he won't sell her any vegetables anymore. Lorelai then counters with 'And since all the produce in the entire world is in his possession and all the produce that will be grown in the future will be in his possession, then we will never again be able to get any produce and all our **vegetarian clients** will die' (1.12, *Double date*).

Emily, Lorelai's mother, is another character who evaluates Vegetarians and not eating meat negatively, as already apparent in example 3 above, and again apparent in her exclamation (concerning Rory's boyfriend) *Oh, I hope Logan's not some kind of vegetarian.* In the remaining occurrences of *vegetarian**, attitudes are not expressed clearly: both occur in the context of explanations with one being used metalinguistically (*The Dalai Lama's a vegetarian, so obviously he's not having the chicken; So, 'vegan' doesn't just mean 'vegetarian'*). Summing up, both Emily and Sookie are protagonists that repeatedly express a negative evaluation of Vegetarians – whether or not we are asked to share this evaluation is ambiguous: Emily is clearly not construed as positive in the series, whereas Sookie is likeable but does not invite identification to the same extent as Lorelai, whose attitude towards Vegetarianism is one of 'professional tolerance' if you will.

Turning now to *vegan**, there are only two occurrences, and both occur in season 7, episode 6, which features Luke on a date with a Vegan, Susan. It is thus interesting to consider this episode more qualitatively.

(12)
RESTAURANT
[Luke and Susan enter]

HOSTESS:	Hello. Two? Okay, right this way. There you go. Your waitress will be right with you.
SUSAN:	Thank you. [To Luke] Oh, no. Come sit with me.
LUKE:	There?
SUSAN:	Yeah. It's cozier.
LUKE:	Oh. Okay.
SUSAN:	I hate being so far away.
LUKE:	[Chuckles, then clears his throat. Looks at the menu] Wow!

SUSAN: I know, right? It's my favorite restaurant. And you said you liked to eat healthy, so . . .

LUKE: Yeah. Huh. I've never eaten <u>this</u> healthy. So, 'vegan' doesn't just mean 'vegetarian.'

SUSAN: No . . . no animal products of any kind. No eggs, no milk, no cheese.

LUKE: Just soy everything.

SUSAN: Soy steak is scrumptious. I swear you totally can't tell the difference.

LUKE: Oh, I bet I can.

SUSAN: So, Luke, let me ask you a question.

LUKE: Okay.

SUSAN: Who would play you in the Luke Danes movie?

LUKE: Huh?

SUSAN: Alive or dead.

LUKE: Uh . . . I-I never really thought about that.

SUSAN: Take your time. Do you wanna know mine?

LUKE: Sure.

SUSAN: [Laughs] Marlene Dietrich.

LUKE: Oh.

SUSAN: Right!

LUKE: I don't know who that is.

SUSAN: Sure you do.

LUKE: No, I don't.

SUSAN: Yes, you do. Think.

LUKE: I don't.

SUSAN: 'Touch of Evil,' um 'The Lady is Willing,' 'Destry Rides Again.' 'Your husband would rather be cheated by me than married to you.' [last quote spoken with accent]

LUKE: Oh, yeah, sure.

SUSAN: My last boyfriend . . . 'the ex' . . . he was always calling me [shouting] 'Marlene!' Oh, you know what? I think you might know him. Bob McCullough, Laura's father?

LUKE: No, I don't think I do.

SUSAN: We lived together for four months, and then he just went totally psycho. [shouting] Psycho! [Luke looks shocked and a little scared] I swore I wasn't gonna date any more single dads after that, but here I am.

LUKE: [Chuckles nervously]

SUSAN: You hooked me.

LUKE: Hmm.

SUSAN: Well, you know what they say . . . third time's a charm.

WAITRESS: Can I get anybody a drink?

LUKE: Yes, please.
(7.06, *Go, bulldogs*; online at www.youtube.com/watch?v=EAlqUcy-dGI, last accessed 23 October 2009)

Considering this episode, and especially this scene, it is very likely that the Vegan's (Susan) behaviour would lead the audience to evaluate her negatively, as some kind of 'weirdo'. She repeatedly breaks normative expectations with respect to appropriate behaviour on a first date and in general. Her behaviour comes across as pushy, inappropriate, strange. For instance, she asks Luke to sit right next to her at the table (a somewhat strange set-up in this situation) and also assumes too much emotional intimacy verbally (*I hate being so far away*; *You hooked me*). She directly contradicts Luke and presumes to know something about his internal state of mind (*LUKE: I don't know who that is./SUSAN: Sure you do./LUKE: No, I don't./SUSAN: Yes, you do.*) and orders him to 'think'. She is also relatively immature in terms of her linguistic style (*I swear you totally . . .*) and the kind of questions she asks (*Who would play you in the Luke Danes movie?*) are pretty 'stupid', with Luke being presented as not knowing what she is talking about. Susan also refers to her ex-boy-friend and starts shouting inappropriately – it is clear here that the impression is that it is not her ex-boy-friend who's the 'psycho' but Susan herself (consider also the titles of the films she lists). This is also reinforced by her tone of voice, facial expression, intonation and other multimodal performance features: the impression viewers get is of her being 'intense' (e.g. 'mad' eyes, intonation shifts, changes in loudness), and strongly coming on to Luke, trying to be 'sexy'. She also has a childish, high-pitched voice, wears girlish (pink) make-up, has styled short hair, and wears relatively old-fashioned clothes. (For a more technical, less impressionistic, description of multimodality, albeit in a different scene, see Chapter 7). In contrast, Luke is clearly uncomfortable throughout, as evidenced by his verbal (frequent interjections and hesitation markers, for example, *oh, wow, huh, uh, oh*) and nonverbal behaviour (chuckling, clearing his throat, looking shocked, scared, nervous and desperately needing a drink).

In a follow-up scene after the date (not reproduced here), the incompatibility of Luke and Susan becomes clear again. Although Luke behaves very 'gentleman-like', in telling his daughter that the date was 'nice' and in not explicitly evaluating Susan negatively, he agrees he did not like the 'vegan food' and that 'she [Susan]'ll just remain "coach Bennett" to me'. He is then portrayed as being made happy through eating pizza with 'real cheese' and sticky buns – again contributing to the overall negative portrayal of both Vegans and Vegan eating practices. As argued above, ideologies carried by unlikeable characters (here: Susan) are unlikely to be invited to be shared by audiences, whereas ideologies carried by likeable characters (here: Luke) are likely to be asked to be shared by audiences. Cohen (1999) hypothesizes that 'viewers are more involved with their favourite characters, remember more about them, and are more likely to be affected by them' (Cohen 1999: 343). In any case, this episode seems to position the audience with 'us' (Luke, meat-eaters, non-Vegans) against the 'other' (Susan, Vegan) and concomitant eating practices.

It may be argued that one positive thing (from the point of view of a Vegan) would be the educational effect of this exchange between Luke and Susan, where Susan offers an explanation of what 'vegan' means:

(12a)

SUSAN:	. . . And you said you liked to eat healthy, so . . .
LUKE:	Yeah. Huh. I've never eaten <u>this</u> healthy. **So, 'vegan' doesn't just mean 'vegetarian.'**
SUSAN:	**No . . . no animal products of any kind. No eggs, no milk, no cheese.**
LUKE:	Just soy everything.
SUSAN:	Soy steak is scrumptious. I swear you totally can't tell the difference.
LUKE:	Oh, I bet I can.

However, Luke then evaluates Susan's answer negatively, assuming Vegan eating means 'just soy everything'. Rather than disagreeing, Susan simply proceeds to evaluate soy steak as positive in terms of taste but also as 'no different' to meat. In so doing she reproduces assumptions that Vegan cooking is not very varied and reinforces the positive evaluation of 'real' steak. Further, Luke disagrees, with his *Oh, I bet I can* additionally implying negative evaluation of the soy 'ersatz'. The potential positive evaluation of Vegan eating practices as healthy offered by Susan (*you said you liked to eat healthy*) is also neutralized by Luke's *I've never eaten <u>this</u> healthy*, implying both that Veganism exaggerates healthy eating and implying negative evaluation (healthy can carry connotations of 'not tasty'). So in this episode Vegans and Vegan eating practices are associated with an unlikeable character (an Other) and evaluated negatively by a likeable character (one of 'us').

The same association of Vegetarian/Vegan practices with an Other becomes apparent when looking at patterns for *tofu**, *soy* and *veggie*. Both *tofu** and *soy* are very strongly associated with Lane's mother, Mrs Kim. All but one occurrence of tofu* are associated with her as well as three of eight occurrences of *soy*, as illustrated by examples (13) to (18):

(13)

LANE:	I'm sorry, but she [Mrs Kim] found a web site that sells **Tofu** in bulk.
LORELAI:	Oh, you're kidding, right?

(1.02, *The Lorelais' first day at Chilton*)

(14)
MRS. KIM: Try the **tofu**rkey. Turkey made from **tofu**.
(3.09, *A deep-fried Korean thanksgiving*)

(15)
ZACH: . . . What else did we get? Squash, zucchini, **tofu**.
MRS KIM: Special calcium-fortified **tofu**.
(7.11, *Santa's secret stuff*)

(16)
LANE: Stash this for me at Miss Patty's, okay?
RORY: Don't you need this for David to bid on?
LANE: Oh no, my mom packed that one. You know, homemade granola, wheat grass juice, **soy** chicken taco.
LORELAI: Suddenly our lunches are looking pretty good.
(2.13, *A-tisket, A-tasket*)

(17)
LANE: Mama, do you need any help?
MRS. KIM: No, thank you.
LANE: I could get out the **soy** scones.
MRS. KIM: If you like.
LANE: **Tofu**tter?
MRS. KIM: Fine.
(3.20, *Say goodnight, Gracie*)

(18)
LANE: Hi, Mama.
MRS. KIM: Hello, Lane. Thank you for having me.
LANE: Did you find the place okay?
MRS. KIM: Yes. Here [passing bowl to Lane]. Multi-grain **soy** pudding. Extra chunky, the way you like it.
(4.21, *Last week fights, this week tights*)

In other words, Vegetarian cooking is strongly associated with an Other, Mrs. Kim, Rory's friend Lane's mother, a Korean immigrant whose 'bizarre vegetarian cooking' (Haupt 2008: 124) is just one aspect of her character that is predominantly portrayed negatively and evaluated negatively by likeable characters such as Lorelai and Rory. While she may have some redeeming features, she is also 'a devout Seventh Day Adventist so rigid in her beliefs and outside the cultural mainstream as to be absurd' (Haupt 2008: 124). Haupt concludes that 'there is no other way to read her than as a narrow-minded and inflexible mother who is seemingly unfamiliar with the concept of nurturance'

(Haupt 2008: 124). Her vegetarian food (such as tofurkey, gluten patties, wheat balls, calcium-fortified tofu) 'mark Mrs. Kim as irretrievably Other', with 'unappetizing food choices' (Haupt 2008: 125). Consequently, this portrayal may invite the audience to share a negative evaluation of such Vegetarian eating practices, and marks it and Vegetarians as not associated with 'Us'.

Of the remaining occurrences of *tofu** and *soy* and the one occurrence of *veggie* a few occur in the context of negative attitudes expressed by particular characters (Emily: *They certainly do like their tofu here, don't they?* where it is clear that she doesn't like it; Lorelai: *So what happens when you guys get serious, the whole place goes soy?* where Luke changes the menu because of his girl-friend and this is evaluated negatively by Rory and Lorelai; Luke's *Just soy everything* as mentioned above; Lorelai's *He'll* ***make me*** *eat a veggie burger!*). There are a few neutral/positive instances of *soy*, but these involve more accepted derivatives of *soy* (*soy milk, soy sauce*), and one of them is uttered by Vegan Susan (as mentioned above):

- Here is your decaf with **soy milk** (1.18, *The third Lorelai*);
- This bowl of rice is all a Burmese prisoner gets to eat in a day. One bowl- that's it. No butter or **soy sauce** . . . (4.17, *Girls in bikinis, boys doin' the twist, aka Gilmore Girls gone wild*);
- **Soy steak** is scrumptious (7.06, *Go, bulldogs*).

With respect to vegetables, a food group not as strongly associated with Vegetarian/Vegan eating practices, only two main discursive patterns can be found. On the one hand, many instances are simply tied to the character of Jackson, Sookie's 'vegetable guy' (and later partner):

- Jackson's vegetables are top-of-the-line, first-rate (7.06, *Go, bulldogs*);
- Jackson invented a new vegetable again (1.11, *Paris is burning*);
- Jackson sells his vegetables all over town (7.06, *Go, bulldogs*).

This pattern contributes to construing Jackson as a character and the relationship between him and chef Sookie. For a discussion of food and the Sookie–Jackson relationship see Coleman (2008: 179–82).

The other pattern is one that is tied to Lorelai's (in particular) and Rory's negative attitude towards vegetables, which is part of their general negative attitude towards healthy food; they famously have 'junk' food, fast food, take away, sweets and lots and lots of coffee most of the time. Here are four examples:

(19)
LORELAI: I swear I would eat my **vegetables** if only they were fizzy.
(7.05, *The great stink*)

(20)

LORELAI: So, what about dinner?
RORY: It should probably be something healthy since we've been eating junk the whole trip.
LORELAI: We had lettuce on our burgers last night.
RORY: You picked it off.
LORELAI: But it left its essence.
RORY: There was lettuce essence on our burgers?
LORELAI: Definitely.
RORY: And that satisfied our **vegetable** requirement?
LORELAI: For the week.
RORY: We can't argue with cold hard facts.

(2.04, *The road trip to Harvard*)

(21)

EMILY: The government says you should have nine servings of fruit and **vegetables** per day.
LORELAI: Imperialist propaganda.
RORY: I think Noam Chomsky would agree.

(5.21, *Blame booze and Melville*)

(22)

CHRISTOPHER: Which one do we get again?
LORELAI: Avoid the words 'made with real **vegetables**'.

(7.10, *Merry fisticuffs*)

This is contrasted with Luke's belief in healthy food, with Luke frequently urging them to eat more healthily, illustrated in example (23).

(23)

[Luke brings their food]

LUKE: All right, pancakes, one fried egg, side of bacon. Chicken noodle soup, side of mashed potatoes.
RORY: Thanks, Luke.
LORELAI: Thanks.
LUKE: How's the cold coming?
LORELAI: It's fine.
LUKE: Any better?
LORELAI: It's fine.
LUKE: It's the third day in a row you've ordered soup for breakfast.
LORELAI: Oh, thanks for the tally.
LUKE: You know what helps get rid of a cold?
LORELAI: Endless vague questioning first thing in the morning?
LUKE: A healthy immune system.

LORELAI:	My second guess.
LUKE:	And you know how you get a healthy immune system?
LORELAI:	Remember when you hated me? That was fun, wasn't it?
LUKE:	Is it eating nothing but crap all day and blowing out your brain cells with coffee?
RORY:	No.
LUKE:	That's right, no.
LORELAI:	Why are you helping him?
RORY:	No seemed like the right answer.
LUKE:	Eat a **vegetable** now and then, maybe some high fiber cereal in the morning.
LORELAI:	Listen, Grandpa, my soup's getting cold.
LUKE:	At least eat the carrots in the soup this time, not just the noodles.
LORELAI:	I promise.

[Luke walks away; Lorelai holds her bowl of soup toward Rory]

LORELAI:	Eat my carrots.
RORY:	Apparently, maturity is extremely overrated in your universe.

(3.02, *Haunted leg*)

Concerning other instances of *vegetable** no clear patterns become apparent indicating a prevailing positive or negative attitude, with many neutral instances and often relating to specific vegetables/cooking (e.g. *I didn't notice the vegetables*; *I was just ordering a ton of extra, you know, vegetables and stuff*; *Fred, why don't you let the vegetables simmer for a while*), some negative ones (e.g. *Well, I christen these vegetables sucky*) and a few that may be classified as positive (*You know what? There is another soup kitchen down on Hadley, and they serve more vegetables than you do. So I would rather work there anyhow*; *Wasting vegetables is wrong*). Vegetables, in contrast to soy, tofu and Veggie products are clearly part of the *Gilmore Girls* universe even if Lorelai and Rory do not particularly like to eat healthy. Whether or not we are asked to share Lorelai/Rory's or Luke's attitude towards vegetables is another matter, as all three are protagonists and likeable characters (compare also the discussion in Section 3.2).

2.3.2 Meat-eating practices

Let us now move on to search terms relating to meat. On account of the predominantly low frequencies for search terms related to Vegetarian/Vegan eating, the discussion was quite detailed. In contrast, because there are more instances for these search terms, I will focus on main discernible tendencies, rather than discussing each search term individually.

First, the vast majority of occurrences for the various search terms does not exhibit an either positive or negative semantic association. Rather, the majority of occurrences are 'neutral' and refer just to what people order/eat (often at Luke's diner or at the Friday dinner with the parents). This cuts across types of meat. Here are just a few examples:

- Scrambled eggs with cheddar cheese and half **bacon**, half sausage. (5.03, *Written in the stars*);
- Ah, here's the **lamb**. (7.05, *The great stink*);
- Uh, six **burgers**, three cheese . . . two cheddar, one Swiss. Two plain **burgers**, one chilli **burger** with cheese and onions on the side. (3.13, *Dear Emily and Richard*);
- We'll make a **fish**-cheese combo course just to be sure. (4.06, *An affair to remember*);
- You can stay for dinner, my mom's making a **roast**. (2.20, *Help wanted*);
- But I'm making my baked stuffed **pork** chops for tonight. (3.02, *Haunted leg*);
- I was just treating Logan to his first Branford dining hall **meat** loaf. (7.10, *Merry fisticuffs*);
- No, that's two orders of garlic gnon, three simosas, and a **chicken** vindiloo. (2.16, *There's the rub*);
- **Chicken** noodle soup, side of mashed potatoes. (3.02, *Haunted leg*);
- I'll have a **turkey** sandwich on wheat and a glass of chardonnay. (7.17, *Gilmore Girls only*).

These can be classified as neutral, but the implication is that people order what they want and like. It is also possible to argue that while these instances are 'neutral', meat-eating is very much naturalized through them, as it becomes part of normal, familiar, commonsense, uncontested behaviour practiced by the majority of characters. They are also an example of how language can encode a particular commonsense world-view making it seem natural rather than socially construed (Fowler 1986: 29). There is an on-going debate between Vegetarians/Vegans and meat-eaters whether or not it is 'natural' for humans to consume animal meat. (Historically speaking, humans were first vegetarians before they switched to meat-eating, although this happened at least 2.5 million years ago [Mayell 2005].) These instances also refer to meat eating without reference to animals, thereby alienating the 'product' from the process of 'producing' it, that is, the (sometimes mis-)treatment of and killing of animals. There are only a few exceptions where explicit reference is made to this:[7]

(24)

JASON:	Here, you want bacon?
LORELAI:	You went out and **slaughtered a pig** between the running and the French toast?

(4.17, *Girls in bikinis, boys doin' the twist, aka Gilmore Girls gone wild*)

(25)

EMILY: Very nice. We'll have lamb.

RORY: So, it will be nice for everybody? Everybody will be nice to everybody? The key word being nice.

EMILY: Yes, very nice.

RORY: Really, really nice?

EMILY: Of course it'll be nice. That's what I just said.

RORY: Good. Nice would be nice.

EMILY: And a nice night it'll be.

LORELAI: Well, **not so nice for the lamb**.

(3.14, *Swan song*)

(26)

TJ: Well then, you could turn it into a weight room. Or a workshop. Or, hey, a pork smoker room! My uncle had a pork smoker room! Big sides of pork hanging all over the place! We called it the **Dead Pig** Room.

(6.03, *The ungraduate*)

(27)

GUY: I had an older brother that got me into them, and when my friends were listening to Hootie and the Blowfish, I was memorizing '**Meat is Murder.'**

RORY: Well, I have a mom who's pretty much cooler than anyone you'd meet, and she did the same thing.

(4.05, *The fundamental things apply*)

(28)

LORELAI: 'For deep water fishing, an angler' – me, again – 'can choose a wire line using a downrigger or a vertical jig. Whatever your technique, the other successful clue to attracting **fish** is the appropriate lure.' Ooh, what about the sequined top I wore to the Christmas party?

(3.12, *Lorelai out of water*)

(29)

RORY: Hey. Oh, no.

LORELAI: Isn't she cute?

RORY: What happened?

LORELAI: The **cork fell off my hook** and Jayne Mansfield over here bit.

RORY: Jayne Mansfield.

LORELAI: Not the brightest fish in the pond, but she's awfully pretty.

RORY: You caught a **fish**.
LORELAI: Yes.
RORY: And you brought it home.
LORELAI: Yes.
RORY: How are you gonna take a bath?
LORELAI: I don't know.
RORY: How long is it gonna live?
LORELAI: Hard to say.
RORY: What are you gonna feed it?
LORELAI: See, this is why I don't fish.
RORY: She is kinda cute.
LORELAI: And she has a great tail swish.
[12 turns]
RORY: Good. So do you think maybe we should try to rehabilitate her and send her back into the wild?
LORELAI: Unfortunately, I think she's already domesticated. Baths and scented candles.
RORY: We'll just have to keep her.
LORELAI: Maybe we can train her to do tricks.
RORY: Tomorrow. Night Jayne.
LORELAI: Night Jayne.
(3.12, *Lorelai out of water*)

For example, in episode 3.12, from which examples (28) and (29) are taken, Lorelai clearly does not want to kill a fish – she has a cork on her hook when fishing and keeps the fish she accidentally catches in a bathtub. Here, hunting and killing animals are not evaluated as desirable by a very likeable character, Lorelai. As said, though, these are exceptions, and it must be pointed out that all of these instances are jokey and not to be taken as serious or as behaviour to be imitated – in example (27), for instance, the memorizing of 'Meat is Murder' is clearly classified as 'uncool'.

There are also a few instances where positive and negative evaluation occurs, which I will discuss only briefly here. Although positive evaluation is by far not as frequent as naturalized, 'neutral' instances, it is more frequent than negative evaluation. From the point of view of how evaluation is expressed in *Gilmore Girls* there are very different ways of evaluating meat, which can be combined (e.g. evaluative adjective plus emotive interjection in *A **nice** burger from Luke's and an ice cream soda, **yum**!*). Table 8.6 below gives a classification of the main evaluative means used to evaluate (the eating of) meat in *Gilmore Girls* in order to show the various ways in which evaluation can be expressed more or less explicitly as well as how it was analysed and classified as positive/negative (valence).[8]

Table 8.6 Expressing evaluation in Gilmore Girls

Evaluator	Example (episode no in brackets)	Valence
Emotion verb	. . . I **love** the bacon. (3.01)	+
	I **like** bacon (2.18)	
	I **love** a good steak on a stick. (5.08)	
	I **love** a lamb shank when it's braised (3.02)	
	. . . people who **love** fish (7.13)	
	I do [**like** lamb] (7.05)	
	I **like** the chicken (3.07)	
	Um, yeah, I **like** roast. (2.20)	
	. . . it was this burger that he seemed to **enjoy** the most. (7.14)	
	Who **doesn't like** a good roast? (5.20)	
	I'm **tired of** it [pork]. (5.15)	–
	Well, I'm **sick of** burgers (3.14)	
	. . . if Oprah decides to **get mad at** beef again. (5.16)	
Expletive	**Who the hell** made chicken and dumplings? (6.09)	–
Interjection	**Ooh, man**, it smells great in here. (4.22)	+
	A nice burger from Luke's and an ice cream soda, **yum**! (3.03)	
	LORELAI: Yes, yes, look. We got, uh, turkey sausage, extra spicy like you wanted - SOOKIE: **Yuck.** (5.09)	–
	Hey, that burger may be a disgusting burger but at least it considers me its equal. **Ugh**. (2.20)	
(intensified) evaluative adjective	This roast beef is **delicious**. (2.20)	+
	His lamb chops. They're **amazing**...(5.19)	
	. . . any of that **really great** braised lamb risotto thing (5.16)	
	It [the lamb]'s **good** (1.01)	
	No, it [the lamb]'s **perfect** (1.01)	
	. . . it [pork chops soaked in saltwater bourbon]'s actually **unbelievably good**. (5.09)	
	I hear the meat loaf is **excellent** here. (4.06)	
	The roast looks **perfect.** (3.14)	
	Mm, god it [meat] smells **good.** (5.08)	
	That lamb was **terrific** (7.15)	
	A **fabulous** leg of lamb (1.20)	
	You're getting my **famous** chicken today (3.03)	
	Seriously good fried chicken. (5.09)	
	This is **amazing** chicken, Mom. I mean it, **really great**. (3.07)	
	This roast beef is **delicious.** It's **lean**, it's **tender**. (2.20)	
	Roast. Sounds **good**. (5.20)	
	It [the roast]'s **really good** tonight, Mom. (4.09)	
	They have **the most delicious** pot roast you've ever tasted. (3.08)	
	It [fish] tastes **good**. (7.15)	
	My **beautiful, expensive**, organically grown turkey. (3.09)	
	It [salmon]'s **marvelous** for you (7.13)	
	Ah well, fish is **good**. (7.13)	

(Continued)

Table 8.6 Cont'd

Evaluator	Example (episode no in brackets)	Valence
	Ooh, man, it smells **great** in here [cooking fish]. (4.22) He does make a **damn fine** burger though. (1.05) The burgers are **delicious**, Luke. (6.09) His burgers are **better**. (6.09)	
	I don't mind paying for my **mushy** meat. (7.10) . . . **unclean** meat fried in unclean oil. (7.16) That **pale misshapen** thing, is that a sandwich or a piece of chicken. (7.13) Ah, we have a **battered** chicken salad (5.08) His turkey burgers are **very dry**. (2.08) This fish is **bland**. (7.15) . . . is it some sort of **precious** fish dish? 'Cause I'm dying for a steak. (5.19) **Disgusting** food [raw fish]. (6.07) . . . that burger may be a **disgusting** burger (2.20)	–
(intensified) evaluative noun	The distinct charred flavor of this meat is like **a delicacy**. (5.16) I hear pot roast is your **favorite**, too. (6.07)	+
	That [coming to the restaurant] was **a total waste** because he couldn't eat dairy, or salt, or meat, so he basically just came in every week for a salad, with no oil, and no mushrooms. (4.11)	–
Negation [implied non-desirability]	**No more** red meat, heavy desserts and you're going to have to exercise regularly. (1.10) If you can travel back in time and make me **not make the veal and ham pate**, I'd appreciate it. **Talk me out of** these things in the future, guys. (6.10)	–
Why-Question [incomprehensibility]	**Why** would anyone ever order that [foie gras with chicken and green shamrock frosting]? (2.17)	–
Verb implying (non-) desirability	And I **promise** you, there won't be any chicken.[9] (5.08)	+
	If **forced**, I may eat this fish, but I absolutely refuse to waste my time having a conversation about it. (7.15) I **don't want** a burger. (5.08)	–
Reference to pos/neg effects (usually health)	. . . and it [salmon] **makes your skin positively glow**. (7.13) . . . fish has been shown **to prevent heart attacks and stroke and has innumerable other health benefits** (7.13)	+
	Red meat can **kill** you. (1.01)	–

In terms of evaluative parameters (see Chapter 3: Section 2.2) then, Table 8.6 shows that I have considered both AFFECT and EMOTIVITY in terms of positive or negative attitudes towards (the eating of) meat. Looking at this with respect to valence (pos/neg evaluation), and taking up Wiggins and Potter's (2003) distinction between *category evaluation* and *item evaluation*,[10] the negative evaluation that does occur is often of specific combinations of food, specific ways of preparing or having food, or food tied to specific locations (school, hospital, work) or is evaluated negatively because a character had too much of it lately, rather than a general evaluation of meat.

(30)
[inappropriate to cultural habits]
LORELAI: Plus you have to eat **fish for breakfast** and you have to eat whales and then polar bears and penguins and Santa Claus . . .
(4.13, *Nag Hammadi is where they found the gnostic gospels*)

(31)
[specific combinations]
LORELAI: You made me **a Santa burger.**
[2 turns]
LUKE: Yeah, I just cut a piece of wonder bread, you know, poured a little ketchup, piped on a little cream cheese.
LORELAI: No one has ever made me something **quite this disgusting** before. I thank you.
LUKE: You're welcome.
(1.10, *Forgiveness and stuff*)

(32)
[specific type]
LORELAI: It's **raw** fish. Dip it in Soya sauce and **swallow it real quick**.
(6.07, *Twenty-one is the loneliest number*)

(33)
[prepared by specific person]
RORY: **Jojo's burgers** could travel to China, and they'd still be just as good.
DEAN: Because they start off **bad**.
(5.05, *We got us a Pippi virgin*)

(34)
[bred specifically]
RICHARD: Pork is bred leaner these days. It has a different taste. Less fat equals less flavor. Yet another example of the great advances man has made, **flavorless pork**. Hurrah for the opposable thumbs.
(3.05, *Eight o'clock at the oasis*)

(35)
[prepared at specific location; hospital food]
EMILY: I hardly know what anything is. That **pale misshapen** thing, is that a sandwich or a piece of chicken.
(7.13, *I'd rather be in Philadelphia*)

(36)
[too much of the same]
BRIAN: Well, **I'm sick of burgers**, so if it could be a place that has more than burgers –
(3.14, *Swan song*)

With respect to the more frequent positive evaluation both seem to occur – evaluation of specific meat cooked at a specific time (*This is amazing chicken*), and evaluation of meat in general (*I like bacon*).[11]

2.3.3 The ideology of eating meat in Gilmore Girls

Summing up the previous sections, we have seen that attitudes towards food can be related to expressive character identity, with different characters exhibiting different attitudes towards food, for instance Luke (non-Vegan) vs. Susan (Vegan), Lorelai/Rory (unhealthy meat-eaters) vs. Luke (healthy meat-eater), Sookie's and Emily's dislike of Vegetarianism. These more or less concern the individual aspect of expressive identity. Many more examples could be found such as the differences in the eating practices between Lorelai/Rory and Richard/Emily, whom Rory has to 'teach' how to eat frozen pizza in one episode. At the same time, many of the characters in *Gilmore Girls* seem to share a set of beliefs about (the eating of) meat, which can be related to ideology as a set of shared values and to the social aspect of expressive identity. We can perhaps talk about this in terms of a 'community of ideology', in analogy to the concept of communities of practice (Wenger 2007). As in Chapters 5 and 6, this analysis can be related to the model for expressive identity introduced in Chapter 6 (Table 8.7).

Table 8.7 Expressive identity: ideology

Macro	stable (repeated) expressive identity: ideology (shared/social expressive identity)	Gilmore Girls main characters: 'meat lovers'
Meso	expressive strategies/actions	Naturalizing meat-eating Positively evaluating meat (eating) Concealing process of production
Micro	expressive features (verbal)	Explicitly evaluative language Implicit evaluations Neutral references to meat

The quantitative and qualitative analyses have uncovered both explicit '*announcements* of beliefs' (Fowler 1986: 132) by characters, such as direct evaluations (e.g. *I don't see how anybody can resist eating meat*) and instances that are more '*symptomatic* of world-view' (Fowler 1986: 132), such as the many 'neutral' references by characters to the eating and ordering of meat.

We can also see that Vegans are made invisible or are portrayed as weird, and Vegetarian food is associated with a negative Other in the series as a whole. The main tendencies in this particular dramedy are the creation of what van Dijk (1998a, b) calls *'ideological polarization'* (van Dijk 1998b: 317). He elaborates: 'many group ideologies involve the representation of Self and Others, Us and Them. Many therefore seem to be *polarized* – We are Good and They are Bad' (van Dijk 1998a: 25). This is usually implemented through positive self-presentation and negative other-presentation expressed through various linguistic meanings and forms (van Dijk 1998b: 317). In the context of *Gilmore Girls,* We are the 'good' meat-eaters, and They are the 'bad' Vegetarians/Vegans. More specifically, Vegetarians are excluded, derogated or tolerated at best, and both Vegans and Vegetarians are associated with a negatively evaluated Other. In contrast, the consumption of meat is naturalized, part of the normal behaviour of 'us', the in-group, more frequently evaluated positively than negatively and separated or alienated from the process of 'production'. Such stereotyping presumably has the purpose 'to make the audience feel part of a cohesive social group, an "us" [here: meat-eaters] that "they" [here: Vegetarians and Vegans], as a "minority" group, are outside of' (Selby & Cowdery 1995: 110). In analogy to the concept of 'heteronormativity' (e.g. Cameron 2005), we can speak of a 'carniverous normativity' which the television series both *legitimizes* and *habitualizes* in Fowler's (1986: 29–33) terms. That is, in giving voice to these meanings, the media as official institution legitimizes them to a certain extent, while at the same time viewers are habitualized to them through recurrent exposure. Although television does not dictate who/what we are supposed to be, it can put pressure on us by showing certain things and not others (Hermes 2005: 103). As one Vegetarian wonders in her blog:

> I wish there were more prominent vegetarian characters on television. I think that would help a lot in showing vegetarianism as a more mainstream lifestyle choice. I believe that when people are exposed to something on TV on a weekly basis, it can help educate them and make them more comfortable with it in real life – as long as it's portrayed positively or neutrally and not as an object of ridicule.
>
> . . . Do you think TV does a good job of portraying vegetarianism? Or is it still portrayed as a 'radical' lifestyle choice? (Sherill 2008)

With respect to *Gilmore Girls,* the answer to these questions, from a Vegetarian point of view, would be 'no, it does not do a good job of portraying Vegetarianism'.

It is not surprising that *Gilmore Girls* portrays the eating of meat so positively because most of its target audience arguably would too, and

> [t]elevision exists, on the whole, to offend as few people as possible. Because of the mass nature of the medium, it is likely that ideologies which are seen to be representative of the majority of viewers are those which are most common. (Mills 2005: 146)

The kinds of ideologies represented in television may be there because of imagined consumer's ideologies, established television practices, and regulation (see below). So the tendencies emerging from the popular television series *Gilmore Girls* may be quite wide-spread in television and popular culture in general. An interesting study on US American popular culture on animated characters also found that '[c]haracters with strongly positive actions and motivations are overwhelmingly speakers of socially mainstream varieties of English. Conversely, characters with strongly negative actions and motivations often speak varieties of English linked to specific geographical regions and marginalized social groups' (Lippi-Green 1997: 101, quoted in Coupland 2007: 87–8). For further discussion of this issue see Section 3.1 below, which looks more broadly at television, ideology and the audience.

3 Ideology and the Audience

Taking the above analyses of *Gilmore Girls* as a springboard for elaboration, this section discusses more generally the relation between ideologies on fictional television and the television audience. While Section 3.1 briefly takes us into a general discussion of television and ideology, because it is such an important topic in relevant research, Section 3.2 brings us back to characterization in discussing relations between fictional characters and the audience in terms of ideology.

3.1 Viewing ideologies on television

Ideology was defined above rather broadly as a set of beliefs or attitudes, and I have demonstrated how it can be analysed in television dramedy with respect to characters' shared attitudes towards the eating of meat. However, it may still be interesting to look at this more closely in terms of power relations between different social groups. In other words, does *ideology* mean 'any set of beliefs' or 'the dominant forms of thought in a society' (Eagleton 1991: 2)? In the case of attitudes towards eating meat in *Gilmore Girls*, the set of attitudes and beliefs at stake is certainly the dominant, or 'hegemonic' one in US American society.

According to a 2006 poll, only 2.3% of adults (18 and older) are Vegetarian, and 1.4% are Vegan (www.vrg.org/journal/vj2006issue4/vj2006issue4poll.htm, accessed 4 March 2009), with about 1 in 200 children and teenagers in the US being Vegetarian (www.msnbc.msn.com/id/28543713/, accessed 4 March 2009). Can one therefore argue that this kind of representation is appropriate because it mirrors (US-American) 'reality' and the views of most (US-American) viewers? No, because on the one hand, we are concerned with ethical issues not with issues of proportional representation. There can be no automatic assumption that something is right because the majority of the population believes in it. On the other hand, even if we were concerned with issues of proportional representation, the question is whether or not television should just reproduce 'reality' even if it is, for instance, unjust? If most members of a particular minority group work in menial jobs, should fictional television series only show members of minority groups in menial jobs rather than as elite professionals? The argument of 'realism' is questionable at the very least in this particular context. In any case, what the above figures show is that the majority of the population (the dominant social group in terms of mass at least) are not Vegetarian and that the shared expressive identity of *Gilmore Girls* in terms of meat-eating is similar to the ideology of the mainstream. This appears to confirm the assumption that '[t]he world of the popular series is . . . the world of the dominant ideology, and its hegemonic [in Gramsci's terms] project is to organise consensus around . . . dominant ideological conceptions' (Thornham & Purvis 2005: 80). Eagleton (1991) notes six strategies of legitimating the power of a dominant social group, and arguably, the corpus-based analysis of *Gilmore Girls* has found that several occur in the context of representing Vegetarianism/Veganism:

> A dominant power may legitimate itself by *promoting* beliefs and values congenial to it; *naturalizing* and *universalizing* such beliefs so as to render them self-evident and apparently inevitable; *denigrating* ideas which might challenge it: *excluding* rival forms of thought, perhaps by some unspoken but systematic logic; and *obscuring* social reality in ways convenient to itself (Eagleton 1991: 5–6, italics in original).

Van Leeuwen's (2008) categories of legitimation (authorization, moral evaluation, rationalization, mythopoesis) are also partially relevant. For instance, we could consider chef Sookie as an 'expert authority' (Van Leeuwen 2008: 107) on food (*authorization*), and we have also seen the role evaluative language plays as well as the naturalization of meat-eating (*moral evaluation*), and the presence of 'instrumental' (van Leeuwen 2008: 113) rationalization (eating fish is good for you).

The fact that positive attitudes towards meat-eating are at present a mainstream ideology in the US has to do with cultural, religious, political and economic factors. While it is beyond the scope of this chapter to offer a detailed discussion, it is clear that powerful economic interests are at stake:

> The meat and poultry industry is the largest segment of United States agriculture. Total meat and poultry production in 2003 reached more than 85 billion pounds. Annual sales for 2002 . . . are estimated at more than $119 billion among the meat packing, meat processing and poultry processing industries. . . . Meat and poultry products represent America's top agricultural export and account for 9.5 percent of the total US meat production. Meat and poultry production and consumption statistics illustrate the impressive size and scope of the industry.
> (American Meat Institute 2007)

Wherever the current mainstream ideology and the representation of Vegetarianism in *Gilmore Girls* stems from, what is the effect of reproducing the mainstream ideology of eating meat in a particular television series? Does it work to perpetuate the meat industry, validate its ideology, the naturalization of eating meat, shaping the audience's thought, construing and framing our social and individual attitudes towards it? Does the fact that Vegetarianism is portrayed as non-mainstream mean that the audience will only be able to see it that way? One view of media and ideology would argue that the media do have a crucial role in reinforcing and maintaining ideologies and shaping thought (van Dijk 1998b: 316, Decker 2004: 11–12, Thornham & Purvis 2005: 28, Beeman 2007: 693). In Althusser's view, the media are an ideological state apparatus. The ideological power of media texts, researchers have argued, lies in their fictional status: 'they allow us to laugh at them, or to dismiss them as unreal, while at the same time getting their message across' (Machin & van Leeuwen 2007: 27). Popular culture hides the fact that it is a field of ideological struggle, by suggesting that it is just there for our entertainment and pleasure (Hermes 2005: 11), but plays a more complex role in our lives. For instance, with respect to her analysis of the television series *The West Wing* (NBC, 1999–2006), Wodak (2009) argues that

> the **representation of everyday politics in the media fulfils important functions, constructing and reinforcing *myths* about 'doing politics', reassuring the public of the rational and good intentions underlying political decisions; which in turn should convey feelings of security and of being protected** (in a necessarily broad sense); in sum, of being able to trust wise *men* to make adequate decisions (Wodak 2009: 26; bold face and italics in original).

However, another strand of media studies research points out that the audience does not necessarily have to accept the ideological positions set up in television texts, as different audiences react differently to them (Decker 2004:

13). Olson (2004) for instance, mentions various studies that have shown that the local consumption of American television broadcasts (e.g. in India, Taiwan, Japan, Nigeria) is very complex, rather than the audience simply taking on 'American' attitudes and beliefs. With respect to hiphop, Pennycook introduces the concept of *transcultural flows* to investigate the 'cultural implications of globalization, the ways in which cultural forms spread and change' (Pennycook 2007: 6), showing how they are localized, appropriated and taken-up in diverse contexts. Other audience studies have put negative claims about television series and their effects on audiences in doubt, having shown 'the complex and personal ways in which audiences function' (Mills 2005: 139). Even fans 'oscillate between consumerism and "resistance"' (de Kloet & van Zoonen 2007: 329). From a socio-cognitive point of view, Van Dijk (1998a, b) makes the point that mental representations have to be taken into account when analysing discourse and ideology (see also Toolan 2001: 87 on the factual and ideological knowledge that readers bring to texts). He argues that we need to consider both social context and 'existing ideologies, attitudes, knowledge, models of experience, current goals and personal interests and so on. This means that ideological influence may not always have the intended effects' (van Dijk 1998b: 318). For instance, Vegetarians will view the representation of Vegetarians and Vegans differently than non-Vegetarians. In media studies, Hall's (1994: 209) three positions for decoding television discourse have been more influential than socio-cognitive theories of mental representations. These three positions are:

1. The **dominant-hegemonic** position: here 'the viewer takes the connoted meaning . . , full and straight, and decodes the message in terms of the reference code in which it has been encoded, . . . is *operating inside the dominant code*' (Hall 1994: 209).
2. The **negotiated** position: here decoders adopt a negotiated code which 'acknowledges the legitimacy of the hegemonic definitions to make the grand significations (abstract), while, at a more restricted, situational (situated) level, it makes its own ground rules – it operates with exceptions to the rule' (Hall 1994: 210). That is, the preferred reading is accepted at an abstract level, but rejected at a more personal level (e.g. when a worker agrees to the hegemonic definition that strike is against the national interest, but is still willing to go on strike) (see Hall 1994: 210f for this example).
3. The **oppositional** position: here viewers decode the message 'in a *globally* contrary way' (Hall 1994: 211, original emphasis) to the hegemonic discourse, and use their own framework of interpretation. For instance, a viewer who '"reads" every mention of the "national interest" as "class interest"' (Hall 1994: 211).[12]

For example, with respect to Vegetarianism in *Gilmore Girls*, viewing it from a dominant-hegemonic position could mean agreeing with the 'carnivorous normativity' completely, both on a theoretical and on a practical level; viewing it from a negotiated position could mean agreeing with carnivorous normativity in general but practising Vegetarianism for personal reasons, and viewing it from an oppositional position could mean viewing the portrayal of Vegetarianism in *Gilmore Girls* critically as hegemonic ideology and advocating Vegetarianism as a mainstream eating practice.

With respect to the ideologies expressed in one particular series such as *Gilmore Girls*, it must also be pointed out that there are always other texts and discourses that audiences have access to, including both personal, private ones (e.g. conversations with Vegetarian/Vegan friends), and public media texts such as television programmes. There are differing representations of Vegetarians and Vegetarianism on television, which may contradict each other. The website www.tvacres.com/vegetarians.htm lists fictional Vegetarians on television (accessed 31 March 2009) and the website www.moveleft.com/moveleft_vegontv_main.html (accessed 31 March 2009) offers descriptions of Vegetarians in 40 sitcoms and dramas. In general, it does appear as if the portrayal of Vegetarianism and Vegetarians on television has some impact on viewers, with a recent study finding that *The Simpsons* (FOX, 1989–) episode where Lisa becomes a Vegetarian ('Lisa the Vegetarian') influenced 9- to 12-year-olds' knowledge and beliefs about vegetarianism (Byrd-Bredbenner et al. 2004).

In view of these issues, it seems reasonable to assume that ideologies on television do have some impact on viewers, but that the relation between media texts, ideology and viewers is extremely complex, and that much more research is needed in this area. On the one hand, this relates to representation in that it is important not just how many characters are, say, Vegetarian, but also how they are portrayed, how other characters evaluate them; what kinds of characters express what kinds of evaluations towards other characters' way of life/ideologies; whether or not we as viewers are invited to share these evaluations and so on. On the other hand, it also relates to viewing/reading, in terms of the audience engaging differently with media texts, mediating their interpretation with mental representations, and engaging with many other texts and discourses. So a textual or linguistic analysis would ideally be complemented by looking at its 'social (post-textual) take-up' (Pennycook 2007: 84). There may also be more than the three reading positions outlined by Hall, with representations on television programmes being able to also be viewed 'ironically'. Indeed, McNair (1999) suggests: 'The effects issue is one of the most difficult and contentious in media studies, despite the vast resources and energies which have been expended in trying to resolve it' (McNair 1999: 26). Regarding journalism, he argues that no matter what the actual effect of the media on the audience is, what is significant is that social actors *assume* that the media has the power to 'manipulate' people. McNair continues, 'From this perspective, the important thing is not the effect of journalistic output on individual attitudes and ideas, but the effect of the widespread perception of journalism's importance on the social process as a whole' (McNair 1999: 26). With respect to entertainment media and fictional television, too, it is clear that there is a widespread view that television has a considerable extent of power and influence concerning social values: The sitcoms *Murphy Brown* (CBS, 1988–1998) and *Ellen* (ABC, 1994–1998) sparked extensive media discussion and public debate about parenthood, family, gay and lesbian issues – for instance, then US Vice President Dan Quayle derogated *Murphy Brown* for advocating single parenthood rather than 'family values'. Another prime example is the controversy caused by *Ellen* when the title character, Ellen, came out in an episode and lesbian issues became a key narrative aspect of the show. In other words, ideologies on fictional television also have an effect on creating numerous additional discourses – whether in public political debate, in the media, or in fan forums and dedicated internet websites. Significantly, then, even if ideologies do not have an immediate impacts on viewers' own beliefs, they still frequently have a *discursive* impact.

However, if we accept for the moment that television has some impact on audiences and that this can be negative in certain cases, one solution would be to argue for regulation in terms of more diversity and variety and less stereotyping on television, for instance in including a relevant principle in a code of ethics. While the Statement of Principles Of Radio and Television Broadcasters adopted in the US (National Association of Broadcasters 1990) already includes the recommendation that

> Each broadcaster should exercise responsible and careful judgment in the selection of material for broadcast. . . . In selecting program subjects and themes of particular sensitivity, great care should be paid to treatment and presentation, so as to avoid presentations purely for the purpose of sensationalism or to appeal to prurient interest or morbid curiosity.

This statement is only advisory and none of the recommended principles are enforced, as they are taken to 'reflect generally-accepted practices of America's radio and television programmers' and '[s]pecific standards and their applications and interpretations remain within the sole discretion of the individual television or radio licensee' (National Association of Broadcasters 1990). Currently, there is also the option of filing complaints with the Federal Communications Commission (FCC), a United States government agency responsible for regulating television as well as other media (www.fcc.gov/aboutus.html). There is one complaint category concerning stereotyping or inappropriate representation labelled 'unauthorized, unfair, biased, illegal broadcasts' but the FCC has been criticized in the past by minority groups for not paying sufficient attention to diversity (National Hispanic Media Coalition 2008). Further, Mills (2005: 105) emphasizes that it takes the regulatory bodies months to investigate complaints and that adjudication won't reach an audience as large as the original media text.

So one argument would be that 'certain kinds of representations, which currently don't exist, should' (Mills 2005: 147), and vice versa, that certain kinds of representation which currently do exist, shouldn't exist. It would follow that some kind of better regulation is needed to ensure this. However, there are a number of significant problematic issues attached to this (see Mills 2005: 146–55 for a discussion relating to sitcom). With respect to dramedy, for instance, would anyone be interested in watching 'politically correct' dramedies? Do we want strict regulation of creativity? How can we preserve elements of comedy in dramedy if it is regulated too strictly?[13] Considering a controversy surrounding a skit about dying children in episode 2 of season 3 of the Australian comedy series *The Chaser's War on Everything* (ABC, Australia, 2006–2009) Jonathan Holmes asks:

> Will the ABC try to lay down what should be the subject of satire, and what shouldn't? Will all satire have to be referred up to Managing Director? The danger is that by changing the processes, we'll end up with comedy that's less edgy and less satirical. (Holmes 2009)

A solution other than regulation would be more media literacy education at all levels, although it is currently by no means clear how televisual literacy can be made an educational goal (Allen 2004: 7). With respect to the United States in particular, Kubey (2003) emphasizes that it 'finds itself in the ironic position of being the world's leading exporter of media products while simultaneously lagging behind every other major English-speaking country in the formal delivery of media education in its schools' (Kubey 2003: 352). This is the solution I would primarily argue for – if we teach media literacy we equip viewers with critical tools to question representations and to understand the rationale behind them no matter what television throws at us. Including television series in the curriculum can also provide motivation and the inclusion of student culture as well as providing texts that can be used in awareness raising (compare Pennycook 2007: 15 on hip-hop in the classroom). In Esslin's view, '*[t]elevision criticism* . . . should become a basic subject of instruction in schools from the earliest grades' (Esslin 2002: 119, italics in original).

3.2 Ideology and bonding/identification

Character, as Toolan (2001) says, 'is often what most powerfully attracts readers to novels and stories' (Toolan 2001: 80), and no doubt it is also important in attracting viewers to television narratives. It is thus worthwhile to briefly consider relations between characters and the audience with respect to ideology.

First, I suggested earlier on that we are invited to share the ideologies or values of likeable characters. However, there may be many ideologies/values that a certain character stands for – are we invited to share each and every one of them? I would argue that characters are more complex than that, and that television characters often have flaws or values that the target audience will not share. Interestingly, audiences can both identify positively and negatively with characters in televisual drama genres, with 'heroines' not entirely flawless and 'antagonists' not entirely 'evil' (Thornham & Purvis 2005: 47). Comic characters in particular are often characterized by both flaws and positive traits (Vorhaus 1994: 30–3). Perhaps we can reason that the more mainstream a character's values are, the more likely it is that we are invited to share them – if characters break communally accepted norms of social behaviour or have values that are not communally accepted by the majority or that go against common sense knowledge, we are not necessarily invited to share them. That does not mean that we do not like to see such characters on television; in fact both adults and teenagers frequently like 'anti-social' characters better than 'pro-social' characters (Cohen 1999: 341). As Cohen notes, it 'remains unclear whether favourite characters are the ones we admire most, feel similar to, identify with, or hold in high esteem' (Cohen 1999: 343). The notion of a 'favourite' character, however, is not necessarily identical with a character that we identify or bond with.

Secondly, I suggest that we identify with, bond with, affiliate with characters whose values, emotional reactions, evaluations etc. we share or that we overlap with to a great extent.[14] In other words, the more like us television characters are in this respect, the more likely we are to identify and bond with them. Giles (2002) notes that 'the expression of an opinion [by a media figure] may chime with the opinion of the user and create a positive judgment based on attitude homophily' (Giles 2002: 296), one of the stages of developing a parasocial relationship. This argument is also in line with Huisman's comment that '[w]hat has been labelled "identification", I suggest, could also be called ideological recognition as it correlates with the value judgements and interpretative orientation of the viewer' (Huisman 2005a: 174). In terms of the communicative context of television and its audience/overhearer design (Chapter 2), it can be argued that it is not just the linguistic style of a television programme but also its ideology that is construed with the audience in mind. The TV audience, then,

> has the power of choice. . . . dissatisfied audience members switch off or tune in elsewhere. . . . only a small minority of the mass audience ever directly contact the media with complaints or suggestions.
>
> Assuming that audience membership usually signifies approval of communicator style [and ideology, M.B.], it follows the media attract the audiences which suit them. If the communicator is unsuccessful in

> accommodating to the audience, the audience will do the accommodating. If the style [and ideology, M.B.] does not shift to suit the audience, the audience will shift to a style [and ideology, M.B.] that does suit. The communicator will then have an audience which was unintended but whose composition in fact suits the style or conceivably no audience at all. (Bell 1991: 107)

But Mills (2005) makes the valid point that 'the oft-invoked argument that anyone offended by television material can simply turn their set off is of little help, for offended viewers are aware that not only have they failed to prevent the material existing, but that it's still likely to be consumed by large audiences' (Mills 2005: 105).

It is also important to note that characters can be like us in one way (e.g. in having positive attitudes towards gender equality) and not be like us in other ways (e.g. in having positive attitudes towards the eating of meat). Group values and identities are not strict dichotomies (in-group vs. out-group); rather there are degrees of shared values and a negotiated identity *space* (Knight in preparation). According to Knight (2010) conversational participants can 'laugh off' values that are unshared between them, commune around shared values and reject unshareable values: 'there are degrees of togetherness by which they [participants] can co-identify' (Knight 2010: 49).

In other words and relating this to television, not identifying/bonding with characters in one way does not prevent us from identifying/bonding with them in other ways. For instance, I may not bond with Lorelai because of certain kinds of values/practices that she stands for, but I may bond with the character because of the witty banter she exchanges with other characters or because of the intertextual references she and Rory make (Chapter 3). In terms of the series as a whole, *Gilmore Girls* creates a world where Vegetarians are excluded as the Other, as the 'not us', and the discourses around the eating of meat serve to include 'meat-eaters' and exclude Vegetarians in its audience. The perspective of the non-Vegetarian characters is privileged in the text; we get their point of view. If Vegetarians notice this happening, then, and it *can* go unnoticed,[15] they can choose to complain or switch off, or to engage with other aspects of the series that include them as viewers (e.g. certain feminist values) or to engage with other characters or other aspects of the series (e.g. humour, witty dialogue). On how pleasure is bound up with ideology see Fiske (1994), and on the needs satisfied by television in terms of 'uses and gratifications theory' see Selby and Cowdery (1995: 186–7).

4 Conclusion

I have taken a somewhat critical look at *Gilmore Girls* as illustrative of mainstream popular culture in this chapter, but this is not to be taken as viewing the series and popular culture in general in a completely negative way as purely reproducing the majority culture. With respect to *Gilmore Girls* itself it does not *exclusively* reproduce the mainstream, and with respect to television series in general, not all of them reproduce the mainstream uncritically. Further, even if the reproduction of the mainstream is viewed as problematic/negative, there are other aspects of fictional television that can be evaluated more positively (e.g. witty dialogue, interesting and believable characters, gripping stories and other 'aesthetic' values). We can say that television series are at the same time a creative achievement and 'cultural commodity' (Fiske 1987, quoted in Burton 2000: 12), a commercial product and an ideological positioning. Clearly then, there are both positive and negative things to say about television series; it is 'a balancing act to both do justice to the pleasures and uses of the popular and reflect on it critically' (Hermes 2005: 3). This chapter limited the analysis of ideology to studying attitudes towards the eating of meat and Vegetarianism, and related this to expressive identity and bonding with viewers. But the analysis of ideology could only go so far. On the one hand we could have related the analysis of attitudes towards the eating of meat to attitudes towards food in general, towards consumption, including transport, energy, for example, from an 'ecolinguistic' (Fill & Mühlhäusler 2001, Bednarek & Caple 2010) perspective, towards globalization, towards the ideology of 'new capitalism' (Fairclough 2004) or towards the overall 'discourse system' (Scollon & Scollon 2001: 183ff) of *Gilmore Girls*, including ideology, socialization, forms of discourse, face systems or its 'ideology-schema' (van Dijk 1998b). Further, the methodology focused on frequency and co-textual patterns, but other discursive construals of ideology such as via metaphor (Goatley 2007) were not taken into account.

And there are many other ideologies to explore – both in *Gilmore Girls* and in other dramedies and other television genres. An example is sexuality – the prevalence of heteronormativity or 'heterosexism' (Collins 2000, cited in Beeman 2007) and the 'othering' of other sexualities (Beeman 2007: 692) in cultural products. Other examples are issues pertaining to love and relationships, such as marriage, finding 'the one', cheating, divorce, what and how relationships are represented, for example, in terms of age, ethnicity, gender, mother–daughter relationships (Walters 1992, Spitz 2005), or nationality (e.g. evaluations of the US compared to other countries) to name but a few. As there is a wealth of past, present and future television programmes there is a rich repository for linguistic (and other) analysis of the construal of diverging residual, dominant and emergent ideologies of all kinds in fictional television.

Notes

[1] The term *mind style* is used in traditional stylistics to 'capture the world view of an author, narrator or character as constituted by the ideational structure of the text' (Archer 2007: 252). In fact, for Fowler, mind style is equivalent to *ideological* point of view (Fowler 1986: 150). Another concept that has similarities with

ideology is Foucault's notion of *discursive formations* – 'historically specific systems of thought, conceptual categories that work to define cultural experiences within larger systems of power' (Mittell 2004: 174). Foucault abandoned the notion of ideology because power, he argues, is everywhere, and the term *ideology* (if tied to power) thus becomes uninformative (Eagleton 1991: 7–8). Also related to ideology are Barthes's *myths* – stories that cultures use to explain reality (Thornham & Purvis 2005: 25) or to 'frame and naturalise one view of the world' (Thornham & Purvis 2005: 54). Barthes's referential or cultural codes of texts also offer 'explanations about culture and the (often) taken-for-granted practices of everyday life' (Thornham & Purvis 2005: 49).

2 However, we also have to look at whether they are primary or secondary characters and how they are depicted. The mere presence of a 'minority' character is not necessarily good practice if it portrays that character in a stereotypical, derogatory or 'voyeuristic' (e.g. lesbian relationships) way. Compare, for example, Calvin (2008a: 17) on racial/ethnic minority characters in *Gilmore Girls*, Hermes (2005: 46) on the portrayal of a lesbian protagonist in the Dutch police series *Dok 12* (RTL4, Netherlands, 2001–2003), Feuer (2001c) and Mills (2005) for debates concerning the representation of homosexuality in *Will and Grace* (NBC, 1998–2006), and Feuer (2001d) for an overview of the 'gay' and 'queer' sitcom. Mills (2005) points out that '[w]hile American sitcom has a (limited) history of gay characters, mainstream success has eluded series whose understanding requires an empathy and understanding towards (some aspects of) gay culture' (Mills 2005: 93), and that research has shown that while gay character increasingly appear in American television and cinema, they are portrayed in limited and repetitive ways (Mills 2005: 122, citing Shugart 2003 and Arthurs 2004). Pennycook (2007) notes: 'Popular culture may indeed be racist, homophobic or misogynist: its frequent articulations of heteronormative sexuality constantly position other sexualities as other' (Pennycook 2007: 82).

3 The search was for *veggie* not *veggie** because I was interested in occurrences where *veggie* is a premodifier or part of a compound and thus quite strongly associated with Vegetarianism (e.g. *a veggie burger*).

4 In Table 8.2 and in the co-textual analysis instances unrelated to the eating of food were excluded (manually deleted). For instance:

- Figurative meanings, idioms, and comparisons (*frozen together like bacon; bring home the bacon; I have no beef with you; not like you resemble beef or anything; the fish on the doorstep; rip apart every other fish in the sea; swim/drink like a fish; the big fish in the small pond* and variants; *two shakes of a lamb's tail; all the little lambs* [religious]; *dead meat; something with a little more meat to it; meat market; cold turkey; turkey legs* [referring to human legs as such]; *lock us up like veal; veal children; the vegetable set*);
- Certain compounds/nominal groups (*fish thermidor; fish lamp; fish bag; fish pan; fish fork; meat thermometer; the turkey-calling contest; turkey heads; 'salute to vegetables' pageant; vegetable business/industry; vegetable grease/oil*);
- Proper nouns and names (*Kevin Bacon; Marlowe, Bacon . . . ; Macon the bacon; beef island(s); burger boy; burger king; fish man; fish girl; meat guy; vegetable guy/supplier; Kentucky Fried Chicken; Go fish; Turkey* [the country]; *Wild Turkey*);

- Double occurrences (e.g. *veggie burger* counted as *veggie*; *turkey burger* counted as turkey – both deleted from *burger* occurrences; *soy chicken taco* counted as *soy* – deleted from *chicken* occurrences etc.);
- Verbs (*to fish*; *to roast*);
- Artefacts (*a dead fish* [stuffed antique]; *electronic fish*; *Billy Bass Fish*; *a plastic dancing pork chop*; *chocolate turkey*; *paper turkey*);
- Other unrelated to food (*chicken pox*; *animal, vegetable or mineral*).

5 However, there are some differences between the frequencies for respective types of meat, as illustrated in Table 8.5.

Table 8.5 Individual types of meat – frequency in *Gilmore Girls* and per capita consumption (American Meat Institute 2007)

Search term	Raw frequency	Per capita consumption in 2005 in US
burger, beef*	125	66.5 pounds pp (including hamburger and other beef cuts)
chicken	82	86.6 pounds pp
turkey	39 (but 11 in one episode)	16.4 pounds pp
lamb	32	0.8 pounds pp
pork	25	50 pounds pp
veal	5 (but 3 in one episode)	0.5 pounds pp

Although these are also similar, burgers/beef and lamb are over-represented in *Gilmore Girls* and pork is under-represented compared to the per capita consumption (where chicken is consumed more than burger/beef and pork more than lamb and turkey).

6 It is at times implied that Michel and a temporary girlfriend of Luke's (Nicole) do not eat meat. In one episode Michel says, 'I don't eat dairy or meat. You know this.' But at other times, he eats turkey and he also talks about eating a burger in other episodes, so he is clearly not Vegetarian. For Nicole, Luke adds three more salads to the menu, adding 'There wasn't really that much for her to eat on the menu' and Lorelai asks 'So what happens when you guys get serious, the whole place goes soy?'. It is thus implied that she may be Vegetarian, but it is not made explicit, and this is the only mention of this in all the episodes that Nicole appears in or is talked about. Further, Nicole is clearly disliked by Lorelai and cheats on Luke (in episode 4.17), so is not portrayed as a role model. It is also reasonable to assume that the audience does not like her as she can be seen as an obstacle preventing the characters of Luke and Lorelai from having a relationship. Overall, Mrs Kim is the only Vegetarian and Susan the only Vegan whose eating practices are explicitly referred to, and will be discussed in more detail below.

7 There is an additional instance where Lorelai talks about locking someone up 'like veal' but because this is a comparison it was not analysed (see Note 4 above).

8 These include evaluative and emotional language (compare Chapter 6: Note 1). See Chapter 3 (Note 12) on references for alternative categorizations of

evaluative resources. Many of these distinguish between the use of emotion terms and other evaluative means (e.g. Wiggins & Potter 2003 on 'subjective' (use of emotion verbs) vs. 'objective' evaluations (use of evaluative adjectives); Martin and White (2005) on Affect (emotion) vs. Appreciation/Judgement (other pos/neg evaluation) to name but two. These evaluative means have different characteristics, a different 'interactional' value (Wiggins & Potter 2003: 521), and are used differently in talk about food (Wiggins & Potter 2003: 526). It is generally assumed that the use of emotion terms is more personalized and more subjective than the use of other evaluative items (e.g. Fiehler 1990: 49, White 2004, Bednarek 2009d for further discussion). Various ways of expressing affect/emotion can further be sub-classified in terms of their subjectivity and personalization (e.g. interjections) – see also Bednarek (2008a) on 'emotional' vs. 'emotion' talk – and in terms of explicitness and implicitness – see Martin and White (2005: 67) on inscribed (~ explicit) and invoked (~ implicit) attitude. In general, explicitly evaluative language is a good example for the claim made in Chapter 6 that language which habitually carries evaluative or emotional meaning can function as expressive resource, whereas the more implicit instances are good examples for the claim, also made in Chapter 6, that expressive features are features that function to construe expressive identity in a given context and cotext.

9 *To promise* means making a desirable offer (Halliday & Matthiessen 2004: 448), thus implying desirability. In turn, chicken is evaluated negatively here because what is promised and therefore construed as desirable is that 'there **won't** be any chicken'.

10 Wiggins and Potter explain item and category evaluation as follows:

> For example, is the evaluation of a specific item, or is it an evaluation of a category or class of things that this item is a member of. Such distinctions are marked in conversation in various ways – for example, grammatical differences such as "I like cheese" or "I like *this* cheese" may be used. Various levels of categorization and particularization are possible in evaluative talk of this kind (Wiggins & Potter 2003: 517).

11 In terms of positive evaluation, fish is very much associated by characters with its known health benefits (especially by Emily and in episodes following Richard's heart attack) and, in terms of negative evaluation, it is frequently tied to its bad smell. In these two aspects fish differs crucially from other types of meat in *Gilmore Girls*. Indeed, fish is in general treated differently from other kinds of meat, as some meat-eaters do not consider fish as 'real' meat (see example (4) above) and some 'Vegetarians' (pescatarians) eat fish. Fish also differs from other meat in terms of cultural value, as it is tied to religious practice and symbolism (like lamb). It is beyond the scope of this chapter to look into differences such as these in detail, but see Section 2.2 above on the special status of veal.

12 The *dominant-hegemonic* and *oppositional* positions have also been called 'compliant' vs. 'resistant' (Huisman 2005b: 162, Martin & White 2005: 206). The notion of a text giving rise to different meanings, or the 'polysemy' approach, which can be traced back to de Certeau (1984, cited in Olson 2004), is related to Hall's concept of reading position/negotiation as follows: 'The fundamental distinction between these two approaches is that negotiation is inherently dialectical, presuming two or three meanings, a few inferred and one implied, with the

production of a synthesized meaning. *Polysemy*, however, presumes that the text is capable of implying, and the reader capable of inferring, a much broader range of meanings; the process is less like negotiation than like selecting from a smorgasbord' (Olson 2004: 121).

13 The issue of representation, ideology and audience is already a complex one, but becomes even more complex when elements of comedy are involved, as is the case in the hybrid dramedy. For instance, comedy depends to some extent on stereotyping (Selby & Cowdery 1995: 109–11, Mills 2005: 82), and there are certain 'genre conventions and expectations within which any portrayal must exist' (Mills 2005: 109). Mills also points out that we can enjoy a joke while disagreeing with it ideologically (Mills 2005: 136). At the same time, the presence of certain kinds of jokes/humour on television tells us what is deemed as acceptable to audiences (Mills 2005: 105); for instance, it is seemingly unproblematic in *Gilmore Girls* to make fun of black (Michel), Korean (Mrs Kim) and Vegan (Susan) characters, although these characters are not necessarily just being made fun of because of their ethnic and 'food' identity but because of other personality/identity issues (as seen in the discussion of 'psycho' Susan). It must also be pointed out that some characters in a television series are used as a 'stereotypical foil against which other characters can be played, and perceived as such by the audience' (Selby & Cowdery 1995: 5).

14 In Media Psychology, audience-media figure interaction is described in more detail as either parasocial interaction, identification, wishful identification or affinity/liking (Cohen 1999, Giles 2002). Parasocial interaction is a particularly well-known concept developed in the 1950s by Horton and Wohl (1956, cited in Giles 2002) and can be considered as 'a user response to a figure as if s/he was a personal acquaintance' (Giles 2002: 289), that is, involves *humanizing* fictional characters, 'imagining characters as if they were real people' (Culpeper 2001: 7). Depending on definitions, the discussion below could be related to parasocial interaction, to identification, where 'a user needs to recognize some salient characteristic in the figure that is shared by themselves' (Giles 2002: 290), and to affinity, which 'stems from liking a character' (Cohen 1999: 329). There might be an argument in including bonding/affiliation as 'parasocial interaction'; including identifying with as 'identification', and to define the notion of 'liking' aesthetically to better distinguish it from parasocial friendships. For instance audiences may 'like' a character for aesthetic reasons, that is, in terms of the character being interesting, having great dialogue, being performed by a fantastic actor and so on. This relates to Clark's (1996) notion of appreciation (Bubel 2006: 58; see Chapter 2).

15 In fact, I had never noticed how 'pro' meat-eating and 'anti' Vegetarian/Vegan *Gilmore Girls* is before starting the detailed analyses described in this chapter. This is either because the observed patterns of usage are indeed not readily apparent to viewers, and can only be uncovered through corpus analysis (see Section 2.1) or because we tend to notice 'major' identities (gender, ethnicity, sexual preference etc.) before 'minor' identities (Lakoff 2006) such as culinary preferences. The latter aspects of individual identity 'are more subtle, perhaps less prone to being problematized, and not linked to group membership in any obvious way' (Lakoff 2006: 143). From a critical perspective it could be said that the less explicit an ideology is, the more difficult it is to uncover it.

Chapter 9

Conclusion

IMAGE 9.1 TV series racks in video store

Images 9.1 and 9.2 show racks stacked with DVDs on fictional television series at a local video store and a local entertainment retailer (company logo blurred), respectively. I include these images here to point once more to the significance of fictional television series in contemporary society.

IMAGE 9.2 TV series rack in entertainment retailer

As I have suggested at the beginning of this book, it is time to take television dialogue seriously and to incorporate its many forms and genres in the linguistic enterprise as a whole. Such genres are a prime example of modern story-telling, skilfully combining various semiotic modes, and are increasingly of high quality, in particular the HBO series (which, although they start out on pay TV in the US, often end up on free-to-air television in other countries). Author Nick Hornby agrees:

> . . . reading appears to be more effortful than watching TV, and usually it is, although if you choose to watch one of the HBO series, such as *The Sopranos* [HBO, 1999–2007] or *The Wire* [HBO, 2002–2008], then it's a close-run thing, because the plotting in these programmes, the speed and complexity of the dialogue are as demanding as a lot of the very best fiction. (Hornby 2006: 4–5)

In some cases, scriptwriters of such series are also authors of fiction in their own right. For instance, writer Dennis Lehane (e.g. *Mystic River*) has written several episodes for *The Wire*; crime novelist Scott Frost (e.g. *Don't Look Back*) used to write for *Twin Peaks* (ABC, 1990–1991), *The X-Files* (FOX, 1993–2002) and other television series. Book series are also often turned into television shows, for example, *Dexter* (Showtime, 2006–) is based on novels by Jeff Lindsay; *Friday Night Lights* (NBC, 2006–) is based on a non-fiction book, and there are many more examples of novels turned into (mini-) television series/serials (e.g. by Jane Austen, P.G. Wodehouse). While reruns of successful television series are still being broadcast in the United States and globally, and spin-offs as well as remakes (e.g. *Melrose Place*, The CW, 2009–; *90210*, The CW, 2008–; the *NCIS* and *CSI* spin-offs) of cult series are produced, new televisual stories and characters constantly arise and compete for the audience's attention, with 23 new fictional television shows in autumn/fall 2009 in the United States (www.tvguide.com/special/fall-preview/, 13 August 2009). This shows the continuing importance of such story-telling in contemporary society.

Further, popular culture in general is bound up with cultural citizenship – 'the process of bonding and community building, and reflection on that bonding, that is implied in partaking of the text-related practices of reading, consuming, celebrating, and criticizing offered in the realm of (popular) culture' (Hermes 2005: 10). Concerning viewers' relationship with television shows Quaglio (2009) notes that 'it is through *language* that this identification is achieved and popular culture is expressed and reflected' (Quaglio 2009: 13), pointing to the importance of linguistic analyses of popular television series. Hermes continues,

> [P]opular texts allow us to bond and build communities. They do so because they are of use to us; they allow us to reflect on our lives by providing 'usable stories' (John Mepham), occasions for fictional rehearsal [a notion

> developed by Stuart Hall] and a domain for what John Ellis calls 'working through'. (Hermes 2005: 155)

From the point of view of education, Kubey asks 'How can we think we are adequately teaching critical thinking if there is no connection made to the thousands of hours that most students spend, before and after school and on weekends, in contact with the media?' (Kubey 2003: 368). Arguably, 'the reach and impact of media language in contemporary social life are indisputable', and 'the media are increasingly inside us and us in them' (Coupland 2007: 28).

In view of these comments, it is disappointing that much academic research outside media/television/cultural studies in fact excludes media content found in popular cultural products. This book is intended as a contribution from linguistics to studying such content, concentrating on fictional television. **Part I** of the book was concerned with the analysis of fictional television, the genre of dramedy and television dialogue. **Chapter 2** outlined the importance of studying television and discussed characteristics of fictional television in terms of its forms and genres, its communicative context, multimodality, the code of realism and the general nature of televisual characters. In **Chapter 3** we looked more closely at the genre of dramedy, introducing the series that provided data for case studies throughout the book (*Gilmore Girls*) and considered how evaluative meanings in DVD cover texts function to construe a target audience for a television series, contributing to the creation of a community of like-minded fans. **Chapter 4** used corpus linguistic methodology to study similarities and differences between dramedy dialogue in terms of frequent words and phrases, showing that they are related to genre (dramedy), the nature of scripted dialogue and the specifics of the series. Concerning Part I, then, here are a number of interesting questions worthy of future investigation:

- What aspects would a more representative corpus of scripted television dialogue reveal about differences between the language of fictional television and spontaneous language (Bednarek in preparation)? And what genre-specific aspects would specialized corpora containing speech from certain fictional genres (e.g. sitcom, drama) show researchers? What are the differences between *film* and *television* dialogue?
- What aspects of the findings are the result of conscious manipulation by professionals involved in writing the script? Of what aspects are scriptwriters themselves aware, what linguistic features do they use consciously? Could linguistic analysis of the kind described in this book result in better handbooks for scriptwriters?
- What influence is there of televisual language on spontaneous language within linguistic varieties, across national varieties and across languages?

- What would an analysis of generic structure/narrative reveal about prevalent 'hybrid' genres such as the dramedy?

Part II dealt with televisual characterization. This aspect of fictional television series was chosen because of the lack of research (Pearson 2007) as well as the significance of characters for stories (Blum 1995: 79) and for audiences (Esslin 2002: 42). In **Chapter 5** I showed how a corpus stylistic approach to characterization in terms of a key word/n-gram analysis suggests that televisual characters are construed as unique and are linguistically differentiated from other characters. Future studies could address how characters are construed in other series, serials, genres and cultures, and include interviews and collaborations with scriptwriters in order to investigate how much of this process is deliberate and how much they are aware of the linguistic features of this process. **Chapter 6** introduced a model for analysing what I argue is a crucial aspect of televisual characterization – expressive character identity. The model includes different levels of analysis and allows for a cognitive or semiotic perspective as well as quantitative and qualitative analysis of dynamic/temporary and stable/repeated character identities. It includes verbal and nonverbal behaviour as well as different aspects of expressivity such as emotionality, ideology, evaluation. Expressive identities, it is argued, are crucial for the audience both in classifying characters and their relationships to each other, and in establishing relationships with them. Aspects of expressivity may also be significant for non-fictional forms and genres of television:

> It is, all in all, a matter of television discourse drawing upon a wide range of semiotic resources in order to foreground emotion – to create the impression that it talks to us, with us and about us in ways which we can not only hear and see but also, and crucially, feel. (Lorenzo-Dus 2009: 184)

Chapters 6–8 illustrated the model with the help of quantitative and qualitative analyses of characterization in terms of emotionality (Chapter 6), the multimodal performance of expressive identities (Chapter 7), and shared ideology (Chapter 8). The chapters looked both at how characters are distinguished from each other by some expressive aspects and how they share others.

Despite the challenges faced concerning the paucity of research on televisual characterization, and the plethora of non-unified research on emotion/evaluation (Caffi & Janney 1994), it is hoped that Part II of this book works as a springboard for future research into the phenomenon of expressive identity. It may be especially useful to address some of the following open questions:

- How do expressive features/resources not closely investigated in this book (e.g. intensity, grading, modulation, epistemic meanings, prosodic

features . . .) contribute to the construal of expressive character identity and what kinds of identities do they construe?
- How do expressive resources cluster as expressive styles (see Tannen 1984 on involvement styles and Selting 1994 on emphatic speech style) to construe expressive identities? How much continuity is needed and how much variability is allowed for a style to be recognizable (Auer 2007b: 15)?
- What sub-types of expressive identity (e.g. emotional types vs. ideological types) are there and how can we best label them in stylistic analysis (e.g. 'warm', 'cold', 'emotional', 'whinger', 'pessimist', 'worriers' – 'feminist', 'conservative', 'religious', 'left-wing', 'vegetarian')? And what expressive dimensions are relevant?[1]
- Are there a finite number of expressive character identity types, 'social stereotypes' (Taavitsainen 1999: 219) or 'stock characters' (Marshall & Werndly (2002: 51)? And what is the relation of these to 'real-life' identity/personality types (Crystal 1997: 23, Fairclough 2003, D'Vari 2005)?
- How do audiences react to different expressive character identities?

With respect to the last question, in particular, it must be said that it was beyond the scope of this book to consider post-textual take-up (Pennycook 2007: 84) or 'the processes involved in the realization of meaning by readers' (Barker & Galasiński 2001: 7) in terms of audience studies (Ang 1985, cited in Hermes 2005, Moores 1994, Gillespie 1995, Livingstone 1998, Burton 2000, Allen & Hill 2004, Hermes 2005). To conclude with the same important televisual character this book started with, not all members of the audience will share Homer Simpson's affective evaluation of television as 'teacher, mother, secret lover' (*The Simpsons*, 6.06, *Treehouse of Horror V*, 30 October 1994).

Note

[1] In studying personal descriptors, Culpeper (2001: 106–7) puts them into dimensions of dis/agreeability; in/flexibility; introversion; psychological strength; negative attitudes; selfishness.

Appendix 1

Table A.1 Cast list (*Gilmore Girls*)

Actor	Character	Seasons
Lauren Graham	Lorelai Gilmore	1–7
Alexis Bledel	Rory Gilmore	1–7
Scott Patterson	Luke Danes	1–7
Kelly Bishop	Emily Gilmore	1–7
Edward Herrmann	Richard Gilmore	1–7
Keiko Agena	Lane Kim	1–7
Melissa McCarthy	Sookie St. James	1–7
Yanic Truesdale	Michel Gerard	1–7
Sean Gunn	Kirk Gleason	1–7
Liza Weil	Paris Geller	1–7
Jared Padalecki	Dean Forester	1–5
David Sutcliffe	Christopher Hayden	1–3, 5–7
Milo Ventimiglia	Jess Mariano	2–4, 6
Matt Czuchry	Logan Huntzberger	5–7
Scott Cohen	Max Medina	1–3
Jackson Douglas	Jackson Belleville	1–7
Emily Kuroda	Mrs Kim	1–7

Appendix 2

Gilmore Girls DVD Cover Texts

Season 1

Welcome to the picture-perfect New England town of Stars Hollow, Connecticut. Founded 1779. Population 9973. And home of 32-year-old Lorelai and her 16-year-old daughter Rory – the *Gilmore Girls.* Heart. Humor. Fan-pleasing DVD extras. They're all in this 21-episode, Year-one collection of the much-loved series. Lauren Graham plays quick-witted Lorelai, manager of historic Independence Inn, mother of Rory (Alexis Bledel) and also her daughter's best friend, confidante and mentor who's determined to help her avoid the mistakes that sidetracked Lorelai when she was a teen. A gifted ensemble plays the colourful Stars Hollow townies. And Kelly Bishop and Edward Herrmann play Lorelai's blue-blooded parents. Once kept at a distance by Lorelai, they're back in her life. So are the issues that originally drove them apart.

Season 2

Those acclaimed *Gilmore Girls* are back for a second season of warmth, charm, zingy repartee and heart-stopping moments of drama. In this 6-disc set are all 22 irresistible year-two episodes about the people you've grown to love: young single mom Lorelai, her super-achieving daughter Rory, her elitist parents Emily and Richard, and a whole town of dreamers and eccentrics. New faces also come to Stars Hollow, including Luke's nephew Jess, whose rebelliousness offends the town, but whose passion for books attracts Rory. Hearts break and mend, careers end and begin, folks stumble and pick themselves up in a series that's 'blissfully brilliant' (Ken Parish Perkins, *Fort Worth Star-Telegram*).

Season 3

More fun, more flames, more flameouts: more Gilmore. This Deluxe 6-Disc Set contains all 22 third-year episodes (plus bonus features) of *Gilmore Girls*, the hit series known for its witty, rapid-fire dialogue and poignant, suds-free storylines.

For mother and daughter Lorelai and Rory Gilmore, it's a year of change. Much of it is expected, like Rory's graduation from Chilton and the anxiety of waiting for college acceptance letters. But much of it is not. Rory starts the year with two boyfriends (that may be two too many). Lorelai rekindles the flame with Max (maybe). Lane meets Mr. Right (at last). Sookie gets a surprise (a good one). And so does the Independence Inn (not such a good one). The girls are waiting (get watching!).

Season 4

Boola boola! Rory starts her first year at Yale. Moola moola! Lorelai finally opens the Dragonfly Inn, although it takes her last dime (and a loan from Luke). The Gilmore girls return for another scintillating, snappy-patter year of . . . *Gilmore Girls*. Welcome, Gilmore groupies, to the fourth season of the series acclaimed for its agile balance of life and laughter. Oh yes, and love. Lorelai has a romantic fling with her father's new, younger partner, but ends the year with the guy every fan has known was right for her all along. For Rory, Cupid seems to be on sabbatical – then Dean *and* Jess re-enter her life. Sookie gets a Davey, Lane gets a life, Kirk gets a girlfriend (!) and you get a 22-episode vacation in Stars Hollow, plus DVD Extras and a mint on the pillow.

Season 5

Gilmore rising: Lorelai. The Dragonfly Inn is a huge success. And Lorelai's romance with Luke (the just-gotta-be relationship fans have waited for!) steams up Stars Hollow. Gilmore going down: Rory. College, boys and career plans crash and burn, leaving the once-confident golden girl reeling. Fasten your seat belt for a fabulously funny and heartbreakingly dramatic Season 5. The wit, charm and eccentricity that have created legions of *Gilmore Girls* devotees are on glorious display in all 22 episodes of the hit series' fifth year. Adding more sparkle is the brilliant array of totally off-kilter, totally engaging supporting characters: Sookie, Paris, Lane, Kirk, Michel, the imperious Gilmore *père et mère* and a townful more. See you in Stars Hollow!

Season 6

Can it be the Gilmore Girls if the Gilmore girls aren't together? At the end of Season 5, Rory dropped out of Yale and moved into Emily and Richard's poolhouse – decisions that broke Lorelai's heart. That's handy, because one half of that heart can be deliriously happy with the big new step in her love affair with Luke. Meanwhile, the other half grieves, and it seems everyone in town wants mother and daughter to reunite. But it may take an unexpected out-of-towner to make it happen.

Of course, there's much more: Lane gets a surprise that leaves her reeling with joy, Luke gets a surprise that may send the Luke-and-Lorelai relationship reeling. What's no surprise is the snappy, wish-I'd-said that Gilmore dialogue, knowing humour and insightful storytelling fans adore. Season 6 starts now!

Season 7

After 20-plus years of single motherhood, after a series of Mr. Not-Quite-Rights, after buying that perfect wedding dress and watching it hang in the closet, Lorelai finally gets married. *Yes, but to whom?* The answer is just one of the deliciously intriguing what's-gonna-happens in these 22 episodes about a mother, a daughter, a town and a world that devoted Gilmore groupies have taken as their own.

Sharpen your wits for the famed, fast-paced Gilmore dialogue – but let your heart do its thing. From Stars Hollow to New York City to Paris . . . from Lorelai's wedding to Lane's baby shower to Rory's graduation . . . from beginning to middle to end . . . here's Season 7.

Appendix 3

Table A.2 Comparison of fan transcript and subtitles in a *Gilmore Girls* scene (from episode 1.11, *Paris is burning*)

Inaccuracies in subtitles	Actual wording	Inaccuracies in fan transcript	Actual wording
do we	*are we gonna*	*cleans out*	*has to clean out*
clean	*clean out*	*compare to*	*compared to*
do	*go through*	*towards*	*toward*
you	*do you*	*bit*	*bite*
bring that up	*bring Skippy up*	*so*	*and*
nothing	*nothing happened to Skippy*		
'd	*would*		
this goes on	*this keeps going on*		
get	*bring me*		
Ø	*hi* (2x)		
Ø	*oh* (5x)		
Ø	*hey* (2x)		
Ø	*cause*		
Ø	*so*		
Ø	*would*		
Ø	*bye*		
Ø	*and* (2x)		
Ø	*look*		
Ø	*well*		

Appendix 4

Conversations included in 140,000 word subset of Santa Barbara Corpus of Spoken American English (part 1):

SBC001 *Actual Blacksmithing*
SBC002 *Lambada*
SBC003 *Conceptual Pesticides*
SBC004 *Raging Bureaucracy*
SBC005 *A Book About Death*
SBC006 *Cuz*
SBC007 *A Tree's Life*
SBC008 *Tell the Jury that*
SBC009 *Zero Equals Zero*
SBC010 *Letter of Concerns*
SBC011 *This Retirement Bit*
SBC012 *American Democracy is Dying*
SBC013 *Appease the Monster*
SBC014 *Bank Products*

(see www.linguistics.ucsb.edu/research/sbcorpus_summaries.html, last accessed on 2 July 2009, for brief summaries)

Appendix 5

Table A.3 Top twenty word forms in *Gilmore Girls* and Santa Barbara corpus

	GiGi[1]	SB[2]
1	*I*	*I*
2	*you*	*the*
3	*the*	*and*
4	*to*	*you*
5	*a*	*to*
6	*and*	*a*
7	*it*	*that*
8	*that*	*it*
9	*of*	*of*
10	*is*	*know*
11	*in*	*in*
12	*what*	*was*
13	*me*	*they*
14	*have*	*like*
15	*this*	*is*
16	*do*	*have*
17	*not*	*yeah*
18	*my*	*he*
19	*for*	*what*
20	*just*	*so*

Table A.4 Top twenty 2-grams in *Gilmore Girls* and LSAC

Top twenty 2-grams in GiGi and LSAC			
2-gram	**Rank in GiGi**	**Rank in LSAC**	**Rank difference**
I don't	1	2	1
you know	2	1	1
in the	3	3	0
are you	4	31	27
and I	5	6	1
have to	6	10	4
going to	7	7	0
I know	8	20	12

(Continued)

Table A.4 (Cont'd)

2-gram	Rank in GiGi	Rank in LSAC	Rank difference
I have	9	24	15
this is	10	21	11
do you	11	14	3
to be	12	15	3
I was	13	9	6
of the	14	13	1
I just	15	35	20
I mean	16	5	11
want to	17	16	1
on the	18	17	1
it was	19	8	11
a little	20	36	16
don't know	21	12	9
I think	22	4	18
to do	31	18	13
and then	49	11	38
uh huh	not in top 100	19	>81

Table A.5 Top twenty 3-grams in *Gilmore Girls* and LSAC

Top twenty 3-grams in GiGi and LSAC			
3-gram	**Rank in GiGi**	**Rank in LSAC**	**Rank difference**
I don't know	1	1	0
what are you	2	30	28
I have to	3	10	7
what do you	4	13	9
are you doing	5	not in top 100	>95
I'm going to	6	7	1
you know what	7	6	1
I don't want	8	20	12
you want to	9	4	5
going to be	10	8	2
a lot of	11	3	8
I want to	12	11	1
don't want to	13	16	3
you have to	14	5	9
do you think	15	32	17
oh my god	16	not in top 100	>84
I don't think	17	2	15
this is a	18	74	56
I have a	19	25	6
have to go	20	70	50
do you want	21	9	12

(Continued)

Table A.5 (Cont'd)

Top twenty 3-grams in GiGi and LSAC			
3-gram	**Rank in GiGi**	**Rank in LSAC**	**Rank difference**
do you have	44	14	30
one of the	80	15	65
to do it	not in top 100	19	>81
you know I	not in top 100	17	>83
a little bit	not in top 100	12	>88
I mean I	not in top 100	18	>82

Table A.6 Top twenty 4-grams in *Gilmore Girls* and LSAC

Top twenty 4-grams in GiGi and LSAC			
4-gram	**Rank in GiGi**	**Rank in LSAC**	**Rank difference**
what are you doing	1	17	16
I don't want to	2	4	2
what do you mean	3	34	31
what do you think	4	19	15
are you talking about	5	100	95
you don't have to	6	6	0
what are you talking	7	not in top 100	>93
I don't know what	8	2	6
I have to go	9	50	41
are you doing here	10	not in top 100	>90
nice to meet you	11	not in top 100	>89
I just wanted to	12	70	58
I'll be right back	13	not in top 100	>87
do you want to	14	3	11
you want me to	15	10	5
I want you to	16	52	36
to talk to you	17	not in top 100	>83
you know what I	18	7	12
where are you going	19	not in top 100	>81
in the middle of	20	35	15
I don't know if	22	1	21
I don't think so	34	13	21
are you going to	36	11	25
I don't know how	38	9	29
if you want to	41	12	29
I was going to	45	5	40
do you want me	66	20	46
I thought it was	77	14	63
I don't know why	not in top 100	15	>85
but I don't know	not in top 100	18	>82
and I was like	not in top 100	16	>84
or something like that	not in top 100	8	>92

Table A.7 Over- and under-represented n-grams in *Gilmore Girls*

N-grams	Over-represented in GiGi	Under-represented in GiGi
2-grams	*are you*	*uh huh*
	I just	*and then*
	a little	*I think*
	I have	*to do*
	I know	*I mean*
	this is	*it was*
3-grams	*are you doing*	*a little bit*
	oh my god	*you know I*
	this is a	*I mean I*
	have to go	*to do it*
	what are you	*one of the*
	do you think	*do you have*
	I don't want	*I don't think*
		do you want
4-grams	*what are you talking*	*I don't know why*
	are you doing here	*but I don't know*
	nice to meet you	*and I was like*
	I'll be right back	*or something like that*
	to talk to you	*I thought it was*
	where are you going	*do you want me*
	are you talking about	*I was going to*
	I just wanted to	*if you want to*
	I have to go	*I don't know how*
	I want you to	*are you going to*
	what do you mean	*I don't think so*
	what are you doing	*I don't know if*
	what do you think	*in the middle of*
		you know what I
		do you want to

Table A.8 Seven-grams in *Gilmore Girls* (f>4)

	N-gram	Frequency
1	*can I talk to you for a*	13
2	*I don't want to talk about this*	10
3	*I don't know what you're talking about*	8
4	*I don't want to talk about it*	8
5	*I just want you to know that*	8
6	*I wanted to talk to you about*	8
7	*what do you want me to do*	8

(Continued)

Table A.8 (Cont'd)

	N-gram	Frequency
8	*I just want you to be happy*	7
9	*I want to talk to you about*	7
10	*if it makes you feel any better*	7
11	*what the hell is wrong with you*	7
12	*don't want to talk about this anymore*	6
13	*have no idea what you're talking about*	6
14	*I have to get back to the*	6
15	*I have to talk to you about*	6
16	*I talk to you for a sec*	6
17	*just want you to know that I*	6
18	*have to get back to the inn*	5
19	*have to talk to you about something*	5
20	*I just wanted to tell you that*	5
21	*I need to talk to you about*	5
22	*of the daughters of the American Revolution*	5
23	*than go to the club with you*	5

Appendix 6

Table A.9 Overview of features associated with expressivity[3]

	Selected resources	Selected references
Nonverbal resources	facial expression (e.g. smile, frown, furrowed brows, crease), body movement, touch, posture, head movement and gaze, gesture (e.g. emblems, symbolic/metaphoric gestures, gaze behaviour, salutation displays, postural echo, tie-signs, triumph displays) indicating evaluative/attitudinal (e.g. disapproval, willingness) or emotional (e.g. disgust) orientation to a situation or a general emotional state of mind	Ekman & Friesen (1975), Ekman (1997, 1999), Morris (1977), Goodwin & Goodwin (2000), Martinec (2001), Tracy (2002), Kendon (2004: 339), McNeill (2005), Baldry & Thibault (2006: 167–72; 207–08), Stivers (2006), Edwards (2007: 39–46), Beeman (2007), Hood (forthcoming)
Verbal resources (linguistic and paralinguistic)	crying, laughing, sighing, pausing, prosody, sound/voice quality, melody, timbre, loudness, intensity, pitch (e.g. leaps), vowel length, sound repetition, density of accentuated syllables, rhythmic organization, intonation, interjections, affective affixes (e.g. pejorative pre/suffixes), pronoun usage, deixis, grammatical markers of stance/assessment (e.g. stance adverbials, comment adjuncts, intensifiers), inversion, terms of endearment, kin-terms, nicknames, forms of insult and contempt, pejorative appellatives, swear words, surge features (exclamations, swearing, pragmatic particles), non-fluency features, stylistic devices (e.g. metaphor, comparison), pos/neg connotations/emotive overtones, emotion lexicon (both literal and metaphorical/metonymical), evaluative lexis	Bühler (1934), Jakobson (1960), Leech (1974), Lyons (1977), Pomerantz (1984), Labov (1984), Tannen 1984, Volek (1987), Ochs & Schieffelin (1989), Stankiewickz (1989), Besnier (1990), Bamberg (1991), Ameka (1992), Selting (1994), Caffi & Janney (1994), Daneš (1994), Foolen (1997), Eggins & Slade (1997: 124), Werth (1998), Taavitsainen (1999), Biber et al. (1999), van Leeuwen (1999), Goodwin & Goodwin (2000), Culpeper (2001), Hunston (2003), Halliday & Matthiessen (2004: 142, 608–12), White (2004), Martin & White (2005), Edwards (2007: 42), Pavlenko (2006), Bednarek (2006a, 2008a, 2009c), Martin (2008b), Norrick (2008), Wilce (2009), Hancil (2009)
Verbal resources (level of speech act/ move/ genre)	*Emotive Äußerungen* (e.g. exclamations, commands, threats) – affective/expressive speech acts (e.g. teasing, insults, joking) – commissive speech acts – argumentative speech acts (e.g. accusations, threats, disqualifications) – agreement/disagreement – politeness/face work/relational work/image work – Assessments – Assessives (illocutions relying on human assessment) – affiliative tokens – speech functions of giving/demanding opinion; supportive sequences; speech genres (e.g. lament, gossip)	Marty (1908), Norrick (1978), Levinson (1983), Pomerantz (1984), Marten-Cleef (1991), Eggins & Slade (1997: 193, 300), Goodwin & Goodwin (2000), Vestergaard (2000), Maynard (2003, cited in Schegloff 2007), Spitz (2005), Stivers (2006), Edwards (2007), Schegloff (2007), Behn (2009), Wilce (2009: 45–9)

Appendix 7

Table A.10 Interjections plus associated most frequent speakers (where f>2)

Interjection	Speaker	Raw frequency	F per 10,000 words
aw	Lorelai	118	3.65
aw/oh man	Luke	11	1.29
bummer	Rory	11	0.59
	[Sookie	2	0.48]
crap	Luke	4	0.47
damn (it)	Luke	3	0.35
ew	Sookie	4	0.95
for the love of god	Lorelai	4	0.12
for x's sake	Emily	16	2.08
geez/jeez	Luke	37	4.3
god	Sookie	13	3.1
my god	Richard	3	0.82
oh god	Sookie	13	3.1
oh my god	Sookie	49	11.69
(oh) my goodness	Emily	13	1.69
	Lorelai	31	0.96
(oh) thank god	Sookie	4	0.95
rats	Lorelai	9	0.28
shoot	Sookie	4	0.95
ugh	Lorelai	151	4.67
	Rory	43	2.33
whoa	Lorelai	75	2.32
wow	Rory	187	10.11
	Lorelai	16	0.49
yay	[Sookie	2	0.48]
	[Sookie	1	0.24]
yuck[4]	Rory	4	0.22
yikes	Rory	7	0.38
whew	Lorelai	3	0.09

Appendix 8

Transcription conventions

(.)	slight pause (less than 2 seconds but noticeable)
(pause: n seconds)	longer pause with duration noted in number of seconds
Underlining	strong salient/marked emphasis
Dotted underlining	less strong salient/marked emphasis
:	elongation of vowels (often indicating emphasis)
°°speech°°	spoken with very low volume ('whisper')
=speech=	saliently/markedly faster than surrounding dialogue
<speech>	saliently/markedly slower than surrounding dialogue
-speech-speech-speech	self-interrupted/'stammering' quality of speech
↓	salient/marked pitch leap downwards
?	salient/marked rising intonation (not necessarily question)
.	salient/marked falling intonation (not necessarily statement)
,	slightly rising intonation
"	marked as 'quoted' speech by intonation/voice quality

All references to images refer to illustrations of screenshots in Chapter 7. For illustration of shots see Table 7.1 in Chapter 7.

Table A.11 Transcript of break-up scene[5]

Long shot with Max in foreground (1a), camera movement from right to left, following Barista's action and then resting on Max and Lorelai		*Coffee shop in Hartford, Max sitting at the counter* *We see Barista pouring coffee into mug and handing it to Max sitting at the counter. Lorelai can be seen in the background entering the coffee shop and walking towards Max; other customers are visible in the background*		
	M	(to barista) Thanks	**Lorelai – nonverbal behaviour**	**Max – nonverbal behaviour**
		(Pause: 7 seconds)		
			enters, walks up to Max,	*observes his hand, takes mug, sighs, lifts up his mug, and starts drinking*
	L	Hey Mister wanna buy a really nice copy of Proust.	*touches Max affectionately on the back; laughs slightly, ending with closed-lip smile – see Image 7.7a*	*almost spills his drink in surprise, turns around to look at Lorelai,* *smiling*
	M	How ya doing?		
	L	<Hmm> <well> you know. You?	*'hmm' = small laugh; raised eyebrows at final 'you'*	*scratches his neck, still smiling*
	M	Ah hmm you know it also.		
	L	Yeah. (Pause:	*one nod* *puts down her bag on a chair (her gaze following), sighs, and sits down*	*his gaze follows bag when Lorelai sets it down, still smiling*
Medium shot with focus on Lorelai (2a)	L	4 seconds)	*open-mouthed smile, lifts both arms and lets them fall on her knees (with audible sound);*	
		So that parent's day is fun.	*ends with open-mouthed smile – see Image 7.7b*	*sighs or laughs slightly after 'so'*
	M	A:h it was a big hit this year (.)	*laughs slightly mid-turn and after Max's comment*	*moves hand to furrowed forehead, shakes head, sighs or laughs slightly at and following 'a:h'*

(Continued)

Table A.11 (Cont'd)

	L		*sighs;*	
		Look (.) the other day, (.) we were going skating and Rory said "why don't we invite Max to come along with us" and that was a little <u>wei:rd</u> for me.	*hands raised slightly at 'look' [but hands mainly invisible because behind counter];* *shaking head at 'weird'*	
	M	Me		
Medium shot with focus on Max (2b)		too, I don't skate. (.)	*laughs*	*laughs a little*
2a (L)	L	She's never really referred to anyone I've dated by their first <u>name</u> before. I-I always kept her out of that part of my life, so it was like "=the=mustache guy"= "the=earring=guy" the: (.) "peg leg guy".	*slight crease above nose;* *small circular movement with left hand at 'always kept her out';* *looking away and gesturing when searching for words at 'final the' (circular/waving movement with left arm)*	
	M	Oh,		
2b (M)		so you have a thing for pirates (.)	*laughs*	

2a (L)	L	She never called anyone by their na:me before. (.)	*fingers of both hands touching each other and moving slightly up and down ('specifying' gesture; see Image 7.5b); then opening both hands up at 'us'; starting at 'and so' takes off her gloves (her gaze following) and puts them on counter; points hand upwards at 'what if'; pushing hair back behind her ear with left hand at 'and then my next thought'; slight shake of head starting at second 'oh my god'*	*gives what seems a self-conscious laugh [after 'by their name before'];*
		She likes you. (.) She likes us, and so my mind instantly went to "oh my god =what=if=we=break=up=she'll=be=crushed", and then my next thought was "oh my go:d what if we break up I'll be crushed".		*sighs at' She likes you. She likes us', turns head, nodding, looking down/in front of him – starts looking back at Lorelai at first 'oh my god'*
2b (M)		And then as you know all hell broke loose.		*brows visibly lowered – 'crease' above nose between eyebrows*
	M	I understand.		*nods*
2a (L)	L	I freaked out. I'm so sorry.	*crease above nose; 'wringing' fingers (see Image 7.5e); breathes in audibly after 'I'm so sorry';*	*puts a hand above eyes to a furrowed forehead [after Lorelai's 'I'm so sorry' – see Image 7.4], rubbing nose with side of hand*
		I-I never meant to treat you like that.		
		I'm-I'm not very good at this. (.) Ask Skippy.	*opening hands at 'I'm not'; forming wide square [hands not touching] – see Image 7.5c*	
	M	Skippy?		
	L		*slight shake of head and closing of eyes in 'irrelevance' or 'never mind' gesture;*	
		I'm so so sorry.	*hands touching each other in triangle and moving up and down a bit at 'so, so' but opening them at 'sorry'*	
2b (M)	M	I was called into headmaster Charleston's office today.		*brows visibly lowered – 'crease' above nose between eyebrows – see Image 7.6*

(Continued)

Table A.11 (Cont'd)

2a (L)	L		*'stop' gesture with both hands/arms;*	
		Let=me=guess, he=put=his=arm=around=you=and=said "=I=don't=understand=why=you=crazy=kids=can't=work=this=out".	*eyebrows slightly raised*	*sighs [starting mid Lorelai's turn]*
2b (M)	M	He said I was jeopardizing my career and my future at Chilton,	*hands on counter, fingers touching and moving slightly occasionally – see Image 7.5 a [continues on to Max's 'I didn't want to' below, sometimes more, sometimes less 'fidgety']*	*brows visibly lowered – 'crease' above nose between eyebrows*
2a (L)	L	Oh ↓	*eyebrows raised*	
	M	And at first I was incensed, outraged and "how da:re, he" (.)		*both hands turn upwards at 'incensed'*
2b (M)		and then I realized that he was right. What happened the other day was completely <unprofessional>. I never in my life would have considered pulling off something like this. (.) He should've fired me.		*brows visibly lowered – 'crease' above nose between eyebrows*
2a (L)	L	But he didn't	*eyebrows raised, pointing gesture with left hand, smile*	
2b (M)	M	Not yet, but the word probation was tossed around quite a bit though.		*nods in agreement, Max's brows visibly lowered – 'crease' above nose between eyebrows*

2a (L)	L	I'm sorry.	*slight shake of head, looking down*	
2b (M)	M	I was the one who started the kiss.		
2a (L)	L	And I'm the one who knocked it up to NC-Seventee:n	*raised eyebrows*	
2b (M)	M	I-I honestly did not think that this was gonna be so complicated.		*exhales, shakes his head, looks down in front of him*
	L	I know.		
	M	I mean you told me it would be. I didn't listen. I didn't want to.		*still looking down in front of him, brows slightly lowered (slight 'crease'), then back at Lorelai at the end*
Medium to medium close-up shot with focus on Lorelai (3a)	L	It's not your fault. If I hadn't acted like a two year old and tried to run away and pretend that you weren't what you are to me then we wouldn't have fought, we wouldn't have kissed, I wouldn't have humiliated my daughter, and the (.) whole thing would've been fine.	*closed-lip smile, wrinkled nose [see Image 7.7c] and shaking head at 'not your fault'* *circular movement with left hand at 'if', crease above nose at first 'and'* *briefly looking down/away* *slight smile – see Image 7.7f*	
Medium to medium close-up shot with focus on Max (3b)	M	(Pause: 4 sec) I-I do not know what to do here.		*turns away to look down in front of him (see Image 7.1), shakes his head, sighs*

(Continued)

Table A.11 (Cont'd)

Medium close-up shot on			*mouth open, very slight crease [sad-looking – see Image 7.1]*	
Lorelai (4a)		I-(pause: 2 sec) I've never been in a relationship like this before, I-	*ending in a sad/affectionate smile (see Image 7.7d)*	
3b (M)		I'm not thinking straight.		*predominantly looking down in front of him, shaking head slightly as speaking*
4a (L)	L	I know.		
		Me either.	*eyes 'to heaven'*	
3b (M)	M			*breathes out 'puh';*
		That was a great kiss.		*shaking head very slightly;* *predominantly looking down in front of him*
4a (L)	L	<u>Beyond</u> great. (Pause: 3 sec)	*sexy open-mouthed smile (see Image 7.7e)*	
3b (M)	M	Maybe we need to take a little time away from each other.		*turns to look Lorelai in the eye, has lowered eyebrows (crease)*
4a (L)	L	(Pause: 5 sec)	*doesn't move for a while, then nods and looks down (see Images 7.3 a–d);*	
		Okay,	*looking at Max again, with crease above nose (see Images 7.3e–f);* *'fidgety' fingers visible again*	
2b (M)	M	You know just to figure out how to do this so it's not so hard.		*still 'crease', mostly looking down, looking back at Lorelai at the end*

2a (L)	L	Su:re, that makes sense.	*nodding at 'sure', looking sideways, not directly at Max, with crease above nose (see Image 7.2); hands on table, still fidgety fingers*	*looking at Lorelai, 'crease',*
2b (M)	M	I just-I don't have any other answers right now.	*looking at Max; still fidgety fingers*	*sighs, turns head to look down in front of him, shaking head*
2a (L)	L	No. You're right. You're-you're absolutely right.	*still fidgety fingers; looking sideways, not directly at Max; crease above nose; audible exhaling ['pf'] after2nd 'you're', hands opening up with left hand pointing upwards (Image 7.5d) then down again at 3rd you're, furrowed forehead, shaking head; sigh*	
2b (M)		(Pause: 3 sec)		
4a (L)		<I really really like you Max Medina.>	*looking directly at Max, face ambiguous but clearly not happy – see Image 7.8*	
3b (M)	M	(.) <I really really like you Lorelai Gilmore.>		*turning away from Lorelai, shaking his head, then turning back to look at her, and nodding slightly as he speaks;* *breathes in and out loudly at the end of his turn [almost a sigh], still has the 'crease' (see Image 7.8)*
4a (L)	L	Well, as long as we have that straightened out.	*turned slightly sideways, face ambiguous but not happy*	

(Continued)

Table A.11 (Cont'd)

		(Pause: 3 sec)		*looks away from Lorelai, nods to himself as if readying himself*
3b (M)	M	Goodbye Lorelai.		*looks at Lorelai again*
4a (L)		(Pause: 4 sec)	*looks at Max,*	*gets up and starts to walk away[out of view]*
	L	°°Bye°°	*nods, presses lips together then whispers, keeps looking down in front of her, sad face. Hands are on table, fingers touching each other, thumbs sometimes moving ('fidgety fingers')*	
Long shot with Lorelai in foreground (1b)				*walks to the door, looking back at Lorelai once as he leaves*

Transcript of scene from 1.11, *Paris is burning*; length: 3 minutes, 28 second

Appendix 9

Table A.12 Evaluations in break-up scene

Parameter	Lorelai	Trigger/Target	Max	Trigger/Target
EMOTIVITY: NEG	*all hell broke loose*	own behaviour	*how dare he*	the headmaster's telling him off
	treat you like that	own behaviour	*unprofessional*	own behaviour
	acted like a two year old	own behaviour	*pulling off something like this*	own behaviour
	we fought	Max/Lorelai's actions [as consequence of own behaviour]	*should've fired me*	own behaviour
	I humiliated my daughter	own behaviour	–	
EMOTIVITY: POS	*nice*	book	*hit, right*	parent's day
	fun	parent's day	*right*	what headmaster said
	fine	situation [hypothetically]	*great*	kiss between Max and Lorelai
	great	kiss between Max and Lorelai		
	right[6]	Max's suggestion		
	right	Max's suggestion		
EXPECTED: KNOWN	*you know*	how Lorelai is doing	*you know it also*	how Max is doing
	as you know	all hell broke loose [what happened]		
	I know	that Max didn't think it was going to be so complicated		

(*Continued*)

Table A.12 (Cont'd)

Parameter	Lorelai	Trigger/Target	Max	Trigger/Target
	I know	that Max's not thinking straight		
+ POWER	*that makes sense*	Max's suggestion	*I understand*	Lorelai's behaviour
	straightened out	what Max and Lorelai's feelings are		
− POWER	*weird*	what Rory said	*complicated*	Max/Lorelai's relationship
	not very good at	relationships	*I do not know what to do*	Max/Lorelai's relationship and its impact
	me either ['I'm not thinking straight either']	Max/Lorelai's relationship and its impact	*I'm not thinking straight*	Max/Lorelai's relationship and its impact
			hard	Max/Lorelai's relationship
			me too ['It's weird for me too']	what Rory said
			figure out how	Max/Lorelai's relationship
			I don't have any other answers	Max/Lorelai's relationship and its impact
AFFEECT: NON-DESIRE	*never meant to*	Lorelai's behaviour	*didn't want to*	listen to what Lorelai said
AFFECT: HAPPINESS	*like*	Max	*like*	Lorelai
AFFECT: UNHAPPINESS	*crushed*	if Lorelai and Max split up	–	
AFFECT: OUTBURST	*oh my god*	possibility of them splitting up	–	
	oh my god	possibility of them splitting up		
	oh	Max's report of what headmaster said		

(*Continued*)

Table A.12 (Cont'd)

Parameter	Lorelai	Trigger/Target	Max	Trigger/Target
AFFECT: INSECURITY	*freaked out*	development of relationship	–	
AFFECT: CONVENTIONALIZED	*sorry*	Lorelai's behaviour	–	
	sorry	Lorelai's behaviour		
	sorry	bad consequences for Max because of what happened between Lorelai and Max		
AFFECT: DISSATISFACTION	–		*incensed*	the headmaster's telling him off
			outraged	the headmaster's telling him off
Other	–		*honestly*	what Max thought
Total Affect	10		4	
Total overall	30		21	

Notes to Appendices

[1] Not in top 20 of SB but in top 20 of GiGi: *me* (N° 51 SB), *this* (N° 21 SB), *not* (N° 55 SB), *my* (not among top 50 in SB), *for* (N° 34 SB), *just* (N° 25 SB).

[2] Not in top 20 of GiGi but in top 20 of SB: *know* (N° 24 in GiGi), *was* (N° 29 in GiGi), *they* (not in top 60 in GiGi), *like* (N° 38 in GiGi), *yeah* (N° 44 in GiGi), *he* (N° 37 in GiGi).

[3] This table just represents an overview, and does not attempt to synthesize the various approaches into a unified framework. The selected references mainly focus on the English language (see, for example, Marten-Cleef 1991 and Schwarz-Friesel 2007 on German). In some cases, research cannot be neatly classified into one cell because it treats several aspects at the same time (e.g. verbal and non-verbal). There is also overlap between concepts used by various researchers, particularly on the speech act level.

[4] Richard also has one occurrence but is quoting Rory on this occasion: RORY: Yuck. RICHARD: Yuck, indeed. (2.18, *Back in the saddle again.*)

[5] Parallel columns are used for descriptions of different semiotic systems following previous studies (Baldry & Thibault 2006, Lorenzo-Dus 2009: 11). Starting from the left-hand side, the first column contains a description of shots (size and focus). The second column includes information on the spoken dialogue, and the third and fourth column show Lorelai's and Max's non-verbal behaviour (in italics). The columns are roughly aligned with each other, although the correspondences are approximate rather than exact. As mentioned before, the focus of the analysis is not on intersemiotic relations, and an approximate alignment is therefore sufficient. The transcription is neither as detailed, nor as complete as possible. (For detailed and technical transcriptions of various modes/modalities see Selting 1994, van Leeuwen 1999, Martinec 2001, Kendon 2004, McNeill 2005, Baldry & Thibault 2006, www.face-and-emotion.com/dataface/facs/description.jsp. For theoretical background see also Chapters 1, 6 and references therein.) Rather, I make use of general and common-sense descriptions for ease of readability and as the focus is on expressive identity rather than on facial expression, gesture phases, or inter-semiotic relations per se. For reasons of scope, I have not done a detailed phonological analysis of rhythm, tempo, intonation or pitch movement (see Selting 1994), but note pauses, emphasis, loudness, sighs, laughter. Minute movements of body parts are not recorded, but distinctive movements of the head (mainly gaze/shakes), hands/arms (gesturing), and face (smile, furrowed forehead, eyebrows) are. Shots are only described in terms of size and focus, without any analysis of editing or lighting, camera position, or angle. However, the various kinds of shots are illustrated with examples in Chapter 6, which features drawings of screenshots. Note that the scene makes use of the conventional shot-reverse shot system (Turner 1994: 123) to represent conversation between participants. To summarize, the transcription is predominantly based on identifying units that are 'noticeable, saliently marked' (Selting 1994: 383), 'perceptually and semiotically salient' (Baldry & Thibault 2006: 183), and

that can be connected to expressive meaning. This means that not *all* non-verbal behaviour is described (e.g. neutral/ambiguous face; obviously conversational functions of gaze/nods – see Chapter 6). In addition to focusing the analysis on expressive meaning and avoiding minutiae, I have tried to avoid technicality, such as technical terms (e.g. prone/supine/oblique for gesture), abbreviations or codes. Note that hearable aspiration is included under the column labelled 'nonverbal behaviour' as are suprasegmental actions like laughing and non-verbal behaviour like gestures.

As Baldry and Thibault (2006) state, transcriptions differ according to the kind of analysis pursued, for instance in terms of the level of detail (what they call 'magnification') provided, and 'the distinction between various types of transcription is only a question of methodological convenience' (Baldry & Thibault 2006: 166). Any transcript, including this one 'is always an artefact of the analyst's own categorisation and selection processes and will therefore always remain an interpretation rather than a faithful reproduction of the primary data' (Lorenzo-Dus 2009: 11, referencing Ochs 1979). Transcribing, Lorenzo-Dus points out, 'is a partial, on-going process' (Lorenzo-Dus 2009: 11). However, note that interested readers can watch the scene in the original, for example, on one of the many websites offering online watching of episodes – a clear advantage of using 'public' data.

[6] Statements like *you're right* are classified as POSITIVE EMOTIVITY, as they express an arguably positive evaluation of what was said by the interlocutor. Because of the nature of evaluative meaning, alternative classifications are always possible. For instance, *crazy kids* (NEG EMOTIVITY attributed to headmaster Charleston, that is, not listed in this table but see transcript in Appendix 8) might be used affectionately (POS AFFECT) and *how dare he* (NEG EMOTIVITY) could be treated as outburst of affect (like interjections) or as a separate category of affect. Note also that some instances of POSITIVE EMOTIVITY are used ironically (*So that parent's day is* ***fun****/Oh, it was* ***a big hit*** *this year*) or hypothetically (*If . . . the whole thing would've been* ***fine***). Phrases like *you know it also* involve a 'Knower' other than the Self but their source is still the speaker who attributes a mental state to the interlocutor and are hence included with the other evaluations concerning the Self (*you know* as discourse marker was not included as evaluative).

References

Abercrombie, N. & Longhurst, B. 1998. *Audiences: A Sociological Theory of Performance and Imagination.* London: Sage.

Adolphs, S. 2006. *Introducing Electronic Text Analysis: A Practical Guide for Language and Literary Studies.* London: Routledge.

— 2008. *Corpus and Context. Investigating Pragmatic Functions in Spoken Discourse.* Amsterdam/Philadelphia, PA: John Benjamins.

Akass, K. & McCabe, J. (eds). 2004. *Reading* Sex and the City. London/New York: I.B. Tauris.

— 2007. 'Analyzing fictional television genres'. In Devereux, E. (ed.), *Media Studies. Key Issues and Debates.* Los Angeles, CA, etc.: Sage, 283–301.

Allen, R. C. 2004. 'Frequently asked questions. A general introduction to the reader'. In Allen, R. C. & Hill, A. (eds), *The Television Studies Reader.* New York: Routledge, 1–26.

Allen, M. (ed.). 2007. *Reading* CSI. *Crime TV under the Microscope.* London/New York: I.B. Tauris.

Allen, R. C. & Hill, A. (eds). 2004. *The Television Studies Reader.* New York: Routledge.

Ameka, F. 1992. 'Interjections: the universal yet neglected part of speech'. *Journal of Pragmatics* 18: 101–18.

American Meat Institute. 2007. 'U.S. meat and poultry production & consumption: an overview'. *American Meat Institute Fact Sheet,* accessed on 1/4/2009 from www.MeatAMI.com.

Ang, I. 1985. *Watching Dallas: Soap Operas and the Melodramatic Identification.* London: Methuen.

Antaki, C. & Widdicombe, S. (eds). 1998. *Identities in Talk.* Thousand Oaks, CA: Sage.

Archer, D. 2007. 'Computer-assisted literary stylistics: the state of the field'. In Lambrou, M. & Stockwell, P. (eds), *Contemporary Stylistics.* London/New York: Continuum, 244–56.

Arthurs, J. 2004. *Television and Sexuality: Regulation and the Politics of Taste.* New York: Open University Press.

Auer, P. (ed.). 2007a. *Style and Social Identities. Alternative Approaches to Linguistic Heterogeneity.* Berlin/New York: Mouton de Gruyter.

— 2007b. 'Introduction'. In Auer, P. (ed.), *Style and Social Identities. Alternative Approaches to Linguistic Heterogeneity.* Berlin/New York: Mouton de Gruyter, 1–21.

— 2007c. 'Introduction to part 3'. In Auer, P. (ed.), *Style and Social Identities. Alternative Approaches to Linguistic Heterogeneity.* Berlin/New York: Mouton de Gruyter, 321–24.

Baker, P. 2003. 'No effeminates please: a corpus-based analysis of masculinity via personal adverts in *Gay News/Times* 1973–2000'. In Benwell, B. (ed.), *Masculinity and Men's Lifestyle Magazines.* Oxford: Blackwell, 243–60.

— 2006. *Using Corpora in Discourse Analysis.* London/New York: Continuum.

Bal, M. [2]1997. *Narratology. Introduction to the Theory of Narrative.* Toronto: University of Toronto Press.

Baldry, A. & Thibault, P. J. 2006. *Multimodal Transcription and Text Analysis. A Multimedia Toolkit and Coursebook.* London/Oakville: Equinox.

Bally, C. [3]1965. *Le langage et la vie.* Geneva: Librairie Droz.

Bamberg, M. 1991. 'Narrative activity as perspective taking: the role of emotionals, negations and voice in the construction of the story realm'. *Journal of Cognitive Psychotherapy* 2: 275–90.

— 2009. 'Positioning emotion – connecting the there-and-then of the story world with the interactive here-and-now'. Paper presented at *11th International Pragmatics Conference,* Melbourne, 12–17 July.

Barker, C. & Galasińksi, D. 2001. *Cultural Studies and Discourse Analysis: A Dialogue on Language and Identity.* Thousand Oaks, CA: Sage.

Barthes, R. 1974. *S/Z.* New York: Hill & Wang.

Bavidge, J. 2004. 'Chosen ones: reading the contemporary teen heroine'. In Davis, G. & Dickinson, K. (eds), *Teen TV. Genre, Consumption and Identity.* London: British Film Institute, 41–53.

Bednarek, M. 2006a. *Evaluation in Media Discourse. Analysis of a Newspaper Corpus.* London/New York: Continuum.

— 2006b. 'Subjectivity and cognition. Inscribing, evoking and provoking opinion'. In Pishwa, H. (ed.), *Language and Memory.* Berlin: Mouton de Gruyter, 187–221.

— 2008a. *Emotion Talk Across Corpora.* Basingstoke/New York: Palgrave Macmillan.

— 2008b. '"What the hell is wrong with you?" A corpus perspective on evaluation and emotion in contemporary American pop culture'. In Mahboob, A. & Knight, N. (eds), *Questioning Linguistics.* Newcastle: Cambridge Scholars Press, 95–126.

— 2008c. '"An increasingly familiar tragedy": evaluative collocation and conflation'. *Functions of Language* 15/1: 7–34.

— 2008d. 'Teaching English literature and linguistics using corpus stylistic methods'. In Cloran, C. & Zappavigna, M. (eds), *Bridging Discourses. ASFLA 2007 Online Proceedings.* Available at: www.asfla.org.au/category/asfla2007.

— 2008e. 'Semantic preference and semantic prosody re-examined'. *Corpus Linguistics and Linguistic Theory* 4/2: 119–39.

— 2009a. 'Corpora and discourse: a three-pronged approach to analyzing linguistic data'. In Haugh, M., Burridge, K., Mulder, J. & Peters, P. (eds), *Selected Proceedings of the 2008 HCSNet Workshop on Designing the Australian National Corpus: Mustering Languages,* Cascadilla Proceedings Project, Sommerville, MA, 19–24. Available at: www.lingref.com/cpp/ausnc/2008/index.html

— 2009b. 'Emotion-talk and emotional-talk: cognitive and discursive perspectives'. In Pishwa, H. (ed.), *Language and Social Cognition.* Berlin: Mouton de Gruyter, 395–431.

— 2009c. 'Polyphony in appraisal: typological and topological perspectives'. *Linguistics and the Human Sciences* 3/2: 107–36.

— 2009d. 'Language patterns and ATTITUDE'. *Functions of Language* 16/2: 165–92.

— 2010. 'Corpus linguistics and systemic functional linguistics: interpersonal meaning, identity and bonding in popular culture'. In Bednarek, M. & Martin, J. R. (eds), *New Discourse on Language: Functional Perspectives on Multimodality, Identity and Affiliation*. London/New York: Continuum, 237–66.

— forthcoming. 'The stability of the televisual character: a corpus stylistic case study'. In R. Piazza, Rossi, F., & Bednarek, M. (eds), *Telecinematic Discourse: Approaches to the Fictional Language of Cinema and Television* (Working title) Book proposal submitted to John Benjamins (for *Pragmatics & Beyond*, ed. Fetzer, A.).

— in preparation. 'The discourse of dramedy.' Unpublished manuscript, University of Sydney, Australia. Available on demand.

Bednarek, M. & Bublitz, W. 2006. 'Enjoy! – The (phraseological) culture of having fun'. In Skandera, P. (ed.), *Phraseology and Culture in English*. (Topics in English Linguistics.) Berlin: Mouton de Gruyter, 109–35.

Bednarek, M. & Caple H. 2010. 'Playing with environmental stories in the news: good or bad practice?' *Discourse & Communication* 4/1: 5–31.

Bednarek, M. & Martin, J. R. (eds). 2010. *New Discourse on Language: Functional Perspectives on Multimodality, Identity and Affiliation*. London/New York: Continuum.

Beeman, A. K. 2007. 'Emotional segregation: a content analysis of institutional racism in US films, 1980–2001'. *Ethnic and Racial Studies* 30/5: 687–712.

Behn, A. 2007. '"My Entire Authority is Gone". Imagearbeit im Coachinggespräch'. Unpublished M.A. thesis, University of Augsburg, Germany.

— 2009. 'Image-related sequence types in coaching interactions'. Paper presented at *i-mean@uwe*, 23–25 April 2009, Bristol, University of the West of England.

Bell, A. 1991. *The Language of News Media*. Oxford: Blackwell.

Bell, A. & Garrett, P. (eds). 1998. *Approaches to Media Discourse*. Oxford/Malden, MA: Blackwell.

Bennison, N. 1998. 'Accessing character through conversation: Tom Stoppard's Professional Foul'. In Culpeper, J. (ed.), *Exploring the Language of Drama: From Text to Context*. London: Routledge, 67–82.

Benoit, W. L. 1995. *Accounts, Excuses and Apologies. A Theory of Image Restoration Strategies*. Albany, NY: State University of New York Press.

Benwell, B. & Stokoe, E. 2006. *Discourse and Identity*. Edinburgh: Edinburgh University Press.

Berliner, T. 1999. 'Movie dialogue and Hollywood realism'. *Film Quarterly* 52: 3–16.

Besnier, N. 1990. 'Language and affect'. *Annual Review of Anthropology* 19: 59–88.

Biber, D. 1988. *Variation Across Speech and Writing*. Cambridge: CUP.

— 2006. *University Language. A Corpus-Based Study of Spoken and Written Registers*. Amsterdam/Philadelphia, PA: John Benjamins.

Biber, D., Johansson, S., Leech, G., Conrad, S. & Finegan, E. 1999. *Longman Grammar of Spoken and Written English*. London: Longman.

Billington, M. 2009. 'Method in the madness'. Available at: www.guardian.co.uk/stage/2009/may/09/stanislavski-method-acting-michael-billington, last accessed 23/7/2009.

Birchall, C. 2004. '"Feels like home": *Dawson's Creek*, nostalgia and the young adult viewer'. In Davis, G. & Dickinson, K. (eds), *Teen TV. Genre, Consumption and Identity*. London: British Film Institute, 176–89.

Blum, R. A. ^{3}1995. *Television and Screen Writing. From Concept to Contract*. Boston, MA: Focal Press.

Bonfiglioli, C. M. F., Smith, B. J., King, L. A., Chapman, S. F. & Holding, S. J. 2007. 'Obesity in the media: political hot potato or human interest story?'. *Australian Journalism Review* 29/1: 53–61.

Bordwell, D. 1985. *Narration in the Fiction Film*. London: Methuen.

Bordwell, D. & Thompson, K. ^{7}2004. *Film Art. An Introduction*. Boston, MA: McGraw Hill.

Brock, A. 2004. *Blackadder, Monty Python und Red Dwarf – eine linguistische Untersuchung britischer Fernsehkomödien*. Tübingen: Stauffenburg.

Brown, P. & Levinson, S. 1987. *Politeness. Some Universals of Language Use*. Cambridge: CUP.

Bruder, M., Cohn, L. M., Olnek, M., Pollack, N., Previto, R., & Zigler, S. 1986. *A Practical Handbook for the Actor*. New York: Vintage Books.

Bruzzi, S. 1997. *Undressing Cinema: Clothing and Identity in the Movies*. London/ New York: Routledge.

Bubel, C. 2006. 'The Linguistic Construction of Character Relations in TV Drama: Doing Friendship in *Sex and the City*'. Unpublished PhD dissertation, Universität des Saarlandes, Saarbrücken, Germany. Available at: www.scidok.sulb.uni-saarland.de/volltexte/2006/598/.

Bubel, C. & Spitz, A. 2006. '"One of the last vestiges of gender bias": The characterization of women through the telling of dirty jokes in *Ally McBeal*'. *Humor* 19/1: 71–104.

Bublitz, W. 2001. *Englische Pragmatik. Eine Einführung*. Berlin: Erich Schmidt Verlag.

Bühler, K. 1934 (^{2}1965). *Sprachtheorie*. Stuttgart: Gustav Fischer.

Burke Erickson, A. K. 2008. 'Drats! Foiled again: A contrast in definitions'. In Calvin, R. (ed.), 63–79.

Burton, D. 1980. *Dialogue and Discourse*. London: Routledge and Kegan.

Burton, G. 2000. *Talking Television: An Introduction to the Study of Television*. London: Arnold.

Butler, J. 1999. *Gender Trouble: Feminism and the Subversion of Identity*. New York: Routledge.

Byrd-Bredbenner, C., Finckenor, M. & Grenci, A. 2004. 'A television program affects children's nutrition knowledge and beliefs'. *Journal of the American Dietetic Association* 104/2: 51.

Caffi, C. & Janney, R. W. 1994. 'Toward a pragmatics of emotive communication'. *Journal of Pragmatics* 22: 32–373.

Calvin, R. 2008a. 'Introduction – "Where you lead": *Gilmore Girls* and the politics of identity'. In Calvin, R. (ed.), 1–22.

— (ed.) 2008b. *Gilmore Girls and the Politics of Identity: Essays on Family and Feminism in the Television Series*. Jefferson/London: McFarland.

Cameron, D. & Kulick, D. 2005. 'Identity crisis?'. *Language & Communication* 25: 107–25.

Cameron, D. 2005. 'Language, gender and sexuality: current issues and new directions'. *Applied Linguistics* 26: 482–502.

Cannon, D. 2009. 'Character building and what makes a truly great actor'. Available at: www.guardian.co.uk/stage/2009/may/09/character-building-great-actor, last accessed 23/7/2009.

Caple, H. 2008. 'Intermodal relations in image-nuclear news stories'. In Unsworth, L. (ed.), *Multimodal Semiotics: Functional Analysis in Contexts of Education*. London: Continuum, 125–38.

— 2010. 'Doubling-up: allusion and bonding in multisemiotic news stories'. In Bednarek, M. & Martin, J. R. (eds), *New Discourse on Language: Functional Perspectives on Multimodality, Identity and Affiliation*. London/New York: Continuum, 111–33.

Caple, H. & Bednarek, M. forthcoming. 'Double-take: unpacking the play in the multi-modal news story'. *Visual Communication* 9/2: 1–18.

Carroll, N. 1996. *Theorizing the Moving Image*. Cambridge: CUP.

Carter, R. & Adolphs, S. 2008. 'Linking the verbal and visual: new directions for Corpus Linguistics'. *Language and Computers* 64: 275–91.

Carugati, A. 2005. 'Interview with Jerry Bruckheimer'. *Worldscreen*, April.

Chion, M. 1999. *The Voice in Cinema*. New York: Columbia University Press.

Clark, H. H. 1996. *Using Language*. Cambridge: CUP.

Claudel, C. 2009. 'Linguistic expression and semiotic translation of emotions in French and Japanese personal emails'. Paper presented at *11th International Pragmatics Conference*, Melbourne, 12–17 July.

Cohen, J. 1999. 'Favorite characters of teenage viewers of Israeli serials'. *Journal of Broadcasting & Electronic Media* 43/3: 327–45.

Coleman, L. 2008. 'Food fights. Food and its consumption as a narrative device'. In Calvin, R. (ed.), 175–92.

Collins, B. 2002. *Getting Into Character. Seven Secrets a Novelist can Learn from Actors*. New York: John Wiley & Sons.

Cook, G. 1992. *The Discourse of Advertising*. London/New York: Routledge.

— 2004. *Genetically Modified Language*. London/New York: Routledge.

Coulthard, M. ²1985. *An Introduction to Discourse Analysis*. London: Longman.

Coupland, J. & Gwyn, R. 2003. 'Introduction'. In Coupland, J. & Gwyn, R. (eds), *Discourse, the Body and Identity*. Basingstoke/New York: Palgrave Macmillan, 1–16.

Coupland, N. 2007. *Style. Language Variation and Identity*. Cambridge: CUP.

Creeber, G. (ed.). 2001. *The Television Genre Book*. London/New York: Routledge.

— 2004. *Serial Television. Big Drama on the Small Screen*. London: Bfi Publishing.

Crystal, D. ²1997. *The Cambridge Encyclopedia of Language*. Cambridge: CUP.

Culpeper, J. 2001. *Language and Characterisation. People in Plays and Other Texts*. Harlow etc: Longman.

— 2002. 'Computers, language and characterisation: an analysis of six characters in Romeo and Juliet'. In Melander-Marttala, U., Ostman, C. & Kyto, M. (eds), *Conversation in Life and Literature: Papers from the ASLA Symposium. Association Suedoise de Linguistique Appliquee (ASLA)* 15. Uppsala: Universitetstryckeriet, 11–30.

Daneš, F. 1994. 'Involvement with language and in language'. *Journal of Pragmatics* 22: 251–64.

Darwin, C. 1965. *The Expression of the Emotions in Man and Animals*; with a preface by Konrad Lorenz. Chicago, IL: University of Chicago Press.

Davis, G. & Dickinson, K. (eds). 2004. *Teen TV. Genre, Consumption and Identity*. London: British Film Institute.

Day, D. 1998. 'Being ascribed, and resisting, membership of an ethnic group'. In Antaki, C. & Widdicombe, S. (eds), *Identities in Talk*. Thousand Oaks, CA: Sage, 151–70.

Decker, J. M. 2004. *Ideology*. Houndmills/New York: Palgrave Macmillan.

De Fina, A., Schiffrin, D. & Bamberg, M. 2006. 'Introduction'. In DeFina, A., Schiffrin, D. & Bamberg, M. (eds), *Discourse and Identity*. Cambridge: CUP, 1–23.

De Kloet, J. & Van Zoonen, L. 2007. 'Fan culture – performing difference'. In Devereux, E. (ed.), *Media Studies. Key Issues and Debates*. Los Angeles, CA, etc.: Sage, 322–41.

Díaz-Cintas, J. (ed.). 2009. *New Trends in Audiovisual Translation*. Clevedon: Multilingual Matters.

Diffrient, D. S. & Lavery, D. (eds) forthcoming. *Screwball Television: Critical Perspectives on Gilmore Girls*. Syracuse, NY: Syracuse University Press.

Dunn, A. 2005. 'The genres of television'. In Fulton et al., 125–39.

Durham, K. 2002. 'Methodology and praxis of the actor within the television production process: facing the camera in *EastEnders* and *Morse*'. *Studies in Theatre and Performance* 22/2: 82–94.

D'Vary, M. 2005. *Creating Characters. Let Them Whisper Their Secrets*. Studio City: Michael Wiese Productions.

Eagleton, T. 1991. *Ideology. An Introduction*. London/New York: Verso.

Eckert, P. 2008. 'Variation and the indexical field'. *Journal of Sociolinguistics* 12/4: 453–76.

Edmondson, W. 1981. 'On saying you're sorry'. In Coulmas, F. (ed.), *Conversational Routine: Explorations in Standardised Communication Situations and Prepatterned Speech*. The Hague: Mouton, 273–87.

Edwards, D. 2007. 'Managing subjectivity in talk'. In Hepburn, A. & Wiggins, S. (eds), *Discursive Research in Practice. New Approaches to Psychology and Interaction*. Cambridge: CUP, 31–49.

Eggins, S. & Slade, D. 1997. *Analysing Casual Conversation*. London/Washington: Cassell.

Eisenstein, J. 2008. *Gesture in Automatic Discourse Processing*. MIT-CSAIL-TR-2008-027. Cambridge, MA: Massachusetts Institute of Technology. Available at: www.people.csail.mit.edu/jacobe/papers/diss.pdf.

Ekman, P. 1997. 'Should we call it expression or communication?' *Innovations in Social Science Research* 10/4: 333–44.

— 1999. 'Facial expressions'. In Dalgleish, T. & Power, M. (eds), *Handbook of Cognition and Emotion*. New York: John Wiley & Sons Ltd, 301–20.

Ekman, P. & Friesen, W. V. 1975. *Unmasking the Face*. Englewood Cliffs: Prentice-Hall.

Elliot, T. 2005. 'Storytellers'. *The Age* Magazine, 21 August.

Ellis, J. 2004. 'Television production'. In Allen, R. & Hill, A. (eds), *The Television Studies Reader*. London/New York: Routledge, 275–92.

Ellsworth, P. C. 1994. 'Sense, culture, and sensibility'. In Kitayama, S. & Markus, H. R. (eds), *Emotion and Culture. Empirical Studies of Mutual Influences*.

Washington, DC: American Psychological Association American Psychological Association, Boston, MA, 23–50.
Englebretson, R. (ed.) 2007. *Stancetaking in Discourse Subjectivity, Evaluation, Interaction.* Amsterdam/Philadelphia, PA: John Benjamins.
Enkvist, N. E. 1964. 'On defining style'. In Enkvist, N. E., Spencer, J. & Gregory, M. (eds), *Linguistics and Style.* Oxford: OUP, 1–56.
— 1973. *Linguistic Stylistics.* Berlin: Mouton.
Entman, R. 1993. 'Framing: towards clarification of a fractured paradigm'. *Journal of Communication* 43/4: 51–8.
Esslin, M. ²2002. *The Age of Television.* New Brunswick, NJ: Transaction Publishers. [Originally published in 1982, San Francisco, CA: Freeman.]
Fairclough, N. 2000. *New Labour, New Language?* London: Routledge.
— 2003. *Analysing Discourse: Textual Analysis for Social Research.* London: Routledge.
— 2004. 'Critical discourse analysis in researching language in the new capitalism: overdetermination, transdisciplinarity and textual analysis'. In Young, L. & Harrison, C. (eds), *Systemic Functional Linguistics and Critical Discourse Analysis: Studies in Social Change.* London: Continuum, 103–22.
Feuer, J. 2001a. 'The unruly woman sitcom'. (I love Lucy, Roseanne, Absolutely Fabulous). In Creeber, G. (ed.), 68–9.
— 2001b. 'Situation comedy, part 2'. In Creeber, G. (ed.), 67–70.
— 2001c. 'Will and grace'. In Creeber, G. (ed.), 72.
— 2001d. 'The "gay" and "queer" sitcom'. In Creeber, G. (ed.), 70–2.
Fiehler, R. 1990. *Kommunikation und Emotion.* Berlin: Mouton de Gruyter.
Field, S. 1984. *The Screenwriter's Workbook.* New York: Dell.
Fill, A. & Mühlhäusler, P. 2001. *The Ecolinguistics Reader. Language, Ecology and Environment.* London/New York: Continuum.
Fine, M. G. 1981. 'Soap opera conversations: the talk that binds'. *Journal of Communication Summer 1981.* 97–107.
Fischer-Starcke, B. 2007. 'Korpusstilistik: Korpuslinguistische Analysen literarischer Werke am Beispiel Jane Austens'. Unpublished PhD dissertation, Universität Trier (Germany).
Fiske, J. 1987. *Television Culture.* London: Routledge.
— 1994. 'Television pleasures'. In Graddol, D. & Boyd-Barrett, O. (eds), *Media Texts: Authors and Readers.* Clevedon: Multilingual Matters in association with The Open University, 239–55.
Fleegal, S. 2008. 'Like mother–daughter, like daughter–mother. Constructs of motherhood in three generations'. In Calvin, R. (ed.), 143–58.
Foolen, A. 1997. 'The expressive function of language: towards a cognitive semantic approach'. In Niemeier, S. & Dirven, R. (eds), *The Language of Emotions.* Amsterdam/Philadelphia, PA: John Benjamins, 15–23.
Forster, E. M. 1987. *Aspects of the Novel.* London: Methuen.
Fowler, R. 1986. *Linguistic Criticism.* Oxford: OUP.
Frye, N. 1957. *Anatomy of Criticism: Four Essays.* Princeton, NJ: Princeton University Press.
Fulton, H. 2005a. 'Introduction: the power of narrative'. In Fulton et al., 1–7.
— 2005b. 'Film narrative and visual cohesion'. In Fulton et al., 108–22.
Fulton, H., Huisman, R., Murphet, J. & Dunn, A. 2005. *Narrative and Media.* Cambridge: CUP.

Galasiński, D. 2004. *Men and the Language of Emotions.* Houndmills: Palgrave Macmillan.

Galtung, J. & Ruge, M. H. 1965. 'The structure of foreign news'. *Journal of Peace Research* 2/1: 64–91.

Garrett, P. & Bell, A. 1998. 'Media and discourse: a critical overview'. In Bell, A. & Garrett, P. (eds), *Approaches to Media Discourse.* Oxford/Malden, MA: Blackwell, 1–20.

Giddens, A. 1984. *The Constitution of Society.* Berkeley/Los Angeles, CA: University of California Press.

Giles, D. 2002. 'Parasocial interaction: a review of the literature and a model for future research'. *Media Psychology* 4/3: 279–304.

Gillespie, M. 1995. *Television, Ethnicity and Cultural Change.* New York: Routledge.

Goatley, A. 2007. *Washing the Brain – Metaphor and Hidden Ideology.* Amsterdam/Philadelphia, PA: John Benjamins.

Goddard, A. 1998. *The Language of Advertising: Written Texts.* New York: Routledge.

Goffman, E. 1967. *Interaction Ritual. Essays on Face-to-Face Behaviour.* New York: Pantheon.

— 1971. *Relations in Public: Micro-Studies of the Public Order.* New York: Basic Books.

— 1974. *Frame Analysis: An Essay on the Organization of Experience.* Cambridge, MA: Harvard University Press.

— 1976. 'Replies and responses'. *Language in Society* 5: 257–313.

— 1979. 'Footing'. *Semiotica* 25: 1–29.

— 1981. *Forms of Talk.* Philadelphia, PA : University of Pennsylvania Press.

Goodwin, M. H. & Goodwin, C. 2000. 'Emotion within situated activity'. Available at: www.sscnet.ucla.edu/clic/cgoodwin/00emot_act.pdf, last accessed 19/5/2009. (Originally published as pp. 33–54 in *Communication: An Arena for Development,* edited by Nanci Budwig, Ina C. Uzgris & James V. Wertsch, Stamford, CT: Ablex, 2000).

Graves, D. A. 1999. 'Computer analysis of word usage in Emma'. *Persuasions* 21: 203–11.

Greimas, A. J. 1966. *Sémantique Structurale.* Paris: Larousse.

Gumperz, J. J. & Cook-Gumperz, J. 2007. 'A postscript: style and identity in interactional sociolinguistics'. In Auer, P. (ed.), *Style and Social Identities. Alternative Approaches to Linguistic Heterogeneity.* Berlin/New York: Mouton de Gruyter, 477–501.

Haddrick, G. 2001. *Top Shelf 1. Reading and Writing the Best in Australian TV Drama.* Strawberry Hills, Australia: Currency Press.

Hänlein, H. 1999. *Studies in Authorship Recognition – a Corpus-based Approach.* Frankfurt: Peter Lang.

Hall, S. 1994. 'Encoding/decoding'. In Graddol, D. & Boyd-Barrett, O. (eds), *Media Texts: Authors and Readers.* Clevedon: Multilingual Matters, 200–11.

Halliday, M. A. K. 2004. 'The spoken language corpus: a foundation for grammatical theory'. In Aijmer, K. & Altenberg, B. (eds), *Advances in Corpus Linguistics. Papers from the 23rd International Conference on English Language Research on Computerized Corpora.* Amsterdam/New York: Rodopi, 11–39.

Halliday, M. A. K. & Matthiessen, C. M. I. M. 2004. *An Introduction to Functional Grammar.* London: Arnold [Third edition].

Hancil, S. 2009 (ed.). *The Role of Prosody in Affective Speech.* Bern: Peter Lang.
Hartley, J. 1999. *Uses of Television.* London/New York: Routledge.
— 2001. 'Situation comedy, part 1'. In Creeber, G. (ed.), 65–67.
Haupt, M. 2008. 'Wheat balls, gravlax, pop tarts. Mothering and power'. In Calvin, R. (ed.), 114–26.
Hayman, R. 1969. *Techniques of Acting.* London: Methuen.
Hermes, J. 2005. *Re-reading Popular Culture.* Oxford: Blackwell.
Hoey, M. 2005. *Lexical Priming.* London/New York: Routledge.
Holly, W. 1979. *Imagearbeit in Gesprächen. Zur linguistischen Beschreibung des Beziehungsaspekts.* Tuebingen: Niemeyer.
Holmes, J. 1984. 'Modifying illocutionary force'. *Journal of Pragmatics* 8: 345–65.
Holmes, J. 1997. 'Women, language and identity'. *Journal of Sociolinguistics* 1/2: 195–223.
Holmes, J. 2009. 'How do you air a bad joke?' *Media Watch* (ABC television, Australia) Episode 18, 8 June 2009. Transcript available at: www.abc.net.au/mediawatch/transcripts/s2592383.htm, last accessed 11/6/2009.
Hood, S. forthcoming. 'Body language in face-to-face teaching: a focus on textual and interpersonal meaning'. In Dreyfus, S., Hood S. & Stenglin M. (eds), *Semiotic Margins: Meaning in Multimodalities.* London: Continuum.
Hornby, N. 2006. *The Complete Polysyllabic Spree.* London: Penguin.
Horton, D. & Wohl, R. R. 1956. 'Mass communication and para-social interaction'. *Psychiatry* 19: 215–29.
Hubbard, E. H. 2002. 'Conversation, characterisation and corpus linguistics: dialogue in Jane Austen's *Sense and Sensibility*'. *Literator* 23/2: 67–85.
Hübler, A. 1998. *The Expressivity of Grammar: Grammatical Devices Expressing Emotion Across Time.* Berlin: Mouton de Gruyter.
Huisman, R. 2005a. 'Soap operas and sitcoms'. In Fulton et al., 172–87.
— 2005b. 'Aspects of narrative in series and serials'. In Fulton et al., 153–71.
Hunston, S. 2002. *Corpora in Applied Linguistics.* Cambridge: CUP.
Hunston, S. 2003. 'Frame, phrase or function: a comparison of frame semantics and local grammars'. In Archer, D., Rayson, P. Wilson, A. & McEnery, T. (eds), *Proceedings of the Corpus Linguistics 2003 Conference. UCREL Technical Papers* 16. Lancaster: UCREL: 342–58.
— 2004. 'Counting the uncountable: problems of identifying evaluation in a text and in a corpus'. In Partington, A., Morley J. & Haarman, L. (eds), *Corpora and Discourse.* Bern: Peter Lang: 157–88.
Hunston, S. & Thompson, G. (eds). 2000. *Evaluation in Text. Authorial Stance and the Construction of Discourse.* Oxford: OUP.
Hunter, K. 2009. 'The body tells a story in itself'. Available at: www.guardian.co.uk/stage/2009/may/09/kathryn-hunter-physical-theatre, last accessed 23/7/2009.
Idato, M. 2009. 'TV facing its own strict diet'. *The Sydney Morning Herald, News Review,* 2–3 May, p. 3.
Iedema, R. 2001. 'Analysing film and television: a social semiotic account of *Hospital: an Unhealthy Business*'. In van Leeuwen, T. & Jewitt, C. (eds), *Handbook of Visual Analysis.* London/Thousand Oaks, CA/New Delhi: Sage, 183–204.
Jagger, G. 2008. *Judith Butler. Sexual Politics, Social Change and the Power of the Performative.* London/New York: Routledge.

Jakobson, R. 1960. 'Closing statement: linguistics and poetics'. In Sebeok, T. (ed.), *Style in Language*. Cambridge: MIT Press, 350–77.

Johns, E. K. & Smith, K. L. 2008. 'Welcome to Stars Hollow. *Gilmore Girls*, utopia, and the hyperreal'. In Calvin, R. (ed.), 23–34.

Johnson, S. & Ensslin, A. (eds). 2007. *Language in the Media. Representations, Identities, Ideologies*. London/New York: Continuum.

Johnstone, B. & Bean, J. M. 1997. 'Self-expression and linguistic variation'. *Language in Society* 26: 221–46.

Kärkkäinen, E. 2003. *Epistemic Stance in English Conversation. A Description of its Interactional Functions, with a Focus on* I think. Amsterdam/Philadelphia, PA: John Benjamins.

Kay, P. & Fillmore, C. J. 1999. 'Grammatical constructions and linguistic generalizations: the what's X doing Y? construction'. *Language* 75/1: 1–33.

Kendon, A. 1967. 'Some functions of gaze direction in social interaction' *Acta Psychologica* 26: 22–63.

Kendon, A. 2004. *Visible Action as Utterance*. Cambridge: CUP.

Kitayama, S. & Markus, H. R. 1994. 'Introduction to cultural psychology and emotion research'. In Kitayama, S. (ed.), *Emotion and Culture. Empirical Studies of Mutual Influences*. Washington, DC: American Psychological Association, 1–19.

Knight, N. 2010. 'Wrinkling complexity: concepts of identity and affiliation in humour'. In Bednarek, M. & Martin, J. R. (eds), *New Discourse on Language: Functional Perspectives on Multimodality, Identity and Affiliation*. London/New York: Continuum, 35–58.

Knight, N. in preparation. 'Sociality through laughter: the pragmatics of Affiliation in conversational humour'. Unpublished manuscript, University of Sydney, Australia.

Konstantinidou, M. 1997. *Sprache und Gefühl*. Hamburg: Helmut Buske Verlag.

Kozloff, S. 2000. *Overhearing Film Dialogue*. Ewing, NJ: University of California Press.

Kress, G. & van Leeuwen, T. [2]2006. *Reading Images: The Grammar of Visual Design*. London/New York: Routledge.

Krishnamurthy, R. 1995. 'The macrocosm and the microcosm: the corpus and the text'. In Payne, J. (ed.), *Linguistic Approaches to Literature*. University of Birmingham: ELR, 1–16.

Kubey, R. W. 2003. 'Why U.S. Media Education lags behind the rest of the English-speaking world'. *Television and New Media* 4/4: 351–70.

Labov, W. 1984. 'Intensity'. In Schiffrin, D. (ed.), *Meaning, Form, and Use in Context: Linguistic Applications*. Washington: Georgetown University Press, 43–70.

Lacey, N. 1998. *Image and Representation. Key Concepts in Media Studies*. Houndmills/New York: Palgrave.

Lakoff, R. T. 2006. 'Identitiy à la carte: you are what you eat'. In De Fina, A., Schiffrin, D. & Bamberg, M. (eds), *Discourse and Identity*. Cambridge: CUP, 142–65.

Lambrou, M. & Stockwell, P. (eds). 2007. *Contemporary Stylistics*. London/New York: Continuum.

Lancioni, J. 2006. 'Murder and mayhem on Wisteria Lane: a study of genre and cultural context in *Desperate Housewives*'. In McCabe, J. & Akass, K. (eds),

Reading Desperate Housewives. *Beyond the White Picket Fence.* London/New York: I.B. Tauris, 129–43.
Lee, D. 2001. 'Genres, registers, text types, domains, and styles: clarifying the concepts and navigating a path through the BNC jungle'. *Language Learning & Technology* 5: 37–72. Available at: www.llt.msu.edu/vol5num3/lee/, last accessed 20/10/2005.
Leech, G. 1974. *Semantics.* Harmondsworth: Penguin Books Ltd.
Leech, G. & Short, M. 1981. *Style in Fiction. A Linguistic Introduction to English Fictional Prose.* London/New York: Longman.
Lemke, J. 1998. 'Resources for attitudinal meaning: evaluative orientations in text semantics'. *Functions of Language* 5/1: 33–56.
Levinson, S. C. 1983. *Pragmatics.* Cambridge: CUP.
Lippi-Green, R. 1997. *English with an Accent: Language, Ideology and Discrimination in the United States.* London/New York: Routledge.
Livingstone, S. ^{2}1998. *Making Sense of Television. The Psychology of Audience Interpretation.* London/New York: Routledge.
Livsey, A. J. 2004. 'A further graying of network televison'. *Media Life Magazine* 15 January. Available at: www.medialifemagazine.com/news2004/jan04/jan12/4_thurs/news3thursday.html, last accessed 17/9/2008.
Lorenzo-Dus, M. 2009. *Television Discourse. Analysing Language in the Media.* Basingstoke/New York: Palgrave Macmillan.
Lothe, J. 2000. *Narrative in Fiction and Film. An Introduction.* Oxford: OUP.
Louw, B. 1993. 'Irony in the text or insincerity in the writer?' In Baker, M., Francis, G. & Tognini-Bonelli, E. (eds). *Text and Technology. In Honour of John Sinclair.* Amsterdam/Philadelphia, PA: John Benjamins, 157–76.
Lury, K. 2005. *Interpreting Television.* London: Hodder Arnold.
Lyons, J. 1977. *Semantics. Vol. 1, 2.* Cambridge: CUP.
Machin, D. & van Leeuwen, T. 2007. *Global Media Discourse. A Critical Introduction.* London/New York: Routledge.
Mahlberg, M. 2007. 'A corpus stylistic perspective on Dickens' *Great Expectations*'. In Lambrou, M. & Stockwell, P. (eds), *Contemporary Stylistics.* London/New York: Continuum, 19–31.
Mandala, S. 2007. 'Solidarity and the Scoobies: an analysis of the –y suffix in the television series Buffy the Vampire Slayer'. *Language and Literature* 16/1: 53–73.
Marshall, J. & Werndly, A. 2002. *The Language of Television.* London/New York: Routledge.
Marten-Cleef, S. 1991. *Gefühle ausdrücken. Die expressiven Sprechakte.* Göppingen: Kümmerle Verlag.
Martin, J. R. 2004. 'Positive discourse analysis: solidarity and change'. *Revista Canaria de Estudios Ingleses* 49: 179–200.
— 2007. 'Genre, ideology and intertextuality: a systemic functional perspective'. *Linguistics and the Human Sciences* 2/2: 275–98.
— 2008a. 'Intermodal reconciliation: mates in arms'. In Unsworth, L. (ed.), *New Literacies and the English Curriculum: Multimodal Perspectives.* London: Continuum, 112–48.
— 2008b. 'Innocence: realization, instantiation and individuation in a Botswanan town'. In Mahboob, A. & Knight, N. (eds), *Questioning Linguistics.* Newcastle: Cambridge Scholars Publishing, 32–76.

— 2010. 'Semantic variation – modelling realisation, instantiation and individuation in social semiosis'. In Bednarek, M. & Martin, J. R. (eds), *New Discourse on Language: Functional Perspectives on Multimodality, Identity and Affiliation*. London/New York: Continuum, 1–34.

Martin, J. R. & Rose, D. 2007a. *Genre Relations: Mapping Culture*. London: Equinox.

— 2007b. *Working with Discourse: Meaning Beyond the Clause*. Second revised and updated edition. London/New York: Continuum.

Martin, J. R. & White, P. R. R. 2005. *The Language of Evaluation. Appraisal in English*. Basingstoke/New York: Palgrave Macmillan.

Martinec, R. 2001. 'Interpersonal resources in action'. *Semiotica* 135 1/4: 117–45.

Martinec, R. & Salway, A. 2005. 'A system for image-text relations in new (and old) media', *Visual Communication* 4/3: 337–71.

Marty, A. 1908/1976. *Untersuchungen zur Grundlegung der allgemeinen Grammatik und Sprachphilosophie*. Tübingen: Niemeyer. [Published originally in 1908, Halle: Niemeyer.]

Matheson, D. 2005. *Media Discourses: Analysing Media Texts*. Maidenhead/New York: Open University Press.

Mautner, G. 2000. *Der britische Europa-Diskurs: Methodenreflexion und Fallstudien zur Berichterstattung in der Tagespresse*. Wien: Passagen.

— 2008. 'Analyzing newspapers, magazines and other print media'. In Wodak, R. & Krzyżanowski, M. (eds), *Qualitative Discourse Analysis for the Social Sciences* Basingstoke: Palgrave, 30–53.

Mayell, H. 2005. '"Evolving to eat mush": How meat changed our bodies'. National Geographic News. Available at: www.news.nationalgeographic.com/news/2005/02/0218_050218_human_diet.html, last accessed 19/5/2009.

Maynard, D. W. 2003. *Bad News, Good News: Conversational Order in Everyday Talk and Clinical Settings*. Chicago, IL: University of Chicago Press.

McCabe, J. & Akass, K. (eds). 2006. *Reading* Desperate Housewives. *Beyond the White Picket Fence*. London/New York: I.B. Tauris.

McCaffrey, M. 2008. 'Rory Gilmore and Faux Feminism. An Ivy League education and intellectual banter does not a feminist make'. In Calvin, R. (ed.), 35–49.

McIntyre, D. 2008. 'Integrating multimodal analysis and the stylistics of drama: a multimodal perspective on Ian McKellen's *Richard III*'. *Language and Literature* 17/4: 309–34.

McKee, R. 1998. *Story: Substance, Structure and Style and the Principles of Screenwriting*. London: Methuen.

McNair, B. ^{3}1999. *News and Journalism in the UK*. London/New York: Routledge.

McNeill, D. 2005. *Gesture and Thought*. Chicago, IL/London: University of Chicaco Press.

Mehl, M. R., Vazire, S., Ramírez-Esparza, N., Slatcher, R. B., & Pennebaker, J. W. 2007. 'Are women really more talkative than men?'. *Science* 6 July, 317/5834: 82.

Mepham, J. 1990. 'The ethics of quality in television'. In Mulgan, G. (ed.), *The Question of Quality*. London: BFI, 56–72.

Merriman, G. 2003. 'Lessons from Liverpool. The Jimmy McGovern workshops'. *Storyline* 3: 13–16

Metz, C. 1974. *Film Language. A Semiotics of the Cinema*. New York: OUP.

Meyer, C. 2002. *English Corpus Linguistics: An Introduction*. Cambridge: CUP.

Miller, T. (ed.). 2009. Special issue of *Television and New Media* on 'My Media Studies'.

Millman, J. 2000. 'The parent trap'. *Salon.com.* 15 November. Available at: www.archive.salon.com/ent/col/mill/2000/11/14/gilmore_girls/index.html, last accessed 17/9/2008.

Mills, B. 2005. *Television Sitcom.* London: British Film Institute.

Mittell, J. 2004. 'A cultural approach to television genre theory'. In Allen, R. & Hill, A. (eds), *The Television Studies Reader.* London/New York: Routledge, 171–81.

Mittmann, B. 2004. *Mehrwort-Cluster in der englischen Alltagskonversation. Unterschiede zwischen britischem und amerikanischem gesprochenen Englisch als Indikatoren für den präfabrizierten Charakter der Sprache.* Tübingen: Gunter Narr.

Mittmann, B. 2006. 'With a little help from *Friends* (and others): Lexico-pragmatic characteristics of original and dubbed film dialogue'. In Houswitschka, C., Knappe, G. & Müller, A. (eds), *Anglistentag 2005, Bamberg – Proceedings.* Trier: WVT, 573–85.

Moores, S. 1994. 'Texts, readers and contexts of reading: development in the study of media audiences'. In Graddol, D. & Boyd-Barrett, O. (eds), *Media Texts: Authors and Readers.* Clevedon: Multilingual Matters, 256–72.

Morris, D. 1977. *Manwatching: A Field Guide to Human Behavior.* London: Grafton Books.

Mushin, I. 2001. *Evidentiality and Epistemological Stance. Narrative Retelling.* Amsterdam/Philadelphia, PA: John Benjamins.

Myers, G. 1994. *Words in Ads.* London: Edward Arnold.

National Association of Broadcasters. 1990. *Statement of Principles Of Radio and Television Broadcasters.* Issued by the Board of Directors of the National Association of Broadcasters.

National Hispanic Media Coalition. 2008. Presentation to Susan Crawford and Kevin Werbach on the Need for Enhanced FCC Commitment to Diversity December 16, 2008. Available at: www.nhmc.org/documents/MediaPolicy/Mtg_with_S_Crawford_K_Werbach_120608.pdf, accessed 8/4/2009.

Neale, S. 1990. 'Questions of genre'. *Screen* 31/1: 45–66.

— 2001. 'Studying genre'. In Creeber, G. (ed.), 1–3.

Norrick, N. R. 1978. 'Expressive illocutionary acts'. *Journal of Pragmatics* 2: 277–91.

— 1993. *Conversational Joking: Humor in Everyday Talk.* Bloomington, IN: Indiana University Press.

— 2008. 'Using large corpora of conversation to investigate narrative. The case of interjections in conversational storytelling performance'. *International Journal of Corpus Linguistics* 13/4: 438–64.

Norris, S. 2002. 'The implication of visual research in discourse analysis: transcription beyond language'. *Visual Communication* 1/1: 97–121.

Norval, A. J. 2000. 'Review article: the things we do with words – contemporary approaches to the analysis of ideology'. *British Journal of Political Science* 30: 313–46.

Oatley, K. 2003. 'Creative expression and communication of emotions in the visual and narrative arts'. In Davidson, R. J., Scherer, K. R. & Goldsmith, H. H. (eds), *Handbook of Affective Sciences.* Oxford: OUP, 481–502.

Oatley, K., Keltner, D. & Jenkins, J. ²2006. *Understanding Emotions*. Oxford: Blackwell.

Ochs, E. 1979. 'Transcription as theory'. In Ochs, E. & Schiefflien, B. B. (eds), *Developmental Pragmatics*. New York: Academic Press, 43–72.

Ochs, E. & Schieffelin, B. 1989. 'Language has a heart'. *Text* 9: 7–25.

O'Halloran, K. L. 2008. 'Systemic functional-multimodal discourse analysis (SF-MDA): constructing ideational meaning using language and visual imagery'. *Visual Communication* 7/4: 443–75.

O'Keeffe, A. 2006. *Investigating Media Discourse*. London/New York: Routledge.

O'Keeffe, A., McCarthy, M. & Carter, R. 2007. *From Corpus to Classroom: Language Use and Language Teaching*. Cambridge: CUP.

Olson, S. R. 2004. 'Hollywood planet. Global media and the competitive advantage of narrative transparency'. In Allen, R. & Hill, A. (eds), *The Television Studies Reader*. London/New York: Routledge, 111–29.

Ortony, A., Clore, G. L. & Collins, A. 1988. *The Cognitive Structure of Emotions*. Cambridge: CUP.

O'Shaughnessy, M. & Stadler, J. ³2005. *Media and Society. An Introduction*. Oxford: OUP.

Paltridge, B. 2006. *Discourse Analysis. An Introduction*. London/New York: Continuum.

— 2007. 'Genre, identity and *Sex and the City*'. Paper presented at *Discourses and Cultural Practices* 29, 30 November & 1 December 2007, Faculty of Education, University of Technology, Sydney, Australia.

Partington, A., Morley, J. & Haarman, L. (eds). 2004. *Corpora and Discourse: A Most Congruous Beast*. Bern: Peter Lang.

Pavlenko, A. 2005. *Emotions and Multilingualism*. Cambridge: CUP.

Pearson, R. 2007. 'Anatomising Gilbert Grissom. The structure and function of the televisual character'. In Allen, M. (ed.), *Reading* CSI. *Crime TV under the Microscope*. London/New York: I.B. Tauris, 39–56.

Pennycook, A. 2004. 'Performativity and language studies'. *Critical Inquiry in Language Studies: An International Journal* 1/1: 1–19.

— 2007. *Global Englishes and Transcultural Flows*. London/New York: Routledge.

Pfister, M. 1988. *The Theory and Analysis of Drama*. Cambridge: CUP.

Planalp, S. 1999. *Communicating Emotion. Social, Moral and Cultural Processes*. Cambridge: CUP.

Pomerantz, A. 1984. 'Agreeing and disagreeing with assessment: some features of preferred/dispreferred turn shapes'. In Atkins, J. M. & Heritage, J. (eds), *Structures of Social Action: Studies in Conversation Analysis*. Cambridge: CUP, 57–101.

Precht, K. 2006. 'Gender differences and similarities in stance in informal American conversation'. Unpublished manuscript Available at: www.kprecht.net/MyWork/Precht%20Gender%202006.pdf

Propp, V. ²1968. *The Morphology of the Folktale*. Austin, TX: University of Texas Press. [Translated by L. Scott.]

Quaglio, P. 2008. 'Television dialogue and natural conversation: linguistic similarities and functional differences' In Ädel, A. & Reppen, R. (eds), *Corpora and Discourse. The Challenges of Different Settings*. Amsterdam/Philadelphia, PA: John Benjamins, 189–210.

— 2009. *Television Dialogue. The Sitcom* Friends *vs. Natural Conversation*. Amsterdam/Philadelphia, PA: John Benjamins.

Rey, J. M. 2001. 'Changing gender roles in popular culture: dialogue in Star Trek episodes from 1966 to 1993'. In D. Biber & Conrad, S. (eds), *Variation in English: Multi-dimensional Studies*. London: Longman, 138–56.

Ridinger-Dotterman, A. 2008. 'Reinventing the bitch: the dynamicism of Paris Geller'. In Calvin, R. (ed.), 50–62.

Rimmon-Kenan. [2]2002. *Narrative Fiction: Contemporary Poetics*. London: Methuen.

Robinson, J. 2005. *Deeper than Reason: Emotion and its Role in Literature, Music, and Art*. Oxford: OUP.

Robinson, J. D. 2004. 'The sequential organization of "explicit" apologies in naturally occurring English'. *Research on Language and Social Interaction* 37/3: 291–330.

Römer, U. 2008. 'Identification impossible? A corpus approach to realisations of evaluative meaning in academic writing'. *Functions of Language* 15/1: 115–30.

Roman, J. 2005. *From Daytime to PrimeTime. The History of American Television Programs*. Westport, CT/London: Greenwood Press.

Romano, A. 2006. 'Dawn of a new network'. *Broadcasting and Cable*. www.broadcastingcable.com/article/CA6364196.html, last accessed 17/9/2008.

Ross, S. 2004. 'Dormant dormitory friendships: race and gender in *Felicity*'. In Davis, G. & Dickinson, K. (eds), *Teen TV. Genre, Consumption and Identity*. London: British Film Institute, 141–50.

Sacks, H. 1992. *Lectures on Conversation*. Jefferson, G. (ed.), Oxford: Blackwell.

Salih, S. 2006. 'On Judith Butler and performativity'. In Lovass, K. F. & Jenkins, M. M. (eds), *Sexualities and Communication in Everyday Life. A Reader*. Thousand Oaks, CA: Sage, 55–68.

Sanger, K. 2001. *The Language of Drama*. London/ New York: Routledge.

Schegloff, E. 2006. 'A tutorial on membership categorization'. *Journal of Pragmatics* 39: 462–82.

— 2007. *Sequence Organization in Interaction. A Primer in Conversation Analysis* I. Cambridge: CUP.

Schwarz-Friesel, M. 2007. *Sprache und Emotion*. Tuebingen/Basel: A. Francke Verlag.

Scollon, R. & Scollon, S. W. [2]2001. *Intercultural Communciation. A Discourse Approach*. Oxford: Blackwell.

Scott, M. 1997. 'PC analysis of key words – and key key words'. *System* 25/2: 233–45.

— 1999. *Wordsmith Tools*. Version 3. Oxford: OUP.

— 2004. *Wordsmith Tools*. Version 4. Oxford: OUP.

Scott, M. & Tribble, C. 2006. *Textual Patterns. Key Words and Corpus Analysis in Language Education*. Amsterdam/Philadelphia, PA: John Benjamins.

Seger, L. [2]1994. *Making a Good Script Great*. Second revised and expanded edition. Hollywood/New York: Samuel French.

Selby, K. & Cowdery, R. 1995. *How to Study Television*. Basingstoke/London: Macmillan.

Selting, M. 1994. 'Emphatic speech style – with special focus on the prosodic signalling of heightened emotive involvement in conversation'. *Journal of Pragmatics* 22: 375–408.

Sherman-Palladino, A. 2005. Interview with Amy Sherman-Palladino, interviewed by Scott Tobias for *The Onion A.V. Club*, 9 February 2005. Available at: www.avclub.com/content/node/23372/print/2, last accessed 14/8/2008.

Sherman-Palladino, A. & Palladino, D. 2006. 'Team Palladino: the interview'. Interviewed by Michael Ausiello for *TV Guide*, 24 April 2006. Available at: www.community.tvguide.com/blog-entry/TVGuide-Editors-Blog/Ausiello-Report/Team-Palladino-Interview/700000966, last accessed 28/8/2008.

Sherrill, C. 2008. 'Vegetarians on TV'. Blog entry posted Friday, 28 March 2008. Available at: www.journalnow.net/index.php/vegginout/2008/03/, last accessed 31/3/2009.

Short, M. H. 1981. 'Discourse analysis and the analysis of drama'. *Applied Linguistics* 2: 180–201.

Short, M. 1998. 'From dramatic text to dramatic performance'. In Culpeper, J. (ed.), *Exploring the Language of Drama: From Text to Context*. London: Routledge, 6–18.

Shugart, H. A. 2003. 'Reinventing privilege: the new (gay) man in contemporary popular media'. *Critical Studies in Media Communication* 20/1: 67–91.

Singer, P. & Mason, J. 2007. *The Ethics of What We Eat: Why Our Food Choices Matter.* New York: Rodale.

Smith, R. D. 2008. 'Still more Gilmore. How online fan communities remediate Gilmore Girls'. In Calvin, R. (ed.), 193–204.

Spencer-Oatey, H. 2007. 'Theories of identity and the analysis of face'. *Journal of Pragmatics* 39: 639–56.

Spitz, A. 2005. 'Power Plays: the Representation of Mother–Daughter Disputes in Contemporary Plays by Women. A Study in Discourse Analysis'. Unpublished PhD dissertation, Universität des Saarlandes (Germany). Available at: www.scidok.sulb.uni-saarland.de/volltexte/2006/595/.

Stankiewicz, E. 1989. 'The emotive function of language: an overview'. In Koch, W. (ed.), *For a Semiotics of Emotion*. Bochum: Bochumer Universitätsverlag, 73–85.

Stivers, T. 2006. 'Stance, alignment and affiliation during story telling: nodding as a token of preliminary affiliation'. Paper presented at the annual meeting of the American Sociological Association, Montreal, Quebec, Canada. Available at: www.allacademic.com/meta/p103670_index.html, last accessed 20/7/2009.

Stokoe, E. 2008. 'Dispreferred actions and other interactional breaches as devices for occasioning audience laughter in television "sitcoms"'. *Social Semiotics* (Special volume: Analysing media discourses) 18/3: 289–307.

Stubbs, M. 2005. 'Conrad in the computer: examples of quantitative stylistic methods'. *Language and Literature* 14/1: 5–24.

— 2008. 'Three concepts of keywords'. Revised version of paper presented to the conference on *Keyness in Text* at the Certosa di Pontignano, University of Siena, June 2007. Available at: www.uni-trier.de/fileadmin/fb2/ANG/Linguistik/Stubbs/stubbs-2008-keywords.pdf, last accessed 7/8/2008.

Stubbs, M. & Barth, I. 2003. 'Using recurrent phrases as text-type discriminators: a quantitative method and some findings'. *Functions of Language* 10/1: 61–104.

Taavitsainen, I. 1999. 'Personality and styles of affect in the *Canterbury Tales*'. In Lester, G. (ed.), *Chaucer in Perspective: Middle English Essays in Honour of Norman Blake*. Sheffield: Sheffield Academic Press, 218–34.

Tagliamonte, S. & Roberts, C. 2005. 'So weird; so cool; so innovative: the use of intensifiers in the television series *Friends*'. *American Speech* 80/3: 280–300.

Talbot, M. 2007. *Media Discourse. Representation and Interaction.* Edinburgh: Edinburgh University Press.

Tallman, J. 1979. 'Ways of Speaking: Styles in Conversation'. Unpublished PhD dissertation, University of California at Berkeley.

Tannen, D. 1984. *Conversational Style: Analyzing Talk Among Friends.* Norwood, NJ: Ablex.

Thompson, G. & Hunston, S. 2000. 'Evaluation: an introduction'. In Hunston, S. & Thompson, G. (eds), *Evaluation in Text. Authorial Stance and the Construction of Discourse.* Oxford: OUP, 1–27.

Thomson, E. & White, P. R. R. (eds). 2008. *Communicating Conflict. Multilingual Case Studies of the News Media.* London/New York: Continuum.

Thornham, S. & Purvis, T. 2005. *Television Drama: Theories and Identities.* Basingstoke: Palgrave Macmillan.

Tognini-Bonelli, E. 2001. *Corpus Linguistics at Work.* Amsterdam: John Benjamins.

Toolan, M. ^{2}2001. *Narrative. A Critical Linguistic Introduction.* London/New York: Routledge.

Totaro, P. 2009. 'Doors open at a creative age'. Interview with Nick Hornby. *Spectrum*, 17–18 October, Sydney: *The Sydney Morning Herald*, pp. 26–27.

Tracy, K. 2002. *Everyday Talk. Building and Reflecting Identities.* New York/London: The Guilford Press.

Turner, G. 1994. 'Film languages'. In Graddol, D. & Boyd-Barrett, O. (eds), *Media Texts: Authors and Readers.* Clevedon: Multilingual Matters in association with The Open University, 119–35.

— 2001a. 'The uses and limitations of genre'. In Creeber, G. (ed.), 4–5.

— 2001b. 'Genre, hybridity and mutation'. In Creeber, G. (ed.), 6.

Turner, J. & Stets, J. E. 2005. *The Sociology of Emotions.* Cambridge: CUP.

van Dijk, T.A. 1998a. 'Opinions and ideologies in the press'. In Bell, A. & Garrett, P. (eds), *Approaches to Media Discourse.* Oxford/Malden, MA: Blackwell, 21–63.

— 1998b. *Ideology. A Multidisciplinary Approach.* London/Thousand Oaks, CA: Sage.

van Leeuwen, T. 1996. 'Moving English: the visual language of film'. In Goodman, S. & Graddol, D. (eds), *Redesigning English. New Texts, New Identities.* London/New York: Routledge, 81–105.

— 1999. *Speech, Music, Sound.* Basingstoke/New York: Palgrave Macmillan.

— 2008. *Discourse and Practice. New Tools for Critical Discourse Analysis.* Oxford: OUP.

van Meel, J. M. 1994. 'Representing emotions in literature and paintings: a comparative analysis'. *Poetics* 23: 159–76.

Vestergaard, T. 2000. 'From genre to sentence: the leading article and its linguistic realization'. In Ungerer, F. (ed.), *English Media Texts Past and Present. Language and Textual Structure.* Amsterdam/Philadelphia, PA: John Benjamins, 151–76.

Volek, B. 1987. *Emotive Signs in Language and Semantic Functioning of Derived Nouns in Russian.* Amsterdam: Benjamins.

Vorhaus, J. 1994. *The Comic Toolbox: How to be Funny Even if You're Not.* Los Angeles, CA: Silman-James Press.

Walters, S. D. 1992. *Lives Together, Worlds Apart: Mothers and Daughters in Popular Culture.* Berkeley: University of California Press.

Weatherall, A. & Stubbe, M. 2009. 'Affiliation during complaint calls in institutional talk'. Paper presented at *11th International Pragmatics Conference*, Melbourne 12–17 July 2009.

Webber, A. 2005. '*Mortified* outline'. Unpublished manuscript, Australian Children's Television Foundation (Melbourne) and Enjoy! Entertainment (Sydney).

Weerakkody, N. 2008. *Research Methods for Media and Communication*. Oxford: OUP.

Wenger, E. c2007. 'Communities of Practice. A brief introduction'. Available at: www.ewenger.com/theory/, accessed 28/7/2009.

Werth, P. 1998. 'On the semantics and pragmatics of emotion verb complementation'. In Athanasiadou, A. & Tabakowska, E. (eds), *Speaking of Emotions. Conceptualisation and Expression*. Berlin: Mouton de Gruyter, 409–40.

Westman, K. E. 2007. 'Beauty and the geek: changing gender stereotypes in the *Gilmore Girls*'. In Inness, S. A. (ed.). *Geek Chic: Smart Women in Popular Culture*. New York: Palgrave Macmillan, 1–10.

White, P. R. R. 2004. 'Subjectivity, evaluation and point of view in media discourse'. In Coffin, C. (ed.), *Applying English Grammar: Functional and Corpus Approaches*, London: Arnold, 229–46.

Widdowson, H. G. 2008. 'The novel features of text. Corpus analysis and stylistics'. In Gerbig, A. & Mason, O. (eds), *Language, People, Numbers. Corpus Linguistics and Society*. Amsterdam/New York: Rodopi, 293–304.

Wiebe, J., Wilson, T. & Cardie, C. 2005. 'Annotating expressions of opinions and emotions in language'. *Language Resources and Evaluation* (formerly *Computers and the Humanities*) 39/2–3: 165–210.

Wierzbicka, A. 2003. *Cross-Cultural Pragmatics. The Semantics of Human Interaction*. Berlin/New York: Mouton de Gruyter.

Wiggins, S. & Potter, J. 2003. 'Attitudes and evaluative practices: Category vs. item and subjective vs. objective constructions in everyday food assessments'. *British Journal of Social Psychology* 42: 513–31.

Wilce, J. M. 2009. *Language and Emotion*. Cambridge: CUP.

Williams, R. 1977. 'A lecture on realism'. *Screen* 18/1: 61–74.

Williams, R. ^{2}1983. *Keywords. A Vocabulary of Culture and Society*. Second revised and expanded edition. London: Fontana.

Wilson, T. A. 2008. 'Fine-grained Subjectivity and Sentiment Analysis: Recognizing the Intensity, Polarity, and Attitudes of Private Sates'. PhD Thesis, University of Pittsburgh. Chapter 7 available at: www.cs.pitt.edu/mpqa/databaserelease, last accessed 5/3/2009.

Wodak, R. 2009. *The Discourse of Politics in Action*. Basingstoke/New York: Palgrave Macmillan.

Woods, F. 2008. 'Generation gap? Mothers, daughters and music'. In Calvin, R. (ed.), 127–42.

Wray, A. 2002. *Formulaic Language and the Lexicon*. Cambridge: CUP.

Wynne, M. 2006. 'Stylistics: corpus approaches'. In Brown, K. (ed.), *Encyclopedia of Language & Linguistics, Second Edition*, volume 12. Oxford: Elsevier, 223–26.

Zappavigna, M., Cléirigh, C., Dwyer, P., & Martin, J. forthcoming. 'Visualising appraisal prosody'. In A. Mahboob & Knight, N. (eds), *Appliable Linguistics: Texts, Contexts and Meanings*. London/New York: Continuum.

Zappavigna, M., Cléirigh, C., Dwyer, P., & Martin, J. 2010. 'The coupling of gesture and phonology'. In Bednarek, M. & Martin, J. R. (eds), *New Discourse on Language: Functional Perspectives on Multimodality, Identity and Affiliation*. London/ New York: Continuum, 219–36.

Zhao, S. 2010. 'Intersemiotic relations as logogenetic patterns: towards the restoration of the time dimension in hypertext description'. In Bednarek, M. & Martin, J. R. (eds), *New Discourse on Language: Functional Perspectives on Multimodality, Identity and Affiliation*. London/New York: Continuum, 195–218.

Zimmerman, D. H. 1998. 'Identity, context and interaction'. In Antaki, C. & Widdicombe, S. (eds), *Identities in Talk*. London/Thousand Oaks: Sage, 87–106.

DVDs

'A Best Friend's Peek Inside the Gilmore Girls' 2007, supplementary feature, *Gilmore Girls. The Complete Seventh Season*. DVD. Warner Bros. Entertainment Inc.

'Gilmore Fashionistas' 2007, supplementary feature, *Gilmore Girls. The Complete Seventh Season*. DVD. Warner Bros. Entertainment Inc.

'Gilmore Girls Goodies and Gossip for "Rory's Dance"' 2000, supplementary feature, *Gilmore Girls. The Complete First Season*. DVD. Warner Bros. Entertainment Inc.

'Gilmore-isms' 2000, supplementary feature, *Gilmore Girls. The Complete First Season*. DVD. Warner Bros. Entertainment Inc.

'International Success' 2004, supplementary feature, *Gilmore Girls. The Complete Second Series*. DVD. Warner Bros. Entertainment Inc.

'My So-called Life Story' 2007, supplementary feature, *My So-Called Life. The Complete Series*. DVD. A.k.a Productions.

'The Gilmore Girls Turn 100' 2005, supplementary feature, *Gilmore Girls. The Complete Fifth Season*. DVD. Warner Bros. Entertainment Inc.

'Welcome to "The Gilmore Girls"' 2003, supplementary feature, *Gilmore Girls. The Complete First Season*. DVD. Warner Bros. Entertainment Inc.

'Who Wants to Argue' 2001/02, supplementary feature, *Gilmore Girls. The Complete Second Season*. DVD. Warner Bros. Entertainment Inc.

'Who Wants to Talk Gilmore' 2005, supplementary feature, *Gilmore Girls. The Complete Fifth Season*. DVD. Warner Bros. Entertainment Inc.

General Index

Index of Television Programmes

Lightning Source UK Ltd.
Milton Keynes UK
UKOW030611040712

195411UK00001B/5/P